Researching Intercultural Learning

Also by Lixian Jin and Martin Cortazzi

RESEARCHING CHINESE LEARNERS: Skills, Perceptions and Intercultural Adaptations (*ed.*)

Researching Intercultural Learning

Investigations in Language and Education

Edited by

Lixian Jin
De Montfort University, UK

and

Martin Cortazzi
University of Warwick, UK

First published 2013 by
PALGRAVE MACMILLAN

Palgrave Macmillan in the UK is an imprint of Macmillan Publishers Limited,
registered in England, company number 785998, of Houndmills, Basingstoke,
Hampshire RG21 6XS.

Palgrave Macmillan in the US is a division of St Martin's Press LLC,
175 Fifth Avenue, New York, NY 10010.

Palgrave Macmillan is the global academic imprint of the above companies
and has companies and representatives throughout the world.

Palgrave® and Macmillan® are registered trademarks in the United States,
the United Kingdom, Europe and other countries

ISBN: 978–0–230–32133–5

This book is printed on paper suitable for recycling and made from fully
managed and sustained forest sources. Logging, pulping and manufacturing
processes are expected to conform to the environmental regulations of the
country of origin.

A catalogue record for this book is available from the British Library.

A catalog record for this book is available from the Library of Congress.

10 9 8 7 6 5 4 3 2 1
22 21 20 19 18 17 16 15 14 13

Printed and bound in the United States of America.

Contents

Part I   Researching Transformations of Cultures of Learning through Internationalization

Part II   Intercultural Learning in Developing Language and Academic Skills

List of Figures

List of Tables

List of Appendices

Acknowledgements

The editors and contributors would like to extend profound thanks to all the participants in the research projects featured in this book. As participants you are learning in many situations, contexts and cultures around the world with different kinds of intercultural learning, and without your help our work and our learning here would not be possible. Your needs encouraged us to research. Thus, in our many languages we give you our gratitude. Thank you.

In the same spirit, the editors would like to say how enjoyable and inspiring it has been for us to work with all the contributors from different parts of the world. We thank all of them.

Finally, we would like to thank the editorial team members of Palgrave Macmillan for their patience. We wish you intercultural blessings.

Notes on Contributors

Some Chinese authors here retain the East Asian name order (family name first) in English while others have adapted to the European order when writing in English (family name last); this means that arranging the names in alphabetical order can become problematic, but here we have followed the authors' own choice about their names in English.

Dr. Inma Alvarez lectured in Spanish language and culture at the University of Michigan (USA), and several universities in the UK before joining The Open University (UK) in 1999, where she is currently a senior lecturer and Head of Spanish Language studies. She holds a PhD in Aesthetics from the Universidad Autónoma de Madrid (Spain). She has authored a variety of Spanish language learning materials and published in the area of languages and intercultural competence as well as on performing arts.

Prof. Sophie Bailly is Professor in Sociolinguistics and in Foreign Language Teaching and Learning (Foreign Languages Didactics) in the Department of Linguistics at the Université de Lorraine. She is the head of the university's French as a foreign language courses centre. In sociolinguistics her main interest is the relationship between gender and language. She studies how essentialist gender ideologies impact discourse and talk-in-interaction in various settings. She is the author of *Les Hommes, les Femmes et la Communication* (2009). In the field of didactics of foreign languages, her research mainly focuses on self-directed methodologies, organizations, devices and tools, whether computer-based or not, with a special interest for the change in roles of learners and teachers in self-directed schemes. Her work contributes to setting goals and contents for the training of language learning advisers.

Prof. Martin Cortazzi is Visiting Professor at the Centre for Applied Linguistics at the University of Warwick, UK. He has taught and trained teachers in Britain, China, Lebanon, Turkey, Iran, Malaysia, Norway, Cyprus and elsewhere. He has published widely on aspects of primary education, applied linguistics, language and cultural issues, narrative and metaphor analysis.

Dr. Phil Glenwright taught English in German grammar schools and German in English grammar and comprehensive schools for ten years before becoming Senior Lecturer in modern languages at a College of Higher Education in the United Kingdom. Since 1987 he taught, until retirement, as Senior Lecturer in English at the Hong Kong Institute of Education where he specialized in teaching methodology and applied linguistics for Teaching English as a Foreign Language (TEFL). He is the author of *The Hong Kong Culture of Learning: Its*

Origins and Effects (2010) and *Dr Phil G's 33 Top TEFL Tips* (2011). He has published in journals including the *Journal of Language, Identity and Education Education and Society* and *Assessing Writing*. His research topics include discourse, curriculum reform, the language proficiency assessment of teachers, teaching practice supervision and the use of multimedia in the teaching of linguistics. This year (2012) he published on the 'Discourse of Amateur Cricket'.

Prof. Eli Hinkel teaches linguistics and applied linguistics at Seattle University. She has taught ESL and applied linguistics, as well as trainee teachers, for more than 30 years, and has published books and numerous articles on learning second culture, and second language grammar, writing and pragmatics in such journals as *TESOL Quarterly, Applied Linguistics, Journal of Pragmatics* and *Language Teaching Research*. Her books include *Culture in Second Language Teaching and Learning* (1999), *New Perspectives on Grammar Teaching* (2001), *Second Language Writers' Text* (2002), *Teaching Academic ESL Writing* (2004), *Handbook of Research in Second Language Teaching and Learning*, vols 1 and 2 (2005 and 2011) and *Effective Curriculum for Teaching Second Language Writing* (in press), as well as several student textbooks. She is also the editor of ESL & Applied Linguistics Professional Series of books and textbooks for teachers and graduate students, published by Routledge.

Prof. Masako K. Hiraga is Professor in Linguistics at the Graduate School of Intercultural Communication, Rikkyo University, Tokyo. Her major publications include 'Special issue on metaphor and iconicity', *The Journal of Pragmatics*, 22 (1) (1994); *Typological, Cultural, and Psychological Perspectives in Cognitive Linguistics* (1999); and *Metaphor and Iconicity: A Cognitive Approach to Texts* (2005). With Joan Turner, she has collaborated in a number of articles on intercultural pragmatic issues of Japanese students studying in Britain. She serves on the editorial boards for *Pragmatics and Society, Pragmatics & Beyond New Series, Cognitive Linguistic Studies in Cultural Contexts* and *Intercultural Pragmatics*. Her research interests are intercultural pragmatics, cognitive linguistics and poetics.

Prof. Jane Jackson is Professor in the Department of English at the Chinese University of Hong Kong. She serves on the editorial board or manuscript review panels of several applied linguistics and intercultural communication journals. She has published numerous articles and book chapters in peer-reviewed applied linguistics, intercultural communication/education and study-abroad journals. Recent monographs include *Language, Identity, and Study Abroad: Sociocultural Perspectives* (2008) and *Intercultural Journeys: From Study to Residence Abroad* (2010). She is currently editing the *Routledge Handbook of Intercultural Communication*. Her research interests include intercultural communication/pragmatics, reticence and anxiety in L2 learners, identity (re)construction and student residence abroad. With the support of competitive research grants, she is investigating the learning of study-abroad students.

Prof. Lixian Jin is Chair Professor of Linguistics and Intercultural Learning and Director of the Centre for Research in Intercultural Communication and Learning (CIRCL) at De Montfort University, UK. She has taught linguistics and English in China, Britain and Turkey, and coordinated research projects in Singapore, Malaysia and China. Her publications and research interests are in intercultural communication, applied linguistics, bilingual clinical assessments and narrative and metaphor analyses. Jin and Cortazzi have for many years jointly researched and published widely on a range of linguistic, cultural and educational issues related to Chinese learners. They are the authors for the teacher's books for New Standard College English series of textbooks (2009, 2010). They are the editors of and contributors to several books, including *Researching Chinese Learners, Skills, Perceptions and Intercultural Adaptations* (2011) and *Researching Cultures of Learning: International Perspectives on Language Learning and Education* (forthcoming).

Dr. Kan Qian is Lecturer in Chinese and also course Chair for Beginners' Chinese at the Open University (UK) since 2009. She holds a PhD in Linguistics from Lancaster University, UK. She taught Chinese language and culture at Lancaster University for three years and students majoring in Chinese at the University of Cambridge for 11 years. She has authored numerous Chinese language learning materials, including *Colloquial Chinese* two editions: (1995, 2009), *Teach Yourself Phone Mandarin Chinese* (2008), *Colloquial Chinese 2* (2007) and with Boping Yuan co-authored *Developing Writing Skills in Chinese* (2002). Her research interests are use of ICT in distance Chinese language teaching and learning and mobile learning. Her co-authored paper, 'Building course cohesion: the use of online forums in distance Chinese language learning', has been accepted by *Computer Assisted Language Learning* journal (2012).

Dr. Xiaohua Liang is an associate professor in Zhongnan University of Economics and Law. She obtained her PhD at The University of Hong kong in March 2011. With long experience of teaching in secondary school and at university, and of researching at kindergarten, primary and tertiary levels, she has been involved in and got very familiar with the complete Chinese education system at all levels. Her research interests include second language acquisition, interaction, bilingualism, intercultural studies and sociocultural theories.

Markus Lux is Head of Good Governance and Education in the Department for International Relations for Central and Southeastern Europe, CIS and China at Robert Bosch Stiftung in Stuttgart. He studied history and politics at the universities of Mainz and Riga. Between 1993 and 1996 he worked at the German public television channel ZDF in Mainz. Between 1996 and 2002 he was a visiting lecturer at several universities in Latvia and a researcher at the Jews in Latvia Museum in Riga. He is currently responsible for exchange programs in the areas of higher education, administration and diplomacy.

Dr. Nick Pilcher is a lecturer in In-sessional English for Academic Purpose in the School of Marketing Tourism and Languages, Edinburgh Napie University. His current research interests are experiences and perception of learning, cultures of learning, Chinese learners, dissertations, nationa qualifications frameworks and issues and methods of qualitative research He is author and co-author of work related to these areas in teaching in higher education, quality in higher education, qualitative research, and in the book *Researching Chinese Learners* (Eds, Lixian Jin and Martin Cortazzi)

Kendall Richards is a lecturer with the role of academic support adviser in the Faculty of Engineering, Computing and Creative Industries at Edinburgh Napier University (UK). He works with many non-traditional, international mature and direct entrant students and also towards the embedding of dis cipline-specific support within programmes and modules across the faculty His research interests cover the areas of academic literacies and academic discourse. He has presented and published in the United Kingdom with the Higher Education Academy, in Europe (ESREA, Seville, 2008) and also in Australia (ATLAANZ, Otago, 2005). He is a founding member of the Scottish Effective Learning Advisors Network (SCOT-ELAS) and also frequently works with students outside the university in Further Education Colleges, and as part of the Lothian Equal Access Programme for Schools (LEAPS).

Dr. Gillian Skyrme is a lecturer in linguistics and second language teach-ing at Massey University, New Zealand, teaching undergraduate and post-graduate students, and English for Academic Purposes for undergraduate international students. She researches the experiences of international students adjusting to the academic culture of a New Zealand university, including their affective and identity issues and the learning of specific skills. Her interest in Chinese international students, the focus of her doctoral research, arises out of many years of teaching Chinese students in New Zealand and China. Her published work includes 'Entering the university: The differentiated experience of two Chinese international students in a New Zealand university', *Studies in Higher Education* (2007); 'Is this a stupid question: International undergraduate students seeking help from teachers during office hours', *Journal of English for Academic Purposes* (2010); and 'Learning to read at university: English L2 students learning on the job', *New Zealand Studies in Applied Linguistics* (2010).

Dr. Gordon Slethaug is Adjunct Professor at the University of Waterloo, Canada, where he teaches in the Department of English and the Department of Speech-Communications and focuses on rhetoric, com-munications, globalization and internationalization. He has most recently been Visiting Professor at the University of Southern Denmark and previ-ously was Lingnan Professor at the University of Hong Kong and Sun Yat-sen University in China. His research centres on international education, cross-cultural pedagogy, cultural studies and American film and literature. Recent books relevant to international education include *Teaching Abroad: The Cross-Cultural Classroom and International Education* (2007) and, with Janette Ryan, *International Education and the Chinese Learner* (2010).

Joan Turner is Senior Lecturer and Director of the Centre for English Language and Academic Writing at Goldsmiths, University of London. Her research focuses on language in higher education, including intercultural communication, academic literacies and English for Academic Purposes (EAP). Recent publications include *Language in the Academy: Cultural Reflexivity and Intercultural Dynamics* (2011); 'Multilingual matters; rewriting writing in higher education: The contested spaces of proofreading', *Studies in Higher Education*, 36 (4), 427–40 (2011); and 'Academic literacies: Providing a space for the socio-political dynamics of EAP', *Journal of English for Academic Purposes*, 11 (1), 17–25 (2012). She is particularly interested in how the dynamics of intercultural encounters and the globalized interaction of differing cultural assumptions and expectations are changing the landscape of international higher education.

Dr. Jane Vinther is Associate Professor and Head of English Studies at the University of Southern Denmark, Campus Kolding. Teaching and research interests include applied linguistics, the language and culture interface and philosophies of education. She has presented papers at conferences in the United Kingdom, Hong Kong and China on these themes. Her most recent publication in this field is 'A Danish Perspective on Teaching Chinese Students in Europe', in G. Slethaug and J. Ryan (Eds), *The Chinese Learner and International Education* (2010).

Wang Jinjing is a PhD student in Linguistics in the University of Lorraine, France, specializing in French as a foreign/second language didactics. She researches the causes of failures of Chinese students learning French in France. Her research involves language didactics, intercultural studies and psychology of learning. Her main research areas are cultures of language learning/teaching in Chinese and French educational systems, Chinese learners' characters and motivations in learning of French in France. She is an assistant lecturer in the Department of Linguistics at the University of Lorraine where she teaches ethnolinguistics, sociolinguistics, language didactics and use of new technology in language teaching.

Dr. Liang Wang is currently an EU-funded language project research assistant based at SOAS, University of London, as well as an associate lecturer in Chinese at the Open University, where he was awarded his Master of Research and PhD degrees in 2008 and 2011 respectively. He also received an MA in Media Technology for TESOL from the University of Newcastle upon Tyne in 2003. He specializes in technology-enhanced language learning, Internet-mediated intercultural foreign language education, teaching and assessing intercultural communicative competence, learner autonomy and blended language teach ing and learning. One of his research focuses is the contribution to establish ing a model of in-class Internet-mediated intercultural learning communitie which complements the prevailing cross-site telecollaborative models. He als develops his interest in investigating the intercultural dimension in CEFF based Chinese language benchmark and doing research multilingually.

Dr. Wang Lixun is Assistant Professor in Applied Linguistics in the Hong Kong Institute of Education, specializing in corpus linguistics, computer assisted language learning, and multilingual education. One of his main re search areas is English–Chinese parallel corpus studies, and he has compiled a 2-million-word English–Chinese parallel corpus, which is freely available and searchable online at http://ec-concord.ied.edu.hk. He is the author of *Introduction to Language Studies* (2011) and co-author of *Academic Writing i Language and Education Programmes* (2011). He has also published in reput able journals such as *System, Computer-Assisted Language Learning, Languag Learning and Technology* and *International Journal of Bilingual Education an Bilingualism*, on topics such as computer-assisted language learning, corpu linguistics, outcome-based learning, the use of multimedia in the teaching of linguistics, and trilingual education in Hong Kong.

Dr. Thushari Welikala is a research fellow at Liverpool Hope University UK, specializing in international higher education, mediation of culture in higher education teaching and learning and narrative research. Before joining Liverpool Hope University she worked at Nottingham University and at the Institute of Education at the University of London. She has man aged and worked for number of research projects funded by major fund ing bodies (European Union Sixth Framework, Higher Education Academy Leverhulme Trust, British Academy and Engineering and Physical Science Research Council). Her contributions to internationalization of higher edu cation include a major curriculum review designed and conducted by her at the Institute of Education, University of London. She is currently the prin cipal investigator of a project on internationalization which is funded by the Higher Education Academy and UK Council for International Student Affairs. Thushari is the co-author of *Improving Intercultural Learning Experiences in Higher Education: Responding to Cultural Scripts for Learning* (2008).

Christian Wochele has studied Philosophy and German Literature at the Universities of Heidelberg and Berlin. In winter 2003/04 he was teaching German as a foreign language at the University of Vesprém/Hungary. From 2004 to 2006 he was a visiting lecturer at the University 'DžemalBijedić' in Mostar/Bosnia-Herzegovina. In 2006 and 2007 he worked for the German Rector's Conference in Bonn. Since 2007 he is responsible for the lecture ship programme of the Robert Bosch Stiftung in Eastern Europe and China as project manager.

Introduction: Research and Levels of Intercultural Learning

Lixian Jin and Martin Cortazzi

Intercultural learning is about how we come to understand other cultures and our own through interaction, how we learn and communicate in cultural contexts, and how we learn culturally. Intercultural learning is vital in current contexts of international, multicultural and social diversity in which all of us increasingly need to interact with members of different cultural communities. We can easily imagine this will be even more the case in the future in globalized educational contexts, with imperatives related to technologies, demographics, economies and businesses, peace, individual and collective self-awareness and ethics (see Martin & Nakayama, 2009). Intercultural learning may be seen as a positive development or as a daunting challenge, yet it might also be empowering for participants – learning whatever we are learning in better ways. To modify a comment made in English for us by a Dutch student, 'Culture is a magnet: it can attract you or repel you. Intercultural learning is an electromagnet: It combines both positive and negative forces in movement to drive a powerful motor.

Here, the term 'intercultural learning' relates especially to issues of learning or teaching which are implicated in contemporary education and language learning in schools and universities around the world. Of course, many curriculum subjects and academic disciplines involve cultures, but foreign and second language learning involve at least two cultures – a 'target' culture and, necessarily, one's own culture, too, by comparison and reflection – so intercultural learning has long been recognized as necessarily part of most language learning (Damen, 1987; Fennes & Hapgood, 1997; Kramsch, 1998; Hinkel, 1999; Corbett, 2010); actually, from a socio-linguistic research perspective, language learning involves many cultures since few languages are used in just one country, most embrace several or many cultures, and relevant societies are in fact multicultural (McKay & Hornberger, 1996). Intercultural learning has nuanced prepositions: It includes learning *about* and learning *in* and *from* different cultural contexts

1

and *with* different communities; engaging in, appreciating and understanding the processes involved in this; understanding and developing the cultural nature *of* all learning processes and the contexts in which they are embedded or the further contexts they construct. This inherent complexity demands a critical awareness of frameworks and ideologies of participants and, arguably, of discourses and counter-discourses of proponents (Holliday, 2011). Intercultural learning in our view focuses primarily on cultural aspects of *how people learn*, but it implicates key features of who participants *are* (their developing multiple identities, senses of self and others: self-esteem, respect and dignity); what they *do* (their behaviour, roles, ways of interacting, meeting and creating expectations, helping others); what they *think* (expectations, interpretations, mental constructions and ways of understanding); what they *feel* (their social and affective relations with others, contentment, trust, responsibilities, motivations and achievements), and other dynamic features of being human and becoming humane.

Researching intercultural learning thus means investigating any intercultural situations and contexts in which such a range of learning take place with a view to gaining knowledge, increasing insights and applying findings in order to solve problems and improve the learning. Envisaged results of researching intercultural learning include helping all participants, as teachers, learners and related others, to engage in learning in contexts in which cultural features are significant aspects so that the learning is better: more effective, more efficient, more satisfying cognitively, affectively and socially (Ting-Toomey, 1999), with better rapport and relationships (Spencer-Oatey, 2000). As all research involves questions, and as research processes help us to understand underlying complexities and raise more and better questions, the research represented here is necessarily exploratory: It should lead to questions. Perhaps it may evoke comments of 'yes, so ...' or 'yes, but ...' and 'yes, now we need to know ...', but not, we hope, the dismissive 'yes, so what?' Since learning is dynamic, changing in extent, depth, sequence or paradigm, intercultural learning is also changing, and as we conduct research in intercultural learning, the nature of what we research may be seen to change and likely we, too, as researchers and people, change – our own sense of who we are, what we do, think and feel becomes different. We examine intercultural learning at three levels:

- A level in which culture is largely 'out there' content but also 'inter' – between cultures
- A level of developing competencies and skills for interpreting one's own and others' cultures
- A reflexive level centring on learning itself as practices and processes in plural social, educational and cultural enterprises

1 Intercultural learning: 'out there' or 'inter'

t one level, intercultural learning is learning about one or more other cultures to promote awareness and knowledge of these other cultures and to be ble to function within them. 'Other' here means a culture distinguishable nd different from that of the learners. This intercultural learning might elate to any particular context in which such knowledge is thought to be ecessary, such as learning a foreign language or participating in business nd professional activities which involve other cultures.

At this level, culture seems 'out there', sometimes far away, and in the effort o compare cultures there may be an 'us–them' orientation. This binary ivision of contrast is reinforced when specific cultures and audiences are nvisaged, as in books in English for Americans who encounter the Chinese Hu & Grove, 1991; De Mente, 2009) or bilingual books for Chinese who ncounter Americans (Wang & Ma, 1999; Fan & Smith, 2003). In the case f language learning, culture refers to the 'target' culture, and sometimes a source' culture of the learners, terms which in themselves often ignore cultural diversity within the area of reference – usually a single country – may mpose a perception of uniformity, and may tacitly ignore how this target anguage is used around the world and, thus, inherently involves many ultures (Cortazzi & Jin, 1999). At this level the target culture needs to be lural – cultures – and in the case of teaching English there are intercultural mplications of world Englishes (Kirkpatrick, 2007). In many older textbooks for learning another language, this level of intercultural learning can be seen embedded as 'background knowledge' or as an aid to understand the literature(s) and society(ies) of speakers of the language. Sometimes the out there' is reversed but is still mono-directional: for example in textbooks for English as a Second language developed for newly arrived international students in North America and in which the focus is on cultural awareness and developing language and communication skills 'in here', in the United States, with brief cross-cultural comparisons (Genzel and Cummings, 1986; Levine et al., 1987; Hartmann, 1992; Levine & Adelman 1993). This level can be seen in current books for travellers and business people – again as facilitative knowledge and as an aid to help visitors avoid problems in meeting local people. The cultural content likely relates to social customs, etiquette, food, festivals and traditions, landmarks in history and the cultural landscape of arts and the media, the uses of a language with typical gestures and communication practices, and perhaps key information about values or attitudes and beliefs. These kinds of books and courses that use them can be incisively humorous, say about Dutch culture (White & Boucke, 1993; Bolt, 1995), or with extensive use of cartoons, or to 'demystify' Chinese culture (Orem et al., 1997; Ostrowski & Penner, 2009). They can informative and valuable as introductions, as in the series to avoid 'culture shock' (Bayraktaroglu, 1996) and become 'culture smart' (Tomalin, 2003). While they are simplified in order to be accessible, they can certainly be starting points for a deeper engagement with cultures; all learning involves simpli fication at basic levels.

The 'inter' of intercultural learning here is that such learning generally leads participants to reflect on specific aspects of their own cultural prac tices and values and perhaps on their cultural identities. In foreign lan guage teaching this is a designed outcome and normally part of the process. However, a telling point is that the indexes and details of the contents of books omit any mention of *learning*: at most, there may be information about the schools and education system of a target country. At this level the nature of the learning in such intercultural learning is ignored, or it is not discussed because it is assumed. There is no consideration of the com petencies involved and how to develop them. The research is generally to ensure accurate and up-to-date content.

I.2   Intercultural learning: competencies and skills of interpreting

A more complex level of intercultural learning stems largely from intercul tural communication and real uses of learned languages. This level moves from descriptive to interpretive and critical perspectives. This involves famil iarity with language functions, close attention to contextual variation and social diversity, the need to suspend judgement and step outside our own frameworks of interpretation, the search for alternative explanations for what surprises, puzzles or irritates us when we interact with people from cultur ally diverse communities. What matters is not just what is said or done, but how, in response to what and, crucially, with what intention and uptake, and within what kind of communication norms and assumed value systems.

Intercultural learning here, usually in education and global business or international relations, goes well beyond cultural knowledge and pays great attention to developing necessary competencies and sets of skills for dis covering and interpreting what is going on culturally (Byram, 1997). This involves knowing one's self and one's own culture and putting one's own values aside to learn those of others and, thus, to adopt an ethnographic per spective of trying to help learners understand participants in other cultures from their own perspectives (Roberts et al., 2001; Byram et al., 2001) and to use ethnographic perspectives to examine intercultural discourses and pro fessional communication (Scollon & Scollon, 2001; Pan et al. 2002). Thus, intercultural learning here means getting an inside view and entering the interpretive frameworks of others, probably with implications of adopting a critical perspective, and sometimes linked to broader educational values, intercultural and citizenship (Guilherme, 2002; Byram, 2008).

This level involves a more nuanced engagement with, and experience of, other cultures with reflexivity upon one's identity and that of others; these

atures of intercultural competency are notably highlighted in later editions
basic texts on intercultural communication for students, while earlier edi-
ons hardly profiled them (Dodd, 2006; Lustig & Koester, 2007; Samovar
Porter, 2007; Samovar et al., 2009). In practice it may include problem
lving though specific training for sojourners with the use of critical inci-
ents which have variant interpretations and outcomes, sometimes with
nsiderations of ethics, emotions, empathy and managing relationships
cultural adjustment (Brislin and Yoshida, 1994; Landis & Bhagat, 1996;
ushner & Brislin, 1996, 1997). It can include visual literacy to interpret
e visual environment, pictures and print (Corbett, 2003), the recognition
f stereotypes and how 'others' and their identities are represented (Hall,
002; Holliday et al., 2004; Lustig & Koester, 2007), the analysis of situ-
tions through mini-projects or work experience, and reflection on social
ngagement with people in other communities through a variety of aware-
ess-raising activities in classrooms (Tomalin & Stempleski, 1993; Kohls &
night, 1994; Corbett, 2010). This level of intercultural learning is more
ophisticated and complex, much more closely based on direct research and
s applications; it is envisaged as a longer term enterprise and can focus
n the processes of learning relevant competencies through systematic
nalysis and reflection on experience (Alred et al., 2003; Spencer-Oatey &
ranklin, 2009). However, a point often missed here, even in international
nd multicultural contexts, is that the learning might itself be a cultural
rocess (again, the indexes and contents details of books significantly omit
learning').

.3 Intercultural learning: learning as a cultural process

A more reflexive level is to observe that, and how, the learning about cul-
ure – or possibly any other learning – is itself a cultural enterprise in a
cultural context which includes the cultural orientations and practices of
hose learning and of those learned about. If culture is seen as a social prac-
ice, then intercultural relations involve social practices. If culture involves
earning (as it does for children who become cultural members through
early socialization and schooling), and if learning involves culture (as it
does when we see different cultural communities around the world engage
in learning in families and schools in quite different ways with diverse
norms and varying expectations), then we may speak of *cultures of learning*
(Jin & Cortazzi, 1993, 2006; Cortazzi & Jin, 1996). This phrase focuses on
how learning has cultural dimensions, how it is a culturally pluralistic process, and that participants in international and multicultural contexts may
well bring quite different social practices and cultural expectations with
them (Cortazzi, 1990; Jin & Cortazzi, 1998).

Internationally, this matters a lot: it could mean teachers and students
expect to teach or learn in ways that can turn out to be different, with

the danger that the process of learning can be interpreted differently. Suc
interpretations can be transferred to those involved: A student behaving di
ferently for cultural reasons might be assessed as a poor student; a teache
teaching in ways perceived as outside the students' expectations may b
seen as a bad teacher. At this level, participants try to acquire inside pe
spectives on each other's ways of doing and interpreting learning. At thi
level, attention is paid to interaction and discourse: how people explair
ask questions, present answers, use their reading and arrange their writing
say what they know, recognize ambiguity and uncertainly, raise doubts o
counter-arguments (Cortazzi and Jin, 1996, 2002). Attention is given to ho
learning is mediated: by a teacher, by peers, by electronic media, by iden
tity, by the language of shifting concepts and differing uses of key terms
Attention is paid to how learning is construed: as a tool of transmission o
medium of construction; as memory or embodied action; as an adventure
exploration or journey of endurance; as a weapon or as a bridge of reconcili
ation (Berendt, 2008; Cortazzi et al., 2009; Jin & Cortazzi, 2011).

This level of learning is lifetime learning: It applies to professional learning
and development as much as to schools and higher education. Researching
intercultural learning involves the learning of the researchers to identify
our own presuppositions, preferences and research cultures (Cortazzi & Jin
2002); so, while the researcher needs to become an insider, in another sense
the research is inside the researcher. Intercultural learning, developed as con
scious intercultural learning of any particular subject or discipline with ar
international or multicultural group, sooner or later itself constructs another
culture of learning, perhaps an immediate face-to-face more local one.

Since these levels complement each other, they might be combined in
modified versions, as seen in this book. Only by researching and applying
insights at these levels will we reach further levels as yet unspecified.

I.4   The chapters in this book

The variety and range of intercultural learning globally is reflected in a
small way in this book, which focuses on intercultural learning in a variety of contexts. Some ideas of the perspectives involved can be gathered
quickly from a consideration that the authors, as researchers, represent a
dozen countries and research traditions. Significantly, many of them work
collaboratively in intercultural teams. These researchers investigate at least
six major cultural settings and geographical locations and refer to around
30 others. They use research methods which include questionnaire surveys,
interviews and focus group discussions, discourse and documentary analysis, classroom observation and analysis of video recordings of teaching
and learning.

To introduce the chapters of this book, we briefly say something about the
context for each chapter, giving an idea of who the authors are (see Notes on

ontributors for more detail); we outline the nature and main idea of the
search involved and show the relationship between different chapters. We
ke each chapter in sequence.

The United States is widely recognized by both outsiders and its citizens
s having a highly diverse and multicultural population and, with its highly
eveloped education and research capacity, is noted as the world's major
ceiver of migrant and international students. In Chapter 1, Eli Hinkel, her-
elf of Russian origin and an experienced researcher and acclaimed editor
n applied linguistics, focuses on writing as a difficult and complex skill
hich international students need to acquire for university entrance and
raduation success. She surveys contemporary research on discourse and lin-
uistic skills, which she relates to the Test of English as a Foreign Language
TOEFL) test, used internationally as a test of English as a foreign language
or prospective university study, and to a specified range of undergraduate
nd postgraduate demands for writing. This raises awareness of the demands
n writing at different levels of university study, and many of her points will
e seen as also valid beyond the American context. A major point in Hinkel's
hapter is that the sociocultural elements in university writing need to be
nade explicit for international students and to Americans themselves (both
tudents and staff), as a source for reflection and further learning. Thus, this
earning is cultural, cross-cultural, and intercultural, and it can be part of
he internationalization of universities. Since huge numbers of international
nd 'home' students engage in academic writing, and they are directly
aught writing or indirectly taught discipline content through writing tasks
y large numbers of teachers, the details of the research presented here need
o be more widely known in order to develop intercultural learning.

Chapter 2 focuses on international students in the United Kingdom. Like
he American university context, the multicultural higher education system
of Britain has long been internationalizing with international students and,
currently, is transforming its vision so that internationalization is increas-
ngly seen to apply to all students (whether they are nominally home or
nternational participants) and staff: this has implications for the curriculum
content of what is studied, how it is studied, and for the interaction and engagement of all participants (not just of international students). In Chapter
2, Thushari Welikala, of Sri Lankan origin and with her own experience
as an international student, uses her research into the learning of international students in the United Kingdom and, more recently, into academic
staff to examine their 'cultural scripts' through their narratives. Drawing
on culture as 'an ensemble of stories', this study investigates cultural scripts
as learning and teaching activities and relationships to show how teachers recognize diversity in learning and attempt complex responses to it,
which, however, may be limited by assumed stereotypes and institutional
pedagogies which overlook subtle features of culture in learning. Welikala
identifies an emerging 'inter-perspective pedagogy' which is potentially a

significant step towards cultural synergy in intercultural learning and inte
nationalization. Developing such a perspective might be further aided by
close reading of other chapters here.

Denmark, in common with other Scandinavian and Northern Europea
countries, is increasingly receiving international students from both withi
and from outside the European Union; some universities in this region, a
part of their internationalization, offer programmes in English and see this a
beneficial for both local and international learners. In Chapter 3, Jane Vinthe
and Gordon Slethaug, both university educators in English studies and com
munication and, respectively, of Danish and American/Norwegian heritage
trace the multiple traditions of higher education in Denmark, where ther
is a German heritage from the philosophy of Wilhelm von Humboldt an
a Danish one through the thinking of N. F. S. Gruntvig with some Englis
influences. The confluence of these heritages emphasizes self-reliance, in
dependence, autonomy and research together with strong ideas about com
munity and 'conversation' in learning; the authors consider these in som
detail with their key concepts and then analyse interview data with Danish
Chinese, European and other students to investigate how, for these students
the traditions enhance or restrict learning. Like the previous chapters, they
suggest that mutual reflection by students and staff on these learning issue
can lead to dynamic renewal and synergies of interpretation. In Denmark
this might be termed 'internationalizing the conversational learning'. By im
plication, readers may see not only the reconciliation of traditions withir
Denmark and how these may be challenged by incoming learners, but how
Danish insights might inform debates on intercultural learning elsewhere.

Hong Kong is another intercultural learning site: here is an obvious nexus
of educational and language traditions which have influenced local cultures
of learning, strands of which relate to the special administrative region's
role internationally and in relation to mainland China. Complementing
migration from mainland China, Hong Kong schools and particularly
universities are receiving more mainland students speaking Putonghua
(Mandarin), and local people in Hong Kong are increasingly learning
this standard language of China; thus the current policy is tri-lingual
(Cantonese, English and Putonghua) and bi-literate (since Cantonese and
Putonghua have nearly identical writing systems, though with very different pronunciation). Strands of learning cultures are complex. Linguistically,
these include the acknowledged substratum of Cantonese with newer layers
of Putonghua and the widespread use of English, besides other minority
languages; educationally, the long-standing British colonial influence sits
alongside Chinese traditions which influence the Hong Kong curriculum. In
Chapter 4, Phil Glenwright and Wang Lixun, British and Chinese authors,
with long experience of teacher education and research in Hong Kong, review the major strands of British and Chinese cultures of learning and a
local educational synergy as the context for their investigation into how

e policy for bi-literacy and trilingualism is realized in one primary school. heir research draws on data from recorded lessons, interviews with teach-s and questionnaires from learners; it shows a current dominance of a hinese culture of learning as different languages are used for different cur-culum subjects, but there are wider educational implications.

Chapter 5 also has a focus on a primary school, this one in southern hina, looking at an immersion class. Compared to primary schools in ost Anglophone and European countries, schools in China are large and ten have large classes, frequently with specialist teachers and a formal ode of classroom teaching, though increasingly pair work and group work n be seen. In this primary school, another language, English, is learned tensively from zero level through its use as a medium for learning major arts of the curriculum. This follows the success of immersion schooling, hich originated in Canada and has spread to the United States, Germany, ungary, Singapore and Japan, and is increasingly attempted in China as way of developing high-level language and cultural proficiency. Xiaohua iang, with Jin and Cortazzi, as a Sino-British team with strong teaching and esearch experience with young learners, draw on observations, video and udio recordings of interaction in and out of class (it is a boarding school) nd teacher interviews to focus on details of peer interaction. Conceptually, hey draw on a Vygotskian model of peer assistance, which originated in the york of Lev Vygotsky in Russia and has been widely taken up and developed n combining activity and extending dialogue in 'scaffolding' learning in Jorth America and Europe, and now in China. They show how children an give nuanced support to each other for English in a teacher-encouraged node of learning; this represents considerable change in learning culture rom the ways of learning found in most primary schools in China. This uggests that the school system as a whole might benefit from this kind of esearch, not only for examining the development of learning another lan-guage to high levels of proficiency but also for insights into the roles of peer nteraction in developing newer cultures of learning.

This focus on the micro-interactional aspects of intercultural learning in a specific educational context continues in Chapter 6. In British universities, as in many higher educational systems, a one-to-one tutorial between an academic and a student is commonly regarded as a major learning context in which, within an expected particular genre of dialogue, students discuss issues in their discipline in depth. Commonly, given the large number of international students, tutorials are intercultural encounters; thus, it cannot be assumed that the nature, purpose and ways of learning in a tutorial are understood, especially when students come from a very different cultural and educational background in which tutorials may be rare or unknown. Often, both academics and students are aware of interactional difficulties in tutorials but are unable to pinpoint what these are. Here, in Chapter 6, Joan Turner and Masako K. Hiraga, as an established British–Japanese research

team who investigate academic cultures and issues in intercultural pragma
ics, analyse two contrasting case studies of Japanese students interacting
tutorials with their British teachers in a UK university. Rather than look
language, they investigate the learning of the discipline of fine arts, whe
the one-to-one interactions of tutorials have a strong role in developin
the learners' understanding of disciplinary principles, largely through ve
balization. Turner and Hiraga draw on video recordings of tutorials and,
year later, on retrospective interviews with the same students, who refle
upon and explain their learning experience. This research strategy allow
the authors to investigate the genre of tutorials and the 'epistemic princ
ples' or the underlying principles which motivate teaching and learnin
in the discipline and, significantly, the extent to which the students hav
adapted or reacted to the British tutorial interactive norms and the discip
line norms underlying this interaction. Significantly, in both these cases th
students are successful but, rather than adapting simply to the host institu
tion's norms and expectations, they work around them; thus the autho
conclude that here the intercultural learning is less adaptive; it is more
matter of permutations of 'different clines of institutional dynamics'. Th
details of this research and the principles revealed are potentially very help
ful to university teachers and students in international contexts.

    The dynamics of institutional learning is further investigated in Chapte
7, which is about local and international students in Britain. Here, Kendal
Richards and Nick Pilcher, a British team who develop innovative research
approaches into aspects of English for Academic Purposes, focus on how
students come to understand terms which are key to academic work: 'dis
cuss', 'analyse', 'define', and similar terms are found especially in instruc
tions and rubrics for tasks and exam questions in which students' learning
is assessed. The details are intriguing. The particular students here are calle
'non-traditional': they are older than the 18–22 age group; they procee
straight into a second, third or fourth year of undergraduate study becaus
they have previous professional working experience (generally British stu
dents) or because in a partnership arrangement with other universities
internationally they have already completed one, two or three years o
study (generally international students, in this case from China). Crucially
both the British and Chinese groups have different cultural orientations to
study compared to 'traditional' learners. Through the use of cascading focus
groups, by which the different groups of students and teachers progressively
come together in discussion, Richards and Pilcher show how a structured
dialogue exposes differences and gaps in understanding the key terms and
how the dialogic process helps to close the gaps. Thus a particular focussed
discussion enhances intercultural learning with indigenous students (here,
within the diverse British students) and with international learners (here,
from China), and between these groups and their teachers. The immediate
application of this research is for teachers and students together to make an

plicit effort to share their understanding of these and similar key terms;
vider application is to identify and discuss with participants any key con-
pts which mediate student learning and assessment.

Chapter 8 also follows international students from China, in this case in a
niversity in New Zealand, closely tracked for three years by Gillian Skyrme,
New Zealand researcher and specialist in teaching writing and English for
ademic Purposes. New Zealand has a long tradition of receiving inter-
ational students from the Pacific Islands and more recently has become
destination for increasing numbers of students from East Asia. Using
ata from a series of interviews and student reflections, Skyrme focuses on
ow these students develop academic writing in a setting of intercultural
arning. The particular students bring a high level of dependency but are
xpected to develop personal analytic thinking skills through writing (see
hapter 1). Thus, beyond development of their English, they face social and
iscourse requirements and a series of tensions between the encouragement to show originality and their need for explicit guidance and models;
etween the local expectation to find their own 'voice' (having something
 say and representing the self in how it is said) and using others' voices
hrough borrowing from models, quoting, and perhaps sliding into pla-
iarism), and considerations of agency and autonomy. Crucially for inter-
ultural learning, Skyrme shows the importance of peer assistance in facing
hese tensions and meeting university requirements in student writing.

The three following chapters look at transcultural adjustment beyond
nglophone situations: in the contexts of learning German, French and
hinese as foreign languages. We think these contexts represent at least
ome other world languages and the present examples of research are sig-
ificant because so much work in intercultural learning, and many other
hapters here, is in the context of international uses of English and mediated
hrough that particular language with its associated cultures (and cultures
f learning and cultures of research). Having at hand examples of research
n intercultural learning related to other languages is important and, in
rinciple, it is vital to investigating the language, cultural and educational
inks to intercultural learning in any contexts and combinations, whether
hey are considered major or minor, global or local, familiar or unfamiliar.
Without a range of research, our thinking about intercultural learning is
n danger of being somewhat restricted and, perhaps, unadventurous and
unimaginative.

In Chapter 9, Markus Lux and Christian Wochele, both international
teachers of German as a foreign language and teacher educators, examine
how young teachers from Germany experience teaching German in universities in unfamiliar contexts in no fewer than 24 Eastern European and
Central Asian countries and in China. This reminds us of the major influence of Germany in Europe and of strong historical and contemporary links
with Eastern Europe. The teaching in focus here is carried out under the

auspices of the work of a non-governmental foundation which sponsors
two-year lectureship programme which has the overall aim of strengtheni
international relations and understanding with Germany through linguis
and cultural education. Lux and Wochele focus on how these teachers he
their students adjust to German cultures and, particularly, how the teac
ers themselves are learning local languages and cultures: In a reciproc
relationship, they later bring back their developed skills, enhanced und
standing and insights for subsequent employment and careers in German
Using a documentary analysis of ten years of archived teacher reports a
some interviews, the authors present a rich picture through the teache
perceptions of, and reflections upon, how they encounter the unfamili
and unexpected: for instance the 'schoolification' and intellectual depen
ence of many learners on teachers, which stems from (the German teache
believe) school-like attitudes, which is contrasted with the teachers' desi
to foster more mature, independent learning and thinking and to use ava
able creative spaces for pedagogic innovations, which are more in acco
with German cultures of learning.

Chapter 10 turns to France, where students from China are learni
and using French, often as a third language after English, since Frenc
although available in a few schools and many universities, is still not co
monly learned in China, while English is learned nearly universally by c
lege students. Like Chapters 3 and 9, this chapter reminds us that ma
international students learn outside Anglophone areas, and that English
not the only language of internationalization: French higher education
also highly multicultural, receiving students from many minority ethn
communities and, internationally, from Francophone and other countrie
Wang Jinjing and Sophie Bailly, respectively a Chinese researcher and a
experienced French applied linguist, use initial interviews with students
the basis for constructing a questionnaire with which to explore the ga
between Chinese students' experiences and expectations and those pr
sented by their French teachers. These gaps relate to both 'language cultur
and 'learning culture'; they create both cognitive and affective discomfo
for the learners. The gaps show up in aspects of learning language skil
attitudes towards using textbooks, reservations about interaction and gro
work, and a different understanding of what is meant by 'autonomy'. 1
close the gaps, teachers need to make explicit the rationale underlying the
pedagogic practices and, as the authors here indicate, respect learners' cu
tures of learning in order to develop cultural synergies.

In Chapter 11, the focus is on how well-motivated Western adult learne
of Chinese develop their intercultural awareness and skills as they encount
features of Chinese cultures, using textbooks but, as students in a distanc
learning programme, largely exchanging their reactions, interpretations an
ideas through electronic media. Chinese is increasingly learned as a foreig
language: The rapid development of this is seen in the worldwide Confuci

stitutes, the introduction of Chinese in schools and universities in many untries, and in the rapid increase in the number of international students ing to China to study Chinese. The exchanges are in English, though a bstantial portion of the learners are Europeans with first languages other an English. Inma Álvarez and Kan Qian, respectively, a specialist in teaching Spanish, dance and performing arts and a specialist in teaching Chinese a foreign language, examine the individual and group positioning on atures of Chinese culture as discussed by participants online in a 'culture rum', through which students reflect on their own and others' cultural rspectives. Through a discourse analysis of forum postings and some follow-up interviews, the researchers analyse 'interculturality in action' and 1ow how in peer dialogues the students argue, draw on outside evidence, 1allenge each other, and offer evidence and explanations on cultural interretations. The authors contextualize the asynchronous online forum as a 1edium of intercultural learning and show, with reservations, how it offers otential for learners to impact each other's intercultural competence.

Chapter 12 offers a contrast by researching how Chinese students from 1ong Kong, through the personal experience of travel in student exchanges, djust to different cultures of learning; the student participants went on xchanges for a semester to three English-speaking countries and five others. he students' learning here is, again, beyond language learning, since students in Hong Kong have been learning and using English for much or most f their school years (see Chapter 4) and English-medium learning is quite amiliar to university students. In Chapter 12, Jane Jackson, a Canadian esearcher with wide experience in Hong Kong, investigates the trajectorzes of their intercultural development using a self-assessment inventory, a tandardized questionnaire and pre-departure and on-return interviews. he shows the details of how the exchange students, compared statistically o a control group and shifted to a greater intercultural worldview. In the 1ew learning contexts, the Hong Kong students had difficulty understanding the purpose of, and engaging in, the expected active class discussions 1nd felt uncomfortable with the communication styles of some host stu-lents; they had expected to receive more guidance from teachers than was ;iven – host teachers expected more independent learning.

Chapter 13, like Chapter 11, is based on an investigation of how the new nedia affect intercultural teaching and learning, here examining how stu-lents in China learn English and may acquire intercultural competence :hrough Internet mediation. Given the extremely rapid global spread and wide use of the Internet and its various uses in education, Liang Wang, a Chinese researcher currently working in the United Kingdom in the field of Chinese as a foreign language, maps out some current possibilities and syn-thesizes a framework for teachers working with a single class or for cross-site collaboration between classes and institutions; details of relevant principles are elaborated. Wang's research surveys 24 higher education institutions

in China with questionnaires and uses interviews and class observatio:
to give detailed characteristics of Internet use in four contrasting ca
study institutions with differing types of students learning various leve
of English. Chinese teachers of English in the study welcome Interne
based banks of resources for teaching and learning, and their studen
especially use the Internet for professional websites as sources of inform
tion – generally working in pairs or groups to prepare class presentation
Many students' attitudes and their usage of social networking possibiliti
for intercultural learning seem ambiguous; this is due to biases in favour
contact with 'native speakers' and against home-based materials, cultur
and 'non-native speakers'. This means that they use online forums less (i
contrast to learners in Chapter 11) and generally simply to express their ow
ideas rather than to actually interact with peers. Thus, it appears that unde
lying social attitudes and cultures of learning influence the use of Interne
mediated intercultural teaching and learning. Teachers, whose knowledg
enthusiasm and role in out-of-class or off-campus online networking ar
crucial for a more engaged use with a wider variety of speakers and culture
of global Englishes, could change this situation, but their own cultures c
learning and intercultural attitudes may need development first.

In their conclusions, Jin and Cortazzi present some critical reflections o
the book as a whole by drawing out some implications of some key theme
related to language, culture and learning; to the roles of teachers, student
and peers; and to collaboration in research. They draw together some sug
gestions for further research.

I.5   Intercultural learning includes all of us

In cultural matters, as researchers and readers we need to be aware of som
cautions: the need to hold both universals and commonalities in mind whil
discussing differences; the need to challenge stereotypes and counterac
them; to beware of making participants into exotic 'others' (or any others a
all); and to take care with simplifications and categories, especially when i
is clear that many or most cultural contexts in education involve multipli
city. Intercultural learning develops interweavings, mixtures and mergers. In
the end, we need to change the pronominal orientation with participants in
education, whether as teachers, learners, researchers or associated others: it is
not *I* and *You* or *They* – but *We*. However, we can learn more from pronouns
in different languages – we can think of Fijian, for instance (Milner, 1972),
as one of those languages which distinguishes in grammar among a much
larger set of 90 or so pronouns with graceful nuances between 'I , the speaker
and one/ two/ three others present but not you the addressee or others', 'I,
the speaker, and you the addressee but not others' and 'I, the speaker and a
few/ more others present and you the addressee'. Such exclusive or inclusive
distinctions, as they are known, mean that a host can say to a guest 'This is

r house' with a grammatical choice of *our* either to exclude the addressee
a passing other or foreigner or to include the guest as one who is truly
•lcome and included as part of the family. In intercultural learning, we
lieve, we need the maximum inclusion of, We as 'speakers, teachers, stu-
nts, researchers and our peoples and all other members of humanity.' The
•int of intercultural learning is that it includes all of us in the same human
•mily. Intercultural learning is a nexus – a complicated series of connec-
•ns around the globe between identifiably different learning communities,
:losely connected group of us learning something central in our lives.

•ferences

red, G., Byram, M. & Fleming, M. (Eds) (2003) *Intercultural experience and education*. Clevedon: Multilingual Matters.
•yraktaroglu, A. (1996) *Culture shock! Turkey*. Singapore: Times Books International.
•rendt, E. (Ed.) (2008) *Metaphors for learning, cross-cultural perspectives*. Amsterdam: John Benjamins.
•lt, R. (1995) *The xenophobe's guide to the Dutch*. Horsham: Ravette Publishing.
•rislin, R.W. & Yoshida, T. (Eds) (1994) *Improving intercultural interactions*. Thousand Oaks: Sage Publications.
•yram, M. (1997) *Teaching and assessing intercultural communication competence*. Clevedon: Multilingual Matters.
•yram, M. (2008) *From foreign language education to education for intercultural citizenship: Essays and reflections*. Clevedon: Multilingual Matters.
•yram, M., Nichols, A. & Stevens, D. (2001) *Developing intercultural competence in practice*. Clevedon: Multilingual Matters.
:orbett, J. (2003) *An intercultural approach to English language teaching*. Clevedon: Multilingual Matters.
:orbett, J. (2010) *Intercultural language activities*. Cambridge: Cambridge University Press.
:ortazzi, M. (1990) Cultural and educational expectations in the language class-room. In B. Harrison (Ed.), *Culture and the Language Classroom*. London: Modern English Publications/The British Council, pp. 54–65.
:ortazzi, M. & Jin, L. (1996) Cultures of learning: Language classrooms in China. In H. Coleman (Ed.), *Society and the Language Classroom*. Cambridge: Cambridge University Press, pp. 169–206.
:ortazzi, M. & Jin, L. (1999) Cultural mirrors: Materials and methods in the EFL classroom. In E. Hinkel (Ed.), *Culture in Second Language Teaching and Learning*. Cambridge: Cambridge University Press, pp. 90–108.
:ortazzi, M. & Jin, L. (2002) Cultures of learning: The social construction of educational identities. In D.C.S. Li (Ed.), *Discourses in search of members, in honor of Ron Scollon*. Lanham: University Press of America, pp. 49–78.
:ortazzi, M., Jin, L. & Wang, Z. (2009) Cultivators, cows and computers: Chinese learners' metaphors of teachers. In T. Coverdale-Jones & P. Rastall (Eds), *Internationalizing the university, the Chinese context*. Houndmills: Palgrave Macmillan, pp. 107–29.
Cushner, K. & Brislin, R.W. (1996) *Intercultural interactions, a practical guide*. Thousand Oaks: Sage Publications.
Cushner, K. & Brislin, R.W. (Eds) (1997) *Improving intercultural interactions, modules for cross-cultural training programs*, Vol. 2. Thousand Oaks: Sage Publications.

Damen, L. (1987) *Culture learning: The fifth dimension in the language classroo*. Reading, Mass; Addison-Wesley.

De Mente, B.L. (2009) *The Chinese mind, understanding traditional Chinese beliefs a* *their influence on contemporary culture*. Tokyo: Tuttle Publishing.

Dodd, C.H. (2006) *Dynamics of intercultural communication* (5th edn). Shangha Shanghai Foreign Language Education Press.

Fan, D. & Smith, S.L.J. (2003) *Cultures in contrast: Miscommunication and misunderstan* *ing between Chinese and North Americans*. Shanghai: Shanghai Foreign Langua Education Press.

Fennes, H. & Hapgood, K. (1997) *Intercultural learning in the classroom*. Londo Cassell.

Genzel, R.B. & Cummings, M.G. (1986) *Culturally speaking, a conversation and cultu* *text for learners of English*. Singapore: HarperCollins Publishers.

Guilherme, M. (2002) *Critical citizens for an intercultural world, foreign language educ* *tion as cultural politics*. Clevedon: Multilingual Matters.

Hall, J.K. (2002) *Teaching and researching language and culture*. London: Longman.

Hartman, P. (1992) *Clues to culture, a cross-cultural reading/writing book*. New Yor Random House.

Hinkel, E. (1999) *Culture in second language teaching and learning*. Cambridg Cambridge University Press.

Holliday, A. (2011) *Intercultural communication and ideology*. Los Angeles: Sage.

Holliday, A., Hyde, M. & Kullman, J. (2004) *Intercultural communication, an advance* *resource book*. London: Routledge.

Hu, W. & Grove, C.L. (1991) *Encountering the Chinese, a guide for Americans*. Yarmouthm MA: Intercultural Press.

Jin, L. & Cortazzi, M. (1993) Cultural orientation and academic language use. I D. Graddol, L. Thompson & M. Byram (Eds), *Language and Culture*. Clevedon Multilingual Matters, pp. 84–97.

Jin, L. & Cortazzi, M. (1998) The culture the learner brings: A bridge or a barrier In M. Byram & M. Fleming (Eds), *Language learning in intercultural perspective* *approaches through drama and ethnography*. Cambridge: Cambridge University Press pp. 98–118.

Jin, L. & Cortazzi, M. (2006) Changing practices in Chinese cultures of learning *Language, Culture and Curriculum*, 19 (1), 5–20.

Jin, L. & Cortazzi, M. (2011) More than a journey: 'Learning' in the metaphors o Chinese students and teachers. In L. Jin & M. Cortazzi (Eds), *Researching Chinese* *learners: Skills, perceptions and inter cultural adaptations*. Houndmills: Palgrave Macmillan, pp. 67–92.

Kirkpatrick, A. (2007) *World Englishes, Implications for international communication and* *English language teaching*. Cambridge: Cambridge University Press.

Kohls, L.R. & Knight, J.M. (1994) *Developing intercultural awareness, a cross-cultural* *training handbook*. Yarmouth, Mass.: Intercultural Press.

Kramsch, C. (1998) *Language and Culture*. Oxford: University Press.

Landis, D. & Bhagat, R.S. (1996) (Eds) *Handbook of intercultural training* (2nd edn). Thousand Oaks: Sage Publications.

Levine, D.R. & Adelman, M.B. (1993) *Beyond language, cross-cultural communication* (2nd edn). Englewood Cliffs: Prentice Hall.

Levine, D.R., Baxter, J. & McNulty, P. (1987) *The culture puzzle, cross-cultural communi-* *cation for English as a second language*. Englewood Cliffs: Prentice Hall.

Lustig, M.W. & Koester, J. (2007) *Intercultural competence, interpersonal communication* *across cultures* (5th edn). New York: Longman.

rtin, J. & Nakayama, T.K. (2009) *Intercultural communication in contexts* (3rd edn). Beijing: McGraw-Hill/Foreign Language Teaching and Research Press.

Kay, S.L. & Hornberger, N.H. (Eds) (1996) *Sociolinguistics and language teaching.* Cambridge: Cambridge University Press.

lner, G.B. (1972) *Fijian grammar.* Suva, Fiji: Government Press.

em, R.A., Wang, S. & Min, B-C. (1997) *Ugly Chinese, ugly Americans.* Seoul: BCM Publishers.

trowski, P. & Penner, G. (2009) *It's all Chinese to me, an overview of culture and etiquette in China.* Tokyo: Tuttle Publishing.

n, Y., Scollon, S.W. & Scollon, R. (2002) *Professional communication in international settings.* Oxford: Blackwell Publishers.

berts, C., Byram, M., Barro, A., Jordan, S. & Street, B. (2001) *Language learners as ethnographers.* Clevedon: Multilingual Matters.

movar, L.A. & Porter, R.E. (2007) (Eds.) *Intercultural communication, a reader* (10th edn). Shanghai: Shanghai Foreign Language Education Press.

movar, L.A., Porter, R. & McDaniel, E.R. (2009) *Communication between Cultures* (6th edn). Beijing: Peking University Press.

ollon, R. & Scollon, S.W. (2001) *Intercultural communication, a discourse approach* (2nd edn). Oxford: Blackwell Publishers.

ency-Oatey, H. (2000) *Culturally speaking, managing rapport through talk across cultures.* London: Continuum.

ency-Oatey, H. & Franklin, P. (2009) *Intercultural interaction, a multidisciplinary approach to intercultural communication.* Houndmills: Palgrave Macmillan.

ing-Toomey, S. (1999) *Communication across Cultures.* New York: The Guilford Press.

malin, B. (2003/2009) *Culture smart! Germany.* Beijing: Foreign Language Teaching and Research Press.

malin, B. & Stempleski, S. (1993) *Cultural awareness.* Oxford: Oxford University Press.

Vang, F. & Ma, D. (1999) *An analytical survey of cultural clashes.* Beijing: Petroleum Industries Publisher.

Vhite, C. & Boucke, L. (1993) *The Undutchables, an observation of the Netherlands: Its culture and inhabitants.* Lafayette, Co.: White Boucke Publishing.

Part I

Researching Transformations of Cultures of Learning through Internationalization

Cultures of Learning and Writing in the US Academy

Eli Hinkel

1 Overview

The past several decades have seen a dramatic growth in international student enrolments worldwide and in the United States, in particular. International students can include, for instance, such sojourners as: college and university students, academically bound learners who seek to obtain language skills prior to the beginning of their careers; professionals, or employees of a broad range of organizations, as well as their family members. Those who undertake to study in the United States often learn English as a second language (L2); here, the term *second language (L2)* refers to English as a second, foreign, or an additional language in bilingual or multilingual contexts. Such learners can come from all walks of academic life and pursue their learning objectives in various types of colleges and universities (Altbach and Knight, 2007).

Due to the ever-increasing pace of globalization and the mobility across national borders, large numbers of international students and new immigrants are enrolled in US colleges and universities (Open Doors, 2011). Both international and immigrant students can be enrolled in the US academy. However, one of the crucial differences between the former and the latter lies in their expected length of residence in the United States: international students are granted temporary visas with the express purpose of obtaining higher education, while immigrants are usually permanent residents or US citizens. In many investigations of these populations, the distinctions between these two groups are frequently not taken into account because considerations of social, cultural, and academic adjustments can apply equally to both cohorts of students. In the discussion below, as in many other studies, the legal status of L2 college and university enrollees is seen as being of little importance.

International learners of all kinds bring to the academic arena a great diversity of cultures of learning that are distinct from those commonly found in US educational institutions (or those in other English-speaking countries) (e.g., Andrade, 2006). L2 students are often faced with a complex adaptation to US academic and cultural norms, and particularly those that pertain to the Anglo-American culture of learning and, more specifically, the cultu of academic writing (Hinkel, 1999; Lee, 2010; Wang, 2000). Martin Cortaz and Lixian Jin (1996: 169) state, for example, that 'any particular culture learning will have its roots in educational, and, more broadly, cultural trac tions of the community, or society in which it is located'. According to J and Cortazzi (2006: 9), the term 'culture of learning' refers to the commor assumed, and taken-for-granted, frameworks of expectations, attitudes, va ues, and beliefs associated with teaching and learning. In this light, cu tural attitudes and values also pertain to writing in the academy and to th educational goals that writing is expected to achieve. Broad-based societ frameworks undergird the culture of learning and writing in the academ These frameworks also apply to how learners understand what is expecte of them in writing assignments and how academic knowledge and writte discourse are evaluated in their studies (Hinkel, 2011; Wang, 2000).

In general terms, culturally determined rules of appropriateness an contextualized relevance in written discourse and academic genres hea ily impact on what content and ideas can be conveyed, how they are t be conveyed in accordance with the sociocultural norms, and how wri ten discourse and text reflect the social contexts in language use. As man teachers know from experience, learning to write in accordance with th rhetorical formats and norms expected in English academic discourse ca be a complicated and protracted process (e.g., Ferris and Hedgcock, 200! Hinkel, 2002, 2011).

Many investigations of L2 skills have continually underscored that aca demic writing represents one of the most vital, and probably the most di ficult, in an enormous range of abilities that newly enrolled cross-cultura learners need to attain. In the United States, the sociocultural elements o constructing academic writing and formal features of written discours place great demands on students' abilities. Thus, first, it seems necessary t take a look at the cultural foundations of student writing and formal writter discourse in US colleges and universities. Based on several recent studies the features of discourse expected in student writing and the specific cri teria for their evaluation in the academy are also discussed, together with a brief description of student writing tasks in university courses.

1.2   Cultural bases of student academic writing in US colleges and universities

Research in the cultures of learning has demonstrated that cultural con structs in discourse and linguistic proficiency in academic writing play an indelible role in learners' success in education. For instance, Cortazzi (2007) outlines a substantial number of variables that impact the attainment of the necessary skills in academic writing in English. These include (ibid.: 1): 'lin guistic, ethnic, social, cultural, and religious background and community embership; educational and social experience, and the role and extent of evious learning and use of English; the purpose of migration, and so on' id.). The author goes on to say that in practically all cases, the general idelines for 'developing writing skills for these learners will need to be odified in relation to school and classroom context and the individual arners' needs'.

In another research report, Jin and Cortazzi (2006: 18–19) similarly point at the many cultural complexities that students encounter when learning construct written academic discourse: 'students are likely to face a num-er of challenges linked to written...learning' due to a range of reasons. hese can be 'a weakness in academic essay writing, due to a relative lack emphasis on developing English writing' in those locations where 'few achers have developed a high ability in writing in English'. In addition, ue to a lack of familiarity with 'discourse patterns expected in' academic ritten prose, 'students may use a background-before-main-point presenta-on of ideas, but this inductive pattern can be misunderstood by...teachers n English-speaking countries] if they do not find main ideas where they xpect them'. Further difficulties in learning to produce appropriate aca-emic writing may stem from students' 'unfamiliarity with academic expec-ations for written assessment, including unfamiliarity with the required ritical responses and style of expressing personal ideas in academic work'. s Jin and Cortazzi explain, in students' academic preparation, learning to roduce formal written discourse receives comparatively little emphasis in ducation in various regions and, thus, it does not become 'part of students' cademic socialization'.

Today, most language teachers and methodologists take it for granted that ritten discourse and language are inextricable from social and cultural ontexts in the academy. Practically all L2 students who prepare to enter de-ree programs in US colleges and universities dedicate vast amounts of time nd resources to learning to produce written academic prose. Unfortunately, s Jin and Cortazzi (2006) note, teachers (or students) in preparatory English anguage programs do not always have a clear picture of the types of writ-ng and written discourse tasks required of students at the university level. n particular, academic learners need to become relatively well-versed in lisplaying knowledge of the subject matter within the formats expected in vritten academic discourse and text (e.g., Hinkel, 2001; Jin and Cortazzi, 1998b, 2006, 2011; Paltridge, 2006). To put it simply, the content of aca-lemic writing must be structured in a manner that meets the reader's cul-tural presuppositions and assumptions in order to enable him or her to discern the writer's intent and identify the stance.

In university writing, the features of written discourse and text need to follow a conventional genre-specific form and meet the sociocultural norms of appropriateness expected in student papers (e.g., Celce-Murcia and Olshtain, 2005; Ferris and Hedgcock, 2005; Hinkel, 1994). It is important

to note that discourse frameworks in various cultures adhere to and val[ue]
different rhetorical conventions (e.g., Hinkel, 1994, 2011; Jin and Cortaz[zi]
2011). For instance, as Jin and Cortazzi (2006) state, in many languages, t[he]
main idea (or the thesis) is not directly stated at the beginning of writing b[ut]
is usually implied or alluded to throughout. In this case, L2 students soci[al]-
ized into such L1 discourse paradigms have to be explicitly taught that f[or]
American academic readers it is the writer who is responsible for making t[he]
main point clear early in the text, rather than it being the reader's task [to]
follow an exposition and draw a conclusion which is intended to be draw[n]
but is not necessarily made explicit.

Research has determined that what is appropriate and inappropriate i[n]
academic written discourse in English is highly conventionalized (e.g[.,]
Hinkel, 2001; Swales, 1990, 2004). Typically, writing instruction focuses o[n]
such fundamental features of formal academic discourse as the organizatio[n]
of information (e.g., introduction, body, conclusion, and other discours[e]
moves), the presence and the placement of the thesis statement, the stru[c]-
ture of the paragraph (e.g., the topic sentence), the rhetorical support fo[r]
the thesis included in every paragraph, and an avoidance of needless digres-
sions, repetition, and redundancy, among many other factors. Thus, th[e]
purpose of writing is often stated explicitly at the outset: that is, a deductiv[e]
framework plays a crucial role in how discourse is constructed and understood (Ferris, 2011; Scollon and Scollon, 2001).

The reason that the features of academic writing are difficult for mos[t]
L2 students to learn is that they represent normative and relatively rigi[d]
characteristics of the academic genre that are not necessarily found in written discourse in rhetorical traditions other than the Anglo-American on[e]
(Hinkel, 1999, 2001). For example, educated L2 learners who are socialize[d]
in other rhetorical traditions are rarely aware of the US academic expect[-]
ation that a clear thesis statement should be placed close to the beginnin[g]
of one's essay (see Jin and Cortazzi, 2006). Furthermore, sociocultural dis[-]
course paradigms prescribe what can or cannot be included in academi[c]
writing or what can or cannot be discussed in an academic essay (e.g. Cai[,]
1999; Coffin et al., 2003). For example, discussions of family affairs, one'[s]
religious beliefs or political views, or certain social attitudes are considere[d]
unacceptable in academic writing. The assumed purpose of student university writing is to display and present knowledge of subject matter in accordance with the sociocultural expectations prevalent in the US academy (e.g.,
Celce-Murcia and Olshtain, 2005; Swales, 2004; Turner; 2011).

1.3   Sociocultural construction of academic writing and discourse

Along with many other researchers, Anna Mauranen (1996: 1–2) observes
that writing and its attendant genre-specific paradigms follow culturally

termined rhetorical practices that manifest themselves in typical discourse and linguistic features that pivot on fundamental sociocultural conducts. She further comments that writers may not be (and often are not) aware of these textual features or the underlying rhetorical practices because they are an integral element of schooling or literacy learning. In cross-cultural settings, the distinctions between writing paradigms 'are more than a difference in cultural tastes' because these impact not merely the readers' expectations of rhetorical elegance and style, but can be seen (in the US academy) as a lack of coherence in writing or even of confused thinking and, thus, seriously damage 'the credibility of nonnative writers'.

It seems that, for L2 students, one of the top priorities in learning to construct academic discourse and text is to identify their needs in learning the US culture of writing (e.g., Paltridge, 2006). Another important consideration is to investigate how learners' own culturally determined beliefs, assumptions, and expectations affect their views on what is appropriate and valued in writing and discourse frameworks in various societies. For instance, to help learners take a different view of how written academic discourse is to be constructed, teachers may need to provide explicit instruction in US cultural norms in academic writing, L2 reader expectations, and the value of explicit argumentation and evidential examples in the Anglo-American student academic genre. This means that US teachers of writing themselves need not only explicit twofold awareness of their own cultural writing and discourse frameworks and of those of their particular international students using English as an L2, but the teachers also need to have relevant pedagogic strategies to relate these together for the students' benefit.

L1 socialization in written discourse paradigms usually has so much influence on learning to write in an L2 that often, even with explicit instruction, learners are not always able to recognize the rhetorical features of L2 discourse in practice (Hinkel, 1994). In addition, however, as with most L2 learning, students need to work with a wide range of sociocultural norms and conventions prevalent in US academy. This factor alone makes it harder for learners to understand and apply what they are instructed to do. In many human societies, writing and literacy represent one of the most highly valued and prized domains of socialization and education. For this reason, many L2 learners may initially choose to adhere to the discourse frameworks acquired in their L1 literacy socialization and the value associated with the appropriateness of writing in a particular way. For example, in English, speakers are expected to present their points in a manner that is more direct than that common among speakers of many other languages (Jin and Cortazzi, 2011; Scollon and Scollon, 2001). Thus, in Anglo-American discourse, indirectness is devalued as a hallmark of politeness in student prose and, hence, should be avoided by students in the United States (Hinkel, 1997).

Despite some amount of variation that can be identified in the features of academic discourse and text across disciplines, many represent what Swales

(1990, 2004) identified as recurring patterns of organization that appear
be greatly consistent across academic genres and university courses in t
Anglo-American academy. Based on Swales's findings, recurring structu
features of academic discourse consist of purposeful and predictable d
course elements, such as a sequence in which there are moves establishi
or introducing the topic and discussing its importance; reviewing earlier
search or other sources of information; preparing and reasoning for the p
sent analysis and/or literature synthesis of information, and constructing
body of evidence. It is important to note that such constructs as introduci
a topic, reviewing earlier research and pertinent sources of information, p
senting analytical reasoning, and relevant evidence, all reflect appropria
and normative cultural attributes of academic discourse and text expect
and taken-for-granted in the US academic discourse community. These, ho
ever, are not necessarily shared or even similarly understood by members
other cultures and sociocultural communities (Cortazzi and Jin, 2002; J
and Cortazzi, 1998a, 2011; Ferris and Hedgcock, 2005; Hedgcock, 2005).

In addition to discourse norms, there are also textual patterns in ac
demic prose. For example, according to Swales (1990), academic writing an
text in published articles in such diverse disciplines as mathematics an
rhetoric share several important characteristics. For example, average ser
tence length remained constant at around 25 words, and the frequency
relative clauses was less than that of noun and adverb clauses of cause an
temporality. In addition, subjects of main clauses included a large numbe
of abstract nouns and nominalized forms (such those with *-ion* and *-ne*
suffixes), and concrete nouns were relatively infrequent. In terms of info
mation organization, practically all articles included reviews of literatur
and earlier research, followed by discussion and conclusion sections, bot
of which can be somewhat lengthy and detailed.

Socially and culturally determined patterns in discourse organization an
recurrent characteristics of academic prose are often neglected in the teach
ing of L2 writing (e.g., Bhatia, 2002; Hinkel, 2002, in press; Paltridge, 2006
To some extent, the reason why the teaching of sociocultural framework
that are ubiquitous in the teaching of L2 academic writing often takes
back seat to other essential language skills has to do with the fact that lan
guage teachers and learners alike often narrowly focus on the linguistic abil
ities needed to do well on tests and exams. As will be discussed in the nex
section, this approach to learning the essentials of language and academic
discourse can be shortsighted.

1.4   Written academic discourse and student
writing in the US academy

Specific characteristics of academic discourse and writing tasks required in
US colleges and universities are usually well-documented in research. In

microcosm, written academic discourse and its attendant values reflect multitude of contemporary and historical considerations in the culture academic writing. In many (if not most) cases, the culture of writing ay occasionally conflict with L2 learners' beliefs, values, and views on hat constitutes effective academic writing. By and large, an individual's pectations of the culture of learning remain fundamentally based on the ciocultural frameworks and the precepts acquired as a part of their first nguage (L1) socialization into educational norms. As Michael Byram and rol Morgan (1994: 43) point out, '[l]earners cannot simply shake off their vn culture and step into another[;] ... their culture is a part of themselves d created them as social beings ...'.

Prior to their studies in their chosen majors, undergraduate students in 5 colleges and universities are required to take general education courses . such disciplines as natural sciences, humanities, and social science. One nplication of this structure in American college education is that the great-t demand on students' language skills occurs during the first two years f their academic careers, when they are expected to read large amounts of iverse types of academic text, write many short and long assignments, and ke numerous tests and exams (Hinkel, 2004; Hinkel, in press).

In the academy in English-speaking countries, the purpose of written ssignments, examinations, and testing is to require students to display nowledge of, and familiarity with, the course material. Examinations vary 1 types and formats that can range from multiple-choice tests to lengthy rm papers, including essay tests and short essay-like responses. Outside f multiple-choice tests, a great deal of writing is expected in most under-raduate courses, and it is not unusual for students to have to produce up ɔ a dozen written assignments per term. Even some multiple-choice tests – uch as the Test of English as a Foreign Language (TOEFL), the American College Test, and the Scholastic Aptitude Test – incorporate writing and ssay components designed to measure test-takers' writing abilities.

It is important to note that practically all writing assignments incorp-rate more than one writing task, such as asking students to engage in an xposition in the introduction, followed by a literature review, an analysis, ause/effect, or comparison/contrast discourse structures and, possibly, to evert back to the exposition in the conclusion. For instance, most types of vriting assignments can include summaries of published works or synthe-es of multiple sources of information or data. In this case, the writing tasks vould also require synthesis (or analysis) of information, paraphrasing, and estatement skills.

In the L2 education at school levels (and even at college levels) in many countries, for example China, students are unlikely to encounter this range of complex demands systematically in writing even over a whole semester, yet alone within a single task. Thus, the writing demands for these students presents a significantly heavy cognitive load as well as requiring a cultural accommodation. Recent curricula and materials to teach L2 writing (in the Chinese case) are changing in this respect, but it may be some time before they have an impact on the issues outlined here.

Beginning in the early 1980s, several studies endeavoured to investigate the types of writing assignments and tasks necessary in undergraduate and graduate courses in academic mainstream education in various disciplines such as the physical sciences (e.g., biology, chemistry, and physics), engineering, business, philosophy, psychology, history, and English, including literature.

1.4.1 Discourse and linguistic skills required in student academic writing

The discourse and writing skills required on the TOEFL, which is decisively the most common standardized test administered to all academically bound L2 writers, seem to provide an excellent synopsis of sociocultural constructs valued in the US academy. Based on the TOEFL writing rubric, it seems relatively easy to figure out the essential characteristics of L2 writing that are considered to be important on the test and, probably, beyond it in the academic world. As has been mentioned, the primary purpose of the TOEFL writing component is to 'measure' students' essential academic writing skills.

The booklet *TOEFL iBT Tips* (ETS, 2005) offers the following outline of written discourse properties that students need to address in their test preparation:

- Identify one main idea and its main supports, such as relevant reasons and examples.
- Think about the essay organization.
- Develop it by using 'reasons, examples, and detail' (p. 20).
- Express your ideas in an organized way.
- Use effective sentence transitions to connect ideas and help the reader understand the connections between your points.
- Use a variety of grammar structures and vocabulary for effective expression.
- Use grammar and vocabulary accurately; use appropriate idiomatic language.
- Follow the conventions of spelling, punctuation, and 'layout'.

This outline in fact mirrors closely the expectations of student writing in US colleges and universities, as is discussed below. It seems clear that the criteria for testing writing on the TOEFL are deeply rooted in Anglo-American values associated with academic prose.

In addition to the discourse and language features of TOEFL writing, a few comprehensive studies have investigated the discourse and writing

aracteristics of academic papers and assignments required in the disci-
nes once students begin their studies. A survey of 155 undergraduate and
5 graduate faculty in 21 US universities specifically identified the essen-
l students' writing skills in courses that ranged from history, psychology,
siness, chemistry, and engineering (Rosenfeld et al., 2001). Ilona Leki
007) also conducted in-depth research of student writing tasks and their
operties, and her findings appear to be remarkably similar.

The data gathered in studies of undergraduate education demonstrate un-
ambiguously that organizing information to convey major and supporting
eas represents the highest-ranked writing skill required of students. In
e rank-based survey by Rosenfeld et al. (2001), discourse structuring is
llowed closely by the requirement to use relevant examples to support
position and, together, discourse organization and exemplification skills
ccupy top priority in the quality of academic writing (ranks 4.19–4.09, re-
ectively, out of 5), just as they do on the TOEFL. It seems apparent from
1e description of these tasks (see Table 1.1) that organizing information,
resenting and taking a position, and selecting relevant examples to sup-
ort it are profoundly sociocultural constructs that may be difficult for L2
udents to figure out, much less to accomplish successfully.

In the teaching of academic writing and discourse, taking a rhetorical
osition that has to be supported by relevant examples is rarely taught as
predominantly Western sociocultural construct. As Swales (1990, 2004)
nderscores, the contemporary formats of academic discourse and text are
ooted in the study of rhetoric and the foundational philosophical precepts
1 the Western literary tradition and early analyses of discourse that draws
n the classical Aristotelian and Greco-Roman rhetorical theory (see also
hatia, 2002 and Cai, 1999, for detailed discussions).

Table 1.1 Discourse and linguistic skills in undergraduate student writing

Task statement/description	Mean importance rating Scale of 0 to 5
Organize writing to convey major and supporting ideas.	4.19
Use relevant reasons and examples to support a position.	4.09
Demonstrate a command of standard written English, including grammar, phrasing, effective sentence structure, spelling and punctuation.	3.70
Demonstrate facility with a range of vocabulary appropriate to the topic.	3.62
Show awareness of audience needs and write to a particular audience or reader.	3.33

In addition, displaying command of standard written English – 'inclu ing grammar, phrasing, effective sentence structure, spelling, and punct ation' – is another high priority requirement (rank 3.70), as is demonstrati 'facility with a range of vocabulary appropriate for the topic' (rank 3.62). these serve to provide evidence of developed linguistic proficiency. On t other hand, showing awareness of audience needs and writing to a partic lar audience/reader is found to be somewhat less important (rank 3.33).

Along these lines, graduate students' academic writing is expected to de onstrate proximate discourse and linguistics skills (see Table 1.2). Gradua faculty rankings of the necessary properties of student writing are close related to those noted by the undergraduate faculty when it comes to t high importance of discourse organization and the role of exemplific tion in academic prose (ranks 4.46 and 4.34, respectively). The importan of language skills – such as grammar, phrasing, effective sentence stru ture, spelling, and punctuation – is substantially higher for graduates tha undergraduates (rank 4.06), as is the usage of appropriate vocabulary (3.74 Unsurprisingly, the awareness of audience needs and targeting a particul reader ranks higher in the requirements of graduate than undergradua writing.

In a separate subset of survey items, both undergraduate and graduate fa ulty also identified the specific writing skills that in their experiences dete mined the success of L2 students in their courses. For undergraduate facult the top three L2 writing skills included (in declining order of importance)

- discourse and information organization (2.40 out of 3)
- standard written English, that is, grammar, phrasing, and sentence struc ture (2.35)
- vocabulary (2.26).

Table 1.2 Discourse and linguistic skills in graduate student writing

Task statement/description	Mean importance rating Scale of 0 to 5
Organize writing to convey major and supporting ideas.	4.46
Use relevant reasons and examples to support a position.	4.34
Demonstrate a command of standard written English, including grammar, phrasing, effective sentence structure, spelling, and punctuation.	4.06
Demonstrate facility with a range of vocabulary appropriate to the topic.	3.74
Show awareness of audience needs and write to a particular audience or reader.	3.62

the graduate level, the top three skills essential for L2 students' success in academic courses consisted of:

discourse and information organization (2.49 out of 3)
command of standard written English (2.37)
using background knowledge, reference materials, and other resources to analyse and refine arguments (2.35)

The usage of appropriate vocabulary received a ranking of 2.27.

In many academic preparatory and writing programs, both teachers and students often believe that their top priority lies in learners' ability to attain linguistic proficiency required in the US academy. In reality, however, such views shortchange the great demands entailed in the sociocultural variables and discourse constructs that are expected – and often taken-for-granted – in formal academic writing. It is essential for students to prepare for writing assignments and tasks required of them once they complete their language training. To this end, both language teachers and students take a close look at cultural considerations that have a direct impact on learners' ability to do their best and succeed in their education in US cultural settings (Cope and Kalantzis, 2000; Hinkel, 2012).

.5   Types of writing tasks and assignments

The most comprehensive study of academic writing tasks was carried out by the Educational Testing Service (Hale et al., 1996) that surveyed eight large comprehensive universities in the United States. The information discussed in this investigation presents a coherent picture of the types and amount of writing expected of L1 and L2 students alike. It seems clear that L2 students are faced with non-trivial demands placed on their discourse and linguistic skills.

Major academic essays typically have a specified length of 5–10 pages, and sometimes more than 10 pages. These papers predominantly take the form of out-of-class assignments and are required far more frequently in humanities courses, such as psychology, economics, history, and English, than in the sciences, engineering, or computer science. Most of these projects also necessitate library research and syntheses of literature and relevant information from a variety of sources. It is interesting to note that according to the findings of Gordon Hale et al. (1996) and Leki (2007), undergraduate courses in the sciences and engineering rarely expect students to write papers as long as 5–10 pages, although, as noted, they are common in humanities courses. It may be worth a note that for writing in English, as L2, in Chinese universities (let alone in schools) non-English majors are very rarely asked to write more than one page in a single task, so these US demands are bound to seem severe when such students arrive in US academic contexts. Also, Chinese

students in China, for example, recognize that writing is the most deman
ing skill, compared to other language skills.

Medium-length essays of 1–5 pages are required as in-class and out-of-cla
assignments in practically all disciplines, with the exceptions of und
graduate courses in physics, mathematics, and engineering. In social scien
and humanities studies, they are expected in a majority of undergradua
courses. Similarly, short written assignments of 0.5–1.5 pages represe
course components in approximately half of all undergraduate courses, i
cluding physics, math, and engineering, and 94 per cent of English cours
(Hale et al., 1996). These essays are assigned both in- and out-of-class
undergraduate and graduate studies alike. Among these assignments, libra
research reports, laboratory or experiment reports with or without inte
pretation, and book reviews represent the most common types of writing
Short writing tasks (also called expanded answers) found in many writte
in-class and out-of-class exams, laboratory reports, case studies, annotatior
of literature, and computer program documentation assignments const
tute the most common type of writing across all disciplines and course
Furthermore, short writing assignments are significantly more common i
undergraduate than in graduate courses, and in in-class than out-of-cla
assignments.

1.6   A final note

Investigations into the discourse and sentence-level features of academi
writing in the disciplines carried out since the 1980s have been very frui
ful, and much useful data have been uncovered to benefit the teaching c
academic writing, curricula, and materials. Other studies have provide
insights into the needs of students in the US academy and into the specifi
characteristics of the various types of academic genre in writing. Althoug
researchers, methodologists, and curriculum designers have learned a grea
deal about the language needs of academically bound learners, their find
ings have had a minimal influence on the teaching of L2 academic writin;
because the prevalent L2 pedagogy in many regions focuses predominantly
on preparing for language testing and exams. However, as has been men
tioned, even on US-based tests, formal academic writing and its discourse
and language requirements cannot be avoided.

It seems striking that the criteria for the evaluation of writing quality –
including that in L2, such as discourse and idea organization, reasoning and
'relevant' evidence and examples, developed and broad academic vocabu
lary, as well as grammatical accuracy – have remained unchanged from the
time when they were first investigated in the late 1970s (Hinkel, 2002; Leki,
2007; Mauranen, 1996; Swales, 1990). In standardized tests and assignment
evaluations, discourse and linguistic features are often believed to indicate
good quality of writing, and that does not appear to have changed, either.

however, the findings of research and methodological innovations in the teaching of language and writing seem to have made little difference in the students' improvements in their writing skills (Hinkel, 2011). In fact, in many cases, L2 university students in the United States become excellent test-takers but not necessarily good writers or learners of discourse and text construction. It is important for university teachers and such students themselves to understand the nature of this apparent paradox and, since the further academic development of the students will be limited by these clear constraints in academic writing, they need to work consciously towards sustained significant development of writing long after 'passing' the required levels of language tests.

There is little doubt that contemporary pedagogical techniques that centre on communicative activities are more enjoyable than teaching students to construct culturally driven discourse structuring or determining what represents reasoned evidence in Anglo-American academic prose. The evaluative criteria of student writing in the disciplines and required courses do not include spoken interaction, group activities, or communicative games. As is the case with language learners in educational institutions, those who seek to advance their L2 writing skills, which are so essential in the US academic arena, need to address cross-cultural and sociocultural learning, which can lead to academic success. The learning of sociocultural discourse and formal writing norms does not need to be detailed, but it needs to be grounded in students' short-term and long-term academic objectives. As Lixian Jin and Martin Cortazzi have emphasized in their work, students' preparation for academic pursuits in US colleges and universities should focus on practical abilities in a complex and substantively different sociocultural milieu.

References

Altbach, P.G. & Knight, J. (2007) The internationalization of higher education: Motivations and realities. *Journal of Studies in International Education*, 11 (3–4), 290–305.

Andrade, M.S. (2006) International students in English-speaking universities. *Journal of Research in International Education*, 5 (2), 131–54.

Bhatia, V. (2002) A generic view of academic discourse. In J. Flowerdew (Ed.), *Academic discourse*. London: Pearson Education, pp. 1–19.

Byram, M. and Morgan, C. (1994) *Teaching-and-learning language-and-culture*. Clevedon: Multilingual Matters.

Cai, G. (1999) Texts in contexts: Understanding Chinese students' English compositions. In C. Cooper & L. Odell (Eds), *Evaluating writing: The role of teachers' knowledge about text, learning, and culture*. Urbana, IL: NCTE, pp. 279–99.

Celce-Murcia, M. & Olshtain, E. (2005) Discourse-based approaches: A new framework for second language teaching and learning. In E. Hinkel (Ed.), *Handbook of research in second language teaching and learning*. Mahwah, NJ: Laurence Erlbaum, pp. 729–42.

Coffin, C., Curry, M., Goodman, S., Hewings, A., Lillis, T. & Swann, J. (2003) *Teach. academic writing: A toolkit for higher education*. London: Routledge.

Cope, B. & Kalantzis, M. (Eds) (2000) *Multiliteracies: Literacy learning and the design social futures*. New York: Routledge.

Cortazzi, M. (2007) Aspects of writing and implications for EAL. Retrieved on May 2011, http://www.derby.gov.uk/NR/rdonlyres/19FA11E5–30C1–48D2-B78 B09D8E966FAE/0/AspectsofwritingandimplicationsforEAL.pdf.

Cortazzi, M. and Jin, L. (1996) Cultures of learning: Language classrooms in Chir In H. Coleman (Ed.), *Society and the language classroom*. Cambridge: Cambrid University Press, pp. 169–206.

Cortazzi, M. & Jin, L. (2002) Cultures of learning, the social construction of educ tional identities. In D.C.S. Li (Ed.), *Discourses in search of members: In honor of R Scollon*. New York: American Universities Press, pp. 47–75.

ETS (2005) *TOEFL iBT tips*. Princeton, NJ: Author.

Ferris, D. (2011) Written discourse analysis and second language teaching. In Hinkel (Ed.), *Handbook of research in second language teaching and learning*, vol. New York: Routledge, pp. 645–62.

Ferris, D. & Hedgcock, J. (2005) *Teaching ESL composition* (2nd edn). Mahwah, N Lawrence Erlbaum.

Hale, G., Taylor, C., Bridgeman, B., Carson, J., Kroll, B. & Kantor, R. (1996) *A study writing tasks assigned in academic degree programs*. Princeton, NJ: Educational Testir Service.

Hedgcock, J. (2005) Taking stock of research and pedagogy in L2 writing. In E. Hink (Ed.), *Handbook of research in second language teaching and learning*. Mahwah, N Lawrence Erlbaum, pp. 597–614.

Hinkel, E. (1994) Native and nonnative speakers' pragmatic interpretation of Englis text. *TESOL Quarterly*, 28, 353–76.

Hinkel, E. (1997) Indirectness in L1 and L2 academic writing. *Journal of Pragmatic* 27, 360–86.

Hinkel, E. (Ed.) (1999) *Culture in second language teaching and learning*. Cambridg Cambridge University Press.

Hinkel, E. (2001) Building awareness and practical skills for cross-cultural commun: cation in ESL/EFL. In M. Celce-Murcia (Ed.), *Teaching English as a second or foreig language* (3rd edn). Boston: Heinle & Heinle, pp. 443–58.

Hinkel, E. (2002) *Second language writers' text*. Mahwah, NJ: Lawrence Erlbaum.

Hinkel, E. (2004) *Teaching academic ESL writing: Practical techniques in vocabulary an grammar*. Mahwah, NJ: Lawrence Erlbaum.

Hinkel, E. (2011) What research on second language writing tells us and what i doesn't. In E. Hinkel (Ed.), *Handbook of research in second language teaching and learn ing*, vol. 2. New York: Routledge, pp. 523–38.

Hinkel, E. (2012) Culture and pragmatics in language teaching and learning. I M. Celce-Murcia, D. Brinton & M. Snow (Eds), *Teaching English as a second or foreig language* (4th edn). Boston: Heinle & Heinle, pp. 443–59.

Hinkel, E. (in press) *Effective curriculum for teaching ESL writing and language building* New York: Routledge.

Jin, L. and Cortazzi, M. (1998a) Dimensions of dialogue: Large classes in China. *International Journal of Educational Research*, 29, 739–61.

Jin, L. and Cortazzi, M. (1998b) The culture the learner brings: a bridge or a barrier? In M. Byram and M. Fleming (Eds), *Language learning in intercultural perspective: Approaches through drama and ethnography*. Cambridge: Cambridge University Press, pp. 98–118.

, L. and Cortazzi, M. (2006) Changing practices in Chinese cultures of learning. *Language, Culture and Curriculum*, 19 (1), 5–20.

, L. and Cortazzi, M. (Eds) (2011) *Researching Chinese learners: Skills, perceptions, adaptations*. Houndmills: Palgrave Macmillan.

e, J. (2010) International students' experiences and attitudes at a US host institution: Self-reports and future recommendations. *Journal of Research in International Education*, 9, 66–84.

ki, I. (2007) *Undergraduates in a second language: Challenges and complexities of academic literacy development*. New York: Lawrence Erlbaum.

auranen, A. (1996) Discourse competence: Evidence from thematic development in native and non-native texts. In E. Ventola & A. Mauranen (Eds), *Academic writing: Intercultural and textual issues*. Amsterdam/Philadelphia: John Benjamins, pp. 195–230.

pen Doors (2011) *Annual Report of the Institute of International Education*. Retrieved on 11 May 2011, http://www.iie.org/en/Research-and-Publications/Open-Doors. aspx.

altridge, B. (2006) *Discourse analysis*. New York: Continuum.

osenfeld, M., Leung, S. & Oltman, P. (2001) *The reading, writing, speaking, and listening tasks important for academic success at undergraduate and graduate levels*. Princeton, NJ: ETS.

collon, R. & Scollon, S. (2001) *Intercultural communication* (2nd edn). Oxford: Blackwell.

vales, J. (1990) *Genre analysis*. Cambridge: Cambridge University Press.

vales, J. (2004) *Research genres: Explorations and applications*. Cambridge: Cambridge University Press.

urner, J. (2011) *Language in the academy, cultural reflexivity and intercultural dynamics*. Bristol: Multilingual Matters.

Vang, X. (2000) Develop and utilize the resources of Chinese students in the United States. *Chinese Education and Society*, 33 (5), 21–30.

2

Inter-Perspective Pedagogy: Rethinking Culture and Learning in Multicultural Higher Education in the United Kingdom

Thushari Welikala

2.1 Introduction

This chapter discusses the key challenges faced by learners from differer cultures when they encounter higher education (HE) pedagogy during the sojourn of learning in the United Kingdom. The empirical work on whic the discussion is based draws on the learning experiences of 30 internation; students reading for postgraduate degrees (2002–06) and on a follow-u study that is based on the teaching experience of 15 academics in three U universities (2007–08).

The study revealed that the higher education pedagogic practices an approaches do not, in the experiences of these students, adequately addres the increasing diversity of student cohorts within the international contex in the United Kingdom. It emerged that learners coming from different cul tures to learn in UK higher education represent diverse cultural scripts fo different activities for learning and for relationships for learning (Welikala 2006). The *culture of learning and teaching* in this study denotes the ensembl of stories we tell ourselves about ourselves (Geertz, 1975), while the notior of *cultural script* is used to refer to the generalized action knowledge which informs how individuals make meaning of a situation and which also guides their actions in a particular context (Welikala and Watkins, 2008).

This research uncovers that different cultural scripts influence how stu dents engage in learning while the pedagogic approaches in their host insti tutions are mainly based on an imagined 'uni-culture' of learning. It wa; revealed that such differences between students' learning scripts and the host university's pedagogic approaches lead to tensions and epistemic gaps. The study further showed that students respond critically to their host uni versity pedagogic approaches, remaking agency and accommodating some

proaches while also showing resistance to hegemonic approaches rather
an just following them for the sake of getting the grades or qualifications.
e study presented evidence that the host academic staff understand the
i-cultural nature of their pedagogic approaches and respond in a complex
anner to these diverse cultural scripts which students bring; these teach-
s provide assistance with the host pedagogic practices, show willingness
mediate between different pedagogic approaches and sometimes show
mbivalence regarding how to tackle diverse ways of creating knowledge
thin these international pedagogic contexts. It emerged that neither the
ademics nor the students engaged in learning and teaching in a simplistic
anner, yet they limited their actions and teaching–learning behaviours
thin commonly assumed national culture stereotypes. Hence, the chapter
gues that the celebratory treatment of the role of culture in learning and
aching can ignore the complexity of the subtle embeddedness of cultures
the process of learning while also ignoring the complex role of culture in
aping international higher education pedagogy.

This chapter deals with three main issues: the *complex responses of teachers
and students* in their confrontation with different ways of going about know-
ng; the challenge of following a particular set of *pedagogic standards and
ractices* within culturally diverse pedagogic encounters; and the nature of
e *emergent multi-perspective pedagogy* within multicultural higher education
ontexts. The emergent themes of this narrative study are not expected to
elineate a generalized grand narrative about pedagogy within international
igher education contexts. However, in order to address diversity in an in-
lusive manner within the context of internationalization, these themes
ill provide important insights into the need for rethinking the context-free
ature of higher education pedagogy in the United Kingdom. Even though
here is an emerging richness of research and literature on international
igher education curricula in the global North, there is a considerable dearth
f literature which focuses on pedagogies within international contexts. The
ew sources which discuss international pedagogies mainly highlight cultural
ifferences in learning and teaching without further exploring the impact
f such differences on the participants' learning and teaching (Ninnes and
Hellsten, 2005). Therefore, this discussion will provide significant insights –
o academics and higher education policy makers, as well as to students who
ngage in education within international contexts – with regard to how the
ncounter of different pedagogic approaches and epistemic views leads to
he emergence of pedagogies which reflect the essence of diversity.

2.2 Internationalization: UK higher education context in brief

For decades, people from different parts of the world have come to the
United Kingdom for higher education. Internationalization, therefore, is
not a new phenomenon. However, the international activities of universities

have expanded in volume, scope and complexity over the years (Altba and Knight, 2007), with a paradigm change from the colonial mode of t 1950s through the commercial mode of the latter part of the twentieth ce tury to an emerging collaborative mode (Lucker, 2008). Today, in the seco decade of the twenty-first century, the concept of internationalization higher education has 'come of age' (Caruana and Hanstack, 2008) in ever increasing commercial mode, with unprecedented competition acro countries in the developed world as institutions seek to maximize forei revenue by recruiting international students (UNESCO, 2009; Gu, 201 Higher education institutions in the United Kingdom now play a key r in the current global higher education market coming only second to t United States in the global list of 'receiving' countries for international st dents. For example, in 2010, 15 per cent of the student population in U higher education institutions, a total of 405,810, consisted of internation students. Compared with 368,970 in 2008–09, this shows an increase of per cent (UKCISA, 2010; King et al., 2010). In 2008–09, the combinati of international fee income and personal off-campus expenditure by int national HE students approached £5bn. This evidences how internation students provide a vital income stream for universities and, indeed, for t wider economy.

2.3 Mapping the research landscape: international students and their learning experience

With the increasing volume of international student recruitment, there i rapid growth in the research and literature which focus on diverse aspects the experience of international students during their sojourn in universiti in global North (Gu, 2009; Trahar, 2010). Much of this research focuses multiple aspects of these sojourners' culture and its impact on their lear ing and living experiences in a different sociocultural context (Anderso 1994; Li, 2002a, 2002b, British Council 2007; Gu, Schweisfurth, and D 2010). The conceptualization of culture within international higher ed cation literature shows a move from celebratory conceptualization of cu ture (Hofstede, 1980; Bochner, 1986) to culture as a resource (Kumar, 200 De Vita and Case, 2003; Murphy-Lejeune, 2003; Carroll and Ryan, 200 and, currently, 'culture as negotiable' (Welikala, 2008; Haigh, 2009; Trah 2011; Parris and Kidd, 2011; Gu, 2011). Figure 2.1 shows how these differe conceptualizations of culture and their alleged role in learning has result in different models and perceptions of international students.

As Figure 2.1 shows, the assumptions about international students and t kind of curricula and pedagogy that can best address their learning nee are mainly based on the way culture is conceptualized within internation contexts of higher education. Empirical research shows that all three mo els are in use today to different degrees within diverse contexts of high

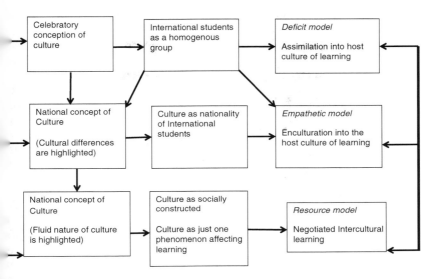

gure 2.1 Different conceptions of culture and models related with international
udents' learning process

ducation in the United Kingdom (Welikala, 2010) and very likely in other
ountries receiving large numbers of international students.

.3.1 Celebrating cultural differences: the risk of homogenizing

he celebratory notion of culture has been influenced by psychological
esearch on international students' sojourns abroad (Bochner, 1986). The
arge-scale, objectivist psychological research on the experience of learn-
ng abroad basically focuses on the emotional adaptation of students and
heir coping strategies while learning in a different cultural location. Such
esearch highlights that living and learning abroad leads to 'stress' and
culture shock', which makes sociocultural adaptation difficult for learn-
rs during their sojourn (Cushner and Karim, 2004). The process of learn-
ng in a different culture is depicted as a difficult, traumatic experience
haped by culture shock; such shock is defined according a medical condi-
ion describing feelings of disorientation following entry into a new culture
Anderson, 1994). Such views resulted in the commonly held assumption
hat international students need support to adapt and assimilate themselves
nto their new culture of learning. This concept of adaptation was influenced by a school of thought primarily encompassing communication theo-
ists (Ruben and Kealey, 1979; Nishida, 1985; Furnham and Bochner, 1986),
who hold that communication is the primary source that decides individu-
ls' ability to interact effectively in all life situations. Cultural adaptation

was given as a major prerequisite for success in overseas learning which p
marily involved learning the communication skills necessary for effecti
social interaction in order to overcome verbal and nonverbal communic
tion failures while learning in a different culture (Furnham and Bochn
1986). Thus, psychological research tends to create a particular construct
international students as a homogenous group that seeks help and suppc
from the host culture of learning in order to survive. The assumption
that, in comparison to the home students, international students are in de
icit in relation to the ways and approaches of knowing. Such assumptio
have resulted in the deficit model of international students and in treatir
international students as a homogeneous group with particular learnir
behaviours.

2.3.2 Following the host university culture of learning: just a one-way process

The second model which encouraged enculturation of international stu
dents into host university learning environments has been influenced b
some behaviourally oriented investigators (Guthrie, 1975; David, 197€
Pedersen, 1983; Bennett, 1986). This model is based on the view that su
cessful adaptation depends on implementing appropriate social behaviou
that are prominent in the new cultural environment. International studen
are, therefore, supposed to follow the home students and teachers to mast€
the rules of the game. Such models encourage enculturation of the inte
national students into the host learning environment. This model is mor
an empathetic than a deficit model; it goes beyond language issues to in
clude cultural behaviour, but does not highlight agency or choice.

2.3.3 A paradox: fluid notion of culture within a nationally located meaning

The third model, which this chapter identifies as 'the negotiation' or 're
source' model, highlights the possibilities of negotiation between differ
ent cultural models of learning. The central concepts, such as intercultura
higher education and intercultural capability, have been influenced by ne
gotiation models which, since the latter part of 1990s, have emerged from
a more qualitative type of sociological research (Trahar, 2011; Bourne anc
Zhao, 2011). Such empirical research has mainly been shaped by socia
constructivist views of knowledge making, cosmopolitanism and ideas o
globalization (Rizvi, 2007; Gunesch, 2007; Coate, 2009; Welikala, 2011a
Trahar, 2011). This model does not reflect culture as being what some
group has, but as what happens when people encounter difference (Agar
1994). International students are often seen, not as a homogenous grour
with deficit cultural ways of learning, but as resourceful individuals with
alternative ways of making knowledge. However, the research that high
lights this notion reflects culture as nationalities paradoxically claiming

lture as a fluid notion (Bruner, 1996; Geertz, 1997). International stu-
nts can offer resources to other students and staff (rather than simply
seen as receivers); they can offer insights and multiple perspectives
host institution academics about alternative cultures of learning in a
ulti-way process of reciprocal learning about learning, or cultural syn-
gy, which potentially strengthens the intercultural competence and
entities of all participants (Jin and Cortazzi, 1993, 1998; Cortazzi and
1, 2002).

One of the major influences of such research was the inclusion of home
udents within the process of internationalization (Nilsson, 2003; Wachter,
)03; Haigh, 2009). Literature and research that consider culture as a fluid,
obal social construct tend to avoid fixed frameworks of culture and under-
and that comparing learning cultures on the basis of cultural models is
roblematic (Gu, 2011).

The general picture of research on internationalization can be summed
p as follows. First, there is an obvious quantitative growth in the number
f studies on international higher education. Second, research on inter-
ationalization is more linked to other areas of education, such as man-
gement, funding, policy planning and globalization issues (rather than to
edagogy). Third, the focus of increasing numbers of studies seems to move
way from the common focus on student experience and higher education
olicy issues and towards institutions, process of knowledge making and
eople within higher education. Fourth, and the most important trend,
treating internationalization as a 'normative topic with strong political
ndercurrents' (Kehm and Teichler, 2007: 262). As Barbara Kehm and Ulrich
eichler hold, internationalization is on the one hand a positive and im-
ortant process. On the other hand, it is a process based on national values
f education and revenue making: internationalization, as it exists today,
eflects global inequalities among nations and regions.

Arguably, we are experiencing a vibrant moment in relation to research
n internationalization of higher education. Within this context almost
ll the universities in the global North are preoccupied with constructing
nternational/intercultural curricula (see Welikala, 2011b). However, there
s very little focus, if at all, on higher education pedagogies within inter-
ational contexts. Therefore, the research discussed in this chapter now
ddresses a current and urgent need that is inadequately addressed in higher
ducation.

2.4   A different story of culture and learning:
the context of the study

The research now discussed is based on two narrative studies (Geertz, 1983,
1997; Sarbin, 1986; Polkinghorn, 1988) conducted during 2002–08. Within
a social constructivist framework, both studies used opportunity sampling

to co-construct stories about learning and teaching in British higher ed
cation by employing active interviews (Holstein and Gubrium, 1995). T
narratives about the experience of learning within a particular British un
versity were co-created with 30 international students studying for po
graduate degrees, while the narratives about teaching in British universiti
were co-created with 15 academics in three British universities. The cy
lical meaning-making process was based on constructivist-grounded theo
approach (Charmaz, 1995).

2.4.1   Why narrative?

The use of narrative approach in this study was formed by the constructivi
view of knowledge making (Berger and Luckmann, 1966). The intentic
to employ this approach was the need to use a culturally–politically infl
enced methodology and a methodologically influenced 'cultural politics' i
the process of constructing meaning.

Narrative is retrospective meaning-making, and it is the primary forr
by which human experience is made meaningful (Polkinghorn, 1995). It
a way of understanding one's own and others' experiences (Bruner, 1996
Contrary to the positivist emphasis on objective science, narrative approac
enables us to engage in an authentic relationship with the research partic
pants. Narrative studies that explore 'educational experience offer researcl
ers the opportunity to import fragments of data from various…events…t
speak to the heart of social consciousness' (Clough, 2002: 8). Such studie
also expose us to the subtle issues of politics and culture as they are actt
ally narrated by people as accounts of their own experiences (Bruner, 198!
Mishler, 1986). Narrative analysis can be seen as 'opening a window on th
mind and[,]…if we are analyzing a specific group of tellers, as opening
window on their culture' (Cortazzi, 1993: 2).

The integration of the main themes and patterns of these studies and c
the meta-narratives depict the experience of learning and teaching withir
international contexts of higher education as being very complex and fa
more than a mere encounter of different Others. The emergent themes o
the analysis of students' stories portrayed that their process of learning i
mediated and shaped by their own cultural scripts for learning: these script
do not necessarily harmonize with the scripts for teaching that emergec
from the analysis of teachers' stories.

2.4.2   Storying learning

The themes emerging from students showed that their learning is medi
ated and shaped by their own cultural scripts for learning. The notion of
culture used here reflects a contextually constructed, fluid meaning which
transcends the notion of national cultures. Clifford Geertz (1983) portrays
the complexity of the notion of culture by citing a passage written by L.
V. Helms delineating a Balinese ritual of ceremonious sacrifice of the lives

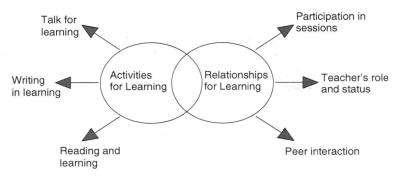

ure 2.2 Cultural scripts for learning
rce: Welikala and Watkins (2008).

the queens during the cremation ceremony of their dead king. Geertz
scribes this cultural act as:

Mysterious conjunction of beauty when it is taken as a work of art, horror
when it is taken as actually lived life, power when it is taken as a moral
vision. (Geertz, 1983: 40)

nce, the studies discussed in this chapter view culture as 'the ensemble
stories we tell ourselves about ourselves' (Geertz, 1975: 448). The learning
d teaching cultures comprise the stories told about learning and teaching.
le emergent themes of the analysis of the students' stories showed that
ere are different cultural scripts for (a) different activities for learning;
ading, writing and talking for learning, and (b) relationships for learn-
g; for peer-interaction, the teacher's role and status, and participation in
ssions. The study revealed that cultural scripts influence teaching and
irning. In the meantime, there was evidence that cultural scripts can be
countered across cultures as well as within cultures. Hence the notion of
ltural scripts does not present a rigid, static meaning.

4.3 Beyond culture shock: cultural scripts for
fferent activities for learning

le studies showed that embarking on a different culture of learning is
uch more than mere culture shock. It was uncovered how international
idents bring different cultural scripts for learning which did not neces-
rily harmonize with the scripts for teaching and learning appreciated
ld expected by the host learning environment. While the sample of stu-
nts comprised mature postgraduate students who held responsible posts
iainly in the field of education) in their home countries, the new culture

of learning provided them with surprises, enriching learning experience as well as with disappointments.

2.4.3.1   What is philosophy in Java is theatre in Bali

Learning is a social act; therefore students experience learning as social beings. It emerged that students often compare their own cultural script for learning with the new ways of teaching and learning encountered in the new learning environment. Rather than making surface-level judgments, the learners responded to the new pedagogic approaches in a mature manner. For example:

> Back home, we wait for the information to come from the teacher. Here it is the job of the learner. There, we think, 'I am here, so teach me'... Here, they tell us 'you are here, so learn yourself'. (IS 1)

This implies that the student is able to make sense of the different ways of going about teaching and learning rather than just noticing differences. Further, learners described how their own scripts for talking, reading and writing for learning can affect the way they respond to the pedagogic requirements of the new culture of learning. A major area commented on by these learners was the 'criticality' encouraged by their host pedagogy during discussions. While some understood critical contributions as enriching their learning experience, others pointed out that their own cultural scripts influenced the way they engaged in verbal interactions for learning:

> Be critical, be critical [;]...we do not talk and that is how we are. The Japanese, the Chinese, yes, we are self-critical. We do not go on criticizing others...openly. We do not like confrontation with the others. (IS 2)

It emerged that talk for learning is not seen as a positive practice by some learners; their cultural scripts for talk for learning has different, socially embedded, meanings and norms. While interactive pedagogies mainly practiced through critical discussions are always appreciated within the Western pedagogy, some international learners find it inappropriate and, at times, disturbing their learning:

> We never argue when the teacher says something [;]...since we are not supposed to disagree and argue with the teacher. We have to respect them. They are our Gurus. But it does not mean that we are just passive learners. If we want to critically engage in discussions, there is time for that in tutorial classes...Here, all the time, students try to show that they are very critical by shouting in the classroom. You see, often, what they say is not relevant. That is very disturbing and wastes our time. I think

the teachers should do something about this. I would like proper critical discussions which will advance our thinking and all that. (IS 3)

hile different cultural scripts shape the way learners go about learning and eir interpretations of the host pedagogic approaches, they seem to mature thin the process of experiencing the encounter of difference. Instead of ndly following the critical pedagogy as constructed by the host institu- n, they expect to experience a kind of 'criticality' which is not alien to em. Criticality also is interwoven with their scripts for living as a member the academic society. In certain cultures, engaging in verbal arguments front of teachers and adults is considered unacceptable, while some feel at open argument means confronting people. Criticality is defined in dif- ent ways in different cultures, and students' engagement in class discus- ns is influenced by such cultural meanings. Some students were reluctant change their scripts for talking unless they found that the change would useful back in their home culture.

4.3.2 Labouring to write: different scripts for writing for learning

ademic writing, and becoming familiar with the rules and norms of writ- g that are appreciated within the host university pedagogy, was a concern the majority of students. For example:

Here … every statement is been referred to, and even when you read some- thing you get disturbed [distracted by references in the text]. Definitely too much. Back home we express things in a better way … any reader can understand. Here, whatever you write you need to refer it to the writer. Otherwise they call it something. Pagaa … ism? [plagiarism] I was very angry about this. (IS 4)

me learners resisted certain highly valued norms and values related to aca- mic writing which were advocated within their host pedagogy. However, is particular student had earlier followed a master's course at the same uni- rsity and achieved very good grades. When asked about how she got good ades for her master's, she mentioned that she followed the 'rules of the game' st to get higher grades, but would not follow those rules for academic writ- g once she is back home. Such complex views about the impact of learning erseas suggest that learning means much more than becoming assimilated to a particular way of creating knowledge. Learning is a socioculturally nbedded process which makes people part of a particular culture. Therefore, e sojourners do not embrace the host pedagogic practices unless they find em useful and acceptable within their own cultural contexts. Nevertheless, ost of the students follow the rules to get the qualification. Yet some learn- s simply 'borrow' features of host learning cultures for short-term purposes, en 'return' them or leave them behind when they go home.

Students willingly accommodate the host pedagogic approaches a‚ norms when they find that such norms enrich their process of knowing a‚ change their understanding about knowledge making:

> I had no idea of writing on our own as they do it here. We always reproduc‚ what the teacher dictated to us. Writing was never developed this way ba‚ home. ... [W]e were trained to do essays after memorising certain things‚ want to learn this way of writing and it is a big challenge to me. (IS 5)

That means that even though learners' responses towards pedagogic pra‚ tices are shaped by their own cultural scripts, the latter do not necessari‚ become barriers in the process of accommodating the host pedagogic pra‚ tices. Hence, learners change their pedagogic behaviours when they fir‚ such behaviours change their learning process and enrich their knowing. ‚ was also found that when students understand that certain pedagogic pra‚ tices do not enrich their learning process, they become active agents rath‚ than becoming blind followers of the unfamiliar:

> You know we set up these study groups. We meet up every other day an‚ discuss our assignments, problems and stuff. That helps a lot. Me and m‚ friend always questioned why we should write in a particular way. What ‚ wrong with our way of doing academic writing? I am not going to follo‚ this once I am back. So, I talked to my teacher. She is very good. She li‚ tens. She said, 'Ok, you have space to be creative and write your thesis in‚ different way. But be careful and remember that this is an academic piec‚ of writing'. And I followed her advice and see, I have got very good con‚ ments from my upgrading panel. They liked my way of writing. (IS 6)

Such stories show that some students create spaces to use alternative ways o‚ knowledge making without altogether following the host pedagogic norm‚ and practices. IS 6 was able to use an alternative style of writing by initiall‚ engaging in discussion with her supervisor and then convincing the super‚ visor about her ability to write successfully in a different way. The analysi‚ of the students' stories showed that enacting agency helped the learners t‚ enrich their process of knowing by making use of multiple perspectives‚ their own cultural perspectives, the perspectives appreciated by the hos‚ pedagogy, and those of their peer learners.

2.5   Cultural scripts for relationships for learning

2.5.1   Teacher in the community: challenging Western assumptions

> We have the rapport all the time. We meet the teacher on the road, in the‚ market place. We call them, 'Hi sir, how are you?' ... We have that bond‚

with the teacher. It is not just teaching something and vanishing. He is there, in the community living with you. (IS 7)

emerged that stories about the teacher–student relationship and its impact
n learning in some cultures demystify the common labelling of particu-
r teaching–learning cultures as 'traditional' in which the teachers are
sumed to act formally and authoritatively. As IS 7 points out above, in his
ulture, the teacher is an intimate member of the community. Their rela-
onship with the teacher is not limited to any pedagogic situations. It is a
ery close relationship flavoured with respect which transcends pedagogic
tuations to their day-to-day lives as community members. The analysis of
udent stories showed that the majority of the learners resist 'disrespectful'
ays of acting (addressing teachers by their first name, arguing with the
acher) towards the teachers during pedagogic situations (though they see
uch ways from local students).

The studies revealed that students are agents of choice: they show resist-
nce when they encounter inappropriate or unfamiliar pedagogic approaches
which have no applicability back in their own culture of learning) and
ccommodate the ones which they think advance their learning process.
his implies that international students, like any other students in higher
ducation, react to the host pedagogy in a complex, but meaningful man-
er. Instead of embracing the new culture of learning as a given, they crit-
ally reflect on its practices, making comparisons with their own cultural
cripts for learning.

.6 Storying teaching

Despite many studies which focus on the student experience within inter-
ational higher education contexts, there is a considerable lack of research
nalysing the experience of academics within such contexts. This chap-
er now reports a study which explored the stories of teaching in British
niversities.

The analysis of teachers' stories reflects that how they go about teaching
nd learning is mediated by different cultural scripts. The different scripts
hat emerged were identified as institutional scripts, disciplinary scripts,
diosyncratic scripts and mixed scripts. These scripts influence teaching in
lifferent ways. It was found that academics often do not limit themselves to
ne specific cultural script during pedagogic situations. Increasing diversity
vithin student cohorts means increasing challenges in terms of identifying
lifferent pedagogical needs of the learners and understanding different
approaches to learning which the different students bring to British pedagogies. Academics' narratives revealed that a mixture of a variety of scripts
hape the way they construct their pedagogic approaches and pedagogic
relationships, which leads to a particular culture of pedagogy that they

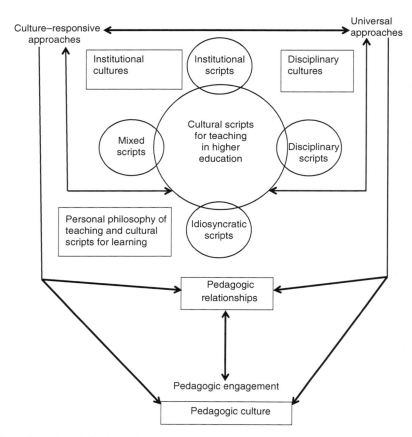

Figure 2.3   Scripts for teaching

think addresses the epistemic challenges. Figure 2.3 shows the scripts whic[h]
emerged and how they are related to pedagogic relationships (between stu[-]
dents–teachers and students– students): these relationships shape particul[ar]
kinds of pedagogic engagement that result in pedagogic cultures.

2.6.1   Encountering diversity: accommodating institutional scripts

There has been far less research into the impact of institutional culture[s]
on teaching–learning experience (Jenkins, 2004 in Ashwin, 2009). In thi[s]
study the analysis of teachers' narratives showed that institutional scrip[ts]
influenced, in a very complex manner, the way teachers go about teachin[g.]
Universities, at all times, retain their identity by maintaining certain uniqu[e]
norms and 'standards'. Individual institutions advocate pedagogic practice[s]

ich help the perpetuation of such 'standards', imagining that they pro-
de a quality learning experience for all. At departmental level within uni-
rsities there are teaching and learning regimes (Trowler, 2005 in Ashwin,
09) which are considered as a 'constellation of rules, assumptions, prac-
es and relationships related to teaching and learning issues in higher edu-
tion[,]...in social relationships and recurrent practices,...and ideologies,
lues and attitudes that underpin them' (Ashwin, 2009: 47). The common
sumption is that academics have the responsibility to see that their peda-
gic practices meet such ideologies, values of teaching and learning regimes.
r example:

> Some are not prepared to argue...[are] used to a didactic...[,] receiving
> pedagogies...like to sit and listen whereas in this institution we accept
> that arguing is very important for successful higher level learning. So we
> try our best to help such students to speak out[,]...to engage in critical
> discussions. (UT 1)

me academics believed that the students cross geopolitical boundaries,
tracted to the 'brand' the particular institution has in the international
arket. Therefore, they mentioned that academics have a responsibility
 help the students master the pedagogic rules appreciated within the
stitution. Thus, it emerged that pedagogic relationships and pedagogic
pproaches were very much shaped by the institutional cultures. Some
ssumed that their teaching should be reshaped to meet certain specific
stitutional needs, such as creating a particular image of the institution for
ternational students:

> When international students come here, we have to show that they are
> important and that their experience counts and so on. We have to treat
> them as customers and...they bring revenue and if we are going to be
> the second highest market for international students, we have to provide
> more and better learning experience. (UT 2)

2.6.2 Playing the game with alternative rules: idiosyncratic scripts for teaching

> The pedagogical task in higher education is both simple and near impos-
> sible...It is that of so releasing students that they come into themselves
> in relation to their curricula challenges. They become beings-for-them-
> selves. They engage with their educational experience *authentically*.
> (Barnett, 2007: 126)

Engaging authentically with the educational experience is only possible
when there is space for the students to make use of their experience and

imagination in a creative manner. Due to numerous institutional fram‌
works and resource constraints, academics find it difficult to let the st‌
dents create spaces where they can be authentic learners. However, th‌
study showed that some academics are reflexive about their own pedagog‌
practices and are willing to allow students to cross pedagogic boundaries,
least to a certain extent:

> I am helping them [the students] to play the game since they have ‌
> pass. On the other hand, I am aware of the fact that I am not engagir‌
> with their experience. ... Arguments and originality are important, n‌
> just the standard and logical sequencing of analysis. I am not particular‌
> concerned about any particular Standard English. I myself do not wri‌
> that way. (UT 3)

This particular academic has allowed students to be innovative in pr‌
ducing their theses and master's assignments. However, she was aware ‌
the risk of criticism by external examiners who go by the 'rules'. Certai‌
dominant institutional narratives about teaching and learning were als‌
criticized, comparing them with individual academic's own theoretic‌
frameworks:

> In the past, people began to realize the heavy structures of power can b‌
> brought into a crisis by critiquing the existing issues[,] ... and critique wi‌
> bring things to crisis. Now things are already in crisis and we do not nee‌
> to critique to bring things to crisis. I now use the notion of design. Peopl‌
> from different parts of the world come here and they design learnin‌
> Critique is something to do with the past. (UT 4)

As Peter Knight (2002) points out, teaching is a web of communication‌
activities, beliefs and working environment, which is the institution. Whil‌
the institution plays a key role in structuring the dominant narratives o‌
teaching and learning, the majority of teachers in this study, using their au‌
tonomy as academics, make use of the teaching web to open up avenues fo‌
learners to be innovative:

> I teach in a particular way and a lot of that is up for discussion ... So i‌
> somebody told me that I ought to deliver straight lectures, and give lec‌
> ture notes, then I wouldn't do it. If somebody told me that people comin‌
> from certain backgrounds were more comfortable with that and that wa‌
> what they expected, I still wouldn't do it. (UT 5)

2.6.3   Acting within the boundaries: disciplinary scripts

The study with these academics revealed how particular disciplines frame‌
their pedagogic approaches. Some pointed out how particular areas o‌

nowledge allow students to cross disciplinary and cultural boundaries and
eate hybrid knowledge, while others highlighted that the nature of certain
nowledge areas does not allow them to negotiate between diverse ways of
nowing.

> I enjoy this diversity to the full, but in a different way. One of my ... students did a wonderful face of a woman last term. I read the face in a complex manner. The Japanese like small round face, the English nose with South Asian kind of eyes ... You see, a mixture of beauties from different parts of the world[,] ... I do always encourage this kind of hybrid work. Art is the best way to tell things in novel ways. (UT 6)
>
> If we're training doctors to do liver transplants then I want every doctor to be able to do a liver transplant. So, some of that stuff is non-negotiable. You have to learn to do it the way it works. If you try to be innovative or use alternatives, there can be a disaster. (UT 7)

here were some teachers who believed in a universal approach to university education in general. For these, learning reflects the successful mastery
f the rules of the game which is predetermined by the university culture,
rrespective of the context or the knowledge boundaries:

> All academia is a game of discourses ... It is not, then, right or wrong ways. And you cannot say that, come here and you don't like the way they play the game here. Some are curious about other cultures, but when it comes to academic rules, if you want to learn football it is not basketball anymore. (UT 8)

.6.4   Addressing diversity using mixed scripts for teaching

Diversity is here to stay. The universities in the global North have to
address the multiple uncertainties related to the process of knowledge
making. Some academics in this study seemed to welcome such epistemic uncertainties by adjusting and embedding their ways of teaching
according to different pedagogic contexts. Their stories seemed more self-reflexive:

> I feel that I am quite rebellious ... I quite wanted to be radical and change the whole nature of curriculum and student writing .... People bring their own stories and reality ... which is much richer and wider from what we are asking them to narrow down here. They come into this room, and lose so much of their richness in order to write the essay, the dissertation or the thesis ... There was this ... girl who did a very creative academic piece of work for her master's module. I allowed her to do it that way [and] even the external examiner was quite happy about her work. (UT 9)

Some academics challenged the accepted stories about Others with Western academia and have learnt to respect and experiment with differe ways of knowing that they encounter in pedagogic situations.

> Chinese learner has been very much considered a 'passive learner' wh does not contribute during lessons. But now, I know that silence is al very important for learning in some cultures. It is learning for me act ally ... now, I learn to be silent sometimes. (UT 10)

2.7   Conclusion

The world is radically unknowable, and there are infinite ways of knowledg making.

> The problem is that there are many knowledges vying for a place withi the university[,] ... and multiple knowledges nowadays knock on the doc of the university, asking to be let in. (Barnett, 2000: 35)

The rapidly increasing internationalization of universities adds volumes c uncertainty to the knowledge-making process of current universities. Th chapter has explored how learners who come from diverse cultures an academics within UK higher education make sense of their learning an teaching experiences. The key findings of the two studies identified diffe ent cultural scripts for learning and teaching within international highe education contexts. These studies reveal that while cultural scripts greatl influence the ways by which students go about learning and how academic frame their teaching strategies, such scripts do not stay static. They chang over time, taking different shapes. The scripts for teaching and learnin were not mainly based on the national cultures. They were, instead, frame by different disciplines, institutional cultures, personal philosophy of learn ing and teaching and previous experience of academics and students.

The studies revealed that even though the scripts for learning are no static, the students are not willing to change their scripts altogether merel because they embarked on a sojourn of learning. Instead, they respond in a critical manner to the complexities of their host university pedagogy; the accommodate when pedagogic approaches seem applicable back home resist when they find certain approaches as unacceptable and of less epi stemic value, and make agency when they want to adjust particular ways o knowing in order to address their own learning needs. These findings prob lematize the deterministic views about the impact of national cultures or learning and assumptions about pedagogic expectations of mature student who come to the United Kingdom for postgraduate studies. It uncovers tha students respond to higher education pedagogy in the United Kingdom in a reflexive, critical manner.

The emergent themes of the analysis of academics' narratives revealed at they are engaged in a reflexive struggle to make sense of the diverse ltures of knowing which they encounter within higher education peda-gies. They try to address different cultural scripts for learning by medi-ing between institutional scripts, disciplinary scripts and idiosyncratic ripts for teaching. The idiosyncratic scripts framed by previous experience teaching and learning, personal philosophy of teaching and learning, lues and beliefs about knowing at university level are found to be the ain factors that frame scripts for teaching. Diversity is taken as a challenge d an exciting resource by almost all these academics. The majority are lling to create pedagogic spaces where they can actively engage in making owledge using different perspectives the students bring to UK pedagogy. emerged that most of the academics consider that the diverse perspectives dents bring to pedagogy should be used to co-create alternative ways of aching and knowing.

Therefore, the emergent themes of these two studies send key messages to licy planners, academics and students to rethink higher education peda-gies within international contexts. Even though terms like 'intercultural rricula', 'cross-border curricular' or 'intercultural capability' are becom-g increasingly fashionable in policy discourse in the United Kingdom, e impact of such curricula on higher education pedagogy is not addressed equately. While universities are preoccupied with constructing inter-tional/intercultural curricula, the meaning of such notions is in practice ll vague. There is very little research which focuses on how to use cultural versity to advance learning and teaching. Studies which focus on such sues do not analyse in depth how different cultures achieve epistemic syn-gy within higher education pedagogies (Ninnes and Hellsten, 2005).

The studies discussed here uncover that the encounter of different cultural ripts for learning and teaching lead to the emergence of inter-perspective edagogies, allowing negotiation between different ways of making know-dge. Inter-perspective pedagogies evolve from pedagogic spaces in which ere is freedom for academics and students to negotiate different ontologies ways of viewing the world) and epistemologies (how knowledge is being eated) and assessment of the process of knowledge making. Such peda-gies can include all the students and academics and their understand-gs and scripts for learning and teaching. Inter-perspective pedagogy can ovide the space to realize local pedagogies of dynamic 'cultural synergies tween cultures of learning' (Jin and Cortazzi, 1993, 1998), can challenge e practicality of notions such as cross-border higher education – since cur-cula and pedagogies designed and developed to bring synergy among dif-rent cultures with geopolitical boundaries make little sense within higher ucation. One common argument is that inclusion of 'foreign' content in e curriculum, and talking about other cultures during sessions and listing ut 'intercultural skills', would work the magic of constructing intercultural

universities. However, these studies showed that both students and teac
ers make meaning of diversity in a complex manner and are willing to, a
do, engage in negotiating multiple perspectives of knowing which they e
counter in pedagogies within international contexts of higher education.
emerged that people with different cultural scripts for learning and teac
ing bring a wide range of perspectives about life and learning into int
national pedagogic contexts. The narrative analysis further revealed th
academics and students have already started making use of these multip
perspectives to co-create knowledge, attitudes and understandings, ev
though this is a complex process which is challenging within the curre
corporative universities.

References

Agar, M. (1994) *Language shock: Understanding the culture of conversation.* New Yo
    William Morrow and Company.
Altbach, P.G. and Knight, J. (2007) The internationalization of higher educatic
    Motivations and realities. *Journal of Studies in International Education*, 11, 290–30
Anderson, L.E. (1994) A new look at an old construct: Cross cultural adaptatic
    International Journal of Intercultural Relationships, 18, 293–328.
Ashwin, P. (2009) *Analysing teaching–learning interactions in higher education: Account*
    for structure and agency. London: Continuum.
Barnett, R. (2000) *Realizing the university in an age of supercomplexity.* Buckingha
    Open University Press and SRHE.
Barnett, R. (2007) *A will to learn: Being a student in an age of uncertainty.* Berkshi
    Open University Press and McGraw-Hill Education.
Bennett, M.J. (1986) A developmental approach to training for intercultural sensit
    ity. *International Journal of Intercultural Relations*, 10, 179–96.
Berger, P.L. and Luckmann, T. (1966) *The social construction of reality: A treatise in t*
    sociology of knowledge. Harmondsworth, Middlesex: Penguin Education.
Bochner, S. (1986) Coping with unfamiliar cultures: Adjustment or culture learnin
    Australian Journal of Psychology, 38 (3), 347–58.
Bourne, J. and Zhao, T. (2011) Intercultural adaptation – it is a two way proce
    Examples from a British MBA programme. In L. Jin & M. Cortazzi (Eds), *Researchi*
    Chinese Learners: Skills, perceptions and intercultural adaptations. Basingstoke: Palgra
    Macmillan, pp. 212–32.
British Council (2007) *Cultural connections: Making the most of the international stude*
    experience. London: British Council.
Bruner, J. (1985). Narrative and paradigmatic modes of thought. In E. Eisner (Ed
    Learning and teaching the ways of knowing. Chicago: University of Chicago Pres
    pp. 97–115.
Bruner, J. (1990) *Acts of meaning.* Cambridge, MA: Harvard University Press.
Bruner, J. (1996) *The culture of education.* Cambridge, MA: Harvard University Press
Caroll, J. and Ryan, J. (2005) *Teaching international students: Improving learning for a*
    Abingdon: Routledge.
Caruana, V. and Hanstock, J. (2008) Internationalising the curriculum: From rhetor
    to reality. In C. Shiel and A. McKenzie (Eds), *The Global University: The role of seni*
    managers. Development Education Association, pp. 31–5.

larmaz, K. (1995) Between positivism and postmodernism: Implications for methods. In N. K. Denzin (Ed.), *Studies in Symbolic Interaction: A Research Annual*, 17.
Greenwich, CT: JAI, pp. 43–72.

ough, P. (2002) *Narratives and fictions in educational research*. Buckingham: Open
University Press.

ate, K. (2009) Exploring the unknown: Levinas and international students in the
English higher education. *Journal of Educational Policy*, 24 (3), 270–82.

ortazzi, M. (1993) *Narrative analysis*. London: Falmer Press.

ortazzi, M. and Jin, L. (2002) Cultures of Learning: The social construction of educational identities. In D.C.S. Li (Ed.), *Discourses in Search of Members, in honor of Ron
Scollon*. Lanham: University Press of America, pp. 49–78.

avid, K.H. (1976) The use of social learning theory in preventing intercultural
adjustment problems. In P. Pedersen, W.J. Lonner and J. Draguns (Eds), *Counselling
across cultures*. Honolulu: University of Hawaii Press.

e Vita, G. and Case, P. (2003) Rethinking the internationalisation agenda in uk
higher education. *Journal of Further and Higher Education*, 27 (4), 383–97.

urnham, A. and Bochner, S. (1986) *Culture Shock*. London: Methuen.

eertz, C. (1983) *Local knowledge: Further essays in interpretive anthropology*. New York:
Basic Books.

eertz, C. (1975) *The interpretation of cultures*. New York: Basic Books.

eertz, C. (1997) Learning with Bruner. *The New York Review*, 10 April.

u, Q. (2009) Maturity and interculturality: Chinese students' experience in UK
higher education. *European Journal of Education*, 44 (1), 37–52.

u, Q. (2011) An emotional journey of change: The case of Chinese students in
UK higher education. In L. Jin & M. Cortazzi (Eds), *Researching Chinese Learners:
Skills, perceptions and intercultural adaptations*. Basingstoke: Palgrave Macmillan,
pp. 212–32.

u, Q., Schweisfurth, M. and Day, C. (2010) Learning and growing in a 'foreign' context: Intercultural experience of international students. *Compare*, 40 (1), 7–23.

unesch, K. (2007) International education's internationalism: Inspirations form
cosmopolitanism. In M. Heyden, J. Levy and J. Thompson (Eds), *The Sage handbook
on research in international education*. London: Sage, pp. 90–100.

uthrie, G.M. (1975) A behavioral analysis of culture learning. In R. W. Brislin, S.
Bochner and W. J. Lonner (Eds), *Cross-cultural perspectives on learning*. New York:
Wiley.

aigh, M.J. (2009) Fostering cross-cultural empathy with non-Western curricular
structures. *Journal of International Education*, 13 (2), 271–84.

ofstede, G. (1980) *Culture consequence: International differences in work related values*.
Beverly Hills, London: Sage.

olstein, J.A. and Gubrium, J.F. (1995) *The active interview*. Qualitative Research
Methods Series. No. 37. London: Sage.

in, L. and Cortazzi, M. (1993) Cultural orientation and academic language use. In
D. Graddol, L. Thompson and M. Byram (Eds), *Language and culture*. Clevedon:
Multilingual Matters, pp. 84–97.

in, L. and Cortazzi, M. (1998) The culture the learner brings: A bridge or a barrier?
In M. Byram and M. Fleming (Eds), *Language learning in intercultural perspective,
approaches through drama and ethnography*. Cambridge: Cambridge University Press,
pp. 98–118.

ehm, B.M. and Teichler, U. (2007) Research on internationalisation on higher education. *Journal of Studies in International Education*, 11 (3/4), pp. 260–73.

King, R., Findlay, A. and Jill, A. (2010) *International student mobility literature revie* Report to HEFCE, and co-funded by the British Council, UK National Agency f Erasmus, HEFCE, UK.

Knight, P.T. (2002) *Being a teacher in higher education.* Buckingham: SRHE and Op University Press.

Kumar, M.K. (2003) Strands of knowledge: Weaving international students' subje ivity and hybridity into undergraduate curriculum. *Melbourne Studies in Educatio* 44 (1), pp. 63–85.

Li, J. (2002a) Learning models in different cultures. *New Directions for Child ar Adolescent Development,* 96, 45–63.

Li, J. (2002b) A cultural model of learning: Chinese 'heart and mind wanting learn'. *Journal of Cross-Cultural Psychology,* 33 (3), 248–69.

Lucker, P. (2008) The internationalisation of higher education: Shifting the par digm. In C. Shiel and A. McKenzie (Eds), *The Global University: The role of seni managers.* Development Education Association Report, Bournemouth Universit pp. 11–14.

Mishler, E.G. (1986) *Research interviewing: Context and narrative.* Cambridge, M, Harvard University Press.

Murphy-Lejeune, E. (2003) An experience of interculturality: Student travelle abroad. In G. Alred, M. Byram and M. Fleming (Eds), *Intercultural experiences ar education.* Clevedon: Multilingual Matters, pp. 101–13.

Nilsson, B. (2003) Internationalisation at home from a Swedish perspective: The ca of Malmo. *Journal of Studies in International Education,* 7 (1), 27–40.

Ninnes, P. and Hellsten, M. (Eds) (2005) *Internationalizing higher education: Critic explorations of pedagogy and policy.* Dordrecht: Springer Verlag.

Nishida, H. (1985) Japanese intercultural communication competence and cross-cu tural adjustment. *International Journal of Intercultural Relations,* 9, 247–69.

Parris-Kidd, H. and Barnett, J. (2011) Cultures of learning and student participatior Chinese learners in multicultural English class in Australia. In L. Jin & M. Cortaz (Eds), *Researching Chinese Learners: Skills, perceptions and intercultural adaptation:* Basingstoke: Palgrave Macmillan, pp. 169–87.

Pederson, P. (1983) The transfer of intercultural training skills. *International Journa of Psychology,* 18, 333–45.

Polkinghorn, D.E. (1988) *Narrative knowing and the human science.* Albany: Stat University of New York Press.

Rizvi, F. (2007) Internationalisation of curriculum: A critical perspective. I M. Heyden, J. Levy and J. Thompson (Eds), *The Sage handbook on research in inte national education.* London: Sage, pp. 390–403.

Rubern, B.D. and Kealey, D.J. (1979) Behavioural assessment of communication com petency and the prediction of cross-cultural adaptation. *International Journal o Intercultural Relations,* 3, 15–47.

Sarbin, T. (1986) *Narrative psychology: The storied nature of human conduct.* New York Praeger.

Trahar, S. (2010) Has everybody seen a swan? Stories from the international class room. In E. Jones (Ed.), *Internationalisation and the student voice: Higher educatior perspectives.* New York: Abingdon, pp. 143–55.

Trahar, S. (2011) *Developing cultural capability in international higher education: A narra tive inquiry.* Oxon, London: Routledge.

UKCISA (2010) *International students in UK higher education: Key statistics 2009–2010* UKCISA, UK.

UNESCO (2009) *Global education digest 2009.* Paris: UNESCO.

Wachter, B. (2003) An introduction: Internationalisation at home in context. *Journal of studies in International Education*, 7 (1), 5–11.

Welikala, T.C. (2010) The idea of internationalisation of curriculum: A new form of social imaginary? Paper presented at the Society for Research into Higher Education (SRHE). Newport, South Wales, UK.

Welikala, T.C. (2011a) Rethinking the internationalisation of the curriculum in higher education: Mapping the research landscape. A position paper commissioned by Universities 21, the network for international higher education.

Welikala, T.C. (2011b) Responding to cultural scripts for learning: Addressing international pedagogies meaningfully. Annual Meeting, American Education Research Association (AERA), New Orleans, USA.

Welikala, T.C. and Watkins, C. (2008) *Improving intercultural learning experiences in higher education: Responding to cultural scripts for learning.* London: Institute of Education Publishers.

3
The Danish Educational Tradition: Multiple Heritages and International Challenges and 'Conversation'

Jane Vinther and Gordon Slethaug

3.1 Introduction

Currently, higher education is in a state of flux, not only with regard to standards, economy, and curriculum, but also student cohorts and pedagogical and didactic approaches. This becomes more apparent every day with increasing internationalization and raises many questions about differing degrees of student readiness for learning and socialization. What happens, for example, when students brought up on the principles of 'Tiger Mothers' (Chua, 2011) meet students from 'laxer' environments? That situation is increasingly frequent as universities, especially in the inner circle of English-speaking countries, enrol growing numbers of students from China and other East Asian countries, not to mention the diasporas. Are the universities – and not least the professors, lecturers, and instructors – prepared to meet the expectations and challenges of the new composition of students? The question implies a potential field of conflict, but that is not the view taken in this chapter. Rather, the situation opens the possibilities of change leading to improvement and beneficial outcomes for all, and this is especially true in Europe.

Within the framework of the Bologna Agreement, the EU has begun the process of unilateralization of higher education. This harmonization of educational structures creates an education dialogue across the EU countries and accommodates the steadily increasing flow of international students but leaves untouched the educational traditions and philosophies of individual countries and cultures. One of the main features of this new educational order is the increasing use of English as the transnational lingua franca for European students, and Melvyn Bragg thinks that the present holds 'the possibility of a world conversation, in English' (2003: iix). Some of this conversation will almost certainly be about the best pedagogical practices for these and similar countries, and Denmark can contribute to is discussion with its pedagogical background drawn from Wilhelm von umboldt and N.F.S. Grundtvig.

This chapter will explore European academic foundations as embedded in anish educational thinking and practice, leading to a conversation about, d an understanding of, the possibilities and difficulties in today's global lucational realities. The 'voices' or participants in the conversation have me from the various traditions and influences from Germany, England, d Denmark to form the current Danish approach to education as part of Nordic interpretation of educational philosophies and pedagogical prac- ces. This formation has become the uniting element between Humboldt d Grundtvig, opening possibilities in learning, but also creating certain iallenges.

.2 The German heritage

he academic branch of Danish upper secondary education was, and to some egree still is, heavily influenced by classical 'Latin schools' (*latinskoler*) and erman education philosophies. The heritage evident in higher education is ie research-based teaching of the curriculum which stems from Humboldt's leas of evidence-based science, his experience as minister of education in russia, his essay on 'Theory of Human Education', and his founding in 310 of the University of Berlin (now called the Humboldt University of erlin). Humboldt (1767–1835) emphasized education in the classics with a lew to forming the educated and civic person who was free to enter into, nd make a contribution to, the new civic society that arose around the me of the Industrial Revolution and the ensuing rise of the middle classes f urban society in the wake of the Enlightenment. Humboldt's principles, icorporated into the University of Berlin, were based upon empiricism and ason, independence of science and research, and, consequently, upon free nd independent universities.

The concept of *Bildung* is closely connected to Humboldt, who detailed its ieoretical foundation in his 1793 treatise, *Theorie der Bildung des Menschen*, 'hich featured the interconnectedness of teaching and research – one of ie tenets which today underpins our university life (Humboldt, 1903–36; ee also translations by Heath, 1999 and Cowan, 1963). The understand- ig of this key construct is challenged by the difficulty of translating the erman term *Bildung* into the English language, although several attempts nd versions of definitions exist. With reference to the German philosopher ant, Wolfgang Klafki defines *Bildung* as incorporating:

self-determination, freedom, emancipation, autonomy, responsibility, reason, and independence. Bildung is understood as a qualification for reasonable self-determination, which presupposes and includes emanci- pation from determination by others. It is a qualification for autonomy,

for freedom for individual thought, and for individual moral decision
Precisely because of this, creative self-activity is the central form in whic
the process of Bildung is carried out. (Klafki, 2000, 87)

Several things become clear from this definition. First, that one word i
English will not suffice to cover the complex content comprised by th
German term. Second, that there is a direct connection between *Bildur*
and the Enlightenment. Third, that *Bildung* is both process and product.
person who has reached the stage of *Bildung* (is *gebildet*: educated in this co
ception) is an educated person who, through the process of being educate
in the right way, becomes knowledgeable and cultured, independent in th
self-construction of life and values. It is implicit that institutions of high
learning need to adhere to and subscribe to these ideals in order to educate
citizenry capable of playing a meaningful role in developing and sustainir
democratic institutions.

This ideal is prevalent in Western universities today, and the applicatio
of the best planning and method of teaching should be brought to be
on any course curriculum in the process of *Bildung*. *Didaktik* (the Germa
spelling, current in Germany and Scandinavia today) signifies this scienc
and the practice as developed in Northern Europe and Scandinavia. In i
autonomy and independence of teachers are key conditions for the focus o
the content, including the selection and mediation of the content for th
benefit of the students. The Anglo-American usage of *didactics* and *didacti*
however, does not get at the heart of this idea and often implies an approac
which is overly directive, patronizing, or boring.[1] The sense in which *dida*
tik and didactics/didactic will be used in this chapter is similar to the on
expressed by Menck (2000: XIII): 'Didaktik is the umbrella concept tha
pulls into one frame a body of traditions that offer ways of thinking abou
the what, the how, and most importantly, the why questions around teach
ing.' *Didaktik* (didactics) comprises theory, reflection, and action at the lev
of general, special, and subject-matter didactics (Gundem, 2000: 236). I
the Humboldtian *didaktik* tradition the content is in focus insofar as th
didactic deliberations serve the purpose of aiding the teacher in enhancin
the learning of the students.

The natural consequence is that the instruction is teacher-centred and/c
learner- centred in the sense that the teacher, being knowledgeable of th
research foundations, chooses the content according to the requirements c
the course and study guidelines, but the didactics approach also subsume
a consideration of the students' level of ability in relation to the best way t
present the content to be learned. The mainstream in language teaching an
learning methodology (presentation, practice, production) adheres to thes
principles (see, for instance, Jin and Cortazzi, 2011). This is schematized i
Figure 3.1: The didactic triangle (for variations of the triangle see Westbur
1998). The arrows signify that interaction is taking place between Teache

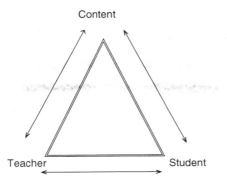

Figure 3.1   The didactic triangle

nd Student, Teacher and Content, and Student and Content. The nature of
ne content determines the way the teacher and the student interact with
 and, equally, the nature of interaction between teacher and student. The
·acher engages with the content, or subject matter, and the student engages
ith the teacher and the subject matter in order for learning to take place.

  An updated version of this German pedagogical heritage[2] owes a great
eal to educator and philosopher, Wolfgang Klafki (1927–). Due to Klafki,
ne individual and the individual responsibility in the learning process have
ecome highlighted, and self-determination may be the primary condition
or teaching and learning, but Klafki's contribution to the interpretation
f the didactic triangle is that the triangle is placed in historical and soci-
tal contexts which need to be taken into consideration. Thus, his critical-
onstructive *Didaktik*

> sets out not only to create awareness by practitioners of pre-requisites,
> opportunities and restrictions of pedagogical action, but is aimed also at
> the possibility of anticipations by didactical theory, suggesting models
> for possible practice, for humane, democratic school and instruction. At
> the same time, it suggests, new models of cooperation between 'practice'
> and 'theory'. (Klafki, 1998: 312)

he 'formation of the individual' (one common translation of *Bildung*)
epends on the interplay of education and society and is primarily the
rocess of becoming independent and autonomous learners and citizens
n democratic participation and responsibility for oneself and the process.
here is, however, an emphasis on models, on the effort to find the 'best'
r ideal way of teaching, on finding the appropriate methods for an effi-
ient transfer of knowledge to the students and, by implication, through
esearch seeking to optimize knowledge of how methodology may support

the development of self-determination and autonomy in education an society.[3] There will always be a dialogic relationship between learner, edu cational community, and society.

3.3　The Danish heritage

In Denmark, university education has sustained the heritage of the Germa Humboldtian tradition, and its renewal by Klafki in particular, though it ha also been influenced by nineteenth-century Danish thinker and education alist, N.F.S. Grundtvig (1783–1872), who was influenced by Humboldt as we as by the English tradition. (In contrast, pre-university education has bee guided primarily by Grundtvig's ideas.) Both the German Humboldt and th Danish Grundtvig theorized higher education that situated knowledge withi a national democratic culture. Higher education in present-day Denma reflects Grundtvig's educational principles in the interaction between profe sors and students, as well as in pedagogical approaches and assessment.

The 'conversation' is a key concept within the teachings of Grundtvi who, among other things, can be characterized as reformer and education alist, theologian and poet, politician and researcher. Lindhardt maintaine (1950: 207) that no single person has influenced Danish society and educa tion so fundamentally and pervasively as Grundtvig.[4] Today's educationa philosophies can be traced back to Grundtvig's contribution and uniqu incorporation of European ideas into his own thinking and, ultimately, int the development of Danish education. Grundtvig's ideas pervade Danis education and teacher education, and his principles of equal participatio set Danish education apart from European education in general.

Grundtvig believed that, in all aspects of its meaning, the 'living wor (*det levende ord*) should form the basis of interaction and interrelationship in all human affairs – education especially. As far as this aspect of educa tion is concerned, Grundtvig was greatly influenced by his experience i the tutorial system at Oxford and Cambridge. The Danish king finance Grundtvig's travels to England from 1829 to 1831. These travels had an aca demic purpose and resulted in his pioneering work on *Beowulf*, for whic he became recognized (Bradley, 2000). Although he spent many month studying documents in various libraries, he also had the opportunity t study English education and societal institutions. He became convince that the great need for the development towards a democratic society wa education, and he advocated the establishment of what he called a 'schoc for life', which also resonates with Humboldt's ideas. Despite Grundtvig theological background, he always put life first; thus, his philosophy c participation is grounded in the belief that any development needs to b embedded in people's life conditions building on a conversation in fre exchange of viewpoints, but leading towards a higher level of realization c enlightenment.

The first realization of Grundtvig's educational ideas took place with the creation of the first 'folk high school', which was a school for young adults over 18 years of age. These schools were renowned around the world from the beginning, as indicated by a South African educator in 1911:

> The object of these schools is to give the peasant a wider outlook, a horizon – a special horizon, a horizon limited by the bounds of nationality and yet unlimited, a horizon very specially Danish and yet European, particular and yet universal. (Marais, 1911: 10)

What Grundtvig advocates is not an academic kind of school, but a school for life, in contrast to the 'Latin schools', which were oriented towards classical education. Thus, the folk high school had no curriculum and no exams. The teaching was ideally a conversation based on matters which would contribute towards formation of 'citizenship';[5] in addition, 'it should be a school with a living, that is, oral, communication between teacher and student to counteract the deadening influence of the printed word' (Knudsen, 1955: 102–3). The dissociation relational to bookish absorption of content without relation to people's lives needs to be seen in the context of the view that the object was to place value on the views and lives of ordinary people, especially the rural population, who were the majority in the latter half of the nineteenth century, and their importance for the democratic process. To Grundtvig, the 'Latin schools' of the elite were the antithesis of true education, which is education for life rather than for livelihood, even though he was a dedicated and recognized scholar himself. As his ideas developed, he reached the realization that formation as a person and continuous conversation among people and between the individual and society are prerequisites and co-companions in further education: 'Grundtvig wanted to show himself and the world that knowledge of books and true education and competence could be achieved without following the beaten track through school with its stultification and examination mentality' (Bradley, 2008).

Higher education in Denmark today carries with it the heritage of both Humboldt and Grundtvig. For the most part, there is no contradiction in this, for both thinkers advocated the formation of independent, self-reliant, and autonomous citizens equipped to become full and responsible members of democratic society and of life. The groundwork for the modern-day (re)discovery of the autonomous learner and the autonomous teacher was laid down by these two reformists. One thing that strikes the outsider in Danish society and education is the lack of hierarchies. The obvious consideration of the opinions and views of students in the partnership of learning stands as tribute to Grundtvig, and it shines through quite clearly in the following examples from the information web page for international students created by the Danish Agency for International Education, under the authority of the Ministry of Science, Technology and Innovation.

3.3.1 The Danish way of teaching

Danish higher education is renowned for its innovative teaching approacl
Our education system promotes independent thinking, analytical rigor, cc
laboration, and self-expression. The learning environment is informal, cr
ative, and driven by the exchange of ideas. We see such interaction as tl
key to fulfilling the student's intellectual potential and as the best possib
preparation for the labour market.

> As a student in Denmark, you will be playing an active role in your ow
> learning process. As well as attending lectures, you will participate i
> discussions to help develop your critical thinking and communicatior
> skills. You will study independently, use your initiative and undertal
> projects – both on your own and with groups of peers. Evaluation will l
> an ongoing process, through oral and written exams. (The Danish Wa
> of Teaching, 2011)

Today's interpretation and lessons from the past help us understand that tl
strong emphasis on 'conversation' is important in several ways:

1. The notion of free and equal exchange among participants in a give
   learning situation
2. The notion of interaction in which each individual engages in tran
   formative development on a personal level
3. The notion of fruition of ideas and traditions in an interactional symb
   osis between past and present, traditional and transitional, individua
   and community

Each of these levels is important and significant in its own right; howeve
as levels in a taxonomy they may comprise the right combination of syne
gies to enhance formation of new insights at a personal, an interpersona
and a systemic plane.

3.4   University student responses

To discover whether Humboldt's and Grundtvig's views of education sti
carry weight, we administered a questionnaire (see Appendix 3.1) to 2
graduate students enrolled in a Media Theory Communications course a
the University of Southern Denmark (SDU). Thirteen of the students wer
Danish (D), and 15 were from: China (C) 2, the Faroe Islands (F) 1, German
(G) 5, Iran (I) 1, Lithuania (L) 2, Poland (P) 3, and Slovenia (S) 1. Thos
from the Faroe Islands and Germany, in particular, might be expected t
share many of the same assumptions as the Danes because of their cu
tural similarity and mutual Humboldtian traditions, and this is generall
the case; but there are some significant differences, especially with referenc

the classroom environment. Other international students might not be expected to accept the Humboldtian or Grundtvigian premises and practices so easily, but this, too, is not necessarily the case.

Most of the students, whether Danish or international, say similar things about the university classroom environment. They find it (or want to find it) different from their secondary school. They believe the teacher to be the key figure in the classroom experience. They value independence and self-direction in their learning. But they often differ in what they find the most attractive classroom environment.

Implicitly, the students understand that there is a significant difference between university education and secondary schooling. For the Danes, study in high school was relaxed, egalitarian, and student-centred with an emphasis on group work, while university study is more formally structured with more individual responsibility. This reflects foundations in Grundtvig's ideas of egalitarianism, conversation, and the 'living word' at the secondary level, and in Humboldt's beliefs in 'self-determination, freedom, emancipation, autonomy, responsibility, reason, and independence' (Klafki, 2000: 7) at the tertiary level. By contrast, the contemporary German high school experience is more akin to the old 'Latin schooling', but the conception of university is similarly Humboldtian. As one German student (G1) notes, '[H]igh school students are spoon fed information; you are told what to learn and have to learn it all by heart. University is less stiff and more informative and open to interpretation. University is self study and requires more motivation and self control.'

All of the students in the target group accept this Humboldtian perspective at the university. The Faroese student (F1) says that university education differs from secondary in having 'more reading material, larger classes, more lecturing, less dialogue in class', and one of the Danish students (D1) adds 'more depending on yourself instead of a teacher: the teacher no longer has the responsibility that you learn, in university it is all up to yourself'. Another Danish student (D2) fills this out by observing that there is 'a higher level with higher requirements. More specialized. Hopefully more student involvement and subjects that link to each other'. Yet another Danish student (D3) notes that in the university classroom, there is 'more focus on the subject than the pupils. I expect them to be "harder" and more challenging and for the teachers not to focus on getting everybody through but getting the majority through'. The fact that all the students echo these ideas suggests that they have accepted the Danish way of university teaching or that, internationally, education has adopted the Humboldtian model. Probably both are somewhat true.

Views on the role of the university teacher reveal more disparity and suggest something from Humboldt and something from Grundtvig. The most common refrain is that the teacher should be above all enthusiastic, inspiring, interesting, and a good communicator with a passion for teaching (a few also say pleasant and friendly), but this is always put in the context of being competent, generally knowledgeable, structured, and able to explain the required theory with relevant examples from his/her own experience.

As one Danish student (D4) puts it: 'A good teacher is dedicated, inspiring, knowledgeable within his/her area. Since good university teaching research based, it is the students' responsibility to figure out why the teacher presents the course material in the way he/she does, i.e. what theoretical background he/she has.'

Another student (D5) remarks: 'It is extremely important that a teacher is able to explain the relation between different theories. Often, it is not difficult to understand a theory, but understand the overall connection between them.' As with these Danish students, all take for granted that this is a research- and theory-based classroom, so the special expertise and assimilative powers of the teacher are necessary. This points to a pedagogical combination of the Humboldtian notions of *Bildung* (the combination of teaching and research) and *Didaktik* (individual responsibility).

Students also assume that teachers should have the freedom to choose their methods, which fits with Humboldt's Enlightenment thinking and squares with his view of a research university in which pedagogy is based upon lecturing but always with the student's own comprehension in mind. Indeed, one of the German students (G2) ties the freedom of teaching method to circumstances in life, as Humboldt would have desired: 'I believe that the professor's freedom of method influences the dynamics of the class (students' participation and discussions), depending on how motivating, structured, and interesting the content is mediated. I find it important our professors have different ways (methods) of teaching as I am convinced that our future co-workers, supervisors/subordinates won't either have one common way of working and it is important to be able to adapt to these styles.'

A Dane (D5) similarly comments: 'It is necessary to have freedom of method in order to feel comfortable with the teaching style. The freedom also means that there are professors that do not give the students the full learning experience. All in all the freedom is a good thing.' However, in commenting about the relationship between teachers and students, one student (D6) says that it is 'good, we're at the same level. As a Dane, I expect it to be this way. Like to be talked to as equal, not inferior'. Non-Danish students do not express this attitude, so in this way, the egalitarian influence of Grundtvig is clearly seen.

The question of the teacher's freedom is also linked to the pedagogical practices in the classroom that go beyond the mastery of content or that relate the content to the assembled students. In being asked whether learning depends on the professor's lecturing and mediation of the content, the students again are in general agreement that the professor is of central importance to the classroom, but they have differing opinions as to whether that should only be through lecturing and PowerPoint presentations or also rough interactive teaching, discussions, and group work – 'conversation'. is at this point that the Humboldtian and Grundtvigian foundational remises and practices pull in different directions.

There is no question about lecturing. All students are for it: none indicate at discussion – though in differing degrees, group work, or presentations – ould be the backbone of courses, though some indicate they should be gnificant parts. This, too, confirms Humboldt's emphasis on research and hierarchy of knowledge. Most students, however, comment on three inter-tive classroom activities and are divided about two of them: students gen-ally favour class discussion, though they are in conflict about group work d student presentations.

With a few exceptions, students think that classroom discussions are an fective learning tool. Indeed, some (D3) argue that there 'could be more of effort to engage students in course activities', and one (D3) says that the eally good' teachers 'are the ones that involve the students in the medi-ion. Discussions can be very educational and are easier remembered than mere lecture'. Most believe that it takes some talent to finesse good discus-ons, and the Faroese student (F1) notes the deficiency of the teacher in elding comments rather than the students: 'One lecturer asks questions class but has pointed out early in the semester that he/she does not want nswers. This I find strange'.

Interestingly, however, it is only the international students who specific-ly advocate an interactive classroom, finding that it relieves the tedium of e lecture and livens up the classroom. One Danish student (D7) is quite utspoken against it, saying, 'Personally, I learn more if the professor teaches opposed to classroom discussion, etc. The professor has the knowledge, d I am not all that interested in finding out what my co-students think a subject. A structured PowerPoint presentation and "monologue" with a inimum of "student interfering" is by far my preference.'

Another Danish student (D8) says much the same thing: 'I think all classes ould be lectures, so we will learn something, not just discuss things with eople on our own level. Often it does not get you anywhere, just gets you onfused about the theory. I want to listen to the teachers, not my fellow udents.' These are the most extreme statements, but other Danes say simi-r things. Given their Grundtvigian heritage, this is somewhat surprising its rejection of egalitarianism and of a group's ability to discover new sights.

While the majority of students valued group work, others find it a waste f time. All but one, 94 per cent, of the international students favour group ork and consider it valuable for their learning, but this affirmation declines 62 per cent for the Danes. One of the Polish students (P1) maintains that roup work is especially good for international students: 'It's really good ay to work at university. Sometimes when you are international students 's harder because you don't know people and you're shy. But I think that

it's good when teacher push a little bit students to work together and than
to that they know each other.' The Iranian (I1) student echoes that vie
affirming that group work 'teaches skills such as communication, bein
a team player, understanding and socializing'. One Chinese student (C
thinks that without group work international students have no chance t
discuss academic work with anyone, but warns that too often groups are s
up on the basis of nationality, which is 'so awful for an international un
versity'. In support of that view, one of the Danish students (D1) notes th
group work and independent work need to be balanced 'because in real lif
that is how it is. We have to be able to work in both ways'.

Another Danish student (D5), one who clearly values the lecture, also fe
that group work has its place: 'At university level I expect a higher degre
of one way communication where the teacher lectures to the students, bu
where questions from students still will be of important matter. Included i
the classes there should also be an amount of group work, either during th
classes or in the free time. This should account for maybe 10 to 25 percent

However, of the five (out of 13) Danish students who hold negative view
on group work, one (D8) says, 'I think all classes should be lectures, so w
will learn something and not just discuss things with people on our ow
level. Often it does not get you anywhere, just get you confused about th
theory. I want to listen to the teachers, not my fellow students, who kno
as little as I do. Furthermore, many students do not prepare for lecture, s
group work is a waste of time in class.'

One of the Chinese students also follows this line of thinking, wantin
the teacher's informed opinion first. A Danish/Vietnamese student (D5
reinforces that view: 'Group work is not a successful method. People are o
different levels and the productivity of it is low. Most people just want to ge
over and done with it.'

The configuration of these comments on group work is a little perplexing
but likely has to do with the Danes' utilitarian view of university education
Based on Grundtvig's belief in egalitarianism and creating a 'conversation
in education, Danish high schools have a relatively relaxed classroom envi
onment with substantial group work and few national examinations; b
contrast, in university Danish students expect a more rigorous content-base
curriculum with independence, and think that the best way to accomplis
that is to focus on the lecture, seemingly minimizing Grundtvig's notion
of community, free and equal participation, and exchange. By contrast, stu
dents from other parts of the world are delighted to share in the democrati
classroom, which helps them understand the material and offers them pos
sibilities for socialization. This could point to a need – which Grundtvig
would be the first to acknowledge, for an explicit discussion of how much
more education is than the uptake of content. To be true education for life
rather than for position or livelihood, it must aim at formation and sustain
democratic ground rules.

Generally, those who respond well to group work also find value in student presentations, and the statistics are not all that different from those relating to group work: 54 per cent of the Danes favour presentations, 31 per cent are against them, and the remainder do not comment on them. Of the international students, 92 per cent expressly favour them, there were no negative expressions, and only one student did not respond. One Japanese/Danish student (D10) says of group work and student presentation that 'they make you involved more in the courses/subjects and they make lectures more interesting instead of just listening which is great'. Following that line of thinking, one Dane (D6) also notes that 'working in teams give you a lot. Social side to it. Learn about cultures as well.' A Lithuanian student (L1) sees two sides to presentations, one negative and one positive: 'I don't find presentations very useful, at least from the studying point of view, learning to present, yes.' One Danish student (D4), however, takes a totally contrarian position, claiming that 'oral presentations seldom work. Most of the time, they haven't been researched properly, and you feel they are a waste of time.' Another Dane (D9) comments that 'personally I don't like presentations, because I focus too much on my own subject and nervousness to be able to concentrate on what the other students are presenting.' One of the German students (G2), however, finds it 'challenging but helpful to have presentations in front of the class (approximately 60 persons) as I learn to handle this kind of stress and how to articulate and present myself and the topic in front of audience'. Students agree that the presenters themselves probably learn some skills from the presentation, but that may be at the expense of the class's learning if the presentations are not well thought out. Some students, however, may simply want to know what the professor thinks, hoping to get the 'right' answer.

For about half the Danes, class discussions, group work, and student presentations are a controversial part of the university classroom experience, though for nearly all international students they are the means of participating and breaking up a solid lecture format. In this sense, the international university students may see a special benefit in learning how to develop their individual voices within class conversations and work within groups. If they have come out of pedagogies built on a teacher–student hierarchy, this can be especially liberating.

Very much in line with Humboldt (especially as redefined by Klafki), most students in this target group affirm the value of independent learning and agree that they need to assume full responsibility for it. As one Danish student (D5) indicates, 'In order to get something out of the study and the lectures, it is my own responsibility to read and prepare.' The role of the teacher in this independent learning is, however, a little cloudy. Independent learning for the Faroese student (F1) means 'minimum interaction with the lecturer'.

For another student (D9), the teacher has a role, but not in determinin answers: 'We are not told how to do many things at the university. You hav to figure it out on your own. I therefore think that working independentl and to take responsibility for our own learning means that we are here b choice and it is our responsibility to get the information we need, to sho up in class, and to figure out how to solve our problems on our own, becaus the teachers are not here to provide us with answers, but they are here t provide us with knowledge.'

The Danish/Vietnamese student (D5), however, says that she prefers 'hav ing a teacher explaining the topic', rather than students having the prim responsibility. Consequently, the definitions of, and attitude towards, pe sonal responsibility are not quite the same, though most accept indepenc ent learning as axiomatic in university education.

One area in which many students do not feel that they can easily take pe sonal responsibility, and in which the university does not do an adequat job of preparation, is that of written examinations and essays. In Denmar academic writing is seldom taught in university and sometimes is not sy tematically addressed in secondary school, so many of the students are le to guess what the process is about. One Danish student (D5) says, 'it is clea what is expected for preparation for class and presentations. Exams on th other hand are more difficult to get an understanding of. A small cours presentation about exams and exam writing in the beginning of the fir semester would be helpful.' Another Danish graduate student (D1) confesse that 'it is the first time for me at the university that I have to write an essa so that type of paper is not so clear to me.' Students then find that the skil of writing essays and examination are too often left to chance.

Another important area left to chance is socialization: partly betwee teachers and students, but mainly among students. As a rule, universit students in Denmark find the relationships between teacher and studen satisfactory. Generally, they do not assume that they will have a socia relationship with their teacher: they all say their relationship is friendl informal, and relaxed but professional (some say impersonal) and based o mutual respect. Students confirm that teachers are helpful in and out c class, respond to questions about the course work, and answer e-mail, whic seems enough to most. On a very positive note, one of the Polish student (P2) remarks: 'At SDU professor is for student, and it is a really good thing professors are always willing to help students and answer every question, a my home university it does not look like that (unfortunately).'

However, many students find the relationships among themselves mor problematic, the Danes having little difficulty but the international stu dents being more perplexed about the process. Danish students are happ with the friendships they have made at university, and none have negativ comments, though one Dane (D4) admits, 'There are a lot of social events although probably more on BA- than MA-level where students tend to b ore "consolidated", but most of them are exclusively social. I miss a mix etween social and educational events.' The Danes admit that their friends nd to develop within their study area rather than across disciplines, so roximity and context clearly matter. They also confess that their friendships nd to be nationally based, and, as mentioned above with group work, this as something to do with the teacher's handling of intercultural relations.

One Danish student (D9) says: 'I have got classes together with a lot of iternational students, and it is very obvious that the class is divided into anish students in small groups and the international students in small roups ("country-groups"), and in that way I think it matters which culture r country you come from. Except that I don't think that it matters which ulture you are from, because everyone is so different at SDU – there is room or everyone.'

Another Danish student (D2) mentions that 'the university itself is not ll ready for multi culture' and does not do as much as it could to promote iternational harmony and integration.

Although one Iranian student thinks that because the majority of stu-ents speak English in Denmark, it is much easier to form friendships at DU than in Germany, for example; most international students noticeably iention that they lack the opportunity to develop friendships. One of the :hinese students (C2) says it the most bluntly: 'Students tend to keep to hemselves or the students they know.' All of the German students com-ient on the difficulty of making friends.

The German students in particular place some blame on the university er se with respect to socialization. As one of the students (G2) observes, infortunately the university did not have enough funds to offer us such ocializing event at the beginning of study. Coming from a different uni-ersity ... it is rather difficult to get to know the students that have obtained heir BA here as they are already among their friendship circles.' Another f the German students (G1) wistfully confirms this structural problem: interaction and socializing happens mostly after class, in the dormitories.)uring class there is not much socializing and it's normal to go to class and lirectly home. I personally find it hard to meet people of SDU as I live away rom the dormitories.' What this student does not understand is that there re few or no dormitories on campus and therefore less opportunity for ocialization out of school. Yet another German (G3) says, 'sometimes the nvolvement of international students and Danish students could be pro-noted in a better way.' Danish universities have generally not seen social-zation as part of their mission, though with the increasing international mphasis in learning, this may be expected. Business colleges in Denmark iave already begun to allocate funds for socialization, so this may well be-·ome important for all institutions of higher learning.

Most students do not lay the blame on the university per se but on indi-·iduals. The Faroese student (F1) says, 'I was expecting to get friends at

SDU. This has yet to be fulfilled, but there are still 1½ years or more left Another German student (G4) thinks the problem is the Danish character 'As I am a foreigner in Denmark, I didn't make much contact with Dane though I would have liked to. They seemed very independent not aiming fc any friendships. The international connection was pretty nice and cohe ent.' Another of the German students (G5) says exactly the same thing, th; 'international people socialize with other international students' and add that is why 'interactions in class are so important to get the Danish an international students closer together.' The Polish and Lithuanian student too, note that, while international students do get together, there is littl opportunity out of class to socialize with the Danes. Indeed, the Lithuania student (L1) makes the case that these separate spheres too often carry ove into the classroom: 'Danes are usually [the] majority' and lecturers brin; 'examples which are known and understood only by Danes, so the dom inant culture can be felt, not in all cases, but too often'. The general cor sensus among the international students, then, is that there may be roor in a Danish university for everyone, but the Danes do not readily welcom international students into their friendship groups.

Some of the comments seem to indicate a culture issue here. The Dane are not considered to be very outgoing, but, if the international student take the initiative and approach the fellow Danish students, they are muc more forthcoming. This lack of connection seems to be an issue at unive: sities around the world, but perhaps it is more pronounced at Danish inst: tutions. It might also be confounded by a lack of institutional framework such as the student fraternities and sororities of the United States or ver active student societies and clubs in the UK. Furthermore, the Danish cu. ture is built on closeness of friendship and inviting and meeting friend in the home rather than in the public domain. The Grundtvigian ideal c community is built not so much on friendship but respect and acceptanc of diversity.

In short, both Humboldt and Grundtvig remain important in the fo; mation of the Danish *didaktik* of university education. The presence c Humboldt is felt and accepted in the connection between teaching an research, in the importance of the teacher, and in the value of independen learning. This philosophy has created a civil and professional atmospher at the university and has promoted good relations between faculty and stu dents. The importance of Grundtvig is also important in the interaction o teacher and students. Grundtvig's ideal of the *foredrag* is especially import ant for class discussions. That is, the teacher's initial exposition and leadin; comments – *foredrag* – provide the basis for subsequent discussion and hel; ferment thoughts and ideas that can crop up later in class or in life, lead ing to character formation and understanding. Although the majority o students do value discussion and learning over time, some believe that the; can learn better in a teacher-oriented classroom than in a student-oriented ne. Moreover, students from the dominant culture may feel comfortable nd happy in relationships with those from their own culture, but they do ot readily extend themselves to international students. This is a feature nat has been noted across the university spectrum internationally, so it is ot unique to Denmark, but some universities might be more open to the nteractive classroom, group work, and presentations as ways to build academic, cultural, and social bridges among students.

.5   Conclusion

is clear that Danish university institutions and many others across the anet are dominated by Humboldt's heritage, in which research and teaching are inextricably intertwined: the teacher is free to teach as he/she pleases n the classroom, and the students are independent agents responsible for neir own education and productivity. In Scandinavia, Grundtvig's views nd ideals are also part of the heritage in higher education but have penetrated this world only so far. Most students – especially the international nes – are attracted by his idea that education be a 'conversation'. While the najority of Danish students support this pedagogy as well, others do not. here can be many reasons for this: some have had enough of group work om their extensive experience of it in primary and secondary schooling; thers do not think of this conversation as a new skill; and still others do ot think they or their classmates can commit enough preparation time) make this an effective tool of learning. Perhaps, too, the embracing of Iumboldt's model for them marks the difference between university and chool. It is evident that one of the effects of globalization is a tendency >wards uniformity of structures and patterns. The growing pressure to do vell in international assessment surveys and tests emphasizes this, minimzing the less quantifiable and measurable qualities of education, such as he formation of free, democratic-minded individuals who take responsibil-y for a wider community and are respectful of diversity in ways of living, ultures, and social standing.

In any case, by reflecting on Humboldt's and Grundtvig's legacy, educaprs can begin to understand the origin of commonly and firmly held pedaogical beliefs and also see and understand trends which go against those alues.

Appendix 3.1: Research Questionnaire

Name:
Age:
Gender:
Nationality:

1. In your opinion what is good university teaching and what makes good teacher?
2. In what ways do you expect classes and teaching at university to be different from those in high school?
3. Is it clear to you what is expected of you at university, for example i preparation for class, presentations, exams, and essay writing?
4. If asked to work 'independently' and take 'responsibility for your own learning', how do you interpret that?
5. Do you find that group work is a well-suited way to work at university level?
6. In your opinion what is the examination form best suited to university courses?
7. Do you agree that your learning depends on the professor's lecturing and mediation of the content?
   If yes, how do you want your professors to mediate the content to be learned?
8. Do you expect more than mediation and lecturing from your professors?
9. In what ways do the professors at SDU involve the students in the course activities? What is your opinion of it?
10. How does the freedom of method for the professors manifest itself, and is it a good thing?
11. Do you obtain more than knowledge of content and subject matter from going to SDU?
12. What do you see as important inspirations and facilitators in bringing forward your development as a person?
13. How do you see the difference between the educational activities at SDU (inside and outside the classroom) and those at your home university?
14. Describe the relationship between students and teachers at SDU as you see it.
15. How would you describe the interaction and socializing among students at SDU?
16. What competences and qualifications do you find important to possess for the future?
17. In what way is culture an element in the classroom?
18. What were you expecting to get from being a student at SDU, and are those expectations being fulfilled?

otes

In this discussion, one difficulty is the way in which terms and concepts are either used with different denotations or do not lend themselves to translation. According to Gundem and Hopmann, 'many of the meaning-conveying educational concepts, terms and words of the German-Scandinavian language area [related to education and *Didaktik*] lack counterparts in English – and resist exact translation. Indeed the term *Didaktik* itself with its comprehensive intertwining of action and reflection, practice and theory, is one such untranslatable concept' (1998: 2).

In influencing the Scandinavian and Danish interpretation of didactic and pedagogical development in the late twentieth century Klafki and Habermas stand out clearer than any educational theorists. Habermas is associated with the so-called Frankfurt school of philosophers who, with their background in Marxist tenets, discussed the dialectic nature of individual and society. Klafki's insistence on the responsibility of the individual distinguishes him from Habermas.

Klafki talks about *Weltbewältigung* and *Personwertung* (1998: 314).

Grundtvig has also been an international influence. Schools after Grundtvig's model and based on his ideas have been established around the world in countries as diverse as the United States, India, and some African countries (Allchin et al., 2000). In addition, Chinese educationalist Liang Shuming, in his approach to the education of the rural population, found inspiration in Grundtvig's educational and social ideas (Thøgersen, 2005).

After the loss of the last remaining part of Jutland to the Germans, the national mood was away from anything German (Prussian) and towards forming a new Danish identity with a focus on Danish language and history.

eferences

llchin, A.M., Bradley, S.A.J., Hjelm, N.A. & Schørring, J.H. (Eds) (2000) *Grundtvig in international perspective*. Aaarhus: Aarhus University Press.

radley, S.A.J. (2000) 'A truly proud ruin': Grundtvig and the Anglo-Saxon legacy. In M.A. Allchin, S.A.J. Bradley, N.A. Hjelm & J.H. Schørring (Eds), *Grundtvig in international perspective*. Aarhus: Aarhus University Press, pp. 147–62.

radley, S.A.J. (2008) *N. F. S. Grundtvig: A life recalled*. Aarhus: Aarhus University Press.

ragg, M. (2003) *The adventure of English*. London: Hodder & Stoughton.

hua, A. (2011) *Battle hymn of the tiger mother*. New York: Penguin Press.

he Danish Way of Teaching (2011) Danish Agency for International Education: Ministry of Science, Technology and Innovation. Downloaded 15 July 2011. http://studyindenmark.dk/live-in-denmark/permits-visas-red-tape/study-in-denmark/the-danish-way-of-teaching-1

undem, B.B. (2000) Understanding European didactics. In B. Moon, M. Ben-Peretz & S. Brown (Eds), *Routledge international companion to education*. London and New York: Routledge, pp. 235–62.

undem, B.B. and Hopmann, S. (Eds) (1998) *Didaktik and/or curriculum*. New York: Peter Lang.

lumboldt, W. von (1903–1936) *Gesammelte Schriften*. Berlin: Preussischen Akademie des Wissenschaften.

lumboldt, W. von (1963) *Humanist without Portfolio: An anthology of the writings of Wilhelm von Humboldt*. Introduction and translation by Marianne Cowan. Detroit: Wayne State University Press.

Humboldt, W. von (1999). *On language: On the diversity of human language constructic and its influence on the mental development of the human species.* P. Heath (Trans.) ar M. Losonsky (Ed.). New York: Cambridge University Press.

Jin, L. & Cortazzi, M. (2011) Re-evaluating traditional approaches to second languaş teaching and learning. In E. Hinkel (Ed.), *Handbook of research in second langua teaching and learning,* Vol. 2. Mahwah, NJ.: Lawrence Erlbaum, pp. 558–75.

Kant, I. (1968) *Kant's Werke: Akademie Textausgabe: Unveränderte photomechanisch Abdruck desTextes der von der Preussischen Akademie der Wissenschaften 1902 begonn Ausgabe von Kants gesammten Schriften.* Berlin: de Gruyter.

Kirchner, A. (2008) *William von Humboldt: Theorie der Bildung des Menschen.* Gri Verlag.

Klafki, W. (1998) Characteristics of critical-constructive didaktik. In B.B. Gunde and S. Hopmann (Eds), *Didaktik and/or Curriculum.* New York: Peter Lang, p 307–28.

Klafki, W. (2000) The significance of classical theories of *Bildung* for a contempo ary concept of *Allgemeinbildung.* In I. Westbury, S. Hopmann & K. Riquarts (Eds *Teaching as a reflective practice.* Mahwah, NJ.: Lawrence Erlbaum Associates, p 85–108.

Knudsen, J. (1955) *Danish rebel.* Philadelphia: Muhlenberg Press.

Larsen, C.A. (1997) *Didaktik. Om didaktikken som planlægningsvirksomhed og om der systematiske placering i pædagogikken.* In E. Jensen (Ed.), *Didaktiske emner – bely gennem 12 artikler af Carl Aage Larsen og C.A. Høeg Larsen.* Copenhagen: Danmark Pædagogiske Bibliotek, pp. 70–92.

Lindhardt, P.G. (1950) Grundtvig and England. *Journal of Ecclesiastical History,* 1 (1 207–24.

Marais, J.I. (1911) *Bishop Grundtvig and the people's high schools in Denmark.* Pretori Government Print and Stationary Office.

Menck, P. (2000) *Looking into Classrooms: Papers on Didactics.* Stamford, CT: Able Publishing Co.

Thøgersen, S. (2005) *A country of culture.* Ann Arbor: University of Michigan Press.

Westbury, I. (1998) Didaktik and curriculum studies. In B.B. Gundem & S. Hopman (Eds), *Didaktik and/or curriculum.* New York: Peter Lang, pp. 47–78.

4

Trilingual Paths: Cultures of Learning and the Use of Cantonese, English or Putonghua within a Hong Kong Primary School

Phil Glenwright and Wang Lixun

4.1 Introduction

After sketching in the political, economic and cultural context of Hong Kong, a vibrant cosmopolitan city with a profoundly Chinese heritage, this chapter reviews recently published work on the Hong Kong culture of learning, which amalgamates powerful educational influences from China and the UK, yet exhibits a number of identifiably local characteristics. This overarching conceptualization of the Hong Kong culture of learning (HKCOL) suggests that disparate impulses converge or diverge in a number of key curriculum areas which are crucial to the teaching and learning of language. However, in either case, there is an ensuing disharmony or confusion that inhibits the effective implementation of educational and language teaching reforms and restricts classroom practices to the more mundane. One such key area of difficulty is the issue of the Medium of Instruction (MOI).

Since the primary focus of this chapter concerns the MOI, the roles of and attitudes towards Cantonese, English and Putonghua in Hong Kong are first considered and relevant government policies are reviewed. The current research then examines how one local primary school in Hong Kong attempts to tackle the complex practical teaching and learning issues arising from the 1997 official policy of bi-literacy and trilingualism. Three sets of data are reported. The first set outlines findings from a discourse-oriented, corpus-based analysis of eight recorded and transcribed lessons in the three MOI languages across a variety of subjects. The second summarizes data from interviews with major stakeholders: the school management (represented by the principal), the subject teachers and the parents. The third presents the opinions of the schoolchildren as reflected in a questionnaire survey. This procedure produces a preliminary, but nevertheless rich, intriguing and

differentiated picture of MOI developments within this one single schoc
It permits an assessment of classroom practices and stakeholder perceptior
that can be understood in terms of the HKCOL. But the case study also po
sesses independent validity in terms of government language policy, as a
parties seek earnestly and sincerely to chart an optimum way forward te
wards the goal of bi-literacy and trilingualism.

4.2   The Hong Kong context

Hong Kong (HK), a cosmopolitan yet intensely Chinese city, has since 199
functioned as a Special Administrative Region (SAR) of the People's Republi
of China. Its stable, executive-led system of government enjoys a relativel
high degree of autonomy whilst retaining its allegiance to the new sove
eign power. Previously, Hong Kong had been a British colony (1841–1997
The HKSAR is a global centre for trade, finance, business and communic
tion which boasts low taxation rates, excellent infrastructure and the rule c
law, and now has a knowledge-based service sector that generates some 9
per cent of GDP. Despite a land area of only 1,090 square kilometres, it rank
as the world's eleventh-largest trading entity; its oft-invoked prosperity an
stability are symbolized by a state-of-the-art US$20 billion airport whic
handles some 45 million passengers a year. With population densities som
times exceeding 53,000 per square kilometre, its dynamism and freneti
often stressful, lifestyle is driven by a powerful work ethic. Education rep
resents the Hong Kong administration's most important long-term soci
investment, accounting for 20 per cent of recurrent annual spending c
some 4–5 per cent of GDP (Information Services Department, 2009).

4.3   The Hong Kong culture of learning

Recently published work on the Hong Kong culture of learning (Glenwrigh
2010) suggests that this represents a complex amalgam of powerful educ
tional impulses from China and the UK. (and other Western influence
together with a number of identifiably local characteristics. A research
based, non-judgmental, visual representation is presented in Figure 4.1 i
which CLT refers to Communicative Language Teaching, TBL to Task-Base
Learning, AL to Audiolingualism, as influential movements in languag
teaching; and TOC refers to Target Oriented Curriculum in Hong Kong.
  Figure 4.1 indicates that powerful elements from a venerated and wel
established Chinese culture of learning (Cortazzi and Jin, 1996) (top lef
have passed unconsciously and largely unchallenged, often through info
mal channels, into the Hong Kong psyche and so into its culture of learnin
(grey borders: Bauhinia flag), as the broader white arrows with continuou
edging indicate. Differing, and often conflicting, ideas about the natur
of learning and language learning emanating from the UK (and the West

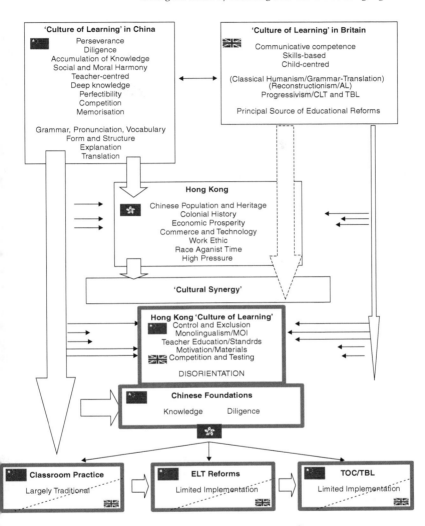

Figure 4.1 The Hong Kong culture of learning: a summary diagram

manifest in the more recent government-propagated, top-down reform initiatives, are represented in the box top right. These consciously and vigorously promoted ideals have had some impact, as indicated by the narrower white arrow on the far right. Nevertheless, in the absence of any process of cultural synergy (Jin and Cortazzi, 1995) – however conceived – they have not usually been deeply absorbed. In formal education, therefore, the

long-standing Chinese culture of learning has more recently either com
bined with, or confronted, the more contemporary CLT and TBL elemen
of the British or Western cultures of learning: in both cases this has ha
unintended inhibiting effects for change and renewal. Clearly, for instanc
knowledge-based and skills-centred conceptions of learning may clas
causing curricular and language teaching reforms to remain adopted rath
than implemented.

Conversely, traditional Chinese culture of learning influences appear a
some point in the remoter past to have absorbed, coalesced with, or bee
strongly reinforced by competitive elements in British classical humanis
with its grammar school traditions. Indeed, this historical merging (ind
cated by the double-tipped black arrow between the two uppermost boxe
may almost have had a defining influence on the development of a Hon
Kong culture of learning and its pedagogical practices. This confluence c
diverging or converging influences finds its expression in the Hong Kon
culture of learning box (Figure 4.1, lower centre), which possesses a mar
edly Chinese base exhibiting a deep respect for, and valuing of, both know
ledge and diligence. The problematic key areas, which most readily exhib
or exemplify tensions within the HKCOL, are listed in the upper sectio
of this box (fringed by external, inward-facing, single-tipped black arrow
that denote the suspected impact of the Chinese and British traditions o
each specific facet of the teaching and learning environment). These area
are inevitably problematic in the apparent absence of any serious attemp
at cultural synergy, (indicated by the 'missing' arrow with dotted edge
and the larger bolded font). This omission has been detrimental to educa
tion, since it renders almost impossible the mediation or resolution of thos
issues shown at the very heart of the HKCOL. The resulting 'disorientatio
of teachers in Hong Kong (which may be transitional), appears due to con
peting British and Chinese traditions and consequent tensions within th
HKCOL. Such current realities are displayed through the three lowest boxe
of the HKCOL diagram, which are arranged (left to right) as general-to-spe
cific outcomes which are all in some sense problematic. Like the Hong Kon
culture of learning box, they reveal the predominance of Chinese influ
ences over Western and local ones. Such non-harmonious outcomes can b
explained (or at least interpreted) by the elements portrayed in the diagra
above them.

This chapter focuses on the Medium of Instruction (MOI) as an issu
related to cultures of learning. We therefore briefly examine the status c
Hong Kong's three main languages. Both English and Cantonese are offici
languages, but Cantonese, not English, remains very much the unmarke
language of choice for intra-ethnic communication – some 95 per cent c
Hongkongers are of Chinese ethnicity (Census and Statistics Departmen
Hong Kong Government, 2007: 39). Cantonese is usually portrayed as th
language of the home and the heart, of identity, solidarity and popula

ulture; its ubiquitous use within the community is maintained with un-diminished vigour and tenacity. By contrast, English, the language of the former colonizer, has often been regarded as the language of a rich, powerful, well-educated elite, the international language of success essential for social mobility and a gatekeeper to higher-level employment in business and commerce. It represents 'important linguistic capital for the continued well-being of "Asia's World City"' (Li, 2009: 73). Putonghua, China's national standard language and symbol of national identity, is increasingly important for business dealings, not only with the mainland but also with entities such as Taiwan and Singapore – and with the ever-increasing in-bound tourists from the mainland. Consequently, since 1995, the Hong Kong government has adopted a needs-driven language policy that seeks to transform the territory into a bi-literate and trilingual community at ease with Cantonese, English and Putonghua, a policy that appears to reflect and foster the evolving realities on the ground. Indeed, long ago, Pennington (1998: 5) suggested that 'incipient *triglossia*' best described 'the complex *multilingual* profile of the community', in which language use varies across genres, situations and media. This complexity is confirmed by a more recent survey by Bacon-Shone and Bolton (2008: 48), whose findings provide 'substantial evidence that Hong Kong is becoming a trilingual society'. Indeed, since 1998, Putonghua has been a compulsory school subject in all government and subsidized schools.

The MOI policy in this linguistically and politically complex setting presents a perennial dilemma for stakeholders. Places in 'prestigious' English MOI secondary schools are often hotly sought by those targeting later tertiary study, whereas schools adopting Cantonese MOI – for sound educational reasons – fear stigmatization and academic disadvantage, especially since English is the dominant MOI in the universities. Prior to the 1997 transfer of sovereignty, mainstream secondary and tertiary students in Hong Kong were supposedly educated in the medium of English (EMI) for the entire curriculum. This official policy emanated from practice in elite schools before the introduction of nine years of universal compulsory education in 1979. But, in the ensuing situation of wider ability ranges, it became – in most cases – a sham: examinations and textbooks were in English, but teacher talk was predominantly Cantonese. Student participation was therefore usually restricted to one-word or single-phrase answers in English or to silence (Littlewood and Liu, 1996; Morris et al., 1996; Johnson, 1997). The consequent desire to promote L1 teaching (of Cantonese) on both political and educational grounds, and the contention that code-switching or language alternation produced proficiency in neither L1 nor L2, led to the much-heralded 'Firm Guidance' on the medium of instruction which stipulated that all public secondary schools should, from September 1998, progressively adopt Cantonese as the MOI, starting from Secondary 1 (S1). However, approximately 30 per cent of schools, able to furnish evidence of both sufficient teacher capability in English and high pupil ability level were granted exceptional approval to continue using English across the cu riculum. At the time local primary schools operated in the mother tongue (Cantonese); English was taught only as a subject.

In the ensuing post-colonial period, unremitting pressure from stakehold ers, particularly from anxious or ambitious parents, for greater flexibility i MOI issues has steadily undermined the mother tongue policy, leading t its ultimate abandonment through a government announcement in 200 stating that 'fine tuning' is necessary. In essence, this permits secondar schools to devise their own MOI policies according to local circumstance Paul Morris and Bob Adamson (2010: 154) therefore suspect that, 'we hav [now] returned to the situation which existed before 1997 and this will re sult in a greater use of EMI, especially for those high-status subjects whic are viewed as important for university.' Policy for primary schools is ine> plicit but, as our case study will show, it appears that each separate inst tution decides when exactly to employ Cantonese, English or Putonghu in the classroom. If this places schools in an unenviable predicament, it i certainly no easier for the children who are expected to begin satisfying so cietal demands for bi-literacy and trilingualism. English remains far more foreign than a second language given the 'absence of a conducive languag learning environment outside the classroom' (Li, 2009: 72) and confront learners with huge phonological and grammatical obstacles, such as stres timing, consonant clusters, a tense system non-existent in either Cantones or Putonghua, and the use of articles. As regards Putonghua, the use of th simplified characters in China rather than the traditional script used i> Hong Kong (and elsewhere) presents some difficulties, but these are far ou weighed by differences in the number and pitch of tones and the diffe> ing pronunciations of the same written characters. In combination suc> obstacles render Putonghua almost a foreign language since Putonghua an Cantonese are not mutually comprehensible to the untrained speaker.

4.4   The current investigation

The current research investigates language policies, practices and percep tions at a single primary school in Hong Kong. This is a government-funde school with students allocated according to standard government criteria It has, therefore, little control over the types of students it accepts. Th children enter primary school at around age six, joining a cohort labelle Primary 1 (P1). They move on to secondary school after the completion o P6, some six years later.

Hong Kong primary schools have various features not necessarily foun in other settings. The daily timetable usually prescribes a sequence of dis crete, subject-specific single or double lessons (e.g., Maths, English) wit 'specialist' teachers who perambulate from class to class almost every tim ιe bell rings. As the teachers have no fixed classroom base, the display of ɹupil work is often limited. Desks are frequently arranged in single or double ɔws, with pupils often seated according to their student number. Pair work ιd group work may, therefore, be somewhat restricted. Convention dic-ιtes that the whole class demonstrates respect for the teachers by stand-ɪg for the mutual greeting at the start of the lesson and to express their ɡratitude for the lesson at the end. In similar manner, individual pupils ιust stand to answer every question from the teacher. Syllabuses are gener-ɑly considered packed, and homework is normally set at the conclusion of ιe major subject lessons – extending the school day well into the evening ιours and imposing considerable burdens on those parents who assist with, ɪr supervise, its completion or are rich enough to employ private tutors. xams occur two or three times a year. Some schools stream pupils from P4 ɪnward in order to prepare elite groups for secondary transfer. A number f such features were evident in the school studied here. Class sizes ranged ɔom 25 to 28 and, if addressed individually, pupils were called upon by ιame (not number).

.5   Methodology

ι order to pursue the government goal of a bi-literate and trilingual soci-ɹty competent in all three languages, the host school in this study has cre-ɑted its own clearly defined trilingual education model: English is the MOI ɔr English, Physical Education (PE) and Visual Arts lessons from P1 to P6. ɹutonghua is the MOI for Putonghua (P1–P6) and Chinese literacy (P4–P6). ɑantonese is the MOI for Maths, General Studies, Music, IT, Chinese literacy ɹ1–P3), and other subjects. Currently, the school is experimenting using ɹutonghua as the MOI in Chinese literacy lessons in one of the three P1 ɹlasses.

To investigate the workings of this policy, both qualitative and quantita-ɪve methods were employed. The data derived from three sources: recorded ɹssons, interviews with staff and a student questionnaire. These generate ɪhree corresponding sets of findings.

.5.1   The recorded lessons

ɪn order to analyse teaching and learning procedures in different lessons ɑught in the three MOIs, eight 35-minute single lessons were recorded and ɾranscribed, namely: three lessons taught in English (English, PE and Visual ɑrts); three taught in Putonghua (Putonghua, Chinese literacy and Chinese ιteracy) and two taught in Cantonese (Chinese literacy and General Studies). ɔo avoid confusion, it should be noted that Putonghua lessons focus exclu-ɪvely on pronunciation whereas Chinese literacy lessons, whether con-ɪucted in Cantonese or Putonghua, are concerned with the acquisition of ιteracy skills.

4.5.2 The interviews

Interviews were conducted with 13 staff members, predominantly females, namely: the school principal, two English teachers, one PE teacher and one visual arts teacher (using English MOI), two general studies teachers (using Cantonese MOI), two Chinese teachers teaching Chinese literacy in Cantonese, two Chinese teachers teaching Chinese literacy in Putonghua and two Putonghua teachers. Most interviews lasted around 30 minutes and the questions focused on the staff's views of the school's trilingual education model, particularly the advantages and disadvantages of choosing certain MOIs for certain subjects, the occurrences and perceived value of code-switching during the lessons and so on.

Interviews with ten randomly selected parents of children across the age range were also conducted, focusing on parental views of the school's trilingual education model, particularly the choice of different MOIs for different subjects, the perceived effects of the model on their children's language proficiency levels and the importance of family support for the children's academic studies. All interviews were audio recorded, with permission, and transcribed word-for-word.

4.5.3 The student questionnaire survey

A questionnaire was designed to ascertain the students' perception of the trilingual education model implemented in the school, and a total of 121 P4 to P6 students were surveyed (P4: 45, P5: 48, P6: 28). All respondents (100 per cent) completed the survey, which employed a five-point Likert scale (Strongly Agree, Agree, Neutral, Disagree, Strongly Disagree). The salient findings are reported, but to save space, the original questionnaire and the Mean and Standard Deviation plot are not included here.

4.6 Findings

4.6.1 Data set 1: analysis of the transcripts of recorded lessons

Lesson transcriptions were analysed to identify the percentage of teacher talk in each lesson, the numbers of turns taken by the teacher and the students, the numbers of questions asked by the teacher and the students, and the patterns of code-switching in different lessons. Figures for each lesson are shown in Table 4.1.

Looking at the overall picture in Table 4.1, it is apparent that the MOI generating the most talk per se is Cantonese, the L1 of both the teachers and the students. The apparent contrast with English is, however, not as acute as might appear, since words and characters are *not* equivalents (most Chinese words consist of two characters). Certainly, in all eight recorded lessons, the teacher's talk predominates: the average teacher–student talk ratio is 88 per cent/12 per cent respectively. The P4 visual arts lesson has the highest *ible 4.1*   Analysis of recorded lessons

ubject (rade)	Medium of instruction	No. of teacher turns (No. of words or characters spoken/ %)	No. of student turns (No. of words or characters spoken/ %)	No. of questions by teacher	No. of questions by students
eneral itudies (P6)	Cantonese	32 (2360/90.5%)	24 (247/9.5%)	34	0
hinese (P1)	Cantonese	85 (5065/88%)	81 (689/12%)	41	7
hinese (P1)	Putonghua	70 (2547/87%)	64 (377/13%)	53	0
hinese (P5)	Putonghua	61 (2859/82%)	56 (622/18%)	35	14
utonghua P1)	Putonghua	86 (2563/83.5%)	86 (510/16.5%)	45	0
isual Arts P4)	English	18 (1188/98.4%)	10 (19/1.6%)	24	0
E (P4)	English	28 (1197/88%)	19 (158/12%)	28	0
nglish (P6)	English	65 (1321/86%)	48 (210/14%)	88	0

ercentage of teacher talk (98.4 per cent), and students only spoke 19 words 1 total: the use of English as the MOI here appears to have had a severely 1hibiting effect on pupil oral participation (although students spent 43 er cent of class time doing artwork on their own). The second-highest percentage of teacher talk (90.5 per cent) is in the General Studies lesson (P6), 1 which Cantonese is the MOI. The P5 Chinese lesson (MOI: Putonghua) ad the lowest teacher–student talk ratio (82 per cent/18 per cent). However, hese figures are somewhat misleading, since a memorized textbook passage f some 150 characters was recited, once chorally by the whole class, once y a small student group, and then by an individual. Although the students rere certainly not expressing their own thoughts, it was decided to treat ach instance of recitation as one turn. These recitations then accounted or around 12 of the 18 per cent of the total student talk recorded in that sson. The memorized passage in question was highly literary and abstract, nd the meaning would be difficult for primary students to grasp. The ndividual recitations were evaluated on the spot – no more than five prounciation errors were permitted for an acceptable performance. Students /ho made no mistakes were awarded bonus points but, more tellingly, here was a stringent focus on the identification and correction of student rrors, which may have generated some tension or nervousness within the lass. Such vigorous and highly competitive evaluation in class was comnon across all the recorded lessons: teachers may consider that this fosters reater diligence and learning. Another scoring difficulty concerned pair nd group work, which in the recorded single lessons occurred only rarely nd, even then, generated little audible student–student oral interaction. /lore extensive pair and group work is said to occur in the later parts of

double lessons with student feedback to the class, which promotes a sens
of learner accountability.

An examination of the classroom discourse reveals, therefore, that th
main task of the pupils is to listen attentively, since in all lessons the teach
ers emphasized diligence, competition, assessment, memorization and th
authority of teacher and textbook. The institutional power of the teach
ers allowed them to nominate the topics, to decide who should speak an
when, and to evaluate student contributions – all this in order to achieve th
preordained pedagogical outcome. In terms of the IRE pattern (Initiation
Response – Evaluation) common in didactic discourse, the teachers had th
right to pose the questions and give feedback, while students, *if* called upo
through a general solicitation or by nomination, were often reduced to pro
viding the answers to a battery of yes or no and/or closed display question
True, the number of speaking turns taken by the teachers and student
totalled 445 and 388 respectively (a ratio of 6 to 5), but it is evident that th
teachers' turns last far longer. Students' turns, by contrast, were frequentl
restricted to short, or one-word answers – despite the average length of stu
dent responses, which amounted to some 5 English words or 7.68 Chines
characters. The surprisingly high average figures for student talk may b
accounted for by student repetition of longer phrases that the teachers use
to prompt answers, and by the repetition of the eventual answers them
selves. The extensive recitations in the Chinese literacy and Putonghua les
sons, and the repeated (verbal) number chains (e.g., 1, 2, 3, 4, 5, 6, 7, 8
accompanying prescribed physical exercises in the PE lesson, also served t
inflate the average student response totals. It was generally noticeable tha
few older students self-selected by bidding for a turn (for instance by raisin
their hand), although younger ones were more spontaneous – possibly thi
suggests increasing oral anxiety as schooling progresses.

It also emerged that, in six out of the eight lessons, the students did no
ask a single question. Questions from students occurred only in one P
Chinese lesson taught in Cantonese and one P5 Chinese lesson taught i
Putonghua. However, even the relatively high frequency of questions (1
in all) in the P5 Chinese lesson is misleading, since the teacher played a
'Ask me a question' game in which students were prompted to pose th
questions. The only instances of students asking the teacher genuine ques
tions (seven instances in total) occurred in the P1 Chinese lesson taught i
Cantonese, in which the use of storytelling aroused their curiosity and le
them to ask related questions, such as 'What is a monk?' 'What does th
poem mean?' and 'What does the story want to tell us?'

4.6.2   Data set 2: interviews with stakeholders

As noted earlier, interviews were conducted with various stakeholders, suc
as the school principal, the teaching staff and the students' parents, to ascer
tain their views on trilingual education.

6.2.1 The principal

one-hour interview was conducted with the principal of the school, who responsible for building its reputation and making the school a popular ïoice for students and their parents.

Established in 2002, the school was always keen to implement the exist-ïg 'trilingual and bi-literate' government language policy, allocating dif-rent MOIs to different subjects and age levels. The principal reported that ï attempt to use English as the MOI for music was abandoned in 2005, ïereas the use of Putonghua as the MOI for Chinese literacy lessons is :adually being extended, experimentally, down the age range, perhaps ïflecting its increasing importance in the lives of educated Hongkongers. :ccording to the principal, the amount of time allocated to different MOIs ïries across different grades, as shown in Table 4.2.

Table 4.2 indicates that Cantonese is the dominant MOI from P1 to P3, though this is gradually changing. The ultimate goal of the school is to :hieve a balanced percentage in the amount of time allocated to the three [OIs across all grades, with a target distribution of 45 per cent Cantonese,) per cent English, and 25 per cent Putonghua – this is currently the situ-:ion in P4–P6. The principal strongly believes that the current model is ïfective, and that the promotion of Putonghua as an MOI is desirable. As :gards attainment levels, the principal stated that students scored well ïove average in the Hong Kong-wide benchmark tests in English, while ïeir Putonghua proficiency level is about average.

In matters of code-switching, the principal suggested that the school ïpport the 'One Language Only' policy, and strongly discourage recourse) Cantonese in lessons in which English is taught as a subject, believing ïat this is a better language-learning environment with greater exposure) English. By contrast, limited use of Cantonese might be permitted in :hinese literacy lessons taught in Putonghua if/when students experience ïfficulties discussing complicated issues in Putonghua.

ible 4.2 Time allocated to different MOIs

rade	Cantonese as MOI	English as MOI	Putonghua as MOI
1 (where *Chinese* ïs taught in ïantonese) ï2 and P 3	62% (*Chinese, Maths, General Studies, Music*, etc.)	32% (*English, PE, Visual Arts*)	6% (*Putonghua*)
1 (where *Chinese* is taught experimentally in ïutonghua)	40% (*Maths, General Studies, Music*, etc.)	32% (*English, PE, Visual Arts*)	28% (*Chinese, Putonghua*)
4, P5 and P6	45% (*Maths, General Studies, Music*, etc.)	30% (*English, PE, Visual Arts*)	25% (*Chinese, Putonghua*)

4.6.2.2   The teachers

Twelve teachers who taught different subjects, using the three differen[t] MOIs, were also interviewed.

(a) English MOI – four teachers   The two English teachers claimed tha[t] they always use English as the medium of instruction in English lesson[s]. However, they permitted the use of Cantonese during student group dis[-] cussions, since this assisted communication and allowed more complicate[d] topics to be addressed.

The PE teacher, using English as the MOI, had been doing this for nin[e] years and consequently felt comfortable with English MOI. She noted tha[t] students in the early years responded more slowly to English instruction[s] but that the extensive use of gestures and movement facilitated receptiv[e] understanding. Indeed, by grades 4, 5 and 6 students had generally becom[e] accustomed to following the teachers' routine instructions in English. Th[e] teacher, therefore, supported the use of English MOI in PE, since physica[l] responses assisted comprehension.

The visual arts teacher, employing English as the MOI, was far less posi[-] tive about the school's language policy, suggesting that students found i[t] very challenging to grasp abstract concepts in English. Much time an[d] energy had, therefore, to be devoted to language issues, leaving insufficien[t] time to cover the subject matter specified in the curriculum. Her strateg[y] was to say everything twice, once in English and once in Cantonese but, i[n] reality, students often ignored her English explanations and simply waite[d] for the Cantonese version. Students were permitted to answer questions i[n] Cantonese, as most were unable to reply in English. The teacher empha[-] sized that brief English instructions for routine activities were effectiv[e] but thought that more complex matters required Cantonese. This teache[r], therefore, expressed doubts about the efficacy of English MOI in enhancin[g] students' English proficiency, although she claimed it familiarized the[m] with the English visual arts vocabulary.

It emerged that these four teachers using English as the MOI to teach thei[r] subjects focused almost exclusively on their own subject, suggesting a vir[-] tual absence of cross-curricular consultation.

(b) Putonghua MOI – four teachers   The two teachers using Putonghua t[o] teach Chinese literacy took a balanced view of school policy. Both sa[w] advantages, since standard written Chinese and spoken Putonghua matc[h] each other directly – that is, formal spoken Putonghua can be written dow[n] word-for-word to form standard written Chinese. By contrast, in Cantones[e] the spoken form varies greatly from standard written Chinese, and man[y] spoken words do not have a written form. In an ideal situation, therefor[e], employing Putonghua to teach Chinese literacy could avoid the mismatc[h] between spoken Cantonese and formal written Chinese. However, Cantones[e]

peakers not sufficiently proficient in Putonghua would not easily be able
to understand instructions and explanations in Putonghua, or effectively
discuss and present ideas in Putonghua. In that case, their Chinese liter-
cy development would suffer. Moreover, the sudden MOI transition from
antonese (P1–P3) to Putonghua (P4–P6) in the teaching of Chinese liter-
cy presents a dilemma, since students who have already developed good
utonghua proficiency will benefit, whereas those with low Putonghua pro-
ciency levels may suffer badly.

As regards the two teachers teaching Putonghua in Putonghua, they
claimed that, since the aim of the subject is to enhance students' Putonghua
roficiency, they try their best to follow the 'One Language Only' policy
nd are quite strict about it. They allow occasional use of Cantonese, but
nly when there is a genuine need, so they are tolerant of Cantonese use in
1, but strongly discourage its use in Putonghua lessons after P2. However,
hese teachers pointed out that the use of Putonghua as the MOI for Chinese
teracy lessons can have a negative impact on the development of students'
antonese proficiency. For example, at school students may have learned
he Putonghua pronunciation of rarer terms and not know how these are
ronounced in Cantonese.

) Cantonese MOI – four teachers   The two teachers teaching Chinese lit-
racy through Cantonese listed a number of advantages. Firstly, the use of
he students' L1 permits learners to follow instructions and explanations
ore easily. Secondly, the learners exhibit a greater sense of language aware-
ess, allowing them to appreciate a story told in Cantonese better than one
old in Putonghua. Moreover, when cultural aspects are discussed, learners
an relate to the content more easily. These teachers noted that there was
o need to use Putonghua at all when teaching Chinese literacy through
antonese.

One of the two Chinese literacy teachers emphasized the importance
f teaching ancient Chinese poems to students, either in Cantonese or in
utonghua. These poems are famed for their rich content, excellent word
hoice, compact language structure and beautiful rhythms. Many poems
arry philosophical stances, cultural values and moral lessons. In mainland
hina, reciting ancient Chinese poems is a very popular method of devel-
ping Chinese literacy, and the teacher believes that it should be equally
mphasized in the Hong Kong Chinese curriculum.

The final interviews concerned the two teachers employing Cantonese
o teach general studies. Both support the use of the students' L1, because
ts use facilitates a grasp of many complicated concepts in the subject, ren-
ering much more effective and efficient the assimilation of subject con-
ent knowledge. They support the school's language policy, believing that
antonese, English and Putonghua should, in a balanced way, all be used
s MOIs. They consider the current percentage of course time allocated to

different MOIs from P4 upwards (around 45 per cent Cantonese, 30 per cen
English and 25 per cent Putonghua) to be appropriate.

4.6.2.3   Parents

All ten randomly selected parents interviewed were in favour of the tr
lingual education model adopted by the school. In their view, English
the most important world language, while Putonghua is gaining status as
world language. Consequently, it is crucial for their children to learn thes
two languages properly if they want to become successful in their studi
and later professional careers. They regard Cantonese as a local languag
which is important for literacy development, but would countenance a fu
ther shift to English and Putonghua if students were able to cope. The
unanimously supported the use of English as the MOI for PE and visu
arts: a number of parents indicated that, from P4 onwards, they would lik
general studies to be taught in English as well. Most also favoured the use c
Putonghua to teach Chinese literacy from P4 onwards, and they welcome
its trial use as the MOI for the Chinese literacy subject from P1.

Bearing in mind the academic pressures of primary school life, most pa
ents indicated that they would provide family support to their children b
for example, reading English and Chinese stories to their children at hom
or employing private home tutors for their children, especially where th
parents cannot themselves speak Putonghua or English. They believe tha
work in the school classroom during the school day cannot, on its ow
help their children to achieve the necessary high levels of proficiency acros
the three languages. Consequently, they are willing to 'spend money' (o
personal tutors, tutorial/cram schools, etc.) in order to help their childre
obtain higher grades and so 'become more competitive in society'.

4.6.3   Data set 3: survey on students' perceptions

The questionnaire made evident that the students are very confident wit
their Cantonese proficiency and feel comfortable using it as the main lan
guage in the school. Their opinions varied on whether they regularly code
switch between English and Cantonese during the study of English, o
between Putonghua and Cantonese during Chinese lessons. In either cas
around 20 per cent of the students strongly agreed and 20 per cent strongl
disagreed. This may mean that the school's 'One Language Only' polic
impacts some students strongly but not others. Answers to other question
naire items reveal that students are generally positive about the trilingua
education model in the school and think that using English as the MO
for the PE lessons is beneficial. They see code-switching as a positive wa
of developing their language proficiency and are confident that they wil
reach high levels of proficiency in written Chinese and Putonghua by th
time they graduate from P6. They are less positive about the use of Englis
as the MOI for Visual Arts and are also not so sure whether it is appropriat

start teaching Chinese through Putonghua from P4. They are less confi-
ent about their English and are not certain whether they would be able to
chieve a high level of English proficiency upon graduation. These personal
eflections of pupils are somewhat at variance with the objective test data
ted by the principal, which suggested that students' English standards are
gnificantly higher than those in other schools, whereas their Putonghua
andards are broadly similar.

.7   Discussion and conclusions

he findings above may be addressed in three ways: firstly, in culture of
earning terms; secondly, in light of Hong Kong's bi-literate, trilingual pol-
y objectives; and, thirdly, by reference to the general educational context.
lowever, before such a discussion, it must be emphasized that no region-
ride generalizations can be made about a single case study: other schools
/ill be seeking different proportions of MOI use; the observed lessons may
ot be thought representative of other lessons taught, either in this school
r elsewhere. Nevertheless, based on our familiarity with many schools, and
ur observations of perhaps 2,000 lessons during our combined 32 years
f teacher education experience in Hong Kong, we consider the sample to
e not untypical in general and certainly they are typical of some other
chools.

1) The recorded lessons   As regards the lessons themselves, the statistical
ata here strongly suggest the dominance of the Chinese culture of learning
/ith emphasis on the accumulation of knowledge through effort, diligence
nd perseverance. The school is obviously seeking to inculcate the virtues of
erious and studious application, to set demanding standards and to engen-
er the sort of rigid determination and commitment designed to enable
tudents to overcome inevitable difficulties and distractions even with dull,
epetitive exercises – perhaps a fainter and more gentle echo of the parental
trategies advocated in the popular account of a Chinese family education
n the United States, *Battle Hymn of the Tiger Mother* (Chua, 2011). Clearly,
he mode of teaching here is transmissive, with the teacher and textbooks
s authorities (only PE and visual arts have no textbook). This is reflected in
he particularly high percentage of teacher talk, (Tsui [1995] suggests 70 per
ent is more usual), the short and limited pupil speaking turns and the gen-
ral absence of learners' questions. Indeed, the pupils' role is largely to listen
nd learn, to memorize and recite. Competitive and stakeholder pressures,
he rigours of tests and examinations, the packed curriculum, the infre-
uency of pair and group work, the arrangement of the school day with its
hort, discrete lessons and perambulating teachers – and even the layout of
he classroom furniture – epitomize the almost 'traditional grammar school
thos' of this primary school, even at P1 level. Certainly, in this particular

case, the limited Western influences on classroom practices as represente
in Figure 4.1 (the three lower boxes) (Glenwright, 2010) appear almost t
have been eradicated. Hong Kong is now very much in China!

(b) The interview data and the student survey   The interview data suggest the
the attempts by this school to formulate and implement a consistent languag
policy enjoy strong general support. The principal enunciates a clear vision c
what must be done and how it must be done, and this receives a large measur
of support from the teachers, parents and children, although mechanism
(and time) to ensure greater cooperation and coordination by subject teacher
using either English or Putonghua as the MOI might be better than the cur
rent isolation of individual teachers. Probably, the need to work towards gov
ernment language policy objectives allows the various parties to perceive, ye
accept, the implicit difficulties and inherent disadvantages in the particula
Hong Kong situation in order to receive the greater, longer-term benefit
for study, career and upward social mobility. Consequently, only the sub
ject teacher expresses serious reservations about the selection of English MC
for visual arts lessons, whereas both the teacher and parents favour Englis
MOI for PE because – very often – only receptive skills are required. There i
also some limited reluctance to adhere strictly to the 'One Language Only
policy, especially where the use of L1 as a resource facilitates the negotiatio
of meaning. Indeed, Angel Lin (1998: 86) had already noted 'the value of th
selective and principled use of L1' in the joint negotiation of meaning, whil
recent publications openly urge teachers to live a guilt-free life and draw ap
propriately on their shared mother tongue (Swain, Kirkpatrick & Cummin:
2011). Overall, however, the fact remains that, in a difficult situation, th
school is making a valiant attempt to meet the linguistic demands of society
Whether the principal's or the children's assessment of learner performanc
and prospects in English or Putonghua is correct remains uncertain – bot
could be right. The children's lack of confidence with English may be just
fied, but they could still be above the general territory-wide standard, whils
their positive assessment of their own Putonghua proficiency could more c
less equate to the Hong Kong-related norm.

4.7.1   Broader implications

The findings above impinge on two other issues, namely: social selectio
and curriculum reform. First, the received wisdom, or 'taken-for-grantec
assumptions, about the essential prerequisites for student success at schoc
serve an obvious social-selection function. This form of selection is achieve
differently in different educational systems: in Hong Kong it is heavily influ
enced by an implicit culture of learning among parents, which manifest
itself in several specific elements. First, some parents themselves provid
extra-curricular tuition; others employ paid private tutors to teach chil
dren after school at home. Second, some students are sent to attend tutoria

olleges after school: there are some 800 tutorial colleges in Hong Kong – a onsiderable industry sponsored by many families who see attendance as ssential for school achievement and later exam success. A third element is ie role of domestic helpers: in Hong Kong there are over 280,000 'domestic elpers' (maids), mostly from the Philippines and Indonesia, some of whom re well educated, well qualified and speak good English, thus reinforcing ie role of English in these families. However, although these elements in ie HKCOL apply to many families, one effect is to restrict the life chances f children from less well-educated and/or poorer families who, understand-bly, cannot support their children's learning in such ways.

As regards curriculum reform, new pathways towards trilingualism are eing charted through the adoption of different MOIs in different pri-iary school subjects, although the consequent heavy linguistic demands n teachers and learners (bi-literacy and trilingualism) may tend to restrict edagogical innovation. More significantly for classroom practice, there ppears to be a strong and abiding local belief in and preference for Chinese ulture of learning essentials, which may partly explain why the sustained nd *seemingly* determined efforts of the Hong Kong government to effect undamental curriculum reform appear, in this particular case, and also iore generally, to have had minimal impact. Indeed, the allegedly restrictive ictors deemed to impede 'Western style' curriculum reform have been ocumented for decades in the Hong Kong academic literature. Curriculum eform is, of course, notoriously difficult to implement (Cornbleth, 1990; ullan & Stiegelbauer, 1991; Snyder, Bolin & Zumwalt, 1992), especially here teachers do not share the particular views of the nature of education nd language learning that are propounded by the authorities (as here). In uch cases, overt or covert practitioner resistance to imported pedagogies ith concealed philosophies of dubious cultural affinity is often an issue ith consequent concealed 'veto' points (Canagarajah, 1999; Dyer, 2000). urthermore, in Hong Kong, it is generally acknowledged that teachers are articularly adept at being 'able to deconstruct the policy text and identify a iessage other than that which prevails on the surface' (Morris & Chan 1998: 59). The severe deficits of the legitimacy of the colonial and post-colonial dministrations (Morris & Scott, 2003) may also intrude. Nevertheless, a eader skimming through the apparently state-of-the-art curriculum guides iight well imagine Hong Kong to be at the forefront of progressive, child-entred, enquiry-based teaching and learning. Yet, long ago, David Carless autioned that, 'learner-centred or discovery-oriented approaches are ... dys-unctional for the examination-oriented approaches prevalent in Hong long' (1998: 235), while Glenwright (2003: 81) concluded that the system s, to a significant extent, held in place by frameworks and attitudes often nimical to [curricular] reform', and 'a high degree of failure [being] ... en-irely predictable both from the history and from the structure, diachronic nd synchronic views converging in meaning'.

4.8   Conclusion

The current investigation has revealed an intricate and intriguing picture of language use across the curriculum in one Hong Kong primary school, where classroom practice is influenced by colonial and post-colonial history by official curriculum and language reform policies – the roles and status of English, Cantonese and Putonghua, the fundamental culture of learning beliefs of the major local stakeholders and the consequent decisions that shape classroom realities as a pathway to trilingualism, tentatively evolving in response to the government's MOI 'fine tuning' announcement. The next phase of this research project will delve further into the objective data to explore issues and instances of classroom language use by teachers and learners, furnishing and evaluating detailed examples of code-switching and turn-taking across subjects.

References

Bacon-Shone, J. and Bolton, K. (2008) Bilingualism and multilingualism in the HKSAR: Language surveys and Hong Kong's changing linguistic profile. In K Bolton and Y. Han (Eds), *Language and society in Hong Kong*. Hong Kong: Hong Kong Open University Press, pp. 25–51.

Canagarajah, A.S. (1999) *Resisting linguistic imperialism in English teaching*. Oxford: Oxford University Press.

Carless, D. (1998) Managing systemic curriculum change: A critical analysis of Hong Kong's target-oriented curriculum initiative. In P. Stimpson and P. Morris (Eds), *Curriculum and assessment for Hong Kong: Two components, one system*. Hong Kong: The Open University of Hong Kong Press, pp. 223–44.

Census and Statistics Department, Hong Kong Government (2007) *Hong Kong 2006 Population By-census Main Report Volume I*, Retrieved 1 April 2010 from http://www. statistics.gov.hk/publication/stat_report/population/B11200472006XXXXB0401.pdf

Chua, A. (2011) *Battle hymn of the tiger mother*. New York: Penguin Press.

Cornbleth, C. (1990) *Curriculum in context*. New York: Falmer Press.

Cortazzi, M. and Jin, L. (1996) Cultures of learning: Language classrooms in China. In H. Coleman (Ed.), *Society and the language classroom*. Cambridge: Cambridge University Press, pp. 169–206.

Dyer, C. (2000) *Operation blackboard: Policy implementation in Indian elementary education*. Oxford: Symposium.

Fullan, M. & Stiegelbauer, S. (1991) *The new meaning of educational change*. London: Cassell.

Glenwright, P. (2003) Education reform and policy change in Hong Kong: A critique of the post-colonial legacy. *Education and Society*, 21 (3), 67–89.

Glenwright, P. (2010) *The Hong Kong culture of learning: Its origins and effects*. Saarbrücken: Lambert Academic Publishing (LAP).

Information Services Department (2009) *Hong Kong 2009*. Hong Kong: Government Logistics Department.

Jin, L. & Cortazzi, M. (1995) A cultural synergy model for academic language use. In P. Bruthiaux, T. Boswood & B. Du-Babcock (Eds), *Explorations in English for Professional Communication*. Hong Kong: City University of Hong Kong, pp. 41–56.

hnson, R.K. (1997) The Hong Kong education system: Late immersion under stress. In R.K. Johnson & and M. Swain (Eds), *Immersion Education: International Perspectives*. Cambridge: Cambridge University Press, pp. 171–89.

, D.C.S. (2009) Towards 'bilteracy and trilingualism' in Hong Kong (SAR): Problems, dilemmas and stakeholders' views. *AILA Review*, 22, 72–84.

n, M.Y.A. (1998) Understanding the issue of medium of instruction in Hong Kong schools: What research approaches do we need? *Asia Pacific Journal of Language in Education*, 1 (1), March, 85–98.

ttlewood, W. and Liu, N.F. (1996) *Hong Kong students and their English: LEAP*. Hong Kong: The University of Hong Kong and Macmillan.

lorris, P. and Adamson, B. (2010) *Curriculum, schooling and society in Hong Kong*. Hong Kong: Hong Kong University Press.

lorris, P. and Chan, K.K. (1998) Cross-curricular themes and curriculum reform in Hong Kong: Policy as discourse. In P. Stimpson and P. Morris (Eds), *Curriculum and assessment for Hong Kong: Two components, one system*. Hong Kong: Open University of Hong Kong Press, pp. 245–62.

lorris, P. & Scott, I. (2003). Educational reform and policy implementation in Hong Kong. *Journal of Education Policy*, 18 (1), 71–84.

lorris, P., Adamson, R., Au, M.L., Chan, K.K., Chan, W.Y., Ko, P.Y., Lai, A.W., Morris, E., Ng, F.P., Ng, Y.Y., Wong, W.M. & Wong, P.H. (1996) *Target Oriented Curriculum Evaluation Project Interim Report*. Hong Kong: In-service Teacher Education Programme, Faculty of Education, The University of Hong Kong.

ennington, M.C. (1998) Introduction: Perspectives on language in Hong Kong at century's end. In M.C. Pennington (Ed.), *Language in Hong Kong at century's end*. Hong Kong: Hong Kong University Press, pp. 3–40.

wain, M., Kirkpatrick, A. & Cummins, J. (2011) *How to have a guilt-free life using Cantonese in the English class: A handbook for the English language teacher in Hong Kong*. Hong Kong: Research Centre into Language Education and Acquisition in Multilingual Societies, Hong Kong Institute of Education. Also available at http://www.ied.edu.hk/rcleams/view.php?secid=1399

nyder, J., Bolin, F. & Zumwalt, K. (1992) Curriculum implementation. In P.W. Jackson (Ed.), *Handbook of research in curriculum*. New York: Macmillan, pp. 402–35.

sui, A.B.M. (1995) *Classroom interaction*. London: Penguin.

Part II

Intercultural Learning in Developing Language and Academic Skills

5

Peer Assistance in an English Immersion Context in China

Xiaohua Liang, Lixian Jin and Martin Cortazzi

5.1 Introduction

Since the late 1990s, English immersion education has been advocated by researchers and teachers in the mainland of China. In an immersion programme, the learners from a common background of a majority or dominant language receive their initial primary and later secondary education through the medium of a target foreign or second language for much or most of the curriculum. The aims of such a program are that within several years children will reach high levels of proficiency in this target language, while adequately learning the curriculum content and maintaining and developing their first language. Such programs began in Canada in the mid-1960s for English speakers to learn French under pressure from parents for their children to become bilingual (Lambert & Tucker, 1972). The generally positive and sometimes surprising evaluation of curriculum learning (Swain & Lapkin, 1983) quickly led to immersion being seen as a form of successful bilingual education which could be used in other contexts (Genesee, 1987) and in many other countries for a wide range of languages, including learning English in Germany, Hungary, Singapore and Japan (Johnson & Swain, 1997). A wide range of types of programs for immersion schooling have been developed, varying from total immersion (for the entire curriculum except the mother tongue as a timetabled subject) to different degrees of partial immersion, to beginning at kindergarten or various primary levels, and including heritage language programs (e.g., to develop Catalan in Spain – an indigenous language – alongside the national language of Spanish), but they all have the explicit aim of developing bilingualism in a kind of dual language program (Christian, 2011) with some features that overlap with content-based second language teaching since a major concern is that students should learn the curriculum content (Lyster, 2011).

In China, this raises the possibility that an immersion program could be used for Mandarin-speaking children (or speakers of other Chinese languages) to learn English within a goal of achieving bilingualism and intercultural education. Crucially, however, an immersion program is no simply a way of organizing language education for bilingual goals; it als implies a different pedagogy, with different ways of using language in th classroom since essentially all students are learning through the medium o a language they are learning, initially at least, as complete beginners (Swai & Lapkin, 1983; Genesee, 1987; Johnson & Swain, 1997). In a Chinese cor text of primary education, this implies a change in the common cultur of learning, with considerable shifts in organizing classroom interactio and developing teacher's and students' talk for learning in much new ways (Cortazzi, 1997, 1998). This is especially a challenge where classes i China are frequently much larger than those found in the West, and whei established classroom cultures have considerable elements of being teache fronted and text-centred; and where, although whole-class interaction ofte has a sophisticated development, the uses of pair work and group work ai relatively new or uncertain to both teachers and learners (Jin and Cortazz 1998, 2002, 2006, 2011)

The first and most influential immersion model in China is the China Canada Collaborative English Immersion Program (CCEI) program (Qiang 2000; Qiang and Zhao, 2000), which was renamed China–Canada–Unite States Collaborative English Immersion (CCUEI) program in 2002 (Zhao an Qiang, 2002). As the names indicate, there was collaborative expertise fror Canada and the United States. Led by Haiyan Qiang of South China Norma University (who had been a key initiator of another immersion program i Xi'an) and   Linda Siegel of the University of British Columbia, the CCUE (then called the CCEI) was first introduced in Xi'an in 1997 (Qiang, 2000 Qiang and Zhao, 2000). The CCUEI is modelled on the Canadian immer sion pattern, which was a second-language situation, and adapted into th Chinese context (Qiang, 2000; Qiang and Zhao, 2000; Qiang and Zhac 2001), which was fully a foreign-language context. English is thus both th teaching content and the teaching medium. The students are immersed i English for up to half of their school time in such subjects as social scienc living sciences and so forth.

The immersion programs differed from the Chinese mainstream school in both curriculum and pedagogy. In the CCUEI curriculum, as expectec some content subjects were taught in English instead of in Chinese, whil mainstream schools were bound to the Chinese-medium, governmen guided local curriculum. The mainstream classroom teaching of Englisr constrained by its focus on linguistic aspects, (or more narrowly on lex ical items and syntax) was characterized by teacher-dominated, knowledge transmitting, whole-class interaction (Cortazzi and Jin, 1996; Deng and Carless, 2009; Zhang and Pei, 2005; Zhang, 2005), while pedagogy in th English immersion classes featured students' active participation in th learning activities, which showed the effort to integrate linguistic and socia cultural elements with educational elements (e.g., needs, goals, motivation arners, teaching materials and teaching methods) (Johnson, 1989; White,)88).

The program marked a departure in English instruction in the Chinese)ntext (where English is usually taught as a foreign language for at most a w hours each week) and also showed autonomy in education given to the ·gion by the central government. In English immersion programs in China, nglish, as the medium of instruction, is taught through integrating it into her content subjects. The aim is to develop fully students' English language :ills, increase their confidence in English language learning, enhance their ritten and spoken English proficiency, ensure satisfactory development in)ntent-based learning and improve their understanding of Western culture 'ithout sacrificing their knowledge of, and appreciation for, Chinese culture ad identity (Qiang, 2000; Qiang and Zhao, 2000). The CCUEI programs in i'an were both effective and successful (Fang et al., 2001; Pei, 1998; Qiang,)00; Qiang and Zhao, 2001; Zhang and Pei, 2005; Zhao and Qiang, 2002), nd English immersion programs were soon introduced into other cities in iainland China (Liang, 2004; Qiang, 2000; Zhang and Yan, 2007; Zhao et l., 2006). However, nearly all the research studies focused on the effective-ess of immersion with an outcome-orientation. Besides researchers such as Iiao Pei (2007), very few researchers took a process-oriented approach to ivestigate the learning process in the CCUEI.

Rather than focusing on the macro-level effectiveness of immersion pro-rams in the mainland of China, this chapter reports a case study in one :hool which examines the students' interaction at micro-level in the learn-ig process, as revealed by data from both in and out of the classroom. nplications can be drawn from the study for English Language Teaching iLT) in mainland China in general and English-immersion programs spe-ifically. The findings offer insights into activities and classroom interaction, specially students' and teachers' involvement in classroom activities.

.2   Methodology

.2.1   The setting

he setting for this case study was a privately funded primary English nmersion boarding school in Guangdong Province. It was selected because : was the first school to adopt English immersion at the school level, not Jst as an experiment with an experimental class and a control class. The etting is a complex school that includes primary, secondary junior, and econdary senior levels. This research was conducted in the primary school; hus, the more specific setting is the primary school.

Since 2004, when the school was first set up, it has offered the English nmersion program. Unlike other English programs in Xi'an, Shanghai, Vuhan and Beijing, where English immersion has been carried out as an

experiment to examine the effectiveness of immersion programs (and h
been limited to experimental and control groups in public schools), th
school in focus here implemented its English immersion program in all fiv
of its grade 1 classes, beginning in September 2004. While virtually all class
in the first four primary grades are immersion classes, very little actual tim
is spent on English immersion content instruction, and English immersio
subjects are limited to social science, living science, P.E. and fine arts. In th
spring of 2008 (when data gathering commenced), the primary school ha
21 English immersion classes and a total of about 800 immersion student
All the classes in grades 1, 2, 3 and 4 were immersion classes except for tw
newly formed classes of newcomers. But in September of 2008, with the a
rival of a new principal, the English immersion program was changed.

5.2.2 The participants

In this study, the total set of participants consists of the principals, th
immersion teachers, the selected students and their parents. However, as th
study focuses on the student activities, the participants here are mainly th
students in a particular class. The class, teacher and students were selecte
as research participants based on the following the criteria:

- The teacher was willing to participate in the research;
- The class was recommended by the school principal on the basis of i
  having a warm and positive classroom atmosphere.
- The students were selected based on their high, intermediate or low pro
  ficiency levels in English.

The selected class had been involved in the immersion program sinc
September 2004. It consisted of 37 students (25 boys and 12 girls) who wer
an average of around 11 years old in 2008. Based on the teacher's recommen
dation, and taking into account the need for gender balance and a variet
of language proficiency levels, a gender-balanced group of six students from
different language proficiency levels was selected: two from the high pro
ficiency level, two from the intermediate and two from the lower, with a
effort to achieve maximum variation. As happens in such a study, one stu
dent dropped out because he was transferred to another school, but anothe
student with similar language proficiency replaced him. A further studen
pleaded to be among the participants; however, he was not selected becaus
he had had the experience of living in Singapore for three years, which
means that he would not represent the mainstream students. Nevertheless
he was observed peripherally.

5.2.3 Data collection and data analysis

A variety of data collection and analysis methods and techniques wer
employed in this case study. Multiple data-collection sources, which fit th

lain of evidence for in-depth analysis, were employed. Observations of hole-class instruction and of the focus students were carried out, both in 1d after class; the observations were recorded in both audio and video for- lats and transcribed. After the observations had yielded information about hat happened in class, interviews were conducted to clarify certain points 1d to deepen the researcher's understanding of what had been observed. he transcripts of the audio and video recordings were a rich database for 1terpretation and reinterpretation. Field notes recorded additional infor- 1ation, such as the atmosphere in the classroom and the flavour of the 1teraction, supplementing the recordings.

The observational techniques used were audio or video recording of 1e activities, taking field notes and collecting physical artefacts. Digital 'corders were attached to the selected students, allowing recording of 1eir interactions in immersion and regular English classes, and their after- ass engagement in evening self-study and other extracurricular activities. udio recordings were transcribed by the researcher, and video recordings 'ere used to capture the classroom atmosphere, whole-class instruction and 1teraction. Field notes were taken with a focus on the eight selected stu- ents in both in-class and after-class observations. Physical artefacts such as 'aching plans, student worksheets, assignments, school slogans and rele- ant school files were collected and examined to enrich the researcher's nderstanding of the collected recorded data and its context.

The data set contained over 120 hours of observations. The classes observed 'ere English immersion classes, regular English language classes, evening 'lf-study classes (since this is a boarding school, students do self-study at :hool), morning reading classes and extracurricular activities. In addition, 1me school events were also observed, such as the school's Science and 'ulture Festival and the opening ceremony of the school's sports games.

The data set also contained almost 25 hours of interviews. Twenty-seven 1dividual interviews were conducted with the selected teacher T1, six with 1e principals (P1, P2), and 18 with the other immersion teachers (T2–10); total of 30 individual and focus group interviews were conducted with 1e selected students (S1–8). In addition, a number of informal personal 0mmunications were noted which occurred in the process of data collec- on, such as lunchtime or dinnertime talks in the canteen, or talks over the hone.

Data on a total of 110 student activities were transcribed in detail and nalysed using three layers of data analysis. Student activities were calcu- ated based on Nina Spada and Maria Frohlich (1995: 30) criterion: 'The eginning or end of an activity is typically marked by a change in the verall theme or content.' First, in order to know their nature, student ac- ivities were examined and categorized into different types, based on the ata. Second, the activities were examined through the optic of the activity ystem, to understand the mediations of activity and unfold the complexity

of its dynamics; third, data analysis was focused on peer discussions, wit
the features of these discussions identified.

5.2.4   Thick description

A rich, thick description provides depth, breadth and richness for the e:
ploration and understanding of the question under study (Flick, 1998
Although some researchers contend that triangulation is incoherent an
empirically empty (Lincoln and Guba, 1985: 307), thick description fror
multiple resources and multiple methods is used to gain multiple perspe
tives for a holistic picture and an in-depth analysis of the case. Henc
Norman Denzin's (1997) and Uwe Flick's (1998) types of triangulation serv
as very important measures for the current study.

Multiple data sources and multiple methods were used to ensure thick d
scription of the case for the purpose of trustworthiness. To achieve a holisti
presentation of the picture, data were collected from difference sources an
a variety of methods were employed in collecting the data. Physical arte
facts were also collected to enrich the understanding of the data. Iterativ
exploration of the data was conducted, and data analysis was conducte
both during the data-collection periods and after completing the fieldworl
To ensure thick description, validation and verification, two additiona
measures were taken, as proposed by Michael Patton (1980: 329):

(1) checking out the consistency of findings generated by different dat;
    collection methods and
(2) checking out the consistency of different data sources within th
    same method

As Patton (1980: 331) explains, consistency does not mean that the data ar
all the same, but that one is aware of the differences, attempts to identif
the reasons for these differences and tries to give 'reasonable explanation
for the differences in data from different sources' in order to contribute t
the validity of the findings.

5.3   Peer assistance as mediation: theoretical dimensions

Neo-Vygotskian theories of student learning have strongly influenced con
temporary approaches to early childhood education, particularly regardin
the roles of talk and activity in constructing learning. These theories, origin
ating with Lev Vygotsky (1896–1934) in Russia (Van der Veer and Valsine
1991, 1994), were gradually translated and culturally transplanted in th
West (Vygotsky, 1962, 1978), inspiring a now widely recognized movemen
for sociocultural ideas about the importance of dialogue to construct learn
ing and thinking and, therefore, to encourage teachers to change traditiona
patterns of classroom interaction so that learning is mediated and scaffolde(

y not only teachers but also by peers (Newman et al., 1989; Tharp and allimore, 1989; Wells, 1999).

Within this theory, learning creates a *zone of proximal development* (ZPD). his notional 'zone' is at the frontier of what a student can do or under- and; the student can achieve understanding within this zone through int activity and discussion with an adult or a more advanced peer; the arner thus has the potential to achieve new levels of development through his kind of mediation and regulation (Lantolf, 2000a, 2000b; Lantolf and horne, 2006; Ohta, 2001; Vygotsky, 1978). For students' ZPD today, their nmediate potential will become their actual level of development, through dynamic and nonlinear process, and the ZPD will have a new extended ontier ready for further learning. Key to this theoretical conception of arning is that it is socially based: learning proceeds from outside inwards, om talk and regulation of activity by others (outside) to internalized anguage, thinking and control (inside or self-regulation). Peer assistance nhances students' learning by helping them to progress from other-regu- ation to self-regulation, and discussion and social interaction is central to his progress in learning (Lantolf, 2000a, 2000b; Lantolf and Appel, 1994a; ygotsky, 1978). As Vygotsky (1978: 78) notes, '[W]hat a child can do with ssistance today she will be able to do by herself tomorrow', a statement choed by numerous researchers (e.g., Ahmed, 1994; van Lier, 1996; etc.). Within the ZPD, peer assistance mediates student learning. There are, how- ver, different kinds of peer assistance which may create or influence differ- nt conditions of learning.

In the current study, peer assistance occurred in nearly all of the collab- rative activities and seems to be a part of the classroom culture. In this sec- ion, the teacher's role in fostering peer assistance in the class is discussed, ollowed by examples of how peers assisted each other in their activities.

.3.1   The teacher's role in fostering the culture of peer assistance

he class shows a culture of peer assistance and active participation, appar- ntly fostered by the teacher, who set its rules and routines – co-constructed y the students, who internalized the set procedures through their interac- ions. The classroom culture is revealed in class-assisting discourse, during which the students frequently help one another.

According to the class teacher, T1 (interview, 26–5–2007), three models f peer assisting had been promoted by him from the very beginning of his class. The first was *one-on-one tutoring*, that is, better students tutoring oorer students; when pairing students, T1 took this model of assisting into onsideration, pairing the proficient S1 with S5, who was less capable than he was. The second model was *the optimum competition model*, that is, each tudent aiming to surpass another student in their studies. For example, S3, 6 and S7 were determined to surpass S8 in their English study. The third as *the mutual-help model*, in which students help each other with their studies. As T1 frequently reminded the students in his class, *'mei ge ren de you shan guang dian, dou you chang chu* ("Everyone has his shining points and his merits")' (Interview, 26–5–2007).

When interviewed (14–03–2008) about the implementation and promotion of his class tutoring and assisting discourse, T1 told me that it was very effective:

> *Xiang hu bang zhu zai xue sheng ho dong zhong xiang dang pu bian. xue sheng men dui bang bie ren he xun qiu bang zhu dou you hen gao ji qing, dou jue e zi ran. wo bu de bu xiang ban fa jiang li ta men – gei zuo de hao de tong xu jia fen.*
>
> (Peer assistance is very common in our student activities, and the students have exhibited great enthusiasm for both offering assistance and seeking assistance very naturally. I have to think of ways to reward those who do well – the awards are additional points on their scores.) (T1)

For their part, the students seem to enjoy assisting each other and being assisted. When asked (group interview, 15–11–2008) how they felt about peer assistance, S7 told me that *'he tong xue yi qi xue xue de geng duo* (we learn more in working with our classmates)', while S6 and S4 both said that *'bang zhu tong xue gan dao hen kuai le* (we feel happy to assist our classmates)'. S added that they *'you yi zhong dang lao shi de gan jue, te bie shi ni jiao yi ge be xue sheng de shi hou ni hui you yi zhong cheng jiu gan* (had a feeling of being teacher, a feeling of gaining achievement especially when teaching a slow student)'. S2 also mentioned benefits she reaped because *'bang bie ren de shi hou, zi ji you zai xue zhi shi* (while helping others, I am learning [that knowledge] again)'.

Aside from fostering the classroom peer-assisting discourse, T1 cultivated the classroom culture as well through class routines and rituals. For example when he greeted the students and began the class, the students would reply loudly in Mandarin, *'Ban ji xing wang wo de zhe ren.* (The prosperity of our class is my responsibility)'. T1 explained (Interview, 14–3–2008) about the ritual *'Zhe ge yi shi neng zen jia xue sheng de rong yu gan. Yi ge ren jin bu bu suan she me, zui zhu yao de shi quan ban yi qi jin bu, na cai shi wo men de guang rong.* (This ritual can enhance the students' sense of honour. That one person is progressing does not weigh as much as that the whole class are progressing together. That is our honour)'. He added, *'Zuo wei ji ti de yi yuan, we men de zhe ren jiu sh bao hut a, bu ran ta shou dao ban dian shang hai.* (As a member of this community, our duty was to protect it from any potential harm). When asked, every student could recite this motto exactly; according to S2 and S4, it meant that *'wo men ying gai re ai ban ji, bao hu ban ji rong yu, hu xiang bang zhu gong tong jin bu.* (we should love our class and protect the honour of our class through helping each other and progressing together.)' (Interview, 14–3–2008).

.3.2   The praxes of the students' peer assistance

he following extracts illustrate how the students assisted their peer inter-
cutors in the activities through peer prompting and waiting; non-verbal
xpressions; correcting errors and modulating speaking volume; trans-
tion; attending to the peer interlocutor's needs; and reciprocating peer
ssistance.

The teacher (T1) asked the students to talk about living and nonliving
ings based on eight pictures (a butterfly, a robot, the Milky Way, an elec-
ronic dog, an orange, a flower, a rock and a jellyfish) in the textbook's
ection, 'Growth and Change', and the criteria introduced in science class.
xtract 1 involves S6 and S4 talking about a butterfly.

.3.2.1   *Peer prompting and waiting*

xtract 1: Talking about butterfly by Pair S6 and S4.

1. S6: This is a butterfly.
2. S4: Is this a living thing?
3. S6: Yes.
4. S4: Why?
5. S6: Because...
6. S4: It can [prompting in a low voice].
7. S6: It...
8. S4: Can [prompting].
9. S6: It can... [0.6] fly.

(13–3–2008, Grade 4, from activity: 'Living things
or nonliving things?')

n this extract, S4 and S6 were trying to reason why a butterfly was a living
hing (in lines 1 to 4). When S6 hesitated and paused, as he could not for-
nulate and articulate the reason (in line 5), S4 prompted in a low voice (in
ine 6) with the two words needed, 'It can', in S6's utterance. S6 picked up
he prompted word 'it' (in line 7), but got stuck there and still had difficulty
o continue. S4 prompted again (in line 8) with the word 'can'. S6 at this
noment picked up the prompt and articulated the reason (in line 9) with
pause of six seconds. From this extract, we see that when S6 had some
ifficulty with the reasoning, S4 patiently assisted him through prompts.
When S6 picked up on the prompts, S4 gave him enough time to talk. Peer
rompting and waiting mediated their activity.

The following three extracts involve S2, S8 and S3 talking about a butterfly
nd a robot and summarizing what they had talked about.

5.3.2.2   Assisting each other through non-verbal expressions
Extract 2: Talk about butterfly by Group S2, S3 and S8.

1. S2: Is this a ... living thing?
2. S8: No, it isn't.
3. It's a living thing.
4. S2: [giggling, indicating he is wrong]
5. S8: Yes, it is.
6. It's a living thing because it can fly.
7. It can – it can.
8. S2: Move [prompting].
9. S8: Move.
10. It can reproduce babies.

(13–3–2008, Grade 4, from Activity 'Living thing
or nonliving things?'

In this extract, when S2 asked S8 whether the butterfly was a living thin
or not (in line 1), S8 gave a contradictory answer: first stating that 'No,
isn't', (in line 2), then stating that 'It's a living thing' (in line 3). S2's gi
gling (in line 4) led S8 to confirm that the butterfly is a living thing (i
line 5). Following that, S8 continued to give reasons for his statement (i
line 6) that 'it can fly'. He repeated the phrase and tried to find out wh
he wants to express (line 7). S2 prompted him (in line 8) and S8 picked u
the prompts (in line 9). In addition, he gave another reason (in line 1(
that 'It can reproduce babies'. This extract shows that, in the peer talk, pe
students' non-verbal expressions (such as S2's giggling) function as assis
ance by indicating an error, and lead to their peer interlocutor's self-repai
According to the seven students (interview, 15–11–2008), they regularl
handed over their turns of speaking through non-verbal expressions, suc
as eye movements or hand gestures. For example, S1 said, '*Shi ge yan se* (Giv
him a hint with our eyes)'; S6 told me, '*Shou shi* (Gestures)'; S3 said, '*Tui ta)
xia.* (Give him a push)'; S2 said, '*Nie ta yi ba.* (Pinch him)'; S3 added, '*Der
ta yi yan.* (Stare at him)'.

*5.3.2.3   Using low voice volume in prompting and correcting
their peer interlocutors*
Extract 3: Talking about the robot by Groups S2, S3 and S8.

14. S8: Is this a living thing?
15. S2: No, it isn't.
16. S8: En ...
17. S3: Why, why, why, why [prompting in a low voice].
18. S8: Why.
19. S2: Because it ... it can ... en ... produce ba– he can ... don't–

20. S8: Reproduce [prompting].
21. S2: It don't produce baby.
22. S8: Isn't this a living thing?
23. S3: No, it is.
24. S8: No, it ISN'T [correcting and prompting in a very low voice].
25. S3: No, it isn't.
(13–3–2008, Grade 4, from Activity 'Living things or
nonliving things?')

ers assisted each other a great deal in the activities, and low voice volume
as used in their assistance. In this extract, the first part from line 14 to line
l is mainly between S2 and S8; however, S3 actively engaged himself in
ie exchange (in line 17), prompting S8 with 'Why' in a low voice when he
und S8 stuttering with difficulty by the pause (in line 16). S8 picked up (in
ne 18) and S2 explained the reason (in line 19), where she showed difficulty
i articulating the reason of 'reproducing babies'. S8 prompted her with the
ord, and S2 picked up, although she felt confused with the words 'prod-
ce' and 'reproduce'. S8 projected the exchange to S3 (in line 22) and asked
im whether the robot was a living thing or not. S3, influenced by the L1 in
iixing that answer of negative and positive, gave the erroneous answer to
ie question with 'No, it is' (in line 23). S8 corrected him and laid emphatic
ress on the word 'isn't' in order to direct S3's attention to the form, but still
i a very low voice. S3 immediately picked up the prompt (in line 25).

Using low voice volume to assist their peer interlocutors was observed to
e a common practice in the student activities in groups. As shown in the
xtract above, S3 was prompting S8 in a low voice (in line 17) and S8 (in line
4) was correcting S3 and prompting S3 with the correct answer in a very
iw voice. When I asked them why (Interview, 15–11–2008), S6 said, '*ying-
ei bie ren ye zai si kao* (because he, too, is thinking about it)'. S2 explained
irther:

> Rruguo ta zai si kao, ni tu ran mao chu yi ju, jiu hui da duan ta de si lu. ta
> ben lai hui, ru guo ni gao yi xiao, ta zai shuo chu da an de hua, lao shi jiu
> hui shuo shi ni gao shu ta de da an. ta hui ren wei na ge tong xue bu hui.
> (If he is thinking about it, he will be interrupted by you when you speak
> out loud your sentence. He himself can work it out, but if you interrupt,
> though he gives the answer, the teacher will believe that it is you who tell
> him the answer but not that student himself can give the answer.) (S2)

l emphasized: '*Bang jiu shi xiao shen ti xing, er bu shi da shen ti ta hui da.*
Assisting means prompting someone in a low voice rather than answering
i a loud voice instead of him.)'

Some students were concerned that their peers might lose face, while
thers did not want to be punished for interjecting. According to S4, '*Yao*

zhao guo qing mian. ([We should] show concern about "face".)' S8 and S7 can
up with the class rule which T1 set to them. S8 said, '*T1 ting dao le jiu you n*
fan le. (If T1 hears it, there will be trouble.)' S7 added, '*hui zuo fu wo chen*
([You will be asked to] do push-ups.)' In short, therefore, they prompted the
peer interlocutors in a low voice to give them a chance to think, to not inte
rupt them, to avoid the teacher's misunderstanding about their peer inte
locutors, to avoid punishment, and to protect their peer interlocutor's 'face

Less proficient students expressed concerns of their own. S6 and S7, for e
ample, had mixed feelings about being offered peer assistance. S6's attitud
towards peer assistance depended on the source of assistance: '*ta ping shi d.*
wo hen hao, wo jiu yuan yi jie shou. ta ping shi dui wo bu hao, wo jiu bu le yi j
shou. wo jiu hui ba ta ji jue kai. (If he is nice to me in our normal time, I wi
accept his assistance. If he is not nice to me in our normal time, I will nc
feel happy to accept it. I will refuse it.)' This may help to explain why S6 wa
sometimes very defensive around S2, who was frequently domineering i
their interactions. S7 explained his frustration with peer assistance, saying

> You shi hou zi ji xue xue xue, hai shi bu hui de shi hou jiu hen shen
> qi le. yao shi you ren lai jiao ni de hua, jiu shi you yi di feng ci zh
> yang zi de shuo fa. Jiu hao xiang bie ren kan bu qi ni, bi shi ni. jiu p.
> (Sometimes when you are learning, learning, learning, still you are nc
> able to work it out, you will feel very angry [with yourself]. If on suc
> occasions someone comes to instruct you, you will feel it ironic [to you
> It seems as if others were looking down upon you, despising you. Yo
> will feel scared.) (S7)

The less intrusive nature of low voice prompting speaks to these concern
and makes it all the more valuable for and important in their learnin
practice.

5.3.2.4   *Assisting each other through translation*

Excerpt 4: Summary by Group S2, S3 and S8.

> 64. S8: Do you know their names?
> 65. S2: Yes.
> 66. This is butterfly.
> 67. This is...robot.
> 68. This is milkway.
> 69. This is er...
> 70. S8: Electronic dog [prompting in a very low voice].
> 71. S2: Electronic dog.
> 72. Er...this is an orange.
> 73. This is water.
> 74. S8: Water animals [prompting in a very low voice].

75. S2: Water animals.
76. This is er... this is...
77. S8: Rock [prompting in a very low voice].
78. S2: A rock.
79. This is a flower.

> (13–3–2008, Grade 4, from Activity 'Living things
> or nonliving things?' continued)

he activity excerpted above should have been a question–answer type,
s the teacher had assigned a task in which 'one asks and one answers'.
owever, the students, in conducting a free conversation about the pictures,
ere using what they had learned and even created, through translation,
new phrase, 'water animal', (in lines 74 and 75) for jellyfish. Extract 5
volved S5 and S1, and they were talking about an electronic dog.

.3.2.5   *Attending to peer interlocutors' needs for assistance*

xtract 5: Pair S1 and S5.

38. S5: Ji qi gou zhen me shuo (How to say 'electronic dog'?}
39. S1: Is this the dog?
40. S5: *Bu shi bu shi* (No no),
41. *Ji qi gou* (Electronic dog).
42. S1: Is this the dog?
43. No, it is the–
44. S5: Chocolate
45. S1: Chocolate [giggling]
46. It's the chocolate dog.
47. It's cool.
48. S5: En, yes?
49. Really?
50. S1: Yes, it is.
51. Is this the no- library [giggling] non- no, no
52. *Shen me de?* (What is it?) [thinking out loud]
53. S5: Nonliving thing (prompting).
54. S1: Yes...

> (13–3–2008, Grade 4, from Activity 'Living things
> or nonliving things?')

n this extract, S5 sought help from S1 when he could not express 'electronic
log' (in line 38). When S1 prompted him with 'Is this the dog' (in lines 39
nd 42), S5 emphasized in the L1 that it was 'electronic dog' (in line 41).
'hen S5 came up with the word 'Chocolate' (in line 44), which had some re-
emblance in pronunciation with 'electronic', and they continued to co-con-
truct the interaction which followed. S1 comments on chocolate dog, 'cool'

(in line 47), but still there was uncertainty about the expression, which mad
S5 inquire about it with 'really?' (in line 49). When S1 wanted to say 'nor
living thing' (in line 51), she suddenly could not express herself, and trie
hard to find the word through thinking aloud in 'private speech' (in lir
52). S5 detected S1's need for assistance by her private speech and prompte
her with the phrase *'nonliving thing'* (in line 53). In the peer exchanges, pee
were learning to attend to each other's needs. This extract shows that whe
the students found their peer interlocutors were struggling, they provide
the assistance needed, and co-constructed the interaction to support the
efforts. In this case, private speech occurred in S1's thinking process, whic
functioned socially and led to S5's provision of assistance.

When asked (Interview, 15–11–2008) how they knew their peer interlocuto
needed assistance, the students indicated that they were responding to a variet
of verbal and non-verbal indicators (stammering, head scratching, extended s
lence, etc.). S7 said, *'ta jiu hui zhe yang zi, er- er- er- zhe yang zi.* (He would talk lik
this, er- er- er- like this}'; S3 said, *'zhua tou.* ([He would be] scratching his head}
S6 said, *'jiu shi zhan zai na li xiang lai xiang qu.* ([He would be] standing ther
and thinking about it}'; S4 said, *'hen jiu mei you shuo hua de shi hou.* ([he would
pause for long}'; S2 said, *'hai you kan zhe bie de di fang.* (Besides, [he would be
looking at somewhere else)'. Their statements show that, in their peer talk, th
students had learned to be aware of and attend to each other's needs. Extract
involved S6 and S4 and they were talking about robot.

5.3.2.6   *Reciprocity of peer assisting*

Extract 6: Talking about robot by Pair S6 and S4.

10. S6: What's this?
11. S4: This is a … robot.
12. S6: Er … is this the …
13. S4: Living thing [prompting in very low voice].
14. S6: Living thing?
15. S4: No, it isn't.
16. S6: Why?
17. S4: Because … it no can – no can grown.
18. S6: Grow [correcting S4]

(13–3–2008, Grade 4, from Activity 'Living thing
or nonliving things?'

In this extract, S4 and S6 were talking about whether the robot was a living
thing or a nonliving thing. When S6 shows his difficulty with his stutter
ing filler 'er …' and hesitation pause (in line 12), S4 offered him prompt
of 'living thing' in a very low voice (in line 13). S6 picked up the prompt
and completed his utterance with the question (in line 14). When S4 hac
some erroneous pronunciation with 'grow' (in line 17), S6 corrected her anc
provided her with the correct pronunciation (in line 18). This extract show

hat reciprocity emerged in student peer assistance, and that less proficient
tudents, such as S6, could also assist their peer interlocutors, even if these
eers were from a higher proficiency level.

To sum up, peer assistance occurred in the activities under several circum-
ances: when the peer interlocutors directly asked each other for assistance;
hen they indirectly showed they were having difficulty through pauses,
ie use of fillers or lengthening of vowels, code-switching, private speech
r non-verbal language; or, when they made an error. Peers used numerous
chniques to assist their interlocutors, including repeating, translating, ex-
mplifying, explaining, clarification and challenging. Peers assisted each
ther in language manipulation, task administration, content selection, be-
aviour monitoring and affective support in language-, task-, content-, be-
aviour- and affect-related aspects. When assistance was offered, the peer
iterlocutors might pick up the prompt or the answer directly, pick up and
eformulate, ask for clarification/repetition, ignore the prompts and con-
nue to talk, challenge and disagree with the reasoning, negotiate with an
lternative answer or defend their answer.

In her study, Amy Ohta (2001: 89) grouped adult learners' peer assistance
ito two contexts: when the peer interlocutor was struggling, or when mak-
ig an error. The current study shows many instances in which the students
ctively sought assistance from their peer interlocutors, and used a wide
ariety of skills in their peer assistance. Their youth, their familiarity with
ssisting classroom discourse, and the positive classroom culture in which
iey interact may account for their sensitivity to their peer interlocutors'
ifficulties, the creative and patient ways in which they tutor and assist
ieir peers and their bold willingness to seek assistance themselves.

.4   Discussion and conclusions

ritical thinking, cultural concerns about 'face' and power-struggles emerged
i the students' responses to the peer assistance. The students were trying,
irough their actual performance in their activities, to gain an understand-
ig and improve their ability to handle their learning difficulties and social
elations. Activities provided a platform for the students to build up rapport,
> learn from each other and to support each other emotionally.

Ohta (2001: 89) reported peer-assisted performance in classroom language
earning in her study about adult learners at university level learning Japanese
s a foreign language. She listed some methods of peer assistance which emerged
i the classroom interaction, such as waiting, prompting, co-construction,
xplaining when the peer interlocutor is struggling and using a next-turn re-
air initiator (to help a peer to realize an error and self-correct) and asking when
he peer interlocutor is making an error. But the assistance was mainly in the
nguistic aspect. Because this research was conducted in an English immersion
ontext, subject content lessons were observed alongside English language les-
ons. Data were collected in class as well as after class. Hence the findings in the

current study extended the findings to the aspects other than linguistic aspec
which consisted of broader range of peer assistance than reported by Ohta. Pee
interlocutors assisted each other cognitively, executively and affectively, an
made activities themselves a motivation for the students' learning.

When this class is compared to other primary classrooms in China, a
of this represents a considerable change in a classroom culture. In China
it is conventionally the teacher who corrects a learner directly or indirectl
using a prompt; some teachers, however, instead of correcting an error ma
simply point out that there is an error and then ask other learners directl
what the error is or to repair it – as a kind of teacher-initiated peer correctio
strategy (Jin and Cortazzi, 1998). This has the advantage that in the whole
class situation, the repair process is not quite so teacher-centred, and the res
of the class can hear the peer correction, but since pair work and group wor
are less common, this peer assistance may not transfer to group situations
The study of this immersion context shows that a teacher can develop
classroom culture in which this peer-initiated assistance is not only possibl
and even normal, but that primary-age students can assist each other in
nuanced and sensitive manner using an unexpected range of strategies t
do so. Here, peers were assisting each other not only cognitively – helpin
each other in the language, in learning subject content, helping each othe
in both the task and in which strategy to use – but also executively in tas
monitoring and behaviour monitoring, and affectively in encouraging, sup
porting and praising. Peer assistance in the activities built up the supportiv
classroom culture, which enhanced the students' learning.

Clearly, this can develop in the primary-level immersion context, and thi
is surely likely to transfer later to secondary levels if teachers are aware o
these possibilities and have developed the pedagogic and classroom manage
ment strategies to facilitate peer assistance. It remains a question of further re
search as to whether it is particularly the immersion context which facilitate
such assistance or whether (and how) peer assistance may be productively
developed in the more usual non-immersion contexts. Since the immersion
context is experimental in China, it may be that program managers, teachers
learners and parents are already prepared for new pedagogies (at least in part)
and that this greatly prepares students for innovation and eases learners into
new peer-assistance practices in the classroom. A further crucial area to re
search is to investigate whether (and exactly how) this peer assistance benefit
the learners' cognitive development in Chinese contexts of second language
learning, as it is widely held to do in neo-Vygotskian theory in the West. Thi
study shows how cultural practices in a Chinese classroom can change: in
this instance using an externally inspired program innovation as a platform
to develop a practice of peer assistance which is perhaps not that unusua
in the West in both immersion and non-immersion contexts, but to date i
rarely encountered in China. The study therefore shows the possibilities of an
intercultural learning at the macro-level of school organization and program
design and at the micro-level of learner-to-learner classroom discourse.

References

hmed, M.K. (1994) Speaking as cognitive regulation: A Vygotskian perspective on dialogic communication. In J.P. Lantolf & G. Appel (Eds), *Vygotskian approaches to second language research*, pp. 157–172. New Jersey Ablex Publishing Corporation.

hristian, D. (2011) Dual language education. In E. Hinkel (Ed.), *Handbook of Research in Second Language Teaching and Learning*, Vol. 2. New York: Routledge, pp. 3–20.

ortazzi, M. (1997) Classroom talk: Communicating within the learning relationship. In N. Kitson & R. Merry (Eds), *Teaching in the primary school, a learning relationship*. London: Routledge, pp. 139–56.

ortazzi, M. (1998) Curricula across cultures: Contexts and connections. In J. Moyles & L. Hargreaves (Eds), *The primary curriculum, learning from international perspectives*, pp. 205–16. London: Routledge.

ortazzi, M. & Jin, L. (1996) Changes in learning English vocabulary in China. In H. Coleman & L. Cameron (Eds), *Change and language*. Clevedon: Multilingual Matters, pp. 153–65.

eng, C. & Carless, D. (2009) The communicativeness of activities in a task-based innovation in Guangdong, China. *The Asian Journal of English Language Teaching*, 19, 113–134.

enzin, N.K. (1997) Triangulation in educational research. In J.P. Keeves (Ed.), *Educational research, methodology and measurement: An international handbook* (2nd edn), pp. 92–102. Oxford: Elsevier Science.

ang, J.M., Wang, J.Y. & Siegel, L. (2001) *Dangdai zhongguo shaoshuminzu shuangyu jiaoxue lilun yu shijian (The Theory and Practice of Bilingual Teaching of Minorities in Contemporary China)*. Xi'an: People's Education Press of Shaanxi Province.

lick, U. (1998) *An introduction to qualitative research*. London: Sage.

enesee, F. (1987) *Learning through two languages: Studies in immersion and bilingual education*. Boston: Heinle & Heinle.

n, L. & Cortazzi, M. (1998) Dimensions of dialogue: Large classes in China. *International Journal of Educational Research*, 29 (8), 739–61.

n, L. & Cortazzi, M. (2002) Cultures of learning: The social construction of educational identities. In D.C.S. Li (Ed.), *Discourses in search of members, in honor of Ron Scollon*. Lanham: University Press of America, pp. 49–78.

n, L. & Cortazzi, M. (2006) Changing practices in Chinese cultures of learning. In T. Coverdale-Jones & P. Rastall (Eds), 'The Chinese Learner', special issue, *Language, Culture and Curriculum*, 19 (1), 5–20.

n, L. & Cortazzi, M. (2011) Re-evaluating traditional approaches to second language teaching and learning. In E. Hinkel (Ed.), *Handbook of research in second language teaching and learning*, Vol. 2. New York: Routledge, pp. 558–75.

ohnson, R.K. (1989) *The second language curriculum*. Cambridge: Cambridge University Press.

ohnson, R.K. & Swain, M. (Eds) (1997) *Immersion education: International perspectives*. Cambridge: Cambridge University Press.

ambert, W. E., & Tucker, G.R. (1972) *The biligual education of children: The St. Lambert experiment*. Rowley, MA: Newbury House.

antolf, J.P. (Ed.) (2000b) *Sociocultural theory and second language learning*. Oxford: Oxford University Press.

antolf, J.P. & Thorne, S.L. (2006) *Sociocultural theory and the genesis of second language development*. Oxford: Oxford University Press.

iang, X.H. (2004) The impact of English immersion on children. *Training and Research: Journal of Hubei University of Education*, 21 (4), 92–94.

incoln, Y.S. & Guba, E.G. (1985) *Naturalistic inquiry*. Beverly Hills, CA: Sage.

Lyster, R. (2011) Content-based second language teaching. In E. Hinkel (Ed Handbook of research in second language teaching and learning, Vol. 2. New Yor Routledge, pp. 611–30.

Newman, D., Griffin, P. & Cole, M. (1989) *The construction zone, working for cogniti change in school.* Cambridge: Cambridge University Press.

Ohta, A.S. (2001) *Second language acquisition processes in the classroom: Learning jap nese.* Mahwah, NJ: Lawrence Erlbaum Associates.

Patton, M.Q. (1980) *Qualitative evaluation methods.* Beverly Hill, CA: Sage.

Pei, M. (1998) The teachers: The key role in English immersion program. *Shaan Normal University Journal* (supplementary issue), 27–31.

Pei, M. (2007) *Scaffolding and participation in classroom interaction: Perspectives fro English immersion teaching in the People's Republic of China.* Unpublished doctor dissertation, The University of Hong Kong, Hong Kong.

Qiang, H.Y. (2000) Jianada di'eryuyan jinrushi jiaoxue chuangju jiqi zai wogu de changshi (Canadian second language immersion and experiment in Chin Research on early cultivation of bilinguals). *Preschool Education Review,* 5, 26–30.

Qiang, H.Y. & Zhao, L. (2000) Jianada di'eryuyan jinrushi jiaoxue chuangju jiqi z woguo de jiejian (Canadian second language immersion and its application i China). *Comparative Education Review,* 4, 38–41.

Qiang, H.Y. & Zhao, L. (Eds) (2001) *Second language immersion.* Xi'an: Xi'an Jiaoton University Press.

Spada, N. & Frohlich, M. (1995) *Communicative Orientation of Language Teachir Observation Scheme* (COLT). Sydney: National Centre for English Language Teachin and Research, Macquarie University .

Swain, M. & Lapkin, S. (1983) *Evaluating bilingual education: A Canadian case stud* Clevedon: Multilingual Matters.

Tharp, R. & Gallimore, R. (1989) *Rousing minds to life.* New York: Cambridge Universit Press.

Van der Veer, R. & Valsiner, J. (1991) *Understanding Vygotsky, a quest for a synthesi* Oxford: Blackwell.

Van der Veer, R. & Valsiner, J. (Eds) (1994) *The Vygotsky reader.* Oxford: Blackwell.

van Lier, L. (1996) *Interaction in the language curriculum: Awareness, autonomy, and at thenticity.* London: Longman.

Vygotsky, L. (1962) *Thought and language.* Cambridge, MA: The MIT Press.

Vygotsky, L. (1978) *Mind in society, the development of higher psychological processe.* Cambridge, MA: Harvard University Press.

Wells, G. (1999) *Dialogic inquiry: Towards a sociocultural practice and theory of educatior* Cambridge: Cambridge University Press.

White, R.V. (1988) *The ELT curriculum: Design, innovation and management.* Oxforc Blackwell.

Zhang, L. & Yan, R. (2007) Impact of different teaching approaches on English worc reading ability for children. *Early Childhood Education (Educational Sciences),* 6, 8–1

Zhang, X.Z. & Pei, M. (2005) Problems in primary school English immersion curriculun and experimental instruction. *Elementary English Teaching Journal,* 5(7), 9–11.

Zhang, Y.F. (2005) *The implementation of the task-based approach in primary school lan guage teaching in mainland China.* Unpublished doctoral dissertation, The Universit of Hong Kong, Hong Kong.

Zhao, L., Pei, M., Liu, H. & Siegel, L. (2006) A new pattern of classroom for Chines children's second language learning. *Journal of Shaanxi Normal University (Philosoph and Social Sciences Edition),* 4 (35), 117–122.

Zhao, L. & Qiang, H.Y. (2002) Ertong zaoqi di'er yuyan jinrushi jiaoxue yu kechen jiangou yanjiu (Research on children's second language immersion and curriculun construction). *Preschool Education Review,* 4, 30–33.

5

Researching Intercultural Communication in a UK Higher Education Context

Joan Turner and Masako K. Hiraga

5.1 Introduction

In this chapter, we undertake four different kinds of analysis towards an understanding of intercultural communication in action. The action is situated in a context where intercultural encounters are common, namely contemporary higher education. Furthermore, the intercultural encounters are discipline specific. They take place in one-to-one tutorials in fine art, in a UK institution. The lecturers are British and the students are Japanese. In the first place, the tutorial interactions are analysed in terms of the tutorial as genre; second, certain recurring exchange types within the tutorial are isolated as examples of what we call *epistemic principles*, namely those underlying principles which motivate teaching and learning in the discipline. Third, and following on from the discourse analytic perspective of the students behaviour, students' own accounts of why they were behaving as they were, and how they understood the tutorial interactions, are explored in a number of retrospective, semi-structured interviews. The stimulus for those interviews were video-recordings of the students tutorials, which had taken place one year earlier, and they were carried out in Japanese. This afforded a fourth kind of analysis, namely the extent to which the students had adapted to or resisted not only the interactional norms of the tutorial, that is behaving like students in a UK context, but also the disciplinary norms which lay behind those interactions. In this final analysis, two students are adopted as case studies, and it is principally, but not exclusively, data from their tutorials and retrospective interviews, which fuel the discussion throughout the chapter. Those two case study examples were specifically chosen for their different degrees of commitment to the expectations of their UK institutional context, and differing levels of engagement with the underlying epistemic principles.

While there is a considerable amount of research into language development in intercultural contexts – for example into pragmatics in language

teaching (Rose & Kasper, 2001; Alcon Soler & Martinez-Flor, 2008), inte
language pragmatics (Kasper, 2001; Kasper & Rose, 2002; Bardovi-Harl
& Hartford, 2005), the embedding of intercultural awareness into Englis
language teaching (Andersen et al., 2006; Corbett, 2003), and the develoj
ment of intercultural competences, especially in foreign language educatio
(Byram, 1997, 2008; Guilherme, 2002) – which has led more recently t
notions of cosmopolitan citizenship (Guilherme, 2007), there is relativel
little research into situated intercultural encounters in education outside c
a language education focus. This chapter provides an example of such re
search. The situated context is one-to-one tutorials in fine art, conducte
in English in a UK institution, and the intercultural nature of the tutoria
is seen as itself a tool for research. Turner (2011) took a reflexive approacl
using the interactions to explore deep-seated cultural assumptions of tutc
and student interaction in a Western context of higher education. Here, th
focus is on the tutorial as a disciplinary activity, realizing disciplinary norm
or epistemic principles, both in terms of the content of what is discussec
and in terms of pragmatic expectations of how the discussion is to be take
up. These pragmatic expectations are implicit, analysed and interprete
through a discourse analytic approach to the interactions and the identif
cation of recurring patterns of exchange, and tutor elicitation moves. Th
extent to which these pragmatic expectations are met, or not, by the inte
cultural interlocutor students (in this case, Japanese students) both help t
get at the underlying epistemic principles of the disciplinary genre and lea
in to research questions as to how the students understand what is going or
In this latter respect, and following on from the discourse analytic perspec
tive of the students' behavior (which identifies points of 'critical pragmati
uptake' which the students tend to miss), students' own accounts of wh
they were behaving as they were, and what they thought was going on, ar
explored in retrospective, semi-structured interviews in Japanese.

6.2   The data and their contexts

In the context of a one-year joint fine art and English for Academi
Purposes (EAP) programme, preparatory to either a bachelor or master'
degree in fine art, one of us observed numerous one-to-one fine art tutori
als over three years, and her observations were fed back into the teachin,
process of EAP. This included work on the kinds of elicitations made b
tutors, the kinds of things students might say in response, as well as vo
cabulary work that would help students describe and evaluate their ow
work. However, this is not the focus of this chapter. For the sake of botl
research and teaching purposes, 21 tutorial sessions were videotaped witl
20 Japanese and one British student and three British tutors. The Britisl
student, who was in his second year of study, agreed to have his routine tu
torial with one of the same tutors videotaped. This was to see if the overal

rythm of the tutorial was similar, if conducted native speaker to native speaker, and also to see what kinds of things the student said in response to similar tutor elicitations. This video was also later used for EAP teaching purposes. A single tutorial is extremely limited as a basis for comparison between British and Japanese students, so it will not be used here in that respect but, nonetheless, it did point up interactional differences and, what is more, was a useful triangulation point for the discourse analysis of this tutorial genre. It confirmed the expectation of particular pragmatic uptakes (i.e., how students were intended to understand – or actually understood – tutors' comments), which a discourse analysis of the tutors' comments and elicitations had identified, and which were often problematic in the intercultural tutorials.

Retrospective interviews in Japanese were conducted with eight students one year after one of their tutorials had been videotaped. The elapse of one year is unusual in the use of stimulated recall methodology (Faerch and Kasper, 1987; Gass and Mackey, 2000). However, its common use as soon as possible after an event – as in, for example, the work of Nanda Poulisse et al. (1987); Andrew Cohen and Elite Olshtain (1994); Zoltan Dörnyei and Judit Kormos (1998); and Doris Dippold (2007) – is usually to identify cognitive processing strategies that may otherwise have been lost to memory. The focus here was not at that micro-level, but rather at a more macro-level of getting a sense of how students understood the underlying rationale and epistemic principles of their tutorial context. In the event, the time elapse was favourable: it was found that the students exhibited a level of met-pragmatic awareness regarding the pedagogical norms of tutor–student interaction that was not the case at the time of the original tutorials. For example, in response to a question in the retrospective interview as to why the student had not asked for clarification about what the tutor meant, our case study student, no. 2 answered as follows:

Excerpt 1: Case study student 2's retrospective interview

I think probably there are differences between the Japanese educational style and that of here. In the Japanese style, we just listen to what the teacher says. Even if the teacher tells us something wrong, we do not have a chance to raise an objection. I think probably I still had that [style] at that time [of the videotaped tutorial]. I might still have it even now. Students here have their own established selves, in regard to what the teacher says. Then, if their teacher says something wrong, the students argue by saying 'your opinion is wrong.' Probably, this is the difference in education. (Translated from the Japanese original)

Regarding the focus in the retrospective interviews, the authors had both viewed the videotapes and discussed particular points of what we are calling

here 'critical pragmatic uptake'. These included: reactions or responses t
tutors' comments or questions about the amount of work done since
previous tutorial; responses relating to the process of development of th
work, including possibly admitting that the work was not progressing, an
being prepared to discuss reasons why; or possibly exploring alternativ
approaches or ways forward. As well as general questions on how well th
students were adapting to their intercultural contexts of the British edu
cation system, the Japanese researcher conducting the retrospective inte
views stopped the tape at these pre-identified points of critical pragmati
uptake and asked the students directly: what they thought the tutor wa
asking them; why they responded as they did; and how they felt they shoul
have responded. The reason for holding the interviews in the students' firs
language was to make them feel they could express themselves more freel
with access to a wider range of lexis and formulation than they would hav
if they were asked the same things in English. This may seem an obviou
choice, but it is recognized that language choice in bilingual research inte
views may have consequences of its own (Cortazzi et al., 2011).

6.3   The fine art tutorial as genre

Joan Turner (2011) analysed the fine art and other creative practice tutoria
as a genre with a three-phase structure, motivated by and turning on how
the student's work as artist/musician/film maker/dramatist is developing
Here, the formulation, 'the students' work', is used as an abbreviation for th
fuller term 'work as an artist'; and it should be understood to emphasize th
importance of the underlying disciplinary principles, both in motivatin
the tutor's elicitations (the topics chosen for discussion) and the kinds c
contribution students were expected to make. In general, the student wa
required to take up a critically reflective stance in relation to her or his ow
work. Such a stance was in effect much more important than the work itsel
which in contemporary art education in higher education can take a wid
variety of different forms.

On one level, the three-phase structure of the tutorial is simply procedura
There is a beginning, a middle and an end. This rather bland description ma
be pedagogically modulated in terms of a 'warm up' phase, a 'nitty gritty
(or detailed and practical) discussion of the work phase, and a wind-dow
'recapitulation' or 'where do we go from here' phase. On another, abstrac
conceptual level, and related to the discipline, the tripartite phasing is dia
lectical. This involves looking at the current state of the work; evaluating it
potential or its deficits; and thinking about how it might be taken forward
The workings of this dialectical epistemic principle in the fine art tutoria
will be discussed in relation to middle phase exchanges exemplified below
and in relation to how two students showed their varied commitments to
wards it.

As in the classroom discourse analysed and discussed by, for example, John Sinclair and Malcolm Coulthard (1975), Hugh Mehan (1979), Sinclair and David Brazil (1982) and Michael McCarthy (1991), the pedagogical transactional phases here are controlled and marked by the tutor, who embodies both the institutional and disciplinary authority vested in and motivating the transactions. The transitional markers between transactional phases (or what Sinclair and Coulthard called 'framing moves') are routinely simple, marked by an emphasis on words such as 'now' or 'so' and occasionally more lexically explicit phraseology, such as 'let's move on now to...'. For example, in the excerpt from case study student 1, below, the tutor marks the transition from an initial 'warm- up' exchange. In this beginning phase of the tutorial, the tutor asks the student whether he went back to Japan over the summer, and there is some discussion about that, such as how long he was there, where he was, what he did and so on. Then the transactional shift to the main purpose of the tutorial, namely to discuss the art student's studio practice, begins as follows:

Excerpt 2:

> British Tutor: Yeah, yea...NOW, have you...let's just go straight to the work, shall we?...Have you been doing any work over the, over the summer? Have you been thinking about studio work?

The following excerpt shows the transactional shift from the main discussion phase to the wind-down phase. This occurs in a tutorial with a different student from those in our case studies.

Excerpt 3:

> British Tutor: Let me just recap. Perhaps the principle change in your thinking has been a shift from what you call hard shapes to soft shapes.
> Japanese Student 3: Yes. First I was drawing with a ruler but now I am drawing without anything.

5.4 The epistemic principle 1: Evidence of work = evidence of thought + disciplinary engagement

While evidence of thought and engagement with the discipline may be seen as a generic desirable of any study context, in the context of fine art tutorials this was particularly tied up with the amount of work available to discuss. In the tutorials observed, there was no set length of time. The unit of teaching time as it were, was the day, and the tutor would speak to individual students in their institutionally allotted studio space in the course of that day. What

determined the length of the tutorial was what was afforded by the studen
and/or her/his work. If there was not much work there to speak about, or
what was there was limited in scope for discussion, the tutorials were rel.
tively short, but others could go on for an hour or more. The length of tim
for the tutorial, then, in itself indicated an implicit evaluation of the student
work. The longer the tutorial, the more it suggested that the work was obv
ously worth talking about, and that it was important to probe the student
approach to and judgments about it. Such evaluations were never explicitl
made, however. They were perhaps indicated obliquely in initial-phase com
pliments, such as 'You've done a lot of work!' (said in an approving intonation
In one retrospective interview on the tutorial in which this tutor complimer
was uttered, and where the student's response at the time was simply 'Yes', th
student (JS 3) revealed that he had not understood the illocutionary force o
compliment and, hence, missed this positive evaluation of the work.

The excerpt below, showing the continuation of Excerpt 2, illustrates th
importance of the epistemic principle of how much work was done.

Excerpt 4: Case study student 1's tutorial

1. B T: Yeah, yea...
2. NOW, have you...
3. Let's just go straight to the work, shall we?...
4. Have you been doing any work over the, over summer?
5. Thinking about studio work?
6. JS 1: Not particularly,
7. But, mm,
8. my perma– job, my job is like making something.
9. BT:...mm...
10. JS 1: Like a sculpture
11. BT:...mm...
12. JS 1: for advertisement.
13. BT:...mm, mm...
14. JS 1: So...
15. BT:...mm...
16. JS 1:...I did do
17. BT:...mm...
18. JS 1: that for summer vacation.
19. BT: So it is related in a way.
20. JS 1: I think so.
21. BT: But, have you been doing any drawings?
22. JS 1: Um, I did in that, that studio
23. BT:...mm...
24. JS 1: (pointing) on July.

25. BT:...mm. Not since then?
26. JS 1: No.

1 this extract, the tutor waits rather patiently while the student haltingly counts what he has done over the summer. While the tutor concedes 1at the student's summer job bears some resemblance to work as a sculptor, the pedagogical crunch point comes in line 21. The student then refers 1ck to work done before the summer vacation, and the tutor's next utter-1ce 'Not since then', works as a veiled rebuke and was identified by the searchers as a 'point of critical pragmatic uptake' related to the epistemic 1inciple. In other words, the expectation was that the student should ave been doing some work for his art, regardless of whether it was vac-tion time or not. The retrospective interview with the student revealed owever, that the student had not realized the significance of the tutor's tterance.

xcerpt 5: Case study student 1's retrospective interview

Japanese Interviewer (I): In the comment, do you think that he was just trying to describe the fact, or do you think he was implying that you should have continued working on it even when you were back to Japan, maybe at least with your sketchbook?
Student (S): In this context, I do not think he was trying to criticise me.
I: So he just wanted to know what his student did during summer objectively.
S: I think so.

(Translated from the Japanese original)
here is triangulated evidence for the discourse–analytic interpretation that 1e amount of work done is an epistemic marker of engagement with, and ommitment to, the discipline. This is given in an explicit comment by 1is same tutor in the course of a tutorial with another student (JS 4). It is similar post-vacation tutorial, in which the student has neither anything) show nor does she appear to have any ideas that she is excited about ex-loring. In this case, the tutor states, albeit in a light-hearted manner:

xcerpt 6:

BT: You must understand that being an art student isn't like being a machine I switch on and off. Becoming a student of art, switch on [STUDENT'S NAME] who now becomes an art student for three hours. It's not like that. You should be thinking about it first thing in the morning and the last thing at night, and in your dreams. All the time.

6.5 Epistemic principle 2: The evaluative process dynamic

The epistemic principle regarding the amount of work done is close[connected with a second principle, which we call 'the evaluative proce[dynamic', whereby the amount of work done is an indicator of ongoing d[velopment in the work. Interestingly, this underlying evaluative dynam[in relation to work and development as an ongoing or continuous proce[was seldom understood by the students in the intercultural tutorials. Th[chimes with a tension between process and product, which recurs partic[larly in creative disciplines in intercultural education contexts. For exampl[Silvia Sovic (2008) drew attention to the product–process distinction whe[it arose as a point of confusion for international students studying the cr[ative arts at the University of the Arts London. She quotes the followin[Taiwanese student, who states the issue succinctly:

> It is slightly different from what I expected. ... Unlike Taiwan, here in th[
> UK I have learned what they are really concerned about is more student
> learning process, and less learning outcomes. My tutors here seem to m[
> to be very concerned about where my ideas come from, how I develop an[
> what research I initiate with my ideas. It is essential that the formatio[
> of ideas, conducting research and completion of my final piece of wor[
> are integrated throughout the whole process, even if the work itself is n[
> very attractive. I am still trying to accommodate this major difference i[
> relation to the teaching and learning approach here. (Sovic, 2008: 12)

Sovic (2008:12) further makes the point that students 'can fail if they do n[understand that tutors expect to see evidence of the design process whe[assessing the work', and mentions the case of a student who had failed h[first year through not realizing this.

The importance of process in the work, the need for ongoing develop[ment, is apparent in the next point of pedagogic transaction in case stud[student 1's tutorial. Still in the important middle phase of the tutorial, bu[signalling also that the wind-down phase is approaching, the tutor move[into the following exchange, in which he encourages the student to loo[forward to what happens next in his work.

Excerpt 7: Case study student 1's tutorial

27. BT: Right. Okay. Do you HAVE ideas about things you WANT t[
    do?
28. JS 1: Next– This term?
29. BT: Yeah.
30. JS 1: Umm. I'd like to do ... like an installation,
31. BT: (hum hum)

32. JS 1: or, of course painting...umm...(8-second long pause) I don't know.

here then ensues a long exchange in which the tutor indicates that he thinks he student is undergoing a period of transition in his work, and there is some iscussion as to what form this will take, whether the student will continue ith painting, or whether he wants to try out working with other materials. he student seems to concur in this assessment, indicating that he is inter-ted in materials but also wants to paint. This leads into the tutor giving a irect illustration of what Turner (2011) called 'dialectical development', and hich we highlight here as another epistemic principle of the discipline.

.6   Epistemic principle 3: Dialectical development

round 33 lines later, with the words 'right' and 'ok', the tutor marks a ansactional shift to the wind-down phase of the tutorial. In this case, the ind-down phase fulfils three different functions. It provides an injunc-on to develop future work; a summary of the current state of the student's ork; and a commentary on the process of change.

xcerpt 8: Case study student 1's tutorial

62. BT: Right. Okay. Maybe now we need to redress the balance by making you do more
63. drawings.
64. JS 1: Yeah, I think so.
65. BT: Mm, but what you're saying, it sounds to me, as though you are in a period of
66. transition.
67. JS 1: What?
68. BT: Change. Period of change. Change from one state to another.
69. JS 1: Yeah.
70. BT: So perhaps previously your work was pretty much contained in painting in a certain
71. way. You now want to move out from painting and experience other materials.
72. JS 1:...mm...

he exchange on the perceived state of transition in the student's work con-nues, as the student self-evidently reveals his state of indecision.

xcerpt 9: Case study student 1's tutorial

83. JS 1: Now I can't say....I don't know. Maybe yes maybe no.
84. BT:...mm. mm. mm.

85. JS 1: Now I am interested in material more than painting.
86. BT: ...mm.
87. JS 1: But I'd like to paint.
88. BT: Mm, mm.

The student then makes a direct request, or plea to the tutor:

91. JS 1: How can I manage?

It is at this point that the tutor expounds the dialectical dynamic:

92. BT: Well, I think...the...surely what you have done now, wha
    you've just said, illustrates one of the necessary agonies of attemp
    ing to be an artist.
93. JS 1: That is necessary.
94. BT: Oh yeah. I think there is a necessary agony.
95. JS1: Yeah.
96. BT: That's trying to, (putting his notebook on the desk) trying t
    reconcile the
97. irreconcilable. Do you understand? Do you understand the wor
    'reconcile'?
98. JS 1: No, I don't.
99. BT: We are trying to bring together two things that seem very fa
    apart.
100. J S 1: Ah, yes.
101. BT: Or putting it another way, I like this, but I also like that. Hov
    can I like them both?

The tutor then goes on to explain that different things can be reconcilec
and that what the student has to do now is to allow different facets of hi
work to show themselves, which comes down to trying everything out. Thi
illustration once more confirms the underlying epistemic principles in th
discipline of producing a lot of work in order to test ideas and let the wor
develop, whatever kind it may turn out to be.

Another instance of the dialectical dynamic occurs with our case stud
student 2, towards the end of a much shorter tutorial (about 26 minutes
This time the focus is on the role of uncertainty as also a constructive moto
of development. This student's command of English is a lot weaker, and he
ideas for taking her work forward are also not very strong.

Excerpt 10: Case study student 2's tutorial

BT: You are beginning to touch on areas of uncertainty. Do yo
understand?
JS 2:...
BT: Uncertainty?
JS 2: No.
BT: Not knowing?

JS 2: What?

BT: There is a doubt? Not knowing? Not having clear thoughts on? Do you understand?

little later, the tutor tries to explain why he is asking her to express her oubts. He states:

xcerpt 11: Case study student 2's tutorial

BT: My function as a teacher is to help to clarify, to make clear doubts and uncertainties.

He then goes on to mark the end of the tutorial by asking the student:

BT: Is there anything else you need to say to me?

JS 2: ... Yes ...

BT: Is there anything else?

JS 2: ...

BT: No? Okay. I don't think there is anything we need to say now. (ends tutorial).

his exchange indicates that the student is in effect centre stage in the tu-
orial. Since the student has not participated or proffered ideas or statements
f doubts, and so forth, there is nothing to discuss.

Some of the reasons for this rather unsatisfactory tutorial may be seen
) lie in the differing expectations of tutor–student interaction, as well as
different understanding of the epistemic principles at stake. In her retro-
pective interview, the student is actually quite clear about these differ-
nces, and while having a better understanding now of what was required,
1e maintains some resistance to doing things in the way that is set up in
1e British educational context:

xcerpt 12: Case study student 2's retrospective interview

I: Do you think it is a bad thing that you cannot express your feelings well, or that you do not have any clear ideas? As you just described, you have to explain to your adviser about your work but you have uncertainty about your work. Do you think it is a bad thing to have such a situation? Did you want to explain more, or was it fine with you just like that?

JS 2: If you follow this school's policy, you have to explain it. But for me, the meaning or process of my work is not very important. If the completed work looks beautiful, it is fine with me. But teachers here and the policy of this school focus on the process of making the work. Teachers are trying to find some interests in me or my work while talk-ing about the process.

(Translated from the Japanese original)

6.7   Framing the intercultural dynamic

This issue of differing pedagogical cultures is much reviewed in the literatu
(Cortazzi, 1990; Chan and Rao, 2009; Ding, 2008; Jin and Cortazzi, 199
2006, 2011; Liu, 2007; Tsui, 1996), as are specific pragmatic aspects of the
such as silence (Jones, 1999; Cheng, 2000; Lee, 2009; Liu and Littlewoo
1997; Liu, 2002; Nakane, 2006; Tatar, 2005; Xie, 2010; Zhang and Hea
2010), or the particularly thorny issue of being critical and giving opinior
(Atkinson, 1997; Koh, 2002; Turner, 2011; Murata, 2011; among many oth
ers). While the above student exhibits the reality of those issues in practic
and expresses them in terms of national cultural differences, we prefer no
to leave the discussion there. As Srikant Sarangi (2011) has warned, there
a danger in what he calls 'analytic stereotyping' by culture, and by dint o
being non-native speakers, in the analysis of intercultural encounters. Tha
chapter is in a compilation, but his original papers were published in the earl
1990s. In a similar vein, but in a different research context, Holliday's (200
23) 'non-essentialist view' aims 'to avoid the political chauvinism of nativ
speakerism by questioning the positioning of the "non-native speaker" Oth
within imagined cultural blocks'. In contemporary contexts of intercultura
communication, such as that of international students studying in a Wester
university (as in the case of this chapter), it seems fair to say that this messag
has been well received. Sensitivity to the issues is widespread, such that blur
analyses which position the student at the root of any miscommunicatio
would be rare. It would be difficult, currently, to find an academic researche
who was not aware of the danger of stereotyping, and there is arguably
greater research literature available, especially over the last decade or so, whic
argues against an 'essentialist' or 'othering' position than a literature whic
assumes and maintains stereotypes. The anti-essentialist stance has becom
the dominant discourse. This reflects also an important epistemological an
methodological shift from a position of 'expert' researcher who conceptua
izes and categorizes the differences observed (Hofstede's 1980, 1991, highl
influential work could serve as an example here) to a more ethnographic pe
spective, whereby participants' voices are heard and their accounts of wh
they are doing/saying/ behaving in the way that they are, become the focus o
attention. Even when (or despite) the fact that the voices in our retrospectiv
interview data sometimes offer 'essentialist' perspectives, this is not the whol
story. Our first student provides an interesting example of the transformativ
dimension of international education.

6.8   Becoming a transnational student (or not)

Taking a closer discourse–analytic perspective on not only what, but how
our first case study student says what he says reveals an interesting insigh
into the live 'intercultural' student. By this we mean that this student no

nly consciously states that he is somewhere in between the two educa-
onal cultures that he has experienced, but he shows in the way he speaks,
is use of code-switching, hesitations, pauses, overlapping, and so forth,
hat he is no longer acting as if within a Japanese context. First of all, hav-
ng been asked whether he feels more Japanese or more British, student 1
ates:

xcerpt 13: Case study student 1's retrospective interview

Well, now, I am not sure... well, I think, I am neither of the two. Not even
between them. Completely different....
(Translated from the Japanese original)

n a particularly telling example, however, his discourse betrays his social-
zation as a UK fine art student. Even though he knows he is speaking to
Japanese university professor in Japanese in his retrospective interview,
e uses the direct formulation *iya*, which translates as 'no' in Japanese, to
orrect an assumption that the professor has made. This would be highly
nlikely in a Japanese context, or would possibly be treated as showing a
ack of due deference. What is more likely is that a student would hesitate,
ay something like *eeto* ('well'), use ambiguous or unclear wordings, or leave
long pause so that the professor eventually infers that the student wanted
o say something different or opposite but had not actually uttered it. The
anscript, shown in both Japanese and English, to make the point clear, is
s follows:

xcerpt 14: Case study student 1's retrospective interview

I: *De, sakuhin wo tsukuru toki wa, dou yatte setsumei shiyou to omotte,
tsukuru?*
(When you work on your piece, do you think about how you would
explain it?)
S: ***Iya***, *saisho ni mou kanngae ga atte*
(**No**, the idea is there when I start.)
I: *Atte, saisho ni kanngae ga atte, sore wo dou arawasouka to omotte, tsukurun
desu ne?*
(So you have some idea and then you work on your piece thinking how
you can express the idea.)
S: *Soo. Kagae ga atte, **materiaru** wa kono kanngae wo arawasu niwa douiu,
tatoeba, **peintingu** ga ii no ka, **sukarupuchaa** ga ii no ka, soretomo **insu-
tareishion** ga ii noka, hanga ga ii noka, bunshou ga ii noka, toka kangaete,
sorekara, dewa, douiu **materiaru** ga ii noka, toka. ...*
(That's right. First I have some idea and I think about what is the
best **material** I use for expressing the idea. I think about whether

I should express it with **painting**, **sculpture**, **installation**, bloc print, or writing. And then, I think about which **material** I shoul use....)

In this last turn, the student uses English loan words in Japanese (boldface above) to talk about his work. These include: 'material', 'painting', 'sculp ture', and 'installation'. This shows his socialization into the disciplinar discourse. Furthermore, what he says at a conceptual level reveals that h is fully engaged with the epistemic principles of the discipline, explicatin the rationale for the tutorial, the importance of trying out different thing and determining the best way forward. He further shows his understandin of the dialectical dynamic in the following statement, comparing how h was at the time of the videotaped tutorial and how he understands what going on now:

Excerpt 15: Case study student 1's retrospective interview

At this time (of recording), I did not realize my problems.... I did no know what was my subject or my theme. But I was in the place that had to explain the concept of my work, which made me think about m problems, or what I needed to do. So my idea became clearer and cleare and at the same time, my work was changing. At this time, I was paint ing. But now I do not do paintings and I am working on installation. M work itself has changed.

(Translated from the Japanese origina

While he is clearly an extremely competent student in his discipline, on could say in this regard that he was a 'transnational' student (cf. Risage 2007); this student also retained an identification with Japanese inter actional norms, especially as regards the use of silence. When asked how h feels about the pauses and silences he witnesses when observing his earlie tutorial, he states as follows:

Excerpt 16: Case study student 1's retrospective interview

I often have a long pause even when I am talking Japanese. And I thin English people always try to explain in detail about what they are talk ing about. Don't you think so? Japanese usually become silent when, fo example, they are nervous. But I think when English people get nervous they become more talkative than usual.

(Translated from the Japanese origina

On this topic of verbalization, the second case study student also make a comparison with the Japanese pedagogic context in which she expect listen to what the teacher says, rather than state her own point of view understanding. She further remarks on the communicative style of the torials, which she finds unhelpful:

xcerpt 17: Case study student 2's retrospective interview

I can manage daily conversations, you know what…in an all-right way. But when I am asked something about my work that I am not sure of, I cannot answer very well. This happens rather often. Teachers here make an effort to keep the conversation going, when students become quiet. They talk about many things, from many perspectives, which drive my idea even messier. Then, I tend to lose confidence about my own work. It happens sometimes.

(Translation from the Japanese original)

1at this student's resistance also applied to the underlying epistemic prin-ples of the discipline was apparent in Excerpt 12, quoted above. She also veals in the following excerpt from her retrospective interview that her 1derstanding is much more recent. She talks about an insight she gained esterday' in a seminar class, which implies that, at the time of her video-ped tutorial, she did not understand its underlying rationale. She goes on:

xcerpt 18: Case study student 2's retrospective interview

[A]nd in the class, I realized, while listening to a Japanese student ex-plain his work, that there is a difference between Western people's way of thinking and that of Japanese. People here try to be theoretical. This, this, and this, so the consequence is this. Though there may be that kind of thing in Japan, I wonder if we usually focus more on the final prod-ucts, or the feel of them, I'm not sure. But, as for myself, I have that way [, focusing on the final product]. …

his student is clearly aware of the epistemic differences in the product–rocess tension, and expresses it very well in terms of differing educational 1ltures. However, she resists moving from her 'Japanese' position on this 1d, by doing so, in a way also reveals herself as a 'critical' player in the edu-1tionally preferred educational mould of the British context.

.9 Conclusion

/hat we have seen here are two very different approaches to the intercul-1ral pragmatic context in which these students find themselves. In this con-xt, the role of verbalization is crucial, but there are varying ways in which 1ese linguistic demands may be taken up. The first student maintains to

some extent the Japanese disposition to the value of silence, while still man
aging to articulate his position as a student and an artist. The other studer
recognizes these demands, but does not adjust to accommodate them an
furthermore, to some extent rejects the underlying rationale for them.

In differing ways, both of these students show that it is not necessar
to fully adapt to the host institutional norms, and that it is possible t
work around them. This shows that intercultural communication in a pa
ticular context is not necessarily an either/or in which either the norm
of one or other background context win out, as it were, or in which th
norms of the 'host' institution have to be fully adapted to in order to b
successful. The important parameter is less one of cultural adaptation, pe
se, and more a question of subtle permutation along different clines in
wider patchwork of intercultural dynamics. It is to be hoped that the tw
lines of permutation that have been exemplified here – those of epistem:
understanding and commitment, and metapragmatic awareness regardin
the norms of tutor–student interaction – may be relevant in researchin
any higher education context within the contemporary global dynamics c
internationalization.

Acknowledgement

This research has been supported in part by Grant-in-Aid for Scientif:
Research C-17520280 (2005–08) from the Japan Society for the Promotio
of Sciences (JSPS), for which we would like to express our gratitude.

References

Alcon Soler, E. & Martinez-Flor, A. (Eds) (2008) *Investigating pragmatics in foreign lan
guage learning, teaching and testing*. Bristol, Buffalo, Toronto: Multilingual Matters
Andersen, H.L., Lund, K. & Risager, K. (Eds) (2006) *Culture in language learnin:
Aarhus University Press.
Atkinson, D. (1997). A critical approach to critical thinking in TESOL. *TESO
Quarterly*, 31 (1), 71–94.
Bardovi-Harlig, K. & Hartford, B.S. (Eds) (2005) *Interlanguage pragmatics: Exploring in
stitutional talk*. Mahwah, NJ: Lawrence Erlbaum Associates.
Byram, M. (1997) *Teaching and assessing intercultural communicative competenc
Clevedon: Multilingual Matters Ltd.
Byram, M. (2008) *From foreign language education to education for intercultural citizer
ship*. Clevedon: Multilingual Matters.
Chan, C.K.K. & Rao, N. (Eds) (2009) *Revisiting the Chinese learner, changing context
changing education*. Comparative Education Research Centre, The University c
Hong Kong. Hong Kong: Springer.
Cheng, X. (2000) Asian students' reticence revisited. *System*, 28, 435–46.
Cohen, A.D. & Olshtain, E. (1994). Researching the production of speech acts. I
E. Tarone, S.M. Gass & A.D. Cohen (Eds), *Research Methodology in Second Languag
Acquisition*. Hillsdale, NJ: Lawrence Erlbaum.

orbett, J. (2003) *An intercultural approach to English language teaching*. Clevedon: Multilingual Matters.

ortazzi, M. (1990) Cultural and educational expectations in the language classroom. In B. Harrison (Ed.), *Culture and the language classroom ELT documents*, No. 132, 54–65.

ortazzi, M., Pilcher, N. & Jin, L. (2011) Language choices and 'blind shadows': Investigating interviewing with Chinese participants. *Qualitative Research*, 11 (5), 505–35.

ing, H. (2008) Living through ambiguity. PhD Thesis, Goldsmiths, University of London.

ippold, D. (2007). Faces, roles and identities in argumentative discourse: The development of facework strategies by L2 learners of German. PhD Thesis, University of Southampton. http://iloapp.myblackboard.co.uk/blog/mylesson?ShowFile&doc=1 183281230.pdf (accessed 08 June 2011).

örnyei, Z. & Kormos, J. (1998). Problem-solving mechanisms in L2 communication: A psycholinguistic perspective. *Studies in Second Language Acquisition*, 20 (3), 349–85.

aerch, C. & Kasper, G. (Eds) (1987) *Introspection in second language research*. Clevedon: Multilingual Matters.

ass, S. & Mackey, A. (2000) *Stimulated recall methodology in second language research*. Mahwah: Lawrence Erlbaum.

uilherme, M. (2002) *Critical citizens for an intercultural world: Foreign language education as cultural politics*. Clevedon: Multilingual Matters.

uilherme, M. (2007) English as a global language and education for cosmopolitan citizenship. *Language and Intercultural Communication*, 7, 72–90.

ofstede, G. (1980) *Culture's consequences*. Newbury Park, CA: Sage.

ofstede, G. (1991) *Cultures and organisations: Software of the mind*. Maidenhead: McGraw Hill.

olliday, A.R. (2005) *The struggle to teach English as an international language*. Oxford: Oxford University Press.

n, L. & Cortazzi, M. (1993) Cultural orientation and academic language use. In D. Graddol, L. Thompson & M. Byram (Eds), *Language and culture*. Cleveland: BAAL and Multilingual Matters, pp. 84–97.

n, L. & Cortazzi, M. (2006) Changing practices in Chinese cultures of learning. *Language, Culture, and Curriculum*. 19 (1), 5–20.

n, L. & Cortazzi, M. (Eds) (2011) *Researching Chinese learners*. Houndmills: Palgrave Macmillan.

ones, J.F. (1999) From silence to talk: Cross-cultural ideas on students' participation in academic group discussion. *English for Specific Purposes*, 18 (3), 243–59.

asper, G. (2001) Four perspectives on L2 pragmatic development. *Applied Linguistics*, 22 (4), 502–30.

asper, G. & Rose, K.R. (2002) *Pragmatic development in a second language*. Malden, MA: Blackwell.

oh, A. (2002) Towards a critical pedagogy: Creating 'thinking skills' in Singapore. *Journal of Curriculum Studies*, 34 (3), 255–64.

ee, G. (2009) Speaking up: Six Korean students' oral participation in class discussions in US graduate seminars. *English for Specific Purposes*, 28, 142–56.

iu, J. (2002) Negotiating silence in American classrooms: Three Chinese cases. *Language and Intercultural Communication*, 2(1), 37–54.

iu, J. (Ed.) (2007) *English language teaching in China: New approaches, perspectives and standards*. London & New York: Continuum.

Liu, N. & Littlewood, W. (1997) Why do many students appear reluctant to partic
pate in classroom learning discourse. *System*, 25 (3), 371–84.

McCarthy, M. (1991) *Discourse analysis for language teachers*. Cambridge: Cambrid;
University Press.

Mehan, H. (1979) *Learning lessons*. Cambridge, MA: Harvard University Press.

Murata, K. (2011) Voices from the unvoiced: A comparative study of hidden valu
and attitudes in opinion giving. *Language and Intercultural Communication*, 11 (:
6–25.

Nakane, I. (2006) Silence and politeness in intercultural communication in unive
sity seminars. *Journal of Pragmatics*, 38, 1811–35.

Poulisse, N., Bongaerts, T. & Kellerman, E. (1987) The use of retrospective verb
reports in the analysis of compensatory strategies. In K. Faerch & G. Kasper (Ed:
Introspection in second language research. Clevedon: Multilingual Matters, p
213–29.

Risager, K. (2007) *Language and culture pedagogy: From a national to a transnation
paradigm*. Clevedon: Multilingual Matters.

Rose, K. & Kasper, G. (Eds) (2001) *Pragmatics in language teaching*. Cambridg
Cambridge University Press.

Sarangi, S. (2011) Intercultural or not? Beyond celebration of cultural differences i
miscommunication analysis. In Z. Hua (Ed.), *The language and intercultural comm
nication reader*. London and New York: Routledge.

Sinclair, J. McH. & Brazil, D.C. (1982) *Teacher talk*. Oxford: Oxford University Press

Sinclair, J. McH. & Coulthard, R.M. (1975) *Towards an analysis of discourse*. Oxfor
Oxford University Press.

Sovic, S. (2008) Lost in transition? The international students' experience projec
from http://www.arts.ac.uk/clipcetl-internationalstudents.htm

Tatar, S. (2005) Why keep silent? The classroom participation experiences of no
native English-speaking students. *Language and Intercultural Communication*, 5(3
4), 284–93.

Tsui, A. (1996) Reticence and anxiety in second language learning. In K. Bailey & I
Nunan (Eds), *Voices from the language classroom*. Cambridge: Cambridge Universi
Press, pp. 145–67.

Turner, J. (2011) *Language in the academy: Cultural reflexivity and intercultural dynamic
Clevedon: Multilingual Matters.

Xie, X. (2010) Why are students quiet? Looking at the Chinese context and beyon
ELT Journal, 64 (1), 10–20.

Zhang, X. & Head, K. (2010). Dealing with learner reticence in the speaking clas
ELT Journal, 64 (1), 1–9.

7

'Discuss, Analyse, Define...' Non-traditional Students Come to Terms with Cultures of Learning in the UK

Kendall Richards and Nick Pilcher

7.1   Introduction

In contrast to students in many countries, British university students are often older than the common 18–22 age range; some are 'non-traditional' students who may have had experience of work in industrial or professional contexts before they study. These students are unlikely to fit the 'traditional' mould (see Figure 7.1 below), and much has been done to support their transition to academic study. However, assumptions about the experiences and knowledge that students bring with them to university are still made. This chapter shows how such assumptions can be made with regard to assessment terms such as 'Discuss', 'Analyse' and 'Define'. Such terms are frequently key elements in the instructions for assignments or in the wording of exam questions. Arguably, these and similar terms are part of a university culture of learning, and staff may assume that students know what they mean and can, therefore, formulate their writing to meet expected patterns of discourse. In this chapter we show how diverse assumptions are made in one university. Variant assumptions about the meanings of such key terms could also be made elsewhere, with these or other terms.

This chapter is based on a study of UK university lecturers and non-traditional students known as 'direct entry' students (or 'direct entrants'). We first look at how 'non-traditional student' is defined and briefly review relevant literature which researches the challenges faced by direct entrants. We then describe an investigation with a series of focus groups to investigate perceptions and interpretations of key assessment terms. The focus groups were staged so that, first, students and lecturers discussed the terms separately before doing so together. This was part of a wider project that also looked at the perceptions of direct entrants from China (and of UK-based Chinese lecturers) and we occasionally draw on the results from this wider project. Following the section on the methods and approach, we present key

results from the study. Through these results we show that non-tradition.
students could have cultures of learning very different to those which a
assumed by their teachers. We discuss the implications of these results an
conclude that what is needed is more classroom dialogue that focuses on th
meanings of such terms.

Direct entrants are students who enter the later years of a degree pro
gramme without having completed earlier ones; possibly, they articula
into the second, third or fourth university year from a tertiary college or g
directly into a later year because their prior learning is recognized. Studen
could also be transferred from universities in other countries: many U
universities now have joint international degree programmes in whic
the first two or three years of study are, for example, in a university i
China or India, while the remaining year or two is completed in Britain fc
a British degree or sometimes a joint UK qualification with one in the or
ginal country. However, there are other types of 'non-traditional' studen
in a UK perspective: a 'mature' student entering university, aged over 2.
or a student from a lower socioeconomic background or a first-generatio
undergraduate, that is, the first in their family to study in university. I
a US perspective, the term 'non-traditional' has been further subclassifie
into 'highly' non-traditional, 'moderately' non-traditional and 'minimall
non-traditional (National Centre for Education Statistics, 2002). These latt
notions draw attention to the absence of university education in the st
dents' immediate families, revealing an assumption that family experienc
can ease students who do have such a family background into a universit
culture of learning.

We draw on the metaphor of different journeys to illustrate the route
students may take before university. For the traditional students (route 1) w
see them as taking a bus straight to university from school which stops ;
year 1. For the non-traditional students (route 2) their journey takes them t
other places (work, tertiary college) before it arrives at university and stor
either at year one, two, three or four. It is also possible for these student
to be the first in their family ('first generation') to go to university. For th
international student (route 3), students arrive by plane rather than bus, an
are flown in to an unfamiliar environment to start in either year one, two
three or four.

The numbers of non-traditional students have increased in many coun
tries, including the United States, Japan, Sweden, New Zealand (Scheutz
and Slowey, 2002) and the United Kingdom (McNicoll, 2004). In the Uk
where different institutions can have quite different percentages of non
traditional students. This is partly a consequence of the deliberate effort
of universities, realized to a greater or lesser extent, to 'widen participation
that is, to attract a broader social range of students and thus include mor
non-traditional ones. One older (pre-1992) UK university recently had 10.
per cent 'mature' students while a newer one (post-1992) had 47.2 per cen

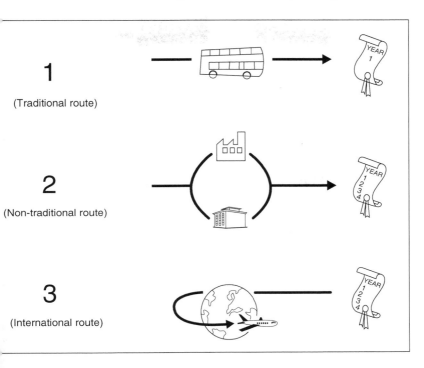

1

(Traditional route)

2

(Non-traditional route)

3

(International route)

Figure 7.1 Possible routes to university

nature' students in their student populations (*Sunday Times*, 2010). Thus, many of the students whom British university faculty meet have had very different educational experiences and, hence, it is likely that these students' social and cultural expectations of learning are also quite different.

Much research highlights the challenges non-traditional students face. Academic staff may make assumptions which generalize about students in groups, yet fail to differentiate between traditional and non-traditional learners, assuming they are all equally familiar with the same content knowledge and share the same understanding of the implicit rules for learning (Mercer, 2007). Assessments of learning are developed within a social and educational context (Lillis and McKinney, 2003) based largely on traditional routes to learning. Classroom discourses are not givens, but are social constructs, which are never neutral or value free (Hicks, 2003) and are perhaps based on the majority of traditional students, with less consideration given to non-traditional constructions of 'talk for learning' or expectations of writing. Science and arts disciplines often have very different expectations for academic writing styles (North, 2005). Further, individual tutors may have different expectations of what the format of an essay or report shoul be, which can confuse students who take courses in different subject are (Godfrey and Richards, 2008). All of these possible gaps of understandir and expectations increase the likelihood that non-traditional students ma misinterpret what is required or expected by a university teacher, which ca lead to misjudgement by the teacher of what the student has understoo and, hence, a misassessment of the student's work.

Students need to develop their own voice and identity in the new learnir environment. Patricia Duff (2003) gives the example that learning scientif discourse involves learning to think, act, speak and write like a scientist i a community of practice. According to Uta Papen (2005), academic literac practices set conventions for writing and standards for achievement: essay and reports are a dominant form of literacy in higher education and, to large degree, a student's success depends on the ability to write accordin to the standards and conventions laid out by the university. Arguably, stu dents reinvent the university each time they sit down to write. The studer has to learn to speak 'our' language, to try out the peculiar ways of knov ing, selecting, evaluating, reporting, concluding and arguing that defir the discourse of our university (Bartholomae, 1985). Crucially, tradition; students' cultures of learning are far more likely to be akin to universit discourses than are those of non-traditional students. The latter could arriv with very different previous cultures of learning, either because they hav been away from the university for a long period of time, or because the were educated in a very different environment or country.

The following approaches to supporting students' academic literacy ca be identified: a traditional 'sink or swim/osmosis' approach; a skills based c a study skills approach; and a 'dialogicality' approach.

In the traditional 'sink or swim/osmosis' approach, it is expected tha students either arrive equipped with the necessary skills or acquire ther quickly. This approach makes no special provision for non-traditional learn ers. In the 'skills based or a study skills' approach, literacy is a set of distinc skills that students can learn in support classes and then transfer to any dis cipline. This approach acknowledges that students need some support, bu it is often implemented by directing them to generic study skills materia. or a generic module without a discipline-related context. However, generi approaches can be unpopular with the students, and teaching sessions ca be poorly attended (Wingate, 2006; Godfrey and Richards, 2008); this sug gests that students may not value or see the purpose of such initiatives.

In the 'dialogicality' approach, students and lecturers engage in dialogu This approach acknowledges a 'deficit' in student knowledge, which need to be reduced through dialogue. This approach is arguably the most e fective of the three for non-traditional students. It helps counter connot; tions of elitism (Freire, cited in Clark, 2002) associated with learning i

niversity and helps make university more inclusive. Many researchers call
r 'dialogue' (Lillis, 2003; Williams, 2005) which makes academic conven-
ons explicit to learners (Lea and Street, 1998; Duff, 2003), including the
leanings of assessment terms used (Williams, 2005). However, dialogue
rguably needs direction or structure; it may need to be initiated or led by
le teacher, in the role of the questioner, rather than the answerer (Aristotle,
opics VIII). Establishing a context for such dialogue and identifying areas
r its focus reveal much about current cultures of learning in the United
ingdom and about how to engage students and teachers in constructive
lalogue. The following section describes how we did this through a series
f staged focus groups.

2   Method: the use of focus groups

or this project focus groups were used to elicit data because the goal was
> create productive group discussion of the meanings and expectations
f the terms. The project investigated how the terms were understood by
oth UK students and teachers, and by Chinese students and UK-based
hinese teachers, and also by Chinese teachers in China. Here we focus
n the UK context. Figure 7.2 shows the process; Figure 7.3 lists the terms
lat were talked about; and Figure 7.4 shows the frequency of use of these
ords across a selection of exams in a variety of subjects. This is repre-
?nted in a word cloud (wordle.net) whereby the frequency of the word
etermines the size of the word in the cloud. Figure 7.4 clearly shows
lat, in terms of hierarchy of use, some terms are used far more than
thers.

As Figure 7.2 shows, the focus group discussions proceeded in a cascade
om four separate groups to two amalgamated groups to one inclusive

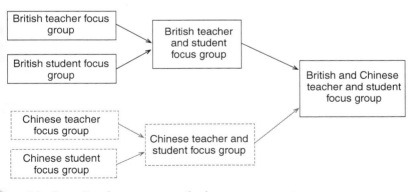

gure 7.2   Cascading focus group method

Account for	Critically evaluate	Distinguish	Interpret	State
Analyse	Define	Evaluate	Justify	Summarize
Comment on	Describe	Examine	Narrate	To what extent
Compare	Relate	Explain	Outline	Trace
Contrast	Discuss	Illustrate		

Figure 7.3   Terms discussed in the focus groups

Figure 7.4   Terms represented in a word cloud to show salience

group. There were two week gaps between each stage. Each focus group was recorded and transcribed, and key points were selected for consideration by the next focus group. This had the advantage that participants focused on the actual terms themselves: it shifted attention away from testing the knowledge and thus promoted a more relaxed atmosphere and created a constructive learning experience for both students and teachers (Padilla, 1993).

Concerning numbers of participants, a figure between 8 and 12 is often recommended for focus groups (Shamdasani and Stewart, 1990), although a figure as low as 3 is recommended for intense focus (Barbour, 2007). The stage-one focus groups generated intense focus as they were smaller (on average 4–5). As the focus groups progressed, they increased in size (to a maximum of 12) but did not become unwieldy. The material from the intense discussion was of an extremely high quality (see below) and provided an excellent basis for the further focus groups. Nevertheless, for this project these group sizes actually occurred fortuitously, and accidentally. The initial focus groups were smaller due to a sudden and unexpected blizzard that prevented a number of participants from attending. Furthermore, the weight of three two-hour focus groups at a critical time for the student workload meant that not all participants could attend all focus groups, so the groups' numbers remained manageable. If all participants had been able to attend all focus groups, the groups may have been unwieldy and

ata would not have been as rich. It is likely that larger groups inhibit
iscussion and do not allow individual participants sufficient time to ex-
ress their ideas. On this basis, we recommend a comparable number of
articipants.

The focus groups also revealed the value of the research process through
howing the meta-value of the groups. This was revealed through the value
tached to focusing on the different meanings of the terms. This was both
ositive (through recognition of the value of the focus groups) and negative
hrough criticism, e.g., of study skills approaches). Regarding the latter, the
eneric study skills approach, 'bolted on' to other courses rather than inte-
rated with them, was criticized. One student said how study skills classes
ad just told a 'big story' about the terms, a story which did not match their
xperience:

> I thought that I knew what they [these terms] meant before I came but we
> were never, even in the introduction class, what's it called ... study skills
> or – biggest waste of time in my life. And we were never sort of warned
> about them[;] ... it's not actually that clear, it's very blurred. If they told
> me one of these words I would know what I have to do, bu, they just tell
> me this big story about it in as simple a way as possible that doesn't actu-
> ally help me.

Many of the differences between students and teachers (see below) confirm
his. Regarding expectations, participants noted how it was assumed stu-
ents would know what to do, and that consequently, such terms were not
xplained. One student noted: 'It's not really explained ... in class and the
ay they [teachers] talk to you it's like they expect it from you ... but when
ou're a mature student and you've not been at school ... for a long time you
end to forget things like this.'

This was confirmed by teachers; one said it was a 'real revelation' to learn
hat students did not know some terms: 'It is the surprise of finding out that
discuss" is so tricky because to me "discuss" is a lovely easy one. ... I always
xplain "critically evaluate" and things like this. Even I know that is a tricky
ne, but "discuss" is a real revelation to me.'

As a positive outcome, the focus group discussions helped raise partici-
ants' awareness of gaps in learning cultures. One student noted how, even
n the third year, they did not really know how to use the terms: 'These
erminologies, this is pretty much ... the first time that I'm actually learn-
ng what they mean and I'm in the third year.' One student championed
ialogue between lecturers and students to help bridge the gap between
ultures of learning: 'What I think would actually help though ... would be
ctually ... talking to academics because then I'd pick it up ... without the
ear of sounding stupid ... because I know what things mean and when they
alk to me I can understand them most of the time ... It's like picking up an

accent, you know, I would start like talking in the same way using the sam
kind of words.'

Rosaline Barbour (2007) notes the importance of analysing focus grou
data in terms not only of what is said by participants, but also in terms of th
interaction between participants. The following extract of dialogue show
different cultures of learning being bridged during the focus group. Teach
A starts with a prior assumption about the efficacy of dictionaries to conve
what is required of the term 'discuss'. This is followed by Student A sugges
ing a different and more comprehensive approach. Then, Student B, follov
ing Student A's comment, returns to Teacher A's point with a convincir
counterargument. Finally, Teacher A acknowledges this as a 'fair point'.

> Teacher A   Dictionary's a hell of a powerful study[;] ... it's a magic bool
> it tells you the meaning of stuff, and in that respect it's brilliant an
> it forces me to then think: If I've written down 'Discuss' would I hav
> written what the dictionary said? And it's written by far clever
> people than me.
> Student A – Well what I find I've started to do ... I'm finding words an
> say small phrases and ... just copy and paste them onto Google c
> Wikipedia ... and reading through what their understanding of it i
> coz ... rather than one sentence you'll get a whole paragraph on it, an
> it actually it helps me understand what actually the word means [ger
> eral agreement] within the sense of what I've originally seen. ...
> Student B – You see the thing is with me ... I would actually disagree wit
> you [Teacher A] ... because the dictionary' ll tell you what it means.
> but it ... doesn't tell you how to put it into context; it might give you.
> maybe one sentence containing the word but it'll no turn round to m
> and say ... I need to use ethnography in this kind of context
> Teacher A – Yeh I know what you mean I could look up ethnography an
> I wouldn't know when to use it exactly, yeh, uh huh, fair point.

Crucially, dialogue serves a twofold purpose: firstly, it exposes gaps in, an
assumptions about, different 'cultures of learning'; secondly, it helps teacl
ers and students bridge these gaps and counter these assumptions. Ope
dialogue that focuses on terms themselves rather than on subject conter
helps shift the focus of the teacher–learner hierarchy. This encourage
discussion.

We argue that the above examples are significant, particularly within th
context of such assumed terms; however, they are not totally new. Tru
there is new discussion in-depth around key assumed terms, but suc
approaches have been done before. However, we now build on this previou
work by deconstructing the understandings of the terms into a scaffold fc
dialogue. Although dialogue is still open, it is guided by the scaffold whic
bridges assumed gaps regarding the terms.

3 Results and discussion

The focus group discussions showed both agreement and difference between lecturers and students with regard to understandings of the key terms. We first focus on agreements and then turn to differences; there were far more differences than agreements.

3.1 Areas of agreement

With the terms 'comment on' and 'evaluate' students and teachers agreed. For 'comment on' one lecturer noted they were 'pleased to see there's no real gap there between students and lecturers'. Also, regarding 'evaluate', one teacher noted: 'I think the definitions on here that the students have offered are very good.' These were the main examples of agreements on terms.

3.2 Areas of difference

3.2.1 Assumptions regarding previous cultures of learning

Results from the first-stage focus groups (teachers and students separate) showed clear differences in actual and presumed cultures of learning: between ideas and concepts actually held by students and those that teachers presumed would be held by the students (but in fact were not). Teachers perceived 'discuss' to be of immense value for its affordance of varied and wide-ranging answers; however, students hated 'discuss' because it was not prescriptive enough. In the culture of learning the students had come from, they had not used 'discuss', yet in university it was expected they could. One student was unclear about what 'discuss' meant: 'Ohh I hate this one. ... I don't really know what it means to "discuss" and I often failed on it ... well not fail but ahh, you know, not do so well ... I read somewhere in one book, that discuss means that you have to highlight the most important points of certain arguments and either compare or contrast them (Facilitator: And does that make sense to you?) (Emphatic) No! (Laughter).' In total contrast, one teacher was glowingly enthusiastic about 'discuss': 'That's good un [sic, meaning "one"] use it all the time[;] ... "discuss" must contain the elements of ... "critically appraise", "analyse", "review" it's got "synthesis" it's got "scholarship" it's got the lot in "discuss"; when you "discuss" something you're expecting students to be able to bring in additional knowledge; when you "discuss" student needs to be able to place it within its subject domain and it actually includes things like "define" '. Other teachers agreed.

Another difference was how 'critically evaluate' was perceived. Students thought it required them to emphasize negative aspects: 'Critically, ummm, I think it's possibly negative cause you're ... actually trying to find fault ... trying to critically evaluate information and that. Finding sort of what's behind the story ... and it may be negative and it may be positive as well, but to me more negative.' In contrast, teachers emphasized that 'critically evaluate' required analysis more than criticism: 'One of the most important

things that a university can give them is a finely tuned bullshit detecto
that comes under "critical evaluation" [also] the thing is "criticism" is to d
with "analysis" it's not to do with "criticism".'

Other terms (for example 'explain') also showed differences in culture
of learning. These differences are key; they show huge gulfs between actua
and assumed cultures of learning with which non-traditional students ca
come to the university. In the second stage of focus groups (teachers an
students together), awareness of such stark differences worried the teacher
who tried to defend the term 'discuss':

> Teacher A – 'Discuss' it isn't too prescriptive for the student ... it's a wor
> that I like to use when I want the student really to ... show me what the
> know about the subject. ... I'm not trying to catch you out ... and ...
> worries me that students would feel like that about it because I thin
> it gives a lot of latitude to students to be able to talk about what they
> like to talk about ... Teacher B – But obviously engenders a fairly ho
> rific reaction. ...
> Teacher A – I know it's a terrible shame. ...
> Students agreed, but wanted more clarity with how to use 'discuss':
> Student A – I agree with what you're saying; it is opening up like, but fo
> me I prefer to have it just clear to know this is what you've done, this
> what you want to talk about, not to 'discuss' then I just don't [unclea
> as you say and does that for me as well like it ...

In the second-stage group, students communicated difficulties directly t
teachers. One student said 'critically evaluate' was extremely difficult:
find this one extremely difficult ... I'm told to "critically evaluate" what I'v
learned ... and I haven't been able to transfer that because I haven't learr
anything so far'. Students also learned from teachers' views. One studer
noted their understanding of the term 'analyse' changed after reading teache
transcripts of the first-stage focus groups: 'Seeing the lecturers' view ... it doe
make more sense to me now when I read it there than when I ... read my ow
view on it ... yeh it has changed ... for me it would have been investigate c
calculate ... but now ... when I read the points here it makes sense.'

In summary, the first-stage focus groups (teachers and students separate
showed many differences in cultures of learning between teachers and th
non-traditional students. The cultures of learning the students had com
from (perhaps a tertiary college or after working for a number of year
meant they wanted direction. In contrast, teachers expected students' cu
tures and approaches to learning would be much broader, and that nor
traditional students would be more independent and require less guidance
Although not the direct focus of this chapter, we also found differences be
tween Chinese and British teachers in approaches to terms; for example th
term 'summarize' was considered straightforward by the Chinese teacher

ut extremely complex by the British teachers. The second-stage groups
howed how dialogue can help bridge these differences and help teachers
how students what these terms mean and how to use them.

.4   Hierarchical cultures of learning

fuch academic literature notes that British cultures of learning can differ
n key features from other cultures, such as Chinese (Cortazzi and Jin, 1996;
m and Cortazzi, 1998, 2011; Coverdale-Jones and Rastall, 2006, 2009): one
·ature is the respect accorded to teachers in China and the far smaller
·ower–distance' gulf between teachers and students in the West (Hofstede,
984), which means that there is less of a hierarchy in Western education.
ccordingly, in the West students are more vocal in class, prepared to
hallenge ideas and question their teachers. However, the non-traditional
:udents who participated in these focus groups were from high power–
istance and hierarchical cultures of learning. For example, in the second-
.age focus group, it was noted that students would not disagree with the
·cturer's statements: 'I mean obviously you are a lecturer I've got to go
long with you.' This applied generally to those in authority, in the words
f one student: 'Somebody in authority like a doctor or a lecturer...you
st automatically go along with what they're saying...you're not gonna
uestion it, you're gonna say well he knows best you know.' This student's
revious experience of a culture of learning had placed distance between
culty and students; and this experience remained influential. Thus, cul-
ires of learning are not simply geographical; they are also temporal (and
herefore can change).

This had implications for understanding some terms, notably 'critically
valuate'. The following dialogue demonstrates the strength of the con-
nuing influence of a previous hierarchical culture of learning. Student A
otes how the terms 'critically' and 'evaluate' are 'daunting' and induce
writers block'; Student B then notes this may have been because they were
rought up' in a culture of learning in which, out of respect for those in au-
nority questioning was not done, and although they felt they were adapt-
g to current cultures of critiquing, it was not easy. Student C highlights
ifferences between education now and 20 years ago:

> Student A – I just find that the words 'critically' and 'evaluate' quite
> daunting...I always get writers block when it comes to something like
> that.
> Student B – I come from the background that...people who are doctors
> or professors or things like that...I've been brought up in a culture
> that...you respect these people because they've got where they are
> today and my first reaction would be not to even question them and
> think well, are there any holes in their argument because I would just

think 'Oh right they must know what they're talking about';...i
changing but God it's hard. ...

Student C – But...I think that probably is actually changing though,
mean, you know, say if you'd asked that twenty years ago you mig
have a totally different response.

Furthermore, understandings of words were not 'mummified'; both teacl
ers and students noted how their understanding of the terms had deve
oped, thus implying two things: firstly that for non-traditional student
the expectations of the education system regarding what they should pro
uce had changed and, secondly, students need time to adapt (which no
traditional students may or may not be given). The following dialogue fro
the second-stage focus group, including Student, Facilitator and Teache
illustrates this:

Student A: I would agree with that.... [a comment from a stage one grou
My understanding of all these words has changed.
Facilitator A: That's great!
Teacher A: Fantastic...and yet I was the person who actually said tha
That's me, I said that. My understanding has changed.

Thus, these students recognized their difficulties; they recognized educatio
had changed, and that they needed to question. Nevertheless, they found que
tioning extremely hard, and the culture of learning they brought with the
made adjustment to the different culture of learning challenging. Unfamiliarit
with questioning also came through from the perspectives of the Chinese st
dents. This barrier of a previous culture of learning could be reduced by di
logue about expectations of assessment (see Section 7.2, Method).

For such adjustment, personality and psychology were considered critica
and the key skill of asking questions of a teacher was thought to depend o
whether a student was shy or outgoing. One student was reluctant to as
questions for fear of sounding 'stupid', and also reluctant to question peop
in authority. This was despite the fact that they agreed some lecturers 'prob
ably' liked to be questioned and, crucially, this student said a situation (i.e
dialogue) like that created by the focus group 'would be fine' to speak
teachers:

If it comes to asking questions I'll be the last one to put my hand u
because...I don't want people to look or laugh at me if I ask a stupi
question. But...to speak to you like this...would be fine. It comes dow
to personality a lot, I think. I would also say...at a psychological level
comes down to an authority thing. You tend not to question people i
authority...And yet some lecturers probably like the fact that you que
tion them. [All teachers agree.]

ne key trait that both teachers and students agreed on was that of having *confidence*:

> Teacher A: It's a confidence thing … of having the courage of your student convictions. … 'Justify', 'Discuss', 'Critically Evaluate', 'Analyse': they're confidence issues; it's having the confidence to just to go for it. [General agreement.]
>
> Student A – See, when it comes to me I'm like, no, that's a stupid question; he's gonna think I'm stupid. I think it's a whole confidence thing. [general agreement].

1 summary, these non-traditional students' former culture of learning influ-1ced their readiness to question 'authority'. They recognized cultural dif-·rences and were slowly adjusting, but this was challenging. Interestingly, estiges of former cultures remain: nor would we necessarily expect – or ·ant – them to disappear, since they are arguably valid in some contexts. ather, we hope non-traditional students will acquire a wider and deeper ·pertoire of learning strategies within a range of cultures of learning and 1en use them appropriately in different circumstances.

4.1 Hierarchies of words

Vithin hierarchical interrelations, 'describe' was considered to be a first xpectation, the initial step of an answer, but 'analysis' was a later and 'bet-·r' one, as the following dialogue from the first focus group stage shows:

> Teacher A – 'Describe' really is just the first step to make sure they've got the boundaries right and the right ballpark.
>
> Teacher B – Yeh, absolutely … and 'describe' is what I usually set as a sort of … let's relax the … students get them into the case study and … if the student spends too long on the 'description' to the detriment of … for example 'analysis' then …
>
> Teacher A – Students … need to be guided that … 'describe' is usually reasonably low-level sort of question.
>
> Such ranking also applied to 'outline' (a lower-level term) and 'summarize' (a higher-level term):
>
> Teacher A – I would use 'outline' for a five-mark question or for a second year where I would use 'summarise' with the fourth years because I think 'summarise' is a really tricky thing to get students to do.
>
> Teacher B – Yeh, I'd consider that hard.

lso, the value or academic expectation raised by the implied meanings of ·rms could be differentiated according to the number of marks awarded) appropriate responses: ' "describe" if it's worth one is very different from describe" if it's worth five'.

Thus, all students, but especially non-traditional ones, have to 'come terms' with these key terms in order to understand and respond successful to them. The terms contain assumed and implied hierarchies. It is implicit assumed that 'describe' responses will be at a 'lower level' than 'analyse', ar yet 'describe' itself (and by implication any other term) could have differe expectations according to the marks attached. It was even possible for som terms to be interchangeable. For the university teachers and their cultur of learning, taxonomies of words exist that tell them which terms to use f different taxonomies of learning (Bloom, 1956, is the classic example, cite in Scottish Government, 2010). However, although the students may hav access to such information, if their previous culture of learning has been ve different, they may not know what is expected, nor be comfortable respon ing to what is expected; unless this is made explicit through dialogue.

7.4.2   Discipline specificity of words

Terms also 'changed' according to discipline. For example, to 'describe' i engineering requires certain subject-specific tests and calculations, and ' actually get an engineer's "description" of soil requires certain tests, requir certain calculations'.

Further, certain terms would only be used in specific subjects. For exampl teachers considering 'narrate' commented: 'I can see where one might u it but not definitely not in anything that I do'; or regarding 'prove': 'obv ously coming from English and film studies "prove" is not really a word th we...really use, it would be more..."justify" your argument'. Similarly, f engineers, 'trace' elicited the following humorous response which referre to a literal enactment: 'Don't ask the engineers that, they'll be out with tl greaseproof paper drawing pictures'.

Some subjects also allowed for vagueness. The following example show how one teacher noted that students were permitted a lot of latitude in the answers:

> Teacher A – in every subject the lecturer sets a question and there is model. ...My subject, I don't have model answers because there is n completely right answer. The student may interpret it differently, the put the order around differently, they may choose to examine som thing in greater depth...so that there is quite a lot of latitude there an an experienced lecturer marks with the view that they want to giv students marks.

Thus, not only is the university culture of learning a set of expectations an processes that non-traditional students may not know or be accustomed t but would arguably only be able to learn what is expected of them throug practice within the context of a particular discipline. Time is required t adapt.

5 Conclusion

This chapter has focused on cultures of learning in the United Kingdom through an analysis of the perceptions of key assessment terms by UK university faculty and British non-traditional students. Direct entrants, as one major group of non-traditional students, are a large and growing group in many institutions worldwide, but their cultures of learning could differ from those assumed by teachers. The chapter used the research method of staged focus group discussion technique whereby teachers and students first talked about the key terms in separate groups before coming together to talk about the terms in a larger amalgamated focus group (which discussed transcribed results from the first-stage group as a focus). Although there were some similarities, the analysis shows mostly differences and complexities in the understandings of the words. These differences showed both the importance of the terms and the need for teachers to recontextualize the terms for this group of non-traditional students so that they can make up for the changes in education and 'cultures of learning' they may have missed by undergoing work and other experience rather than joining the university directly in the traditional route.

The focus group discussions showed the surprise (and sometimes the worry) of teachers that students reacted in such negative ways to some terms. Although some teachers previously believed dictionaries to be an aid (although not all did), the discussions also showed how the students generally found these inadequate, since dictionary meanings were necessarily recontextualized. It was generally felt that, in order to fully engage with these terms, recontextualization through discussion of their specific use in discipline is required. The success of opening a dialogue based on the terms was shown by the second stage of the focus groups. We have shown that the teachers were not previously aware of these differences between the assumed 'culture of learning' that they expected students to be familiar with and what the reality of non-traditional students understand and believe. Teachers expected students to know the meanings and implications of these apparently simple words; and it is likely that many 'traditional students' already do, since they come directly from levels of school education in which, largely through exam preparation, the terms are emphasized. One email response from a fourth-year traditional student to the initial call for participants to help with this research shows that many traditional students believe they know the meanings of these terms, and that dialogue is unnecessary: 'Sounds like stupid crap, no…p.s try dictionary.com'. However, this study reveals that the awareness of non-traditional students, and teachers' false assumptions of the cultures of learning of non-traditional students shows that 'dictionary.com' would be of little use and, more importantly, talking about such terms is anything but 'stupid crap'. Rather, engaging in dialogue about the implied meanings of these terms, about the kinds of

responses which are expected from them and their likely rankings in a hie
archy of academic values will help non-traditional students 'come to term
with the key terms.

References

Aristotle (2006) *Topics*. WA *Pickard*-Cambridge (Trans.). Digireads.com.
Barbour, R.S. (2007) *Doing focus groups*. London: Sage.
Bartholomae, D. (1985) Inventing the university. In M. Rose (Ed.), *When a writer can write: Studies in writer's block and other composing-process problems*. New York an London: The Guilford Press, pp. 134–66.
Bloom, B.S. (Ed.) (1956) *Taxonomy of Educational Objectives: The Classification Educational Goals: Handbook I, Cognitive Domain*. New York: Longmans, Green.
Cortazzi, M. & Jin, L. (1996) Cultures of learning: Language classrooms in Chin In H. Coleman (Ed.), *Society and the language classroom*. Cambridge: Cambridg University Press, pp. 169–206.
Coverdale-Jones, T. & Rastall, P. (Eds) (2006) The Chinese learner (special issue *Language, Culture and Curriculum*, 19 (1).
Coverdale-Jones, T. & Rastall, P. (Eds) (2009) *Internationalizing the university, th Chinese context*. Houndmills: Palgrave Macmillan.
Duff, P.C. (2003) Problematising academic discourse socialisation. In H. Marrio T. Moore & R. Spence-Brown (Eds), *Learning discourse and the discourses of learnin* Melbourne: Monash University Press.
Godfrey, H. & Richards, K. (2008) Developing academic support strategies for non traditional entrants to university. ESREA Access, Learning Careers and Identiti Network Conference, 10–12 December 2008, University of Seville, Spain.
Hicks, D. (2003) Discourse, teaching and learning. In S. Goodman, T. Lilli J. Maybin & N. Mercer (Eds), *Language, literacy and education: A reader*. Stoke o Trent: Trentham Books, pp. 3–24.
Hofstede, G. (1984) *Culture's consequences, international differences in work-relate values*. Newbury Park: Sage.
Jin, L. & Cortazzi, M. (Eds) (2011) *Researching Chinese learners: Skills, perceptions an intercultural adaptations*. Houndmills: Palgrave Macmillan.
Lea, M. & Street, B. (1998) Student writing in higher education: An academic lite acies approach. *Studies in Higher Education*, 23 (2), June, 157–73.
Lillis, T. (2003) Student writing as 'academic literacies': Drawing on Bakhtin to mov from critique to design. *Language and Education*, 17 (3), 192–207.
Lillis, T. & McKinney, C. (2003) *Analysing language in context: A student workboo* Stoke on Trent: Trentham Books.
McNicoll, S. (2004) Access to higher education among lower socioeconomic groups: historical perspective. *Journal of Access Policy and Practice*, 1 (2), 162–70.
Mercer, N. (2007) *Words and minds: How we use language to think together*. Londor Routledge.
National Centre for Education Statistics (2002) U.S. Department of Education. Institut of Education Sciences. Special Analysis 2002 Non-traditional Undergraduate http://nces.ed.gov/programs/coe/2002/analyses/nontraditional/sa01.asp Accesse November 2010.

orth, S. (2005) Different values, different skills? A comparison of essay writing by students from arts and science backgrounds. *Studies in Higher Education*, 30 (5), 517–33.

ıdilla, R. (1993) Using dialogical research methods in group interviews. In D. Morgan (Ed.), *Successful focus groups: Advancing the state of the art.* California: Sage.

ıpen, U. (2005) *Adult literacy as social skills: More than skills.* London: Routledge.

:heutze, H.G. & Slowey, M. (2002) Participation and exclusion: A comparative analysis of non-traditional students and lifelong learners in higher education. *Higher Education*, 44 (3–4), 309–27.

:ottish Government (2010) Using Learning Outcomes. Available at http://www. scotland.gov.uk/Publications/2004/09/19908/42705 Accessed December 2010.

ıamdasani, P. N. & Stewart, D.W. (1990) *Focus groups: Theory and practice.* Applied social research methods series, v. 20. Newbury Park, CA: Sage Publications.

ınday Times (2010) University guide, 2011, 12 September.

'illiams, K. (2005) Lecturer and first year student (mis)understandings of assessment task verbs: 'Mind the gap'. *Teaching in Higher Education*, 10 (2), April, 157–73.

'ingate, U. (2006) Doing away with 'study skills'. *Teaching in Higher Education*, 11 (4), 457–69. Wordle.net http://www.wordle.net/

8
'It's Totally Different': Undergraduate Chinese Students Learning to Write in a New Zealand University

Gillian Skyrme

8.1 Introduction

This chapter examines the responses of Chinese international students to th writing demands of their undergraduate study of business in a New Zealan university. While writing in English was only one among many planes i which they experienced an enormous amount of intercultural learning, it wa significant as a major means by which they demonstrated their universit learning to their teachers and entered into some sort of communication wit them. The chapter reveals that in spite of these learners' growing understanc ing of, and even in some cases alignment with, the values of the universit there were occasions when they did not adopt ways of writing favoured withi this host culture of learning, as a result of either inability or strategic choice.

8.2 Learning academic cultures

Students learn what it means to be a student in particular contexts – cor texts which respond to wide influences, from the macro-level of goverr ment education policy and historical cultural understandings of learnin to the micro-level of how daily interactions with faculty and other studen socialize them to be and do the identity of 'student' (Gee, 2004) in th classroom. These experiences build into cultures of learning, which Jin an Cortazzi (2006: 9) describe as 'taken-for-granted frameworks of expecta tions, attitudes, values and beliefs about how to teach or learn successfully which are implicitly learned not only through 'one's own social actions bu also through one's interpretation of other people's behaviour' (Kato, 200: 52). Sharing such understandings engenders a sense of membership and c who one is within a community.

This learning is far from static: adjusting to each new classroom an stage of learning is a norm of the experience, even within one institutiona ational or cultural context, as studies of the first-year experience of native speaker university students attest (e.g., Pascarella and Terenzini, 2005). However, when the new stage is in an academic culture apparently unrelated to previous learning experiences, and in which expectations about teaching and successful learning are not met, the challenge is much greater, and the sense of personal development along a trajectory can be lost.

Although Jin and Cortazzi (2006) point to changing practices within Chinese cultures of learning, differences between the learning environments in which the participants in this study had had their early education and those of the Western academy have been widely noted (and often misunderstood, for example, see Biggs, 1996). Knowledge of the milieu of one's own world is taken for granted, which makes it difficult for participants to see dispassionately either its salient features or those of contrasting worlds, so examining the nature of any particular culture of learning is fraught with the possibility of oversimplification. However, recurring themes have emerged from investigations of Chinese academic culture. These include a value placed on mastery as a basic process in learning, establishing a thorough understanding of existing authorities within a field before aspiring to critique, so that students are not asked to express their own ideas at a stage when they feel they do not 'know enough to say or do something original' (Cortazzi and Jin, 1997: 86). Knowledge is seen as a social construct rather than the subject of individual ownership (Chandrasoma et al., 2004). To achieve mastery, perseverance and hard work are highly valued, and success tends to be attributed to effort rather than to high ability (Jin and Cortazzi, 2006; Parris-Kidd and Barnett, 2011).

Another factor of significance here is the dual nature of Chinese education (Dooley, 2001), producing contrasting cohorts of students. Zhang (2003: 54), reporting on Chinese students studying abroad, proclaims 'good academic foundations, strong abilities, and hardworking diligence' of students from elite institutions have 'commanded admiration in the countries to which they have gone'. However, Xuesong Gao (2006: 61) describes very different traits and motivations in students from a 'low-profile tertiary vocational college', in particular, their excessive teacher dependence. He attributes this to learning strategies developed in similarly low-profile high schools to optimize the chance of passing exams. The participants in this study, typical of many who have chosen New Zealand as a destination, were from the latter group; if they had had any Chinese tertiary educational experience, it was at sub-university 'college' level in the type of university described by Gao.

These students were entering a culture of learning, which, in spite of the university's geographical position in the Asia Pacific region, can be seen as a manifestation of Western institutions of higher learning. Such institutions do not always make their values explicit to newcomers such as international students: Theresa Lillis (2001: 14) attributes to them 'an ideologically inscribed institutional practice of mystery'. However, there have been attempts to explain their values more explicitly. For example, Peggy Nightingale ar Mike O'Neill (1994) do so by defining quality in higher education as a tran formative process resulting in 'autonomous, critical, reflective and articula students' empowered and enhanced to a degree that enables them to critiqu their experience and themselves (p. 10), and they suggest that fostering suc 'higher order intellectual capabilities in their students no matter who the are and at what stage of their studies' is 'one overarching purpose that a [such institutions] share' (p. 11).

This focus on the development of personal analytical thinking skills wa conveyed directly to students in this university at the time of the stud through their engagement with a widely used text designed to induct the into academic writing practices (Emerson, 2005) in which Romuald Rudz (2005) underlines the importance of evaluation and critique: 'You are able t make informed judgements (based on your analysis and synthesis) as to ho good (or bad) something is'; and, at the highest level of achievement, of th creation of new knowledge: 'such individuals are able to create new know ledge through research and new approaches through innovations' (p. 13).

Whether such values have the universal reach suggested has been que tioned. Ryuko Kubota (2004) points out that the autonomous studer engaged in critical classroom interaction implied in the above text (ofte contrasted with the 'reticent' Asian student) is the exception rather tha the norm. Others have noted that even the institutions that promote the: values put limitations on them. Ranamukalage Chandrasoma and othe (2004: 189) assert, 'We want our students to be critical thinkers, to do thing for themselves, but only along the narrow guidelines that we set for accep able criticality.' The tension between trying to be independent and yet d what was expected of them – and deemed acceptable in the new culture of learning – was a major challenge to the students in this study.

One method of investigating the challenge is through explicit instructio by means of such texts as Lisa Emerson (2005) cited above, or participe tion in first semester study skills seminars. However, Jean Lave and Etienn Wenger (1991) demonstrate that less explicit methods are also vital, an that newcomers to a community of practice such as this need opportuniti to participate in its practices alongside willing old-timers who accept the novice status and recognize the legitimacy of their 'peripheral practice Ideally, support is provided to help them perceive and adopt the normalize ways of being, doing, speaking and writing within that community. This a process that inevitably reaches deeper than simply a few new behaviour it leads to an adoption of the community's 'perspectives and interpretation seeing the world in the same ways and taking on an identity as a member of that community' (Hyland, 2002: 1092). On the other hand, unfortunatel this kind of willing guidance is not always visible to students and they ca find it difficult to find out about the appropriate terms of participation. Th can create a sense of marginalization and disempowerment: 'In practice, w now who we are by what is familiar, understandable, usable, negotiable; we now who we are not by what is foreign, opaque, unwieldy, unproductive' Venger, 1998: 153).

.3   Writing as an expression of the culture of learning

'riting can be seen as a key and complex element within the process of :culturation into academic cultural values. In many courses, it is through riting that disciplinary learning is judged and grades awarded, the ul- mate (though not the only) test of membership in the learning community. 'riting, as a social practice (Abasi and Akbari, 2008; Gee, 2004), typically akes place in a web of discourses, including assignment instructions, con- ›nt-based classes, reading research and student discussion. Acquiring ex- ›ertise is not simply about the level of English language proficiency, but 1volves social perspectives such as finding out the requirements of a dis- ›urse by reading and writing relevant texts and seeing what is considered nportant (Lea and Street, 1998; Weigle, 2005). This is complicated by the ict that discourses vary between disciplines (Harwood and Hadley, 2004; utz, 2004; Lea and Street, 1998; Moore and Morton, 2005), so that students aking early introductory courses across a range of core papers (as in the 1siness degree program in which these students were enrolled) have to :spond to often conflicting writing demands. There are also areas of appar- 1t permissiveness which turn out to have significant limitations, bounded ; they must be by what constitutes 'knowing' within the discipline (Lea nd Street, 1998). One example, which coexists confusingly for many inter- ational students with instructions to adopt a specified style, is the invita- on to show creativity or originality in writing. Desmond Allison (2004:)5) suggests that this invitation can be an 'illusory freedom' to those who ack access to ... how to innovate acceptably in writing'.

An aspect of writing that has been given wide attention in recent years, 1d in which international students have often been implicated, is that of lagiarism (Abasi and Graves, 2008; Holmes, 2004; Le Ha, 2006; Liu, 2005; ›wden, 2005; Walker, 1998). The notion seems straightforward to many Vestern academics; however, a little investigation reveals complex incon- stencies and a widespread norm of textual borrowing. Academic writers emonstrate their central participation within a discourse by drawing on he repertoire of voices they have encountered in their experience of par- cipating in genres and discourses' and by uniquely recombining these in 1eir texts (Ivanič and Camps, 2001: 6). The manner of drawing on the rep- rtoire can be indirect, adopting a style of writing associated with the genre 1 question, or more direct, through citations and quotations. Students are, 1erefore, asked to distinguish their own voices from words that are 'owned' y individual authorities through referencing conventions, while at the ame time they are encouraged to adopt shared ways of writing and talking

about their discipline which are seen as in the public domain. Alastai
Pennycook's question is pertinent:

> Because all language learning is, to some extent, a practice of memoriza
> tion of the words of others, on what grounds do we see certain acts o
> textual borrowing as acceptable and others as unacceptable? (1996: 202

This can be perplexing for new writers of academic English.

Under such circumstances, the 'moral outrage' (Pennycook, 1996: 204
shown by many academics at apparent plagiarism seems often to have dubi
ous justification, particularly as students new to a discipline are inevitabl
dependent on authoritative sources (Lea and Street, 1998). Plagiarism is on
of the few aspects of academic writing which is typically addressed overtl
in instructions in university courses. However, it is generally discussed i
very legalistic terms of copyright and ownership, or punitively, explaining
the penalties if plagiarism is detected in students' writing. Instructions ofter
do not address the underpinning philosophy (Angelil-Carter, 2000; Lea and
Street, 1998; Wingate, 2006), or discuss the pedagogical value of absorbin
new concepts into a deeper structure of internally held knowledge, whic
makes it possible for students to re-express them.

If the incorporation of other voices into writing is a key area of learnin
for new students, so is the notion of *voice* in the singular. Two of the poten
tial meanings encompassed by this term which Roz Ivanič and David Camp
(2001) investigate are of value in this study. The first of these is voice as *self-re*
resentation. They see this as inevitable in any text, as it is created by the choice
that writers make at the level of elements of syntax, lexis and so on, which re
sult in writing that represents them as aligning with some sort of social group
As Mikhail Bakhtin (1986: 124) says, 'there are no voiceless words that belon
to no one.' There are constraints in the choices open to students: '[T]he ver
sion of self that will be rewarded may be determined by the tutor who will b
assessing the work' (Ivanič and Camps, 2001: 6). In the university, it is ofter
the challenging variety known as academic English that reaps rewards.

The other meaning of *voice* Ivanič and Camps (2001) discuss is *voice a*
having something to say. This is a more specific presence, that of 'the writ
er's own views, authoritativeness, and authorial presence' (p. 7) within th
text. This is not necessarily the 'neo-romantic' expression of individualit
discussed and rejected by Vai Ramanathan and Dwight Atkinson (1999) o
Rena Helms-Park and Paul Stapleton (2003), but the requirement to develo
a position by making an argument, which Mary Lea and Brian Street (1998
and others (e.g., Hyland, 2002) have found to be a requirement across disci
plines. This sense links to the notion of the 'autonomous, critical, reflectiv
and articulate students' imagined by Nightingale and O'Neill (1994).

However, Ron Scollon (1991, in Ramanathan and Atkinson, 1999: 53
suggests a fundamental difference in the role of writing within Chines

ltures of learning: it is not intended to reveal the writer's own voice, ut is 'for the purpose of becoming integrated into a scholarly community. ...One is writing to pass on what one has received'. From a stance of hared scholarship, a writer can expect readers to recognize allusions and ontribute to interpretation, and an absence of overt explication may be voured since readers are credited with the ability to draw out implicaons for themselves. This stance carries, too, implications for the use of the ords of others within one's writing, and the attitude to textual borrowing as certainly been less strident (Jin and Cortazzi, 2006; Sowden, 2005) han in Western universities. There is some dispute in the literature about hether unattributed use is permitted (Liu, 2005), and in current practice any university teachers in China show a deepening concern about rising vels of plagiarism among students. However, in the colleges where they ad studied, this had been raised as an issue for very few of the participants this research.

.4   The study

he data reported in this chapter were collected as part of a doctoral research roject based largely on semi-structured interviews carried out between 003 and 2006 with a total of 24 undergraduate Chinese international students studying business and information sciences in a New Zealand university (Skyrme, 2008a). The study sought to uncover their expectations, the sues that faced them, and the changes that they experienced. It included oth a retrospective perspective based on single interviews with students earing the end of their study, and a longitudinal perspective, initially following 12 students through their first semester at the university, and then ve of those during the entire course of their degree study. All interviews ere transcribed and analysed through a process of multiple readings in rder to identify units of meaning and emerging themes, and to note their elation to those of other participants and to data from other interviews ith the same student. This was done through a recursive process involving ollow-up questions and member-checking the researcher's interpretations the longitudinal study (Tesch, 1990). A more extensive account is proided in Skyrme (2011). The participants cited here are coded CSR for those the retrospective study, and CSL for the longitudinal study; these codes re followed by the number code for the interview from which the comment ame from (see Appendix 8.1).

The study was not focused on writing but, to both researcher and students, this was a significant area of interest which threaded through interiews. As the source of data was interviews, this chapter is not about the ritten texts that students produced, but it records their perceptions of the riting processes they experienced and their emerging identities as writers or the university.

8.5   Finding your own academic voice

8.5.1   Recognizing the distance

Pre-sessional preparatory English courses and feedback on early assign
ments made participants very aware of the distance to be travelled and c
their disadvantageous starting point, compared to students who were mor
familiar with the expected conventions in academic writing in English. On
of them described her Chinese writing as allusive: 'I think I can do tha
beautifully, I can hide my idea. ... Maybe I can describe a flower or weathe
and in that side maybe have my exposition of my general idea, in ther
(CSR1). She had been quick to discover that, in this context, such subtlet
was not an asset: 'Totally different .... You need to present the key senten
first. Don't hide them. It's totally different.' CSL1 found that achievement c
the English language criterion of a score of 6 within the widely recognize
International English Language Testing System (IELTS) which was require
for enrolment was not indicative of readiness: 'Oh, feel terrible, because I g
to the IELTS, I got 6 point for the writing so I think my writing is all righ
but the essay ... let me to know my writing is terrible' (Y1.3).

The next sections will show some of the struggles involved as student
tried to bridge these gaps and some strategic decisions that were made t
limit the stretch.

8.5.2   Finding the recipe or being creative?

These students had the clear expectation that learning required effort, an
they were not averse to doing so on the university's own terms by adop
ing its culture of learning. They were alert to messages given to them abou
how to do that, and these messages suggested that there was a formul
available. CSR1 had learned about '[T]he structure, three part', and anothe
mentioned the 'very traditional report format, one, one two three, exampl
(CSL2 Y1.3). Or perhaps it was even a recipe: in a first semester study skil
workshop, CSR1 was told that if 'lecturer want chocolate cake, but you thin
you can cook fruit cake is the best, so you present your fruit cake, but yo
will got zero.' This message was reiterated by more experienced friends, wh
told her: 'The lecturer just want to know this, this and this, so what [yo
are] thinking is rubbish.' There seemed no invitation for her to develop he
own voice.

Nevertheless, in spite of the apparent importance of such recipes, the
found it curiously difficult to gain access to them. Academics are notor
ously more able and/or willing to recognize 'good' academic writing tha
to explain its features to students (e.g., Lea and Street, 1998), and what i
counted as 'good' can vary across disciplines or even across teachers withi
the same discipline (Harwood and Hadley, 2004; Lea and Street, 1998; Lilli
2001). For these students, sources of enlightenment were absent. Participant
craved samples to flesh out any emerging 'formats', lamented inadequat

xplanations of new genres, felt confusion about different tutors contrast-
ıg requirements, and resorted to the supposed 'expertise' of near peers,
ɔrrowing marked assignments from previous semesters:

> I borrowed the assignment from my friend…because she got B+ on the
> first assignment, oh very good, because something I can keep using, and
> this is very good and we have discussion. You should avoid this because it
> is not good on the assignment, you will lose the mark. (CSL3 Y1.2)

ı the face of institutional mystery, second year international students were,
ɔ new arrivals, significant instructors in the art of writing. This may not be
situation that teachers see as ideal, but it is certainly understandable.

By the end of the first year, students seemed more at ease with familiar
.signment genres, though when they were asked to produce a new kind,
ıch as a briefing paper or a literature review, this could still send them
:urrying for the elusive recipes and it led to deep frustration. An invita-
on to ask questions about an assignment, for example, was no substitute
ɔr clear instructions: 'I've never heard of, you know, briefing paper. I don't
ave any questions, I don't know what I don't know' (CSL4 Y1.4).

At this point, though, one of the students received new understanding
ɔout the nature of the recipe, that there was room for variation:

> [I]n Western country one thing is really important for people is creative,
> so you don't need to follow another people's idea to copy.…So, yeah,
> trust yourself. (CSL3 Y1.4)

SL3 was enthusiastic about an invitation to originality which he had not
ıus far recognized. It seemed to allow him to exercise more autonomy in
resenting his own voice. However, next time we met he revealed that he
ad made a judicious decision not to take up the invitation:

> At least I know, I followed this to do, I will get pass. That's what all I need.
> Maybe if I make it creative, two result for me is worse, is best, 'cause sometime
> I never tried it, I don't want to take this risk because it's too risky. Especially
> every assignment or every work for me is important, they all count in the
> internal the result so I don't want to take such a big risk. (CSL3 Y2)

ı the conditions that prevail in the university, often the only writing on
ʰich students receive feedback is that proffered for high-stakes internal
ssessment. This works fundamentally against the experimentation ne-
essary for students to feel confident in deviating from the 'format' and
ʲercising more personal choice. This was not an environment in which
ew writers could trust that their 'peripheral practice' would be recognized
s legitimate and acceptable (Lave and Wenger, 1991). The challenge of

innovating acceptably (Allison, 2004) was too great. CSL3 returned to pr
ducing 'chocolate cake' with a sense of regret that he had not taken up tl
challenge of a more autonomous strategy.

8.5.3 Borrowing voices

Some aspects of academic writing had been brought to the focal studen'
attention in pre-sessional courses, and they knew they would be required
write from relevant sources. This seemed, as suggested above, to have bee
presented largely in legalistic terms: '[Y]ou have to gone into the APA styl
and if you broken this law you will lose lots of mark in your assignment.
is very base problem for Chinese students' (CSL3 Y1.1).

Their interviews showed that quoting sources was seen as a way of boos
ing the word count, helping to bridge the gap between the familiar IEL'
250-word essays and the more challenging university assignments of ov
1,000 words, even to the point of obliterating personal voice (as *havi*
something to say) in the writing. For example, faced with a choice betwee
two topics, one student chose the least familiar, about genetically modifi(
(GM) food, because she could find more references for it, even though sl
felt she could have written half the words on the other topic from her exis
ing knowledge:

> [B]ut later I think if I find a GM I can borrow heaps and heaps of bool
> and I can write that one and try to do it and I can get more book, so lat
> I choose to GM food. (CSL1 Y1.2)

Having references, then, seemed more important than having idea
Inevitably, in the absence of any personal understanding of the topic, sl
became reliant on the references and found herself forced to copy too muc
material from them, which earned her the reprimand of her teacher.

For a considerable number of the students, the first round of universit
assignments brought awareness of the tension between using other people
ideas and expressing their own. The problems lay in two directions. On
was the lack of cohesion that arose where there was no framework provide
by a process of personal analysis:

> Cut paste, cut paste, cut paste. Because that is not my work, so it is unlog
> cal, you know, but just 'you said,' 'she said,' 'I said,' you know, all con
> bined together, so it's quite rubbish. (CSL2 Y1.3)

The other was the failure to distinguish their own words from those (
others:

> I found the plagiarism – at that time I was, wah! Because Chinese studen
> we don't know that we should mention the author or something. Ol

don't want to be cheating but I just don't know how to do that. I learned from blood lesson. (CSR1)

This ignorance had persisted through a three-month pre-sessional language course in which such matters had been covered, 'but at that time I don't understand fully. Maybe just some writing style or culture, Western, so I just, yes, do some. I forgot, immediately actually' (CSR1). These students' pre-sessional courses had not delivered 'blood lessons' in the form of assessments, since the writing was formative rather than summative. The most important writing at that stage had been the IELTS exam, where they did not have to write from other sources.

Over the course of the first semester, it was clear that a number of students aligned themselves more closely with the university's understanding of the nature of plagiarism, as Ken Hyland (2002) suggests. One student, for example, rejected the practice, clearly recognizing both the legalistic and the pedagogical aspects: 'I think that's illegal, and it's useless. Why people teach student just copy what another people said, that's useless for you' (CSL6 Y1.2). However, avoiding it remained a problem.

Limited linguistic resources created a barrier here, in view of the need for academic English to establish their legitimacy as writers for the university. This was a variety of which they were not yet competent speakers or writers:

> I didn't use my own words. Because after I reading the book, it just give me the idea, the sentence structure perfectly. How can I change?...I change the academic language to kindergarten language. (CSR1)

To present herself so inappropriately would dash her hopes of claiming membership in this new culture of learning.

Finding approved ways to express themselves was particularly challenging when, as with CSL1 above, they were writing about matters unfamiliar to them:

> Actually I find it's a little bit hard, like how to paraphrase other people's work to get yourself away from being plagiarism, because it's hard, you know, it's really fine line...it's not general information, it's not general knowledge, so you've got to get someone else's idea. (CSL4 Y1.2)

CSL4 was tripping up on the dilemma of having, in the text, the visible presence of the ideas of authorities within the constraints imposed by the danger of being accused of plagiarism. Students who are struggling to achieve this in linguistically challenging contexts often adopt a rather superficial approach to paraphrasing, 'copying from a source text and then deleting some words, altering grammatical structures, or plugging in one-for-one synonym-substitutes' (Howard, 1992: 233). Howard points out, though, that this, which we might see as *paraphrasing by manipulation*, can be seen as a first step towards understanding of and competence in borrowing voices. We might therefore expect to see a gradual development of greater expertise, a normal progression of novices negotiating the new role, appropriating practices accepted as legitimate, so that eventually they are able to express concepts drawn from sources in more personally voiced ways, which we might call *paraphrasing by integration*.

However, once again the data provide a clear example of withdrawal from a level of autonomy as a writer, which is one of the markers of quality in this cultural context identified by Nightingale and O'Neill (1994) above. One of the students, CSL1, had impressed me as a learner made in the image of the university values because of her quest for personal understanding; her interviews were peppered with statements like: 'And now I try to understand what the tutor is talking about, I try to conclusion by myself, by my sentence' (Y1.2). From an early stage, she attempted to internalize new ideas and express them in her own voice. She provided an account of this practice in recalling a discussion with friends during her second year:

> I just asked them, 'When you write the assignment you just read through all the book and then you get your own idea and combine together and just write down your own words?' (Y2)

Her friends adamantly advised that she should stay close to the original text, adopting a tactic of paraphrasing by manipulation, because 'your all idea come from that book so you need to paraphrasing the book, you can't just write down on your own sentence' (Y2). This advice reversed her fortunes as a writer, a skill she had always struggled with and, from time to time, failed at. She flourished in university writing only when she ceased to call primarily on her own voice to develop her position and, instead, remained closely parallel to the original texts. Her grades immediately improved.

As she spoke to me, CSL1 made persistent grammatical errors, a challenge which had not abated by the end of her undergraduate study. As an experienced listener to learner English, I rarely found it difficult to understand her message and readily detected the committed student and inquiring mind behind her words. It is certainly possible, though, that her teachers found it more difficult to recognize the argument that she was developing, which suggests that when one's voice is heavily accented, it is considerably less welcome in academic writing.

Once again, it seemed that success lay in retreating from a more autonomous practice.

8.5.4   Owning an idea

I will return finally to the question of *voice* as having something to say. The data indicated that, from the first assignment, it was demanded that

udents have an encompassing concept which provided cohesion and pur-
ose to the ideas in the text – as we saw in CSL2's realization that his 'cut
aste' offering was 'rubbish.' At the same time, CSL3 was striving to invest
is writing with this element: 'Even if the main idea is came from the book,
ut I make understanding and use my own, myself's opinion, relevant about
nis idea' (CSL3 Y1.2).

The concept of a claimed position is related to critical thinking, since it
mplies reading with an expectation of evaluating others' ideas as either
upporting the reader's argument or not. As such, it requires a degree of
onfidence that these views will be acceptable within the current forum.,
y the end of their studies, most of the participating students alluded to
pproaches to reading for assignments that encompassed this sort of fil-
ering process. Right to the end of the programme, though, it remained a
ifficulty for one of the students. In her final semester, she noted that 'the
ommon problem of my assignment is I do not own an idea myself. That
s the weak point of me' (CSR2). What particularly interested me was that
ne expressed the final comment in a whisper, giving it the air of a shame-
ul confession. This was in spite of having previously described herself as a
onfident student and active participant in class. The final step in making a
ull claim to identity as a New Zealand university student eluded her, to her
bvious disappointment.

I will examine this aspect further through the experiences of two con-
rasting students, CSL5 and CSL2 (see also Skyrme, 2007). CSL5 gave prom-
nence to framing assignments around his own views and experience. In
is second semester, he expressed a balance between his ideas and those of
ne books he read: 'The first I will write what I think and what I read at the
ooks' (Y1.4). Already he prided himself that he had learned to 'read the
uestion in a different way. Sometimes…I can read the book in different
vay and I get the opinion in my own' (Y1.4). CSL5 continued measuring his
rowth as a student in terms of his independence, and in his final semester
f study he determinedly referred everything back through the filter of his
wn understanding:

> First I will get the topic of this class, of this paper and then I will think
> about my previous experience and if I'm no experience then I will look-
> ing for some book, some sources, and then relate to the situation, to the
> experience, to the real world. (Y2)

t was his experience and knowledge of the world which was the pivot of his
pproach to writing.

In contrast, CSL2 was dependent on his teachers to a degree that seemed
n direct contravention of Western university values. His first response on
eceiving an assignment topic was to read it, think about it a little, then
o and discuss it with the teacher to find out what was required, rather

than try to 'guess' the intention, as he put it, through a process of pee
discussion:

> I'm very very enjoying to ask lecturer question.... I can go their offic
> maybe ten times, twenty times only for assignments and keep annoyin
> them. ... Rather than I ask my friends ... I think it's totally rubbish. Becaus
> all the assignments is all from the lecturers. So why we need to do assigr
> ments? How the assignments will achieve his opinion and what's about h
> idea to analyse this assignment, what's he think about assignments. (Y3)

It must be noted that this approach was not universally welcomed by h
teachers: some gave him short shrift. In his major area of study, howeve
teachers appeared to accept it and this resulted in some excellent assigr
ment grades. The contrast with CSL5, though, was striking: not only di
CSL2 not feel driven to own an idea, but he did not even see himself as th
owner of his own writing.

Neither CSL5 nor CSL2 was a particularly spectacular student: both ha
failures in their undergraduate careers. What interested me in examining th
adaptation to the new culture of learning was the fact that two such very di
ferent approaches – one apparently aligned with the university's demand fc
autonomy, and the other seeming to eschew everything it stood for – coul
both make their way to the Holy Grail of a completed degree. Was adherenc
to the university's core values as important as might be supposed?

8.6   Discussion and conclusion

As their words show, the participants in this study were aware of a nee
to adjust to a new culture of learning, and they craved explicit guidance
What guidance they did find was often contradictory or unattainable a
their current level of linguistic and academic proficiency, as in the cas
of avoiding plagiarism. Although some help was available within the un:
versity, other disciplinary-specific support was puzzlingly unavailable: fc
example, the provision of models, which suggested themselves as obviou
to the students (since they are commonly provided in China, where thi
is widely considered 'good' teaching). In this environment, one of th
key sources of enlightenment for these new writers of English was mor
advanced peers through such means as advice (CSL1) and 'model' marke
assignments (CSL3). The importance of peers in promoting learning ha
been highlighted in the work of Vygotsky and those who followed hin
(see, for example, Cortazzi et al., 2001; Lantolf, 2002). However, the assist
ance peers give may not always be perfect and would ideally be supple
mented by experts in the field. Here, then, are implications for disciplinar
teachers to reflect on how novices can learn appropriate discourses, and t
consider how they might take a role in making their discourses more ex
plicit in ways which would enable these students to write more correctly

or example, Karen Macbeth (2010) makes a considered case for the use of models in this process.

From time to time during the period of my research and beyond, I have heard university teachers talk of international students who 'only want to get a degree'. In my research I found no student who *only* wanted to get a degree, for all that this was a key goal. They dreamed of many other gains from their sojourn. As Lave and Wenger (1991) point out, learning over such long trajectory involves the negotiation of new identities, both interim and future. The aspiration to the imagined identity of graduate was supported by the desire for a sense of membership in the current community, of an interim identity as a competent and confident New Zealand university student (see Skyrme, 2008b), and it was clear that most students recognized elements of autonomy that were implied in the full enactment of this identity. The excitement with which CSL3 initially embraced the notion of new freedoms in his writing is one manifestation of this.

Kelleen Toohey and Bonny Norton (2003: 68), however, caution that 'the conditions under which language learners speak [or write] are often highly challenging, engaging the learners' identities in complex and often contradictory ways' – ways which bring questions of power into strong focus. Given the conditions that prevailed – the high-stakes assessment for almost all the writing on which they received feedback, the frequent demands for new genres, and perhaps the influence of their earlier cultural initiation to a preference for mastery over autonomy – it is hardly surprising that a degree of trade-off between the two desired identities was demanded. As CSL3 put it, the more autonomous path was often 'too risky'. There was certainly a sense of disappointment in that decision for CSL3, and in CSR2's whispered confession. This disappointment is in itself a sign of the partial alignment they had reached with the new culture of learning, recognizing, even if unable to attain it, that confidence in one's own thinking was an indicator of legitimate, enacted New Zealand studenthood.

Being myself thoroughly enculturated in the Western academy, these instances of withdrawal from, or lack of access to, the ideal of autonomy left me, too, initially with a sense of disappointment. I was more warmed by CSL5's pursuit of his own understandings than by CSL2's determined dependence on his teachers (successful though it proved to be). However, as I considered the strategic thinking and diligence with which they pursued their goals, I found a more useful lens to consider it through, one that also related to selfhood, the notion of *agency*.

Autonomy (as used in the higher education literature that I have cited) can be seen to refer to the individual's relationship with a discipline, indicating an ability to act in some sense independently as a member. It is generally used as a more public notion than *agency* (as used in sociocultural literature), which tends to refer to more personalized ways of claiming identity and acting intentionally in the world. The distinction is made by Nesta Devine and Ruth Irwin (2005), who see agency as a wider concept accounting for spaces in which individuals can 'accept, modify, alienate or find alternatives to the prevailin[g] paradigm' (p. 327), including the 'motives, practices and self understandin[g] of human beings in relation to the tangled complexities of the environmen[t]' (p. 326).

The effective tertiary writer's exercise of autonomy would include bein[g] able to use the library, research a topic, reflect on the ideas encountered an[d] integrate them into one's own understandings, then independently produc[e] an assignment which meets course requirements without excessive depend[d]ence on teachers, fellow students, sources or other models of the genre i[n] question. However, finding more subterranean passages through the univer[r]sity which are less visible to and approved by others, but which serve one'[s] own ends as a student. These might include borrowing a student's marke[d] assignments or making multiple visits to teachers.

Is it possible to envisage autonomy in the absence of agency? Hardly, sinc[e] the personal investment that is associated with agency drives the acquisitio[n] and exercise of autonomy. On the other hand, we might see CSL2's choic[e] to retain dependent relationships with teachers, and his success in doing s[o] as an illustration of the exercise of agency without autonomy. Ultimatel[y] agency may be the more important quality for the participants in this stud[y] both within and outside the university, since their own aspirations wer[e] not an exact match with those of the institution itself, and their eventua[l] imagined identity was as an agent in their own lives in the world beyond. I[t] certainly allowed these students to find ways to subvert to some extent th[e] culture of learning in which they were immersed. Agency enabled CSL2, fo[r] example, who greatly favoured oral communication over written, to experi[i]ence the university the way he wanted in his frequent consultations with hi[s] teachers.

Lave and Wenger (1991) point out that when novices negotiate new iden[n]tities within communities of practice, resulting change is inevitably mutua[l] as the existing community learns in some way to accommodate this ne[w] identity. The possibilities for reciprocal learning, when Western teachers mee[t] Chinese learners, have been discussed by others such as in Cortazzi and Ji[n] (1996) and Tianshu Zhao and Jill Bourne (2011). Cortazzi and Jin advocat[e] a 'cultural synergy' (p. 201) leading to enhanced intercultural competenc[e] on the part of both groups, which can be seen as an optimal outcome of th[e] presence of international students within the university. One aspect of th[e] resultant change may be a wider interpretation on the part of Western uni[i]versities of what autonomy may mean (see for example, Littlewood, 1999).

In fact, within the interviews there was evidence that participants wer[e] exercising a degree of intellectual autonomy beyond the confines of th[e] university: for example, using concepts learned in their study to reflect o[n] the news (CSL5), or to analyse relationships and structures in a tiresom[e] holiday job and imagine improvements to them (CSL2). Ultimately, it wa[s] heartening that these Chinese students achieved their imagined identity a[s] New Zealand university graduates and were able to carry their learning int[o]

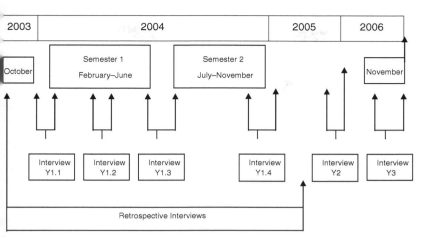

ppendix 8.1   Timeline of data collection

1eir own worlds, even though they might not have been an exact fit with 1e university's graduate profiles.

.eferences

basi, A.R. & Akbari, N. (2008) Are we encouraging patchwriting? Reconsidering the role of the pedagogical context in ESL student writers' transgressive intertextuality. *English for Specific Purposes*, 27 (3), 267–84.

basi, A.R. & Graves, B. (2008) Academic literacy and plagiarism: Conversations with international graduate students and disciplinary professors. *Journal of English for Academic Purposes*, 7, 221–33.

llison, D. (2004) Creativity, students' academic writing, and EAP: Exploring comments on writing in an English language degree programme. *Journal of English for Academic Purposes*, 3, 191–209.

ngelil-Carter, S. (2000) *Stolen language? Plagiarism in writing*. Harlow, UK: Pearson Education.

akhtin, M.M. (1986) *Speech genres and other late essays*, V.W. McGee (Trans.). Austin, TX: University of Texas Press.

iggs, J.B. (1996) Western misconceptions of the Confucian heritage learning culture. In D.A. Watkins & J.B. Biggs (Eds), *The Chinese learner: Cultural, psychological and contextual influences*. Hong Kong: Comparative Education Research Centre, pp. 45–68.

handrasoma, R., Thompson, C. & Pennycook, A. (2004) Beyond plagiarism: Transgressive and nontransgressive intertextuality. *Journal of Language, Identity & Education*, 3 (3), 171–93. doi: doi.org/10.1207/s15327701jlie0303_1

ortazzi, M. & Jin, L. (1996) Cultures of learning: Language classrooms in China. In H. Coleman (Ed.), *Society and the language classroom*. Cambridge: Cambridge University Press, pp. 169–206.

ortazzi, M. & Jin, L. (1997) Communication for learning across cultures. In D. McNamara & R. Harris (Eds), *Overseas students in higher education: Issues in teaching and learning*. London: Routledge, pp. 76–90.

Cortazzi, M., Jin, L., Wall, D. & Cavendish, S. (2001) Sharing learning through narr tive communication. *International Journal of Language and Communication Disorde* 36 (Supplement), 252–7.

Devine, N. & Irwin, R. (2005) Autonomy, agency and education: He tangata, he tan ata, he tangata. *Educational Philosophy and Theory*, 37 (3), 317–31. doi: doi:10.111 j.1469–5812.2005.00122.x

Dooley, K. (2001) Re-envisioning teacher preparation: Lessons from China. *Journal Education for Teaching*, 27 (3), 241–51.

Emerson, L. (Ed.) (2005) *Writing guidelines for business students*. Southbank, Vie Thomson Dunmore Press.

Gao, X. (2006) Understanding Chinese students' teacher dependence. In T.S.(Farrell (Ed.), *Language teacher research in Asia*. Alexandria, VA: Teachers of Englis to Speakers of Other Languages, pp. 61–74.

Gee, J.P. (2004) Learning language as a matter of learning social languages withi Discourses. In M.R. Hawkins (Ed.), *Language learning and teacher education: A soci. cultural approach*. Buffalo, NY: Multilingual Matters, pp. 11–31.

Harwood, N. & Hadley, G. (2004) Demystifying institutional practices: Critical pra, matism and the teaching of academic writing. *English for Specific Purposes*, 2 355–77.

Helms-Park, R. & Stapleton, P. (2003) Questioning the importance of individualize voice in undergraduate L2 argumentative writing: An empirical study with ped gogical implications. *Journal of Second Language Writing*, 12, 245–65.

Holmes, P. (2004) Negotiating differences in learning and intercultural communic tion. *Business Communication Quarterly*, 67 (3), 294–307.

Howard, R.M. (1992) A plagiarism pentimento. *Journal of Teaching Writing*, 11 (2 233–45.

Hyland, K. (2002) Authority and invisibility: Authorial identity in academic writin, *Journal of Pragmatics*, 34, 1091–112.

Ivanič, R. & Camps, D. (2001) I am how I sound: Voice as self-representation in L writing. *Journal of Second Language Writing*, 10, 3–33.

Jin, L. & Cortazzi, M. (2006) Changing practices in Chinese cultures of learning. I T. Coverdale-Jones & P. Rastall (Eds),The Chinese Learner, special issue of *Languag Culture and Curriculum*, 19 (1), 5–20.

Kato, K. (2001) Exploring 'cultures of learning': A case of Japanese and Australia classrooms. *Journal of Intercultural Studies*, 22 (1), 51–67.

Kubota, R. (2004) Critical multiculturalism and second language education. In I Norton & K. Toohey (Eds), *Critical pedagogies and language learning*. Cambridg Cambridge University Press, pp. 30–52.

Kutz, E. (2004) From outsider to insider: Studying academic discourse communitie across the curriculum. In V. Zamel & R. Spack (Eds), *Crossing the curriculum: Multilingu learners in college classrooms*. Mahwah, NJ: Lawrence Erlbaum, pp. 75–93.

Lantolf, J.P. (2002) Sociocultural theory and second language acquisition. In R.I Kaplan (Ed.), *The Oxford handbook of applied linguistics*. Oxford: Oxford Universit Press, pp. 104–14.

Lave, J. & Wenger, E. (1991) *Situated learning: Legitimate Peripheral Participation*. Ne York: Cambridge University Press.

Le Ha, P. (2006) Plagiarism and overseas students: Stereotypes again? *ELT Journal*, 6 (1), 76–8. doi: 10.1093/elt/cci085

Lea, M.R. & Street, B.V. (1998). Student writing in higher education: An academic li eracies approach. *Studies in Higher Education*, 23 (2), 157–72.

Lillis, T.M. (2001) *Student writing: Access, regulation, desire*. London: Routledge.

ttlewood, W. (1999) Defining and developing autonomy in East Asian contexts. *Applied Linguistics*, 20 (1), 71–94.

u, D. (2005) Plagiarism in ESOL students: Is cultural conditioning truly the major culprit? *ELT Journal*, 59 (3), 234–41.

acbeth, K.P. (2010) Deliberate false provisions: The use and usefulness of models in learning academic writing. *Journal of Second Language Writing*, 19, 33–48.

oore, T. & Morton, J. (2005) Dimensions of difference: A comparison of university writing and IELTS writing. *Journal of English for Academic Purposes*, 4 (1), 43–66.

ightingale, P. & O'Neill, M. (1994) Defining quality. In P. Nightingale & M. O'Neill (Eds), *Achieving quality learning in higher education*. London: Kogan Page, pp. 7–14.

arris-Kidd, H. & Barnett, J. (2011) Cultures of learning and student participation: Chinese learners in a multicultural English class in Australia. In L. Jin & M. Cortazzi (Eds), *Researching Chinese learners: Skills, perceptions and intercultural adaptations*. Basingstoke, UK: Palgrave Macmillan, pp. 169–87.

ascarella, E.T. & Terenzini, P.T. (2005) *How college affects students*, Vol. 2. San Francisco: Jossey-Bass.

ennycook, A. (1996) Borrowing others' words: Text, ownership, memory and plagiarism. *TESOL Quarterly*, 30, 201–30.

amanathan, V. & Atkinson, D. (1999) Individualism, academic writing and ESL writers. *Journal of Second Language Writing*, 8 (1), 45–75.

udzki, R. (2005) On being a business student. In L. Emerson (Ed.), *Writing guidelines for business students* (3rd edn). Southbank, Vic.: Thomson Dunmore Press, pp. 10–13.

xyrme, G. (2007) Entering the university: The differentiated experience of two Chinese international students in a New Zealand university. *Studies in Higher Education*, 32 (3), 357–72.

xyrme, G.(2008a) Expectations, Emerging Issues and Change for Chinese International Students in a New Zealand University. Unpublished Doctoral Thesis, Massey University, Palmerston North, NZ.

xyrme, G. (2008b) *I am who I am: New senses of self in a New Zealand university*. Paper presented at the CLESOL 2008, Auckland, New Zealand.

xyrme, G. (2011) Getting the big picture: A longitudinal study of adaptation and identity in a New Zealand university. In L. Jin & M. Cortazzi (Eds), *Researching Chinese learners: Skills, perceptions and intercultural adaptations*. Basingstoke, UK: Palgrave Macmillan, pp. 188–211.

owden, C. (2005) Plagiarism and the culture of multilingual students in higher education abroad. *ELT Journal*, 59 (3), 226–33.

esch, R. (1990) *Qualitative research: Analysis types and software tools*. New York: The Falmer Press.

oohey, K. & Norton, B. (2003) Learner autonomy as agency in social settings. In D. Palfreyman & R.C. Smith (Eds), *Learner autonomy across cultures*. New York: Palgrave Macmillan, pp. 58–72.

Walker, J. (1998) Student plagiarism in universities: What are we doing about it? *Higher Education Research & Development*, 17 (1), 89–106.

Weigle, S.C. (2005) Second language writing expertise. In K. Johnson (Ed.), *Expertise in second language learning and teaching*. Basingstoke, UK: Palgrave Macmillan, pp. 128–49.

Wenger, E. (1998) *Communities of practice: Learning, meaning and identity*. Cambridge: Cambridge University Press.

Wingate, U. (2006) Doing away with 'study skills'. *Teaching in Higher Education*, 11 (4), 457–69.

Zhang, S. (2003) An analysis of the situation of persons in the Beijing area with ac demic histories at or above the junior college level who go abroad for self-fund studies. *Chinese Education and Society*, 36 (2), 44–62.

Zhao, T. & Bourne, J. (2011) Intercultural adaptation – it's a two-way process: Exampl from a British MBA programme. In L. Jin & M. Cortazzi (Eds), *Researching Chine learners: Skills, perceptions and intercultural adaptations*. Basingstoke, UK: Palgra Macmillan, pp. 250–73.

Part III

Transcultural Adjustment and Bridging Distances

9

Teaching German in Eastern Europe and China: Reciprocal Relationships between Teaching and Learning Cultures

Markus Lux and Christian Wochele

> Those who teach in a foreign country are forced to do something that is inherently difficult: to relativize ideas and ideologies, facts and values that have shaped and determined their childhoods and youths and which they perceive as unalterable. These teachers must distance themselves from their own educational systems, which have become second nature as they fought their way through them themselves – with more or less success and ease. And they must realize that in the countries where they are now, other values and ideas are just as unalterable and self-evident.
>
> Sigrid Freunek, teacher in Nižnij Novgorod, Russia, 2001–04 (Freunek, 2005: 50)

.1 The context for programs of teaching German

⸮n the mid-1980s, Mikhail Gorbachev's policies of *glasnost* ('openness') and *?erestroika* (political and economic 'restructuring') marked the beginning ⸮f a transformation process in Central and Eastern Europe. The collapse of ⸮ommunism in this region from 1989 onwards resulted in a new openness ⸮r Western foreign languages and new methods of teaching them. As a con-⸮equence, an increasing number of teachers from Europe and the United ⸮tates were sent to Eastern Europe and later also to Asia (mainly to China), ⸮arting in the early 1990s. Germany and Austria took the lead in this devel-⸮pment for two reasons. One is their geographical proximity, and also the ⸮istorical ties that had been severed more than 40 years before. The other ⸮ the German language, which had played an important role in the USSR. ⸮erman was the most important Western foreign language. It was, after all, spoken in the German Democratic Republic (GDR [East Germany], 1949–90) one of the 'socialist brother countries'. Therefore, these German-speaking countries promoted their language so that German, rather than English would attain the status of a *lingua franca*. As we now know, those attempts were futile; English has become the *global language* in this region, too, and has even turned into an *emblem of a global identity* (Jackson, 2010: 9).

During this period, a multitude of programs were developed for sending teachers and lecturers to Central and Eastern Europe to teach German at schools and universities. Sponsors were mainly governmental or semi-governmental organizations such as the German Academic Exchange Service (DAAD) and the Pädagogischer Austauschdienst (Educational Exchange Service) (PAD) in Germany and the Austrian Agency for International Mobility and Cooperation in Education, Science and Research (OeAD) in Austria. Private-sector institutions were active, too, especially the Robert Bosch Stiftung GmbH (RBSG) in Stuttgart, which has been promoting German-Polish relations since 1974. Promoting the German language abroad and, reciprocally, the languages of Germany's neighbouring states in Germany has always been a cornerstone of the foundation's activities. This goes back to its founder, the entrepreneur Robert Bosch, who regarded languages as the key to international understanding (Robert Bosch Stiftung, 2001) and central to the foundation's aims of developing science, health, education, culture, and international relations.

One measure that has survived to the present day is the lectureship program for universities in Central Europe and later for Eastern Europe and China, which started in 1993. Based on reciprocity, this program drew from the experience of a tutoring program, started in 1992, which filled teaching positions at universities in the former GDR with young French and American teachers. The lectureship program, coordinated jointly by RBSG with the Eastern Europe Centre at the University of Hohenheim since 1999, aims to address the demand for lecturers who are native German speakers and, in addition to their field of expertise, communicate a young, vibrant image of Germany at universities in Eastern Europe and China. The program also allows university graduates to gather professional experience at universities abroad. The lecturers become qualified through teaching and carrying out projects as well as by learning the respective language of their host country – strengthening the relationship between Germany and their host country in the process.

Wherever they go, these teachers of German come into contact with very different learning cultures – cultures that invariably differ significantly from the ones in which they themselves grew up. In order to convey an appropriately up to date picture of the target foreign language's cultural sphere (in this case, Germany), teachers must also be familiar with the learning culture and teaching methods current in Germany. The young lecturers and their students often find themselves torn between the local teacher roven, familiar methods and the guest teacher's interesting but sometimes ard-to-adapt-to methods. However, this tension also constitutes an oppor- inity for the lectureship program. The young teachers are encouraged to se their stay not only to teach but also to learn from a foreign culture, if nly by reflecting on their experiences. This chapter addresses this under- ring conflict.

.2   Key questions and the research approach

he lectureship program offers the opportunity to study the impact, on oung teachers, of longer-term teaching positions in countries in tran- tional development. At the same time, we can take stock of the various arning cultures in Eastern Europe and China and how they have changed ver the last 10 years. We can ask:

What are the challenges that await guest lecturers at their teaching posi- tions in Eastern Europe and China?
To what extent were cultural synergies possible – how and when do both sides profit from learning about the other's teaching/learning culture?
How has the encounter with other teaching/learning cultures impacted on the teachers' working methods after their lectureships have ended?

fter finishing their lectureships, the majority of lecturers found employ- ient at universities, schools and further education facilities or by start- ig their own businesses (Hüsken, 2011: 21). Thus, an inventory of various arning cultures in Eastern Europe and China, together with the ongoing nanges over the past decade, is emerging through their reports. Fortunately, iost teaching locations are at smaller universities far removed from the iajor urban areas, and so it is possible to study the periphery, which more ften than not falls by the wayside in research. Of course, we must recog- ize the vast differences between the developments in the educational land- :apes of Central and Eastern Europe and China, which makes comparisons ifficult. Similar to the development of democracy, we find an East–West ivide (Poland–Russia) and also a North–South divide (Baltic states–Balkan :ates) in the educational systems of the Eastern Europe region, especially 'ith respect to the universities' technical facilities (Peters, 2006: 173f.).

The RBSG lectureship program differs somewhat from the placement pro- rams run by (semi-) governmental institutions such as the DAAD or the •eAD. Even though the main objective is establishing good relations be- veen Germany and the target countries via teaching the German language nd conveying an authentic image of Germany, the program is designed ） be a further education program for young professionals from German-)eaking countries. The formal expression of this is the fact that the lec- ırers receive a grant from the foundation to sustain themselves, and that they enter into a formal employer–employee relationship with the host in stitution. More important, however, are the close guidance and continuing education elements. In addition to teaching and carrying out projects, the lecturers also complete a professional training program entitled 'Educatio Management at Universities in Eastern Europe and China'. This train ing program, started in 2006 and specially developed for the lectureship program in cooperation with the Organization Studies Department at the University of Hildesheim, uniquely combines theoretical knowledge with practical experience based on the concept of life-long learning. At the same time, the training program constitutes a basis from which lecturers can launch their careers after completing the lectureship. Increasingly, the lectureship program can be regarded as a building block for the process of life-long learning. As a consequence, the grant invariably ends after two years; until 2006, it was possible to extend it to three years. Evaluations have shown that a third year did not produce any improvements in the fields of teaching quality, motivation or project intensity among partic pants (Deckers, 2008: 22); thus, a two-year period of service seems to meet the developmental aims for the participating lecturers.

Since our study analyses the perspectives of these teaching participants (as evidenced in their reports and some interviews), their status needs to be recognized. The lecturers are graduates, comparatively young when they start their lectureships for teaching German, and they do not usually bring previous professional teaching experience with them: not even 20 per cent of them had taught professionally prior to starting the lectureship (Deckers 2008: A7–3). On the other hand, more than half of all lecturers had already worked in a professional or self-employed position (Hüsken, 2011: 18). The prospect of a professional qualification is one of the most important incen tives for applying for a lectureship; however, the continuing development of one's own personality is at least as important to applicants (Deckers, 2008 18). Notably, their sojourns were for two years, during which their goal included becoming familiar with local languages, people and cultures, in line with explicit program aims and the professional qualification they sought.

In this study, we examine the period between 2000 and 2010. This limi tation was chosen for program-internal as well as program-external rea sons. Many countries in Central and Eastern Europe have since joined the European Union (EU) and participate in the Bologna Process, which aim to develop comparable and compatible degrees, promote student mobility and ensure high quality teaching within and beyond the EU. This partici pation has caused major changes in their educational systems. In addition the RBSG program has undergone several reforms. The spectrum of coun tries shifted as a consequence of the withdrawal from Central Europe and expansion into China; also, continuing education has joined teaching and project work as a third major element of the program. The primary emphasis

f this study is, therefore, on the learning cultures in Eastern Europe. The
rogram has been active in China only since 2008 (for studies on Chinese
arners in Anglo-American and Chinese research, see Coverdale-Jones,
006, 2009).

The basis of the study is documentary analysis of the program evalua-
ons (Deckers, 2008; Litta and Peters, 2009; Hüsken, 2011) and especially
ie internal reports by the lecturers. These are submitted twice a year to the
rogram coordinators and offer insight into the local situation, classroom
nd project work, and also into the personal development of the lecturer.
s they were not meant for publication they allow an unfiltered view of
ich lecturer's perception (to preserve anonymity, names and places are not
iven here, only the country and year). Overall, 312 reports during the study
eriod were analysed to distil common themes from 25 countries: Albania,
rmenia, Bulgaria, Bosnia-Herzegovina, Belarus, China, Estonia, Georgia,
:roatia, Kazakhstan, Kyrgyzstan, Latvia, Lithuania, Macedonia, Moldova,
oland, Russia, Romania, Slovakia, Serbia, the Czech Republic, Tajikistan,
.ungary, Ukraine and Uzbekistan.

Former lecturer Andreas Umland deserves special credit for publishing
ur volumes of field reports and analyses by German guest lecturers in
astern Europe (Umland, 2005; Berghorn et al., 2006; Bürgel and Umland,
009). These contributions were used, as were the unpublished term papers
iat some lecturers wrote as coursework in Hildesheim University's con-
nuing education program (cited here with only the writer's initials (HA),
ountry and year). The results were reviewed by conducting interviews with
lected participants.

.3   Perceptions of teaching and learning cultures –
hallenges for lecturers

Vhen starting their lectureships, as recent graduates of no more than five
ears standing, the lecturers experience a fundamental shift of perspec-
ve. They are now career starters, and switch roles: former learners become
achers in a more or less alien environment. They are required to make
ie transition from the familiar to the unknown. The key for approaching
ie unknown is the acquisition of its terminology, and this is what Sigrid
'reunek did once she had started her lectureship in Russia. It is also true
or the entire post-Soviet area. She notes, 'If you attempt to think through
ie unknown in your own words and in your own terminology, you risk a
iisunderstanding in the truest sense of the word' (Freunek, 2005: 51). For
istance, terms such as *hardworking* (*trudit'cja*) or *learn by heart* (*vyučit' nai-
ıst'*) have positive connotations in Russian, but in German, they tend be
egative. Even if *education* and *obrazovannie* are formal linguistic equiva-
nts, they are used in different ways: the Russian term encompasses *train-
ıg*, which the German term does not (Freunek, 2005: 56ff.).

It is these terms recurring in the lecturers' reports that characterize the perception of learning cultures in Central and Eastern Europe and Chin. The terms that make a regional differentiation across the entire decade a most impossible are: *schoolification, hierarchy, corruption,*[1] *lack of motivatior plagiarism;* also: *composure, adaptation, freedom, self-confidence, intimacy, an* so forth. These terms are mentioned regardless of the lecturers' location which prompts us for the present purpose to regard Eastern Europe an China as one study area (though we recognize much differentiation in oth spheres). From our point of view, this grouping is not only possible, but a tually preferable. Although Chinese learning culture is heavily influence by the Confucian cultural heritage, the mark of more than 60 years of s cialism and the impact of a rapidly evolving educational landscape cann be simply ignored, and calling in this tradition as the sole basis of learnin in China means relying on a deficient model (Clark and Gieve, 2006). It important to remember that China in the 1950s and 1960s was strongl influenced by the Soviet Union, particularly in the many fields of languag training and continuing education. This influence deteriorated in the 198C and has virtually disappeared today, although, mutual interest has bee rekindled. It is understood that the Soviet Union exerted formidable inflι ence on all other then-socialist countries in Eastern Europe between 194 and 1990.

The many parallels to the perception of teaching and learning traditior in the successor states of the former Soviet Union suggest that, for Chini ideology has a stronger impact on learning than is often assumed. One le turer observed (Report China, 2009–10): 'Working at the university giv me ... good insight into the Chinese working world and the Chinese educ: tional system. I find the relationship between politics and the education: system particularly interesting. What happens in the classroom is directl related to it, and vice versa.'

However, there appears to be a major structural difference betwee Eastern Europe and China: ultimately, education in China enjoys a muc higher priority. This can be explained not only by the much larger publi investments China makes in its educational system, which evokes a sense c advance and progress in many places, but also by the 'Soviet' division int research (Academy of Sciences) and education (university), which is still i place in much of Eastern Europe. Teachers in Eastern Europe have a muc stronger background in teaching than in research. The teaching of factu: knowledge prevails. If a teacher attempts to introduce scientific discussio and critical methods, the students often feel overtaxed. 'The teaching sta therefore rarely calls for systematic changes, and, what is perhaps worse: th students do not demand a systemic change either' (Tischer, 2006: 127f.).

Despite negative population growth in all these countries (again, e> cluding China) university studies became much more attractive. Only i the last two years can stagnation be observed (for Russia: Rostat, 2010; fc

hina: National Bureau of Statistics of China, 2011). Since 1989, the number
f students in the Russian Federation alone has almost tripled. The causes
an usually be found in the relatively short time at school and in the lack of
pportunities for vocational training. A lecturer notes for Belarus:

In addition, approximately 60 to 70 per cent of high school graduates
begin studies at university because of the absence of other training
opportunities and because vocational schools have an extremely bad
image. (Report Belarus, 2008–09)

he selection of study subjects is mainly pragmatic and career-related.
tudying here is not so much regarded as voluntary acquisition of know-
dge (and thus an opportunity), but rather as a mere necessity' (Report
ussia, 2005–06). This is remarkable since foreign-language studies, along
ith the management disciplines, law, and engineering sciences, count
mong the more popular options because they open the door to university
udies abroad. University studies usually require the payment of tuition
es and successfully passed admission tests. These are partly conducted
entrally (in China by the *gaokao* national university admission test) and
artly by the faculties or departments. Thus, in most cases the choice of the
eld of study depends on the probability of achieving as positive a result as
ossible on the certification test.

At the same time, starting university studies signifies clear guidelines
egarding the timetable and, besides disciplinary specialization, participa-
on in general education subjects such as physical education, political geog-
aphy, world history, literature and so forth. A lecturer describes an extreme
ase:

The students are required to participate in a range of subjects that
have nothing to do with their chosen subjects (e.g., ecology, history of
Kazakhstan, Kazakh language). This general teaching is supplemented by
the relevant specialist teaching and a large amount of language tuition
(English and German). This adds up to a teaching workload of up to 36
hours per week plus homework. (Report Kazakhstan, 2008–09)

hese factors have a direct impact on the motivation of students in the
lassroom: students aim to achieve a degree in the shortest possible time.
ow much effort the students make in the course of their studies depends
rimarily on the expectations formulated in the tests. The general guideline
: 'Do not think, but write (copy down), learn (by heart) and pass (the test)'
ürgel, 2006: 47). 'For the tests, something is learned by heart and quickly
rgotten soon after' (Report Albania, 2008–09). Memorization is the most
ommon learning strategy for learning foreign languages in both regions.
China, this is often legitimized by referring to Confucianism (Li and

Cutting, 2011). In the post-Soviet area, this is explained with reference t
Lenin's demand for 'learning, learning and more learning' – in spite of th
fact that Lenin never actually explained what should be learned and ho
(Freunek, 2005: 51).

The number of *extrinsic constraints* is another factor that cannot be unde
estimated; these range from the division into study years with fixed cla:
allocations and compulsory attendance to the threat of deregistratio
for the failure to pass an exam. Thus, German lecturers often regard the:
students as being *dependent*. In Kiev, Antje Kirchhof is puzzled by the intere:
of her students in learning the German language 'without content, as a kin
of pure form', and she criticizes the lack of awareness 'that a foreign lar
guage means a different world view' (Kirchhof, 2006: 84f.). As a methoo
lecture-style teaching meets the needs of her students for specific, tangibl
facts quite well. Not surprisingly, therefore, encouragement to look for cre
ative interpretation approaches in class is often perceived by the studen
as 'disturbing and is thus blocked out and branded as impractical' (Repo
Estonia, 2004–05). Lecturers are acutely aware of this: 'Students usually pe
ceive attending lecturers' classes as a burden because they want to obtai
their degrees with as little effort as possible' (Report Albania, 2009–10).

This may well be the reason that free discussion rarely occurs, even afte
explicit encouragement from the lecturer. Students have the feeling tha
'There is always one correct answer – to every question' (Report Chin:
2009–010). Consequently, they are reluctant to give a wrong answer du
ing a discussion. This view fundamentally contradicts the value placed o
free discussion at the university, which in Germany is regarded as a place c
opinion-forming.

This contradiction is most obvious when plagiarism among studen
occurs.

> The local teachers, who themselves perform scientific work flawlessl
> and by Western standards, measure the written work of students wit
> lower or unscientific criteria. ... Among the students there is virtually n
> awareness of the problem of plagiarism; plagiarism is not perceived as
> violation. On the contrary, the compilation of information about a sp
> cific topic using verbatim adoption of text blocks is regarded as legitimat
> or even 'scientific'. (Salimi-Asl, 2005: 87)

The term used most frequently to describe the higher education system
from the perspective of a lecturer is *Verschulung* ('schoolification') or *ve
schult* ('organized like a school'); it seems that this is the key term applicabl
in all these countries and throughout the entire decade for the perceptio
of the teaching and learning culture in the host country of the lecture:
from German-speaking countries (e.g., Report Czech Republic 2001–02: *d
noch starke Verschulung der Studiengänge* ('the even stronger schoolification c

ourses of study') or Report China 2009–10: *sehr verschultes System* ('a system greatly organized like a school'). Literally, *schoolification*, means the dumbing down or infantilization of the European higher education system by making it more like school, with more attendance requirements and graded homework and less independent learning. University is associated with academic freedom on the part of the teachers as well as the students, while school is associated with studying in classes along with fixed curricula. Thus saying that academic teaching is *verschult* means it is similar to teaching in school, with little freedom to decide what to learn at what time and in what way. Such fixed-group classes, compulsory attendance, and rigid curricula are an alien concept at universities in Germany and Austria, as are personal attention from the instructor and study modules such as tutorials. This may change for German students, though, in the Bologna Process with the gradual introduction of bachelor and master's courses.

Only a few lecturers note the similarity to the more regulated system at German universities of applied sciences (*Fachhochschulen*) (Report Croatia, 2005–06). Rarely do the lecturers define the term *Verschulung* as accurately as did a lecturer in Poland:

> By this I mean that many students know little about practices of self-study and sometimes assume the role of a mere consumer. ... Open tasks or questions are met ... with bewilderment. Scientific standards and methods are not sufficiently taught at the university and (if at all) are only applied during final examinations. There are no opportunities for choice or specialization in the course of the studies. Literature and authentic materials are utilized very late and – in my opinion – not nearly sufficiently. (Report Poland, 2008–09)

However, the frequent use of this term offers insight into the – sometimes limited – self-reflection of the lecturers. It shows that, despite its drawbacks, the German university system is highly appreciated by these graduates because of its greater freedom and individualism in comparison to school. It is just this absence of freedom and teaching flexibility that is perceived by the lecturers particularly strongly in their new roles as teachers since, for them, it is part of an authentic image of Germany. This is often expressed in very emotional terms: 'Students have no chance of an individualized study program due to an ancient study structure and an outdated idea of equality' (Report Russia, 2009–10). Universities are compared with schools: 'Sometimes I had the impression of teaching at a girls' school' (Report Ukraine, 2007–08). Students are sometimes referred to as children: 'The students are very young. ... Accordingly, they behave like adolescents. They have to be reprimanded and called to order much more frequently than would be the case in Germany' (Report Russia, 2008–09).

In many cases, of course, the perception of a foreign teaching and learning culture also leads the lecturers to reflections such as the following: 'From my own experience from Germany, France, and Italy, I know that in Europe the lecture is the most common form of instruction and that university teachers generally have no training in modern teaching methods and didactics' (Salimi-Asl, 2005: 83).

'The most remarkable factor for someone from a German university is the much more intense personal relationship between students and university teachers' (Klement, 2005: 74). Being a stranger in a foreign country, many lecturers appreciate this close contact with colleagues and students. However, it is also regarded as problematic: 'Those friendly relations, however, foster a kind of "intellectual dependence" of the students on the opinion of the teacher' (Report Ukraine, 2008–09).

In addition, an unfamiliar and often stressful issue unfolds: the personal closeness brings with it the responsibility 'to be accountable for the performance of students and their grades' (Report Ukraine, 2005–06). Ultimately, the lecturers experience the conflict of balancing their own expectations and experiences, the demands of the university and the students' needs: 'My task, then, is to satisfy three parties that cannot be reconciled with sound teaching' (Kirchhof, 2006: 86). 'I often had the feeling of being stuck in a vicious cycle of appalling teaching and utter disinterest on behalf of the students' (Report Lithuania, 2004–05). From the perspective of the students, the conflict certainly looks very different: 'The German lecturers expect them to reflect and form an opinion; the Czech teachers expect them to be intelligent, inquisitive and quiet' (Report Czech Republic, 2005–06).

9.4 Reactions of the lecturers: their opportunities in the host learning culture

There comes a point when the ideas of the lecturers about self-directed learning and the freedom of the learner to acquire self-selected content collide with understanding the foreign culture. At some point, almost every lecturer asks himself or herself the classic questions: 'Should I apply the [W]estern standards that I brought with me on a one-to-one basis? Or should I take a step back, adapt, and enjoy the small but nevertheless undeniable successes?' (Peters, 2006: 175f.). The lecturers therefore seek some free space to adjust their own ideas about the teacher's role. This search usually begins with discussions with the local contact persons, department employees or the department management. The readiness to question proven principles and traditions, forever established in the teaching and learning culture, varies considerably. However, even in places where the grammar–translation method for learning a language has been deemed expedient, knowledge about alternatives can be found. For many years, teacher-training institutions such as the Goethe Institute and language schools that use more recent textbooks from Germany have informed people about the benefits of the communication- and activity-oriented teaching of a foreign language. Thus, they create at least some readiness in university departments to look into those 'modern methods'. Lecturers are therefore often regarded as ambassadors of a modern teaching approach, which they are to practice on the students (albeit within existing and prescribed limits). Specific exceptions exist whereby a 'common departmental culture or an exchange of approaches and methods' do not exist (Report China, 2009).

From the lecturers' reports it is clear that a lecturer in a host university department can always factor in a certain degree of exoticism. There is no need to answer the question if this exoticism is attributable to themselves or to their personal conduct. Their involvement in the department puts the lecturers in an exposed position: although there is an employment contract and thus integration into the formal hierarchical system of the host institution, the lecturer, as recipient of a grant, is not nearly as dependent on the salary as are many local colleagues. At the same time, his or her perspective is limited to a maximum stay of two years. It is observable that lecturers act within their host institutions with a limited risk awareness when it comes to dealing with superiors or circumventing rigid rules and standards: 'On the outside, teaching is tightly organized in a school-like manner. On the inside, however, I have great latitude in implementation' (Report Moldova, 2007–08).

This fact should not make us ignore the considerable resistance that lecturers have to face in their attempts to apply their 'new methods'. There are numerous cases in which lecturers had to make their claims slowly and over a long period of time. At the same time, even those departments that claimed to be interested in communicative teaching methods did not adapt their structural framework for teaching. Thus, it is not unheard of that a lecturer for timetabled 'conversation' practices the skill of speaking with his students, but they then have to take a written test in that same subject. However, lecturers are often provided creative spaces within which they can practice their preferred forms of teaching. Lecturing is a testing ground for them, especially if they want to make teaching a career: 'Most of all, I benefited from being able to prepare my lessons and test whether my teaching is successful' (Report Latvia, 2004–05).

Creative spaces are opened either directly, if, for example, the department management launches a project to improve the quality of teaching by defining standards with reference to the European framework for languages (HA China, 2008), or if the dean asks the lecturer 'to organize teachers' training, so that lessons become more varied and topical' (HA Ukraine, 2008). In the majority of cases, however, the creative possibilities open up indirectly: 'It is the responsibility of the teacher/lecturer that the student passes the examination!' (Report Russia, 2009–10); how they achieve that is up to the lecturer.

Antje Kirchhof in Kiev chose to place emphasis on 'skills' rather tha
on content, and teaches methodologically diverse lessons by using, amon
other things, radio plays and comic books (Kirchhof, 2006: 87). Other le
turers use their own principles to move in a similar direction. For exampl
they strive to 'focus on the needs of the learners', 'transfer more respor
sibility for classroom work to individual learners', to 'not be at the centr
of attention all the time', 'create a pleasant learning atmosphere', or 'se
themselves as learning facilitators'. One lecturer explains that she sees h
role as 'bringing as many methods to my classes as possible that promot
learner autonomy, require creativity and commitment and, above all, mak
learning fun' (Report Russia, 2009). Over time, many lecturers recogniz
the necessity of adapting parts of their students' learning cultures that ar
initially cumbersome but useful: 'You should definitely incorporate learn
ing by heart into your teaching. And to know something by heart does no
mean you cannot think for yourself' (Klement, 2005: 72).

It would be wrong, though, to suggest that lecturers use the approach c
purposefulness for indoctrination towards a better method or even 'mis
sionary work'. Creative freedom, that innovative concept expected by th
department, those self-developed but hardly ever realized ambitions tha
lecturers hold as career starters, the high degree of responsibility for thei
own students – all these often develop into a special challenge. In som
cases, especially in the early days, such challenges frustrate and overwhelr
the lecturer. Consequently, the turning away of lecturers from the initiall
diagnosed 'dependence' of the students in the host culture results in th
urgent need for them to be clear about the objectives and methodology c
their own teaching work:

> Initially, the school-like university system discouraged me. But over tim
> I've also learned to appreciate the positive aspects of this system an
> learned not to disqualify everything as negative just because the system
> grew up in uses different methods. (Report Ukraine, 2004–05)

In the course of time, there was even increased understanding for the highl
bureaucratic and hierarchical structures within the university: 'I did learn tha
freedom also needs a framework' (Report Bosnia-Herzegovina, 2005–06).

In hindsight, most lecturers appreciate the benefits of 'learning by doin
as teachers in the classroom; this is the effective opportunity to try out ne
methods and observe reactions to them, and 'the ability to develop innova
tive approaches and solutions to problems that are alien to you' (Repor
Armenia, 2008–09). Often, the lecturers have no exact ideas about th
teaching situation in the department, and they have to approach the targe
audience and the ambitions and needs (of both the group and the lecture
carefully: 'Teaching was a process in which I had to constantly reflect o
and adapt myself and my approaches in order to be successful in workin

ith students' (Report Russia, 2009–10). A lecturer in China (HA China, 009) describes her approach:

> Through a variety of tasks in group work, I noticed, for example, that almost all learners are very musically talented, like to sing and memorize lyrics easily. Many of the students also have excellent creative and artistic skills that they regularly showcase during photo and poster exhibitions.

s this example shows, culturally induced detachment can work as a con-uit for an open mind for the follow-up teaching opportunities that lectur-rs find with young adults in the classroom. Without this knowledge, the epartment's interest in communicative teaching approaches would erode ooner or later, as the same lecturer notes reports elsewhere:

> In the area of teaching practice, I can realize my vision to the extent that the learners and their willingness permit. Experiments, however, should not be too daring, because the risk of failing in the classroom should always be kept as small as possible.

n their quest for greater self-determination among their students, many cturers go beyond classroom teaching and initiate projects as extra-curric-lar activities. These include writing workshops, environmental seminars, istory workshops and applied theater exercises. In addition, lecturers also evelop joint projects such as summer schools or seminar weeks, some with lements of experiential education, which enable the students to expand heir (linguistic) knowledge beyond the usual learning environment, for xample, in other cities or countries. This utilization of extra-curricular earning environments is being observed by many host institutions with rowing interest: since 2001, the Foundation has financially supported xtra-curricular project work on the part of the lecturers with partial fund-1g. In 2006, the lecturers' teaching load was reduced from 12 to 6 hours er week in order to open up more room for project work at the host institu-on. Remarkably, the program has not lost its appeal in any way for the host 1stitutions. Also, the annual number of applications from potential new ost universities to be incorporated in the program has remained constant.

In recent years more and more lecturers have asked themselves whether 1e knowledge transfer could take place in both directions (Polk and Reif, 009: 188). The introduction of the accompanying training program in 006 and the associated intensification of project work resulted in increased ooperation between the guest lecturers and local junior and senior man-gement. Since the mid-1990s, we have witnessed increasingly high student 10bility within Europe, but also the mobility of Chinese and Central Asian tudents to Europe and the emergence of the European Higher Education rea (under the provisions of the Bologna Process). All these provided the basis for the joint tackling of the challenges brought about by the mutual recognition of degrees and qualifications and more competence-based curricula in all participating countries (including Germany). The proportion of projects 'at eye level' has increased notably. One example is the development of a curriculum framework at the Udmurt State University in Izhevsk, Russia. The usual paradigm of communication between 'Western European experts' and 'Eastern European patients' was broken up (Polk and Reif, 2009: 182).

9.5   The effect of the lectureship on participants' future careers

Teaching abroad was helpful for almost 60 per cent of the former lecturers and was even a decisive factor for their present-day professional activities (Deckers, 2008: A7–10); more than 70 per cent agree, even years after completion of their lectureship, with the statement: 'I have acquired skills through the lectureship that I still apply today' (Hüsken, 2011: 9). They also realize that teaching without a doctorate from a German university would hardly have been possible (Report Hungary, 2004–05). One example is the statement that they 'have gained more professional experience in this year than during one year at a German university and still enjoyed more freedom' (Report Romania, 2005–06). Asked about the individual elements of the program and their importance for the professional development of lecturers, mentioned first are living abroad and teaching (Litta and Peters, 2009: 163). But what do these statements mean in practice? The follow-up study of 2010 shows that 'skills to address particular situations' are of particular importance even today:

> The highly self-responsible work and the acknowledged 'elevated' status have taught me to work confidently and purposefully with individuals and groups – this helps me today and I am very grateful. (Hüsken, 2011: 43)

In the reports, lecturers often refer to softer factors such as gain in composure, flexibility, security, self-assurance and routine, as well as the knowledge of not having to always understand everything, and that 'satisfying feeling of making a difference' (Report Russia, 2005–06). Teaching abroad also helped many lecturers to increase their improvisational talents. However, after their return, this ability was not always called for: 'I had become so accustomed to improvisation that my first seminar in Germany was promptly evaluated as "chaotic"' (Tischer, 2006: 132).

After finishing the lectureship, almost 40 per cent of the lecturers found their place in the field of educational work: as a teacher, lecturer, speaker or teacher of German as a foreign language. Some stayed abroad but switched to a different region. They were surprised to find that the differences between he learning cultures were sometimes not so great after all. Michaela lement, who moved from Russia to Great Britain, notes: 'Are there differences between my Saratov and Cambridge students? Far fewer than you ould expect! ... The urge to learn seems comparable in both groups of students, but the motivation is different' (Klement, 2005: 79).

In interviews, a number of former lecturers were asked to assess the impact of their teaching in China or Eastern Europe from today's professional erspective. The results of analysing these interviews will be outlined using hree examples. In the first case, a former specialist lecturer in economics escribes how concerned he was that his students were more interested in earning subject-specific German and not so much on the theories about which he lectured. The students were more interested in learning skills to se to their advantage in locally owned German companies than in learning about cutting-edge science: 'Teaching in Győr, Hungary forced me as lecturer to orient myself to the interests of students. This helped me to dically focus on the key question: What do the students find interesting?' One of the many answers was job interview training according to German standards. Prior to his time in Hungary, the lecturer had had a nior teaching appointment at a German university. His approach to the ctureship proved beneficial for him; he had received, by his own account, negative evaluation for his static, *sight-read* lectures. Today he is a proessor at a German university and he can unite both extremes: 'With regard content, I teach what I want to, but I make sure that the participants are ith me.'

In the second case, too, a lecturer experienced the difficulty of inspiring is students on issues that did not concern them personally. In this respect, e notes, they are similar to the students he now teaches at a high school Hamburg. When teaching in Belarus, his aim was to get the students volved with practical language exercises. This was a different approach ompared to the classical, text-heavy seminars of his local colleagues. He ade the students juxtapose contrasting views during discussions so that hey could get insight into the pluralist worldview of Western democraies. Methodologically, the lecturer achieved this by using collaborative pproaches. Students were expected to consolidate their knowledge on speific topics, to exchange information in rotating working groups and to proose independent views. During his mandatory training for the teaching rofession, the lecturer was informed that this form of cooperative learng complies with the guidelines of the Institute for Teacher Education in amburg.

When I was teaching a seventh grade class, I was confronted with the question of how to make the subject of the 30 Years' War interesting without delivering endless lectures. We then discussed a vicious circle: mercenaries are hired by warlords for money to not starve; they devastate

the land, cause famines, after which more and more hungry men ge
hired as mercenaries. The seventh-graders had to decide whether th
mercenaries should be regarded as victims or as perpetrators, and the
were to justify their opinions with facts. This approach led to a seriou
discussion.

He appreciates that the two years of lecturing in Belarus gave him the oppor
tunity to independently tap into this form of learning, and he regards it a
an important issue for his future as a school teacher: while many teacher
orient themselves quickly to the teaching culture of their school after thei
teacher training and also continue the tradition of lecture-style teaching, h
has discovered the right approach for himself; one of which he is convinced
and which he will retain.

Both these former lecturers have stressed that they still benefit from hav
ing taught non-native speakers: whether it is because the students, as a resul
of the language barrier, forced a slowing of the pace and thus a simplified
representation of complex issues, or because the awareness grew that lan
guage acquisition using word lists, standard phrases, and so forth, may wel
(contrary to some recent Western methodologies) prove methodologically
useful to German learners.

For the third interviewee, this fact would certainly not have come as a sur
prise. She studied German as a foreign language, so from the outset she wa
in touch with the methodology and didactics of foreign language teaching
Her studies had prepared her well to meet the challenge of very differently
motivated learners in one group, and she was also well-equipped in term
of classroom management (planning, methodology, implementation). She
found it rewarding to put the tools acquired during her studies to the tes
with a consistent group of learners for two years.

> I could put the structures, criticized as rigid by many others, to excellen
> use over a longer period of time in my investigation of the efficiency o
> my methods. In Germany, this opportunity would have been open to m
> only as a school teacher.

Today she works as a teacher of German as a foreign language at a German
university and invariably has foreign students (especially from Easter
Europe and China) in her seminars.

> I can appreciate the Eastern European cultures to some extent. My cross
> cultural knowledge about the different teaching and learning culture
> helps me to estimate whether the learners are accustomed to voicing
> their opinions in front of the teacher. My observation is that Russian
> students quickly assimilate once they are in the German system and the
> get involved easily. This does not apply to Chinese students since the

rote-learning approach is rooted much deeper. However, during my lectureship I had learned to deal with unfamiliar students.

nterestingly, she also observes at German universities a trend toward *Verschulung'*. The students receive a more structured timetable, and the teacher is regarded as a person who cares, gives instructions and offers orientation. 'In this respect, German and Eastern European and Chinese students re similar: at first they all are unstructured and dependent.'

.6   Conclusion

s is apparent from these accounts, these German lecturers are frequently xposed to an unfamiliar working environment. Especially during the arly days of their lectureship, they find ways of dealing with a teaching–learning operation that they often find 'regimented' and in need of undamental change. They are confronted with the demands of their superiors and students in the host country and must be aware of the limits of their adaptability. They also need to decide to what extent they can make changes and not lose their audience in the process. Synergies emerge when lecturers recognize their limits, make them visible to themselves and to others, and move beyond them; for example, by opening up new methodological paths for their students to approach the German language and culture in a playful manner, without sacrificing seriousness or jeopardizing success in the university examinations. If this happens, each side benefits from the learning process of the other and from learning about each other's cultures of learning in *cultural synergy* (Cortazzi and Jin, 1996: 01–2). Teaching abroad or pursuing overseas studies means crossing borders in order to bring back an irrevocably altered perspective; in this case, the design of teaching-learning processes. And, of course, a part of the lecturers will always remain where their activities were performed in the form of joint experiences.

Note

It is interesting to note that lecturers frequently discuss corruption (see e.g., Report Bosnia-Herzegovina, 2006–07), but were never personally affected by it ('There is much corruption, especially with regard to examinations. However, I am a foreigner, so I was not involved and I was never under any pressure' [Report Albania, 2007–08]).

References

erghorn, G., Keith, Th. & Umland, A. (Eds) (2006) *Geistes- und sozialwissenschaftliche Hochschullehre in Osteuropa II: Deutsche und österreichische Impressionen zur Germanistik und Geschichtswissenschaft nach 1990*. Frankfurt: Peter Lang.

Bürgel, M. (2006) Zur Situation der Germanistik in Russland, oder: Wer kann Dornröschen aus dem Schlaf erwecken? In G. Berghorn, Th. Keith & A. Umland (Eds), *Geistes- und sozialwissenschaftliche Hochschullehre in Osteuropa II: Deutsche und österreichische Impressionen zur Germanistik und Geschichtswissenschaft nach 1990* Frankfurt: Peter Lang, pp. 41–53.

Bürgel, M. & Umland, A. (Eds) (2009) *Geistes- und sozialwissenschaftliche Hochschullehre in Osteuropa IV: Chancen und Hindernisse internationaler Bildungskooperation* Frankfurt: Peter Lang.

Clark, R. & Gieve, S.N. (2006) On the discursive construction of 'the Chinese Learner'. In T. Coverdale-Jones & P. Rastall (Eds), 'The Chinese Learner'. *Language, Culture and Curriculum*, 19 (1), pp. 54–73.

Cortazzi, M. & Jin, L. (1996) Cultures of learning: Language classrooms in China. In H. Coleman (Ed.), *Society and the language classroom*. Cambridge: Cambridge University Press, pp. 169–206.

Coverdale-Jones, T. & Rastall, P. (Eds) (2006) 'The Chinese Learner'. *Language, Culture and Curriculum*, 19 (1).

Coverdale-Jones, T. & Rastall, P. (2009) *Internationalizing the university: The Chinese context*. Houndmills: Palgrave Macmillan.

Deckers, B. (2008) *Evaluation Lektorenprogramm der Robert Bosch Stiftung. Endbericht Januar 2008*. Köln: Institut für Potenzialberatung (unpublished).

Freunek, S. (2005) Učit'sja, učit'sja und nochmals učit'sja: Einige Schlüsselbegriffe des russischen Hochschulbetriebs und was dahintersteckt. In A. Umland (Ed.), *Geistes- und sozialwissenschaftliche Hochschullehre in Osteuropa I: Eindrücke, Erfahrungen und Analysen deutscher Gastlektoren*. Frankfurt: Peter Lang, pp. 49–69.

Hüsken, S.P. (2011) *Verbleibstudie 2010 Lektoren-Alumni Robert Bosch Stiftung. Evaluation des beruflichen Verbleibs ehemaliger Lektoren und Lektorinnen in Osteuropa und China*. http://www.bosch-stiftung.de/content/language1/downloads/LB Verbleibstudie_2010.pdf

Jackson, J. (2010) *Intercultural journeys: From study to residence abroad*. London: Palgrave Macmillan.

Jin, L. & Cortazzi, M. (Eds) (2011) *Researching Chinese learners: Skills, perceptions and intercultural adaptions*. London: Palgrave Macmillan.

Kirchhof, A. (2006) Deutsche Literatur in Kiew unterrichten: Studierende, Lehrstuhl und Boschlektorin – unvereinbare Ansprüche. In G. Berghorn, Th. Keith & A. Umland (Eds), *Geistes- und sozialwissenschaftliche Hochschullehre in Osteuropa II Deutsche und österreichische Impressionen zur Germanistik und Geschichtswissenschaft nach 1990*. Frankfurt: Peter Lang, pp. 82–9.

Klement, M. (2005) Einmal Saratov – Cambridge, bitte ...: Eindrücke aus der russischen und britischen Universitätslandschaft. In A. Umland (Ed.), *Geistes- und sozialwissenschaftliche Hochschullehre in Osteuropa I: Eindrücke, Erfahrungen und Analysen deutscher Gastlektoren*. Frankfurt: Peter Lang, pp. 70–9.

Li, X. & Cutting, J. (2011) Rote learning in Chinese culture: Reflecting active Confucian-based memory strategies. In L. Jin & M. Cortazzi (Eds), *Researching Chinese learners: Skills, perceptions and intercultural adaptions*. Houndmills: Palgrave Macmillan, pp. 21–42.

Litta, S. & Peters, T.B. (2009) Pioniere der Völkerverständigung? Deutsche Gastdozenten in Mittel- und Osteuropa. In M. Bürgel & A. Umland (Eds), *Geistes- und sozialwissenschaftliche Hochschullehre in Osteuropa IV: Chancen und Hindernisse internationaler Bildungskooperation*. Frankfurt: Peter Lang, pp. 151–73.

ational Bureau of Statistics of China (2011) *Press release on major figures of the 2010 National Population Census*. www.stats.gov.cn/was40/gjtjj_en_detail. jsp?searchword= higher+education&channelid=9528&record=1, 28 April 2011.

eters, T. (2006) 'Ostblock' ade? – Das (Hochschul-)Abenteuer Osteuropa. In G. Berghorn, Th. Keith & A. Umland (Eds), *Geistes- und sozialwissenschaftliche Hochschullehre in Osteuropa II: Deutsche und österreichische Impressionen zur Germanistik und Geschichtswissenschaft nach 1990*. Frankfurt: Peter Lang, pp. 173–6.

olk, A. & Reif, L. (2009) Alte Herausforderungen und neue Wege in der Hochschulzusammenarbeit zwischen Ost und West am Beispiel des Lektorenprogramms der Robert Bosch Stiftung. In M. Bürgel & A. Umland (Eds), *Geistes- und sozialwissenschaftliche Hochschullehre in Osteuropa IV: Chancen und Hindernisse internationaler Bildungskooperation*. Frankfurt: Peter Lang, pp. 174–93.

obert Bosch Stiftung (2001) *Sprachen als Schlüssel zur Völkerverständigung: Initiativen zur Sprachenförderung in Deutschland und Europa*. Stuttgart: Robert Bosch Stiftung.

ostat (2010) *Higher Vocational Education Institutions*. www.gks.ru/bgd/regl/b10_12/IssWWW.exe/stg/d01/08–10.htm

alimi-Asl, C. (2005) Strukturelle und kulturelle Rahmenbedingungen sozialwissenschaftlicher Hochschullehre in Kasachstan: Eine Problemauflistung. In A. Umland (Ed.), *Geistes- und sozialwissenschaftliche Hochschullehre in Osteuropa I: Eindrücke, Erfahrungen und Analysen deutscher Gastlektoren*. Frankfurt: Peter Lang, pp. 81–92.

ischer, A. (2006) Die akademische Geschichtswissenschaft in Lettland: Ein Erfahrungsbericht. In G. Berghorn, Th. Keith & A. Umland (Eds), *Geistes- und sozialwissenschaftliche Hochschullehre in Osteuropa II: Deutsche und österreichische Impressionen zur Germanistik und Geschichtswissenschaft nach 1990*. Frankfurt: Peter Lang, pp. 125–35.

mland, A. (Ed.) (2005) Geistes- und sozialwissenschaftliche Hochschullehre in Osteuropa I: Eindrücke, Erfahrungen und Analysen deutscher Gastlektoren. Frankfurt: Peter Lang.

10
Chinese Students' Attitudes towards Their Learning of French in France
Wang Jinjing and Sophie Bailly

10.1 Introduction

For more than a decade, increasing numbers of Chinese students have chosen European countries, especially Spain, France and Germany, as their overseas study destination. The reasons for this choice generally are: to acquire a foreign language that is not commonly taught at school in China but is widely used in the world; to increase opportunities in finding employment after returning in China; to pursue personal interest concerning the chosen country; and to avoid continuing learning English because of low performance at school (since study in a Chinese university commonly means passing tests in English before graduation). Thanks to an action plan developed by the French government in 1998 to promote its universities worldwide and attract a larger number of international students, there were more than 216,000 international students attending French universities in 2008, a 77 per cent increase compared to 1998; 14.4 per cent of these international students were from Asia (Bangou and Bourdet, 2010). In 2009 there were more than 35,000 Chinese students registered in French universities (People' Daily Online – Le Quotidien Du Peuple En Ligne). France was ranked in fifth place behind the United States, Britain, Australia and Japan for receiving Chinese students. As the French language is rarely taught in the Chinese education system, most students have to learn it on their arrival in France before enrolling at the university. For those beginners, the language learning process may take from one to two years, or more.

We have observed in our environment that Chinese students sometimes encounter difficulties in their learning of French in the classroom and in their daily life. Some fail to master the language, or even have to give it up completely. As they are studying in a new cultural environment, the question of adaptation to a new learning/teaching style may be relevant for both students and teachers.

In order to understand further the reasons for acquisition difficulties of Chinese learners in France, we conducted a study focusing on one actor: the cultural distance between language learning beliefs and habs acquired previously through the Chinese educational system, and ome of the main teaching modalities encountered in their French course n France. The results of this research indicate that there is a distance etween Chinese students' expectations of how language teaching should e conducted and the pedagogical modalities that they actually encounter n France, thus confirming certain aspects of cultures of learning tackled y the literature about Chinese language learners. Also, some charactertics, such as preference for authentic learning documents and for findng learning resources by themselves, have been discovered among these Chinese students.

0.2   Literature review

0.2.1   Cognition and beliefs

n a learning activity, cognition and beliefs play important roles because ow well acquisition occurs depends both on the individual's mental funcon as well as on the knowledge they have previously built up. Reuven euerstein, with his collaborators (Feuerstein et al., 1980; Feuerstein and alik, 2000; Feuerstein et al., 2003) proposed the idea that anyone can beome a fully effective learner. He propagated the theory of *structural cogitive modifiability*, which is the idea that people's cognitive structures are nfinitely modifiable: no one ever achieves the full extent of their learnng potential, but people can continue to develop their cognitive capacity hroughout their lives (quoted in Williams and Burden, 1997: 41). Thus, ental construction is a dynamic activity that can be modified whenever eople are in touch with something new.

Herbert Puchta employed the term 'individual map' to represent human ognitive construction, and explained that 'Our senses (or representational ystem), together with our unique experiences, beliefs, culture, language, nterests and values act as filters that we use in the creation of our maps' Puchta, 2002: 247). Humans interact with the world around them on the asis of their own inner map of the world. The construction of the 'individual map' may be described as consisting of rational as well as irrational bjects.

In education, beliefs and cognitive topography are important in guiding earners' positive or negative emotional orientation which might affect their earning outcomes:

Strong supportive beliefs do not automatically guarantee success, but they help students access learning states. ... Negative beliefs influence our students' expectations. Low expectations lead to a low level of motivation and every failure is seen as confirmation of the initial beliefs. (Puchta, 2002: 257)

Although our cognitive construction is continually modified during contacts with new things, some beliefs reside in our head for a long time and interfere with learning actions. In education, beliefs are defined as a set of attitudes and ideas, sometimes stereotypes, which the subject conveys in an unconscious way, and which will affect his/her learning (Barbot and Camatarri, 1999: 58). The beliefs are often thought to be related to 'emotion'. Emotion is an affective state, which consists of sensations, either positive or negative, which has a precise beginning and is related to a precise object (Kirouac, 1993: 44). In learning, a learner's beliefs and emotional states could influence his/her motivation about the learning subjects, perhaps even the learning outcomes.

10.2.2   Language culture and learning culture

In the field of language learning and acquisition, the notion of *language culture*, a term introduced by Henri Holec (1991), encompasses the social beliefs involving languages and communication that orient our vision regarding what has to be learned in order to master a foreign language. The language culture provides answers to a set of questions related to language learning. For instance, what is lexis? Is it a virtually undifferentiated 'bag of words' that learners have to learn one by one without the possibility of grouping them in sets and hierarchies? Is the lexis of a foreign language a set of labels different from the mother tongue that express the same things? Could the expression of an idea be reduced to finding the 'right word' in the other language? The set of ideas about language culture in a given sociocultural group could interfere with the content of foreign language teaching programmes and curricula.

In foreign language teaching and learning, the linguistic content is important, but the ways the language is taught and learned cannot be neglected. Holec (1991: 4) proposed the term *learning culture* to refer to a set of preconstructed ideas about teaching and learning modalities and resources. For him, learning culture, like language culture, is made of certain beliefs that sometimes need to be re-examined. For instance, he suggested that we have to be careful about what we think of the 'good' learner and 'good' learning.

Although Martin Cortazzi and Lixian Jin prefer the term *culture of learning*, they clearly agree with Holec's definition when they state that 'much behavior in language classrooms is set within taken-for-granted frameworks of expectations, attitudes, values and beliefs about what constitutes good learning, about how to teach or learn, whether and how to ask questions, what textbooks are for, and how language teaching relates to broader issues of the nature and purpose of education' (Cortazzi and Jin, 1996: 169). In language courses for foreign students, there may be 'largely unnoticed gaps between the expectations of the teacher and students, or between different groups of students' (ibid.). Cortazzi (1990) maintained that it was the degree f proximity of the congruence of teacher–student expectations that played significant role in the success or failure of language teaching and learn-ng. Likewise, Ron Scollon and Suzanne Scollon (1995) considered that the ducation or experience which was valued in one system could be devalued 1 other systems to which a person belonged. For example, Western and :hinese cultures of learning have been analysed in terms of contrasting aps of expectations and beliefs with social, psychological and academic istances between them, and in which each dimension of distance has dis-.nct features (Jin and Cortazzi, 1998: 115).

The notion of culture of learning is at the intersection of the notions of ulture and cognition. It is also at the heart of a study we conducted with :hinese students in order to try to understand the reasons for their difficul-.es in learning and acquiring the French language.

0.3   Methods

)ur research is based on interviews and questionnaires. The interviews are sed to provide ideas for constructing the items of the questionnaire. We 1ink that using students' own opinions to inquire about their peers is a etter method than imposing our own ideas or those of some previous find-1gs, because this enables us to include as few preconceptions as possible. his approach provides a more 'inside' view or ethnographic perspective 3rewer, 2000); when the learners themselves become aware of the findings bout their own opinions and experiences, this may be a step towards the :arners becoming ethnographers as part of a culturally based approach to 1ore advanced language learning (Roberts et al., 2001).

0.3.1   Phase 1: interviews

Ve interviewed eight students from different areas of China about their 1nguage learning before and since their arrival in France. The ages of the 1terviewees ranged from 19 to 31 years. They had been staying in France ·om one to eight years at the moment of interview. Each interview lasted bout 20 minutes and followed the guidelines below:

What are the characteristics of language courses in China and France? Give concrete examples, especially about teaching activities, interaction between teacher and students, use of teaching material and modalities of teaching, and so forth.
Which style of teaching, Chinese or French, better suits you?
What are your principal difficulties in learning French?

ll the interviews were entirely conducted and transcribed in Chinese. Ve used this transcription as a basis for a content analysis from which we xtracted apparently relevant elements for a larger scale questionnaire. The items of the questionnaire were formulated as closely as possible to what had been stated in the interviews.

10.3.2   Phase 2: questionnaire

The questionnaire contained 18 Likert-type scale items. Anchors of the six point scale were 'I do not agree at all' and 'I totally agree'. The respondents were also given the possibility to choose 'I don't know' as the answer and write down some complementary comments about the proposed items. The questionnaire was written in Chinese (see Appendix 10.1 for an English translation).

10.3.3   Procedure

This research was conducted in 2009 in Nancy, a city in Eastern France. To maintain confidentiality, the participants filled in the questionnaire anonymously.

For those students who were studying French in language schools, we handed out the questionnaire at the end of courses, and it was filled in our presence. Therefore, if any student needed more information, we could reply directly. For those students who were already in a special field of discipline study other than French, we met them at their residences to give and then pick up the questionnaire.

10.3.4   Data

A sample of 45 students composed of 22 men (49 per cent) and 23 women (51 per cent) answered our questionnaire: 25 of them were studying French in a university course for French as a second language (FSL); 20 had finished their French courses and were in their special fields of study at university. The students were aged 20 to 30 years with a mean of 24.5 years; the lengths of stay in France were from 1 to 7 years with a mean of 3 years and 7 months.

10.4   Results and discussion

10.4.1   Results

In the following Tables 10.1–10.3, the questionnaire items are presented according to the general tendency of the responses: items 1 to 9 display the ideas on which the respondents tend to agree (65 per cent to 85 per cent of agreement); items 10 to 13 show strong points of disagreement (64 per cent to 90 per cent disagree with opinion expressed); items 14 to 18 reveal the opinions that most divide the respondents.

In Table 10.1, the items which received the most confirmation are represented in descending order of agreement. The items are 'difficulty in writing activities' (item 1), 'feeling lost during listening activities' (item 2), 'missing drill use' (item 3), 'missing teacher's guiding' (item 4), 'disagree with teacher

Table 10.1　Students' agreement about French language courses in France

Items	Agree	Disagree	Don't know
They rather agree...			
French teachers are demanding; writing in French is very difficult	38 (85%)	6 (13%)	1 (2%)
I feel hopeless in comparison with my European or American classmates during listening comprehension activities in class	38 (85%)	3 (6%)	4 (9%)
French teachers do not make enough use of drills that would help me improve my skills in French	36 (80%)	9 (20%)	0 (0%)
French teachers do not tell me what is important to learn in class	33 (74%)	10 (22%)	2 (4%)
French teachers should not forbid me to use my dictionary in class	31 (69%)	14 (31%)	0 (0%)
In France we lack French textbooks	31 (69%)	14 (31%)	0 (0%)
French teachers do not teach enough grammar	30 (66%)	12 (26%)	3 (8%)
I feel uncomfortable when the teacher asks me to talk to the class; I'm afraid that my classmates laugh at me when I make mistakes	29 (65%)	16 (35%)	0 (0%)
There is too much work in groups during the class; I feel uncomfortable when working with European or American students	29 (65%)	15 (33%)	1 (2%)

Table 10.2　Students' disagreement about French language courses in France

Items	Agree	Disagree	Don't know
They rather do not agree...			
0. I do not like to learn with authentic documents	5 (10%)	40 (90%)	0 (0%)
1. I do not like it when French teachers ask me to find learning resources by myself	11 (33%)	34 (77%)	0 (0%)
2. French teachers do not control me enough in my learning process; they let me have too much freedom	14 (32%)	30 (66%)	1 (2%)
3. French teachers spend too much time on speaking activities	16 (36%)	29 (64%)	0 (0%)

Table 10.3   Students' dissimilarities about French language courses in France

Items	Agree	Disagree	Don't know
Several agree, others no ...			
14. The change in the way of teaching a foreign language in China and in France impedes my learning of French language	25 (55%)	17 (39%)	3 (6%)
15. French teachers do not teach enough vocabulary	23 (51%)	22 (49%)	0 (0%)
16. French teachers ask me for too many personal opinions, I do not know what to say most of the time	22 (49%)	23 (51%)	0 (0%)
17. I am not used to making notes during classes; I often miss things	22 (49%)	21 (47%)	2 (4%)
18. I prefer to learn in class rather than through self-study in the resource centre	21 (47%)	15 (33%)	9 (20%)

about dictionary use' (item 5), 'missing the textbook' (item 6), 'missing th grammar teaching' (item 7), 'afraid of speaking target language' (item 8 and 'disliking group work and collaboration with other foreign student (item 9).

In Table 10.2, the items which students did not agree with are classified i descending order. The items involved are 'liking authentic documents' (iter 10), 'liking to look for learning resources autonomously' (item 11), 'needin teacher's control' (item 12) and 'disliking speaking activities' (item 13).

Table 10.3 represents items which did not receive significantly dissimila frequencies between 'agreement' and 'disagreement'. Thus, the proportio between the two trends in these mixed responses is more or less 50 pe cent, except the item, 'I prefer to learn in class rather than through sel study in the resource center' (item 18), for which 20 per cent of the student did not give an answer. The other items are 'feeling impediments becaus of changes of cultures of learning' (item 14), 'enough vocabulary teachin₰ (item 15), 'disliking giving out personal opinions in speaking activitie (item 16), 'feeling lost in class for lack of skills in taking notes' (item 17).

10.4.2   Discussion

10.4.2.1   *Writing skill*

According to certain Western teachers, Chinese students' writing is unclea with confused logic (Houston, 1994: 100); this may be related to the inte ference of their mother tongue. For instance, at the level of the sentence w can observe in Chinese students' writing some uses of transfer from Chines such as: *because ... so ...* or *although ... but ...* (Young, 1994; Scollon and Scollor 1995), which are typical Chinese syntactic constructions, but in French on art would be redundant. At the level of discourse, a number of researchers (Hinds, 1990; Young, 1994; Scollon and Scollon, 1995) noted that Chinese students prefer an inductive mode of expression in which there is a delayed introduction of the main point, which could confuse readers expecting a more deductive approach. In our research, 38 of 45 students (85 per cent) validated this aspect. Thus, the distance between Chinese and French syntactic constructions may explain why our sample has massively agreed with the idea that French teachers demand too much of them as regards writing skills and think that writing is a difficult skill to acquire.

0.4.2.2 Drill training and grammar learning

. Charmet and E. Martin observed in a French as a second language course that Chinese learners have a preference for writing activities. Describing them as very well trained to accomplish numerous pages of grammatical exercises, they call this automatic behaviour of Chinese learners, a 'well-oiled machine' (Charmet and Martin, 2002: 107). Rebecca Oxford and Neil Anderson explained this phenomenon in terms of preferred patterns of mental functioning. The Chinese learners are said to prefer classrooms where (grammar) rules are emphasized and learning is inductive (Oxford and Anderson, 1995). In our research, 36 and 30 of 45 students (80 per cent, 66 per cent) think that French teachers do not give them enough drill and grammar training, which respectively would enable them to improve their language competences. In other words, they feel that they lack these activities in French courses in France.

0.4.2.3 Dictionary use and textbook use

As Jean-Michel Robert described, Chinese students consider that the incomprehension of a given word is a personal problem. They think that it may be more polite and efficient to look for it in the dictionary than to ask the teacher. Also, letting others know that they do not understand a word is considered an act of losing face. However, the French teachers apparently compel students not to use the dictionary but rather to listen to the teacher's explanations (Robert, 2002: 140). Robert explained Chinese students' dependence on dictionary by the syntactic differences between Chinese and French. In an Indo-European language, the misunderstanding of a word is less likely to disturb the understanding of the sentence, because syntactically at least we know that it is a noun, a verb or an adjective, and so forth. But in Chinese, a word can have several syntactic functions depending on its place and the meaning of the sentence. Therefore, for a Chinese learner, the misunderstanding of a word is not only semantic, but also categorical in syntax (ibid.). For this reason, they need to frequently check each word that they want to use, and thus they tend to construct a linear meaning (word by word) rather than a global one (looking holistically at a paragraph or text). In our research, 31 of 45 students (69 per cent) think that French teachers should not forbid them to use the dictionary during classes, thus expressing a legitimate and specific need.

As for the use of textbooks in class, Robin Scarcella (1990) noted tha many Asian cultures view the book as containing all knowledge an wisdom. In a research study between Chinese and native students carrie out in New Zealand, Ken Levinsohn (2007) found that Chinese student preferred teacher-guided study, primarily using textbooks. In our researcl 33 (74 per cent) of 45 students feel that the French teachers do not inforr them enough about what is important to learn, and 31 (69 per cent) thin that they lack textbooks in French courses in France. These findings corre pond to the previous ones.

10.4.2.4 Interaction and group work

Learners from the Confucian Heritage Culture (CHC) are often observe by their foreign teachers as being reticent in class. According to certai researchers, the reason for this is their worry about losing face; they dar not speak out with personal ideas, either for fear of being thought silly c for fear of making others feel humiliated (Cocroft and Ting-Toomey, 1994 Ting-Toomey, 1988). Chinese learners' apparent 'passivity' is interpreted b Cortazzi and Jin as 'reflection'; 'Chinese students value thoughtful question which they ask after sound reflection [;] ... less thoughtful questions may b laughed at by other students' (1996: 191). Meihua Liu and Jane Jackson als confirmed this (Liu and Jackson, 2011). In our research, the students do nc feel comfortable to talk to the class. Their reticence may be provoked by th fear of losing face in case they make mistakes: 29 of our 45 students (65 pe cent) confirmed this.

Cortazzi and Jin noticed that Chinese learners were unwilling to wor in groups and preferred whole-class work or individual work, because the desired to concentrate on learning tasks without the distraction of talkin to their peers (Cortazzi and Jin, 1996: 185). Another explanation, argued b Susan Shirk (1982, cited in Agelasto, 1998), involved the specific Chines educational system. Shirk found that Chinese people had less cooperatio in academic study than in labour or extracurricular activities: '[In China study was organized individually, with no collective goal'. Therefore, th Western approach of learning in groups may be culturally unfamiliar t Chinese learners, although recent widespread introduction of pair work an some (but less common) use of group work in language classrooms in Chin should make this interaction much more familiar to younger Chinese stu dents (Jin and Cortazzi, 2006).

Another problem which affects Chinese students' participation in a intercultural class discussion is the presence of European or America students. In an FSL course, Robert (2002) described how when a Chines student hesitated to answer a question, another student, often with a Lati language as mother tongue, intervened and responded for the student wh was first asked. This behaviour was judged impolite by the Chinese st dents, and they were surprised that the French teacher did not restrain c reprimand the intervener. For Chinese students, European and American students are too competent; they already speak or write French, because to the Chinese (from the point of view of their own Chinese mother tongue) English, Spanish or even German do not seem too different from French. This may engender a feeling of linguistic inferiority among Chinese students. The students in our research confirmed this point: 29 of 45 (65 per cent) feel that there is too much work in groups, and they do not like to work with European and American students.

In comparing certain issues of our study to previous research, it appears that most of our students' behaviours in French learning in France are similar to the Chinese students' behaviours and attitudes in an English-speaking context. These findings therefore suggest that there is less distance between French and English teaching cultures than between Chinese teaching culture and occidental norms in language education. Although many Chinese students may adapt themselves to new learning conditions, some others could benefit from specific help which takes into account specific learning needs related to their original culture of learning (item 14).

10.4.2.5   Learners' autonomy

Throughout the questionnaire, the dimension of attitude towards autonomous learning is involved in several items (items 5, 11, 12, 18); our results both validate and disconfirm other research raising this theme.

'Autonomy' is the capacity to take charge of one's own learning (Holec, 1981). Learners' development of responsibility for their own learning is important in this theory. Phil Benson (2001) also stated that autonomy varies according to people, because everybody has this capacity at different levels, but autonomy can also be variable across cultures (Palfreyman and Smith, 2003). Learners' autonomy in learning is a skill that is more and more promoted by teachers of FSL courses in France. Bouvier (2003: 404) observed that French teachers tend to encourage students to be autonomous in their learning, but Chinese students are more used to remaining in a passive stance to receive information from teachers. Joseph Kee-Kuok Wong (2004) stated that Chinese learners preferred a teacher-centred style: they learned better when most information was given by the teacher and did not learn well when discovering by themselves. Our study both validates and disconfirms this view (items 4 and 11). Individual variability of the students should be taken into account; some adapt better than others in this matter.

Simon Gieve and Rose Clark, in research within a self-directed language learning framework at a British university, concluded that 'the Chinese students felt that they were able to benefit linguistically from self-directed and Tandem learning at least as much as the European students' (Gieve and Clark, 2005: 272). Thus, they reject the notion that autonomy for Chinese students is controversial.

In our research, 34 of 45 (77 per cent) students are positive towards the idea of finding learning resources by themselves. As for the item preference for self-study at a language centre or learning in class, 20 per cent of the students did not answer; maybe because they had not yet experienced self-studying at a language centre or had never asked themselves that question.

Another indicator of autonomy can be found in the preference of Chinese learners for using drills and looking up words in a dictionary. This means that those learning skills are acquired as part of the useful knowledge for learning a language. The mastery of those skills enables them to work in more independent way if they have to or want to.

Perhaps, the meaning of 'autonomy' should be understood culturally. In the Western definition, individual learner autonomy is reflected in a cluster of related concepts: agency, locus of control, attribution of outcomes and self-efficacy (Oxford, 2003). In the Asian context, any concept of autonomy must involve the person in relationship to the group. Sung Dynasty scholar Chu Hsi (quoted by Pierson, 1996: 56) supported 'sharp, independent thinking, but this autonomy does not imply that the individual can operate without consideration of his or her own rank in society and in the family'. In our opinion, Chinese learners' autonomy always depends on the other members of the group to which they belong. For instance, when asked why they use their dictionary so much in class, Chinese students' rationale often is that they respect the teacher and other students, so they do not want to interrupt the class and waste their time with a problem which they can solve by themselves. Therefore, we should be careful with the assumptions that instructional approaches in Asia generally fail to encourage students to take responsibility for their learning. It is possible that some Western concept of individual autonomy do not fit well into many traditional Asian culture (Oxford, 2008: 50) because of its stress on the self to the detriment of the relationship with others of the group.

10.5 Limits of the research

We are aware of various methodological weaknesses in our research. Firstly, the items proposed in the questionnaire are extracted from interviews which have their limitations. An interview, also called a self-reported communication event, is based on autobiographical memories which are episodic memories recalled long after their occurrence in an individual's life (Woike, 2008). These memories have been found to decline in frequency over time (Crovitz and Schiffman, 1974). Thus, interviews are always re-interpretations of actual events or feelings, and are not in themselves the objective reality. Furthermore, there still remains a scientific doubt concerning at what point the interviewer's views interfere with the interviewee's: this is the paradox of observation, that a researcher's presence may itself interfere, plus the notion of interview as a dialogue in which the interviewer's voice contributes much more than simply questions.

Secondly, the transformation of interviews into questionnaires is a delicate phase as it has at least two risks. The first risk of bias happens during the content analysis, or research of categories, when researchers could, even unconsciously, let their own preconceptions influence their analysis. The second risk to write questionnaire items avoiding ambiguous or irrelevant questions.

Although we have tried to limit as much as possible the biases in our research protocol for this preliminary research on Chinese students' language learning culture, we did not avoid all the traps. As a consequence we will not draw definitive conclusions from our results, but we can make some suggestions to improve our methodological tools.

10.6   Conclusion

Investigating the learners' opinions about their language learning experience in the host country is a good way to understand what could promote or prevent their learning of other languages. To this extent, this research contributes to the understanding of Chinese learners learning attitudes and behaviours in the French context, as well as in other contexts. Identifying Chinese students' expectations and becoming aware of the gap between these expectations and the teaching modalities that they are exposed to should encourage teachers to further negotiate with students the methodological approaches they use in class. As for students, understanding why teachers act in the ways they do could help them develop new learning strategies or make better use of the courses. This means that research into cultures of learning among Chinese students of SL in France (or in similar cases) should aim for a mutual application to help both students and teachers understand each other's cultures of learning, with a view to working towards *cultural synergy* and avoiding any implication that one culture of learning is 'better' than another (Jin and Cortazzi, 1998).

Our study also shows that even though there are some strong points of agreement revealing underlying 'Chinese' norms in the sector of languages education, all the respondents do not think alike, and individual variability is present in the answers. Previous school experiences are imprinted on the learners' cultures of learning, and the chances to adapt to new ways of 'doing learning' (i.e., new cultures of or for learning) are most likely related to many other types of experience than the school experience. Our study highlights disagreements among students in France about what they like or dislike in their learning, but it does not clearly link those declared feelings to the students' actual academic success or lack of success in their French learning. More research could be done on the effect of affect (feelings and emotions) on those particular students and their achievements.

In the future we will examine whether the cultural gap, which seems to cause those students cognitive and affective discomfort while learning

French in France, is a significant variable in the prediction of success or
failure in acquiring a language in the target language sociocultural context. We could also introduce additional questions to raise some clues about
which other languages students know and how they learned them, as attitudes towards learning of French as a second language are impacted by the
fact that non Indo-Europeans either have or have not learned English before
learning French (Bailly et al., 2009). Such information could add context
for more accurate interpretations and allow a potential measurement of cultural distances experienced by learners between several languages.

Another interesting thing to do would be to compare the results of our
study to studies conducted amongst French (or other languages) learners of
Chinese (or other languages) as a second language. It is only by continuous
comparative studies that we can hope to clarify the meaning of the term
'culture of learning' and understand fully its role in the learning process.
Research in the field of cultures of learning and teaching still has many
doors to open to our understanding of the complexity of human learning.

Appendix 10.1: Questionnaire on the culture of learning of French

Age
Sex
How long have you been living in France?

Please fill in the questionnaire below with a cross in the boxes.
1. I do not agree at all.
2. I do not agree.
3. I slightly disagree.
4. I more or less agree.
5. I quite agree.
6. I totally agree.

	1	2	3	4	5	6	I do not know	Remarks
1. The changes in the way of teaching a foreign language in China and in France impedes my learning of French language								
2. French teachers should not forbid me to use my dictionary in class								
3. I do not like to learn with authentic documents								

4. In France we lack French textbooks								
5. I am not used to making notes during classes; I often miss things								
6. French teachers do not make enough use of drills that would help me improve my skills in French								
7. French teachers spend too much time on speaking activities								
8. French teachers do not teach enough grammar								
9. French teachers do not teach enough vocabulary								
0. French teachers ask me for too many personal opinions; I do not know what to say most of the time								
1. French teachers are demanding (about the style, organization of ideas and overall consistency); writing in French is very difficult								
2. I do not like it when French teachers ask me to find learning resources by myself								
3. I prefer to learn in class rather than through self-study in the resource centre								
4. French teachers do not control me enough in my learning process; they let me have too much freedom								
5. French teachers do not tell me what is important to learn in class								
6. I feel uncomfortable when the teacher asks me to talk to the class; I'm afraid that my classmates laugh at me when I make mistakes								
7. I feel hopeless in comparison with my European or American classmates during listening comprehension activities in class								
8. There is too much work in groups during the class; I feel uncomfortable when working with European or American students								

References

Agelasto, M. (1998) Educational disengagement: Undermining academic quality at Chinese university. Retrieved 5 April 2011, from http://www.agelastos.com/diser gagement/

Bailly, S., Boulton, A., Chateau, A., Duda, R. & Tyne, H. (2009) L'anglais langu étrangère: langue d'appui pour l'apprentissage du français langue étrangère. I G. Forlot (Ed.), *L'anglais et le Plurilinguisme: Pour une Didactique des Contacts et d Passerelles Linguistiques.* Paris: L'Harmattan, pp. 35–57.

Bangou, F. & Bourdet J.-F. (2010) Teaching French as a second language to Chines students: Instructional staff adaptation and intercultural competence develor ment. *International Journal of Intercultural Relations,* 34 (6), 561–70.

Barbot, M.-J. & Camatarri, G. (1999) *Autonomie et apprentissage innovation dans la fc mation.* Education et formation. Pédagogie théorique et critique. Paris: Presses un versitaires de France.

Benson, Ph. (2001) *Teaching and researching autonomy in language learning.* Harlov England: Longman.

Bouvier, B. (2003) Chinois et français : quand les habitudes culturelles d'apprentissag s'opposent. *ELA,* 4 (132), 399–414.

Brewer, J.D. (2000) *Ethnography.* Buckingham: Open University Press.

Charmet, A. & Martin, E. (2002) Convenance et Resistance en F.L.E. (Français Langu Etrangère): Le Cas des Étudiants Chinois. *Verbum,* 4 (1), 105–15.

Cocroft, B.-A.K. & Ting-Toomey, S. (1994) Facework in Japan and the United State *International Journal of Intercultural Relations,* 18 (4), 469–506.

Cortazzi, M. (1990) Cultural and educational expectations in the language clas room. In B. Harrison (Ed.), *Culture and the language classroom.* Hong Kong: Moder English Publications and the British Council, pp. 54–65.

Cortazzi, M. & Jin, L. (1996) Cultures of learning: Language classrooms in Chin In H. Coleman (Ed.), *Society and the language classroom.* Melbourne: Cambridg University Press, pp. 169–206.

Crovitz, H. F. & Schiffman, H. (1974) Frequency of episodic memories as a functio of their age. *Bulletin of the Psychonomic Society,* 4, 517–18.

Feuerstein, R., Rand, Y., Hoffman, M. & Miller, R. (1980) *Instrumental enrichment: A intervention program for cognitive modifiability.* Baltimore, MD: University Park Pres

Feuerstein, R. et al. (2003) *Feuerstein's theory and applied systems: A reader.* Jerusalen ICELP Press.

Feuerstein, R. & Falik, L.H. (2000) Cognitive modifiability: A needed perspective o learning in the 21st century. *College of Education Review,* 12, 127–43.

Gieve, S. & Clark, R. (2005) 'The Chinese approach to learning': Cultural trait c situated response? The case of a self-directed learning programme. *System,* 33 (2 261–76.

Hinds, J. (1990) Inductive, deductive, quasi-inductive: Expository writing in Japanes Korean, Chinese, and Thai. In U. Connor & A.M. Johns (Eds), *Coherence in writin Research and pedagogical perspectives.* Alexander, VA: TESOL, pp. 87–110.

Holec, H. (1981/1979) *Autonomy and foreign language learning.* Oxford: Pergamor Strasbourg: Council of Europe.

Holec, H. (1991) Autonomie de l'apprenant : de l'enseignement à l'apprentissag *Education Permanente,* 107, 1–5.

Houston, A. (1994) Learn writing through writing: The Chengdu approach to teacl ing written composition. *Teaching English in China,* 26, 100–10.

in, L. & Cortazzi, M. (1998) The culture the learner brings: A bridge or a barrier? In M. Byram & M. Fleming (Eds), *Language learning in intercultural perspective, approaches through drama and ethnography*. Cambridge: Cambridge University Press, pp. 98–118.

in, L. & Cortazzi, M. (2006) Changing practices in Chinese cultures of learning. In T. Coverdale-Jones & P. Rastall (Eds), *The Chinese Learner*, special issue of *Language, Culture and Curriculum*, 19 (1), 5–20.

irouac, G. (1993) Les émotions. In R.J. Vallerand & E.E. Thill (Eds), *Introduction à la psychologie de la motivation*. Laval : Edition Etudes Vivantes, pp. 41–82.

e nombre d'étudiants chinois en France dépasse les 35 000'. *People's Daily Online – Le Quotidien Du Peuple En Ligne*. 15 January 2010. Retrieved 2 April 2011 from http://french.peopledaily.com.cn/Sci-Edu/6870375.html

evinsohn, K. (2007) Cultural differences and learning styles of Chinese and European trades students. *Institute for Learning Styles Journal*, 1, 12–22.

iu, M. & Jackson, J. (2011) Reticence and anxiety in oral English lessons: A case study in China. In L. Jin & M. Cortazzi (Eds), *Researching Chinese learners: Skills, perceptions and intercultural adaptations*. Houndmills: Palgrave Macmillan, pp. 119–37.

)xford, R.L. (2003) Toward a more systematic model of L2 learner autonomy. In D. Palfreyman & R. C. Smith (Eds), *Learner autonomy across cultures: Language education perspectives*. Houndmills: Palgrave Macmillan, pp. 75–91.

)xford, R.L. (2008) Hero with a thousand faces: Learner autonomy, learning strategies and learning tactics in independent language learning. In S. Hurd & T. Lewis (Eds), *Language learning strategies in independent settings*. Clevedon, UK: Multilingual Matters, pp. 41–66.

)xford, R.L. & Anderson N.J. (1995) A crosscultural view of learning styles. *Language Teaching*, 28 (4), 201–15.

'alfreyman, D. & Smith, R. (Eds) (2003) *Learner autonomy across cultures, language education perspectives*. Houndmills: Palgrave Macmillan.

'ierson, H.D. (1996) Learner culture and learner autonomy in the Hong Kong Chinese context. In R. Pemberton, E.S.L. Li, W.W.F. Or & H.D. Pierson (Eds), *Taking control: Autonomy in language learning*. Hong Kong: Hong Kong University Press, pp. 19–58.

'uchta, H. (2002) Creating a learning culture to which students want to belong: The application of neuro-linguistic programming to language teaching. In J. Arnold (Ed.), *Affect in language learning*. Cambridge: Cambridge University Press, pp. 246–59.

'obert, J.-M. (2002) Sensibilisation Au Public Asiatique – l'exemple Chinois. *ELA*, 2 (126), 135–43.

'oberts, C., Byram, M., Barro, A., Jordan, S. & Street, B. (2001) *Language learners as ethnographers*. Clevedon: Multilingual Matters.

'carcella, R. (1990) *Teaching language minority students in the multilingual classroom*. Englewood Cliffs, NJ: Prentice Hall.

'collon, R. & Scollon, S.W. (1995) *Intercultural communication: A discourse approach*. Oxford: Blackwell.

'hirk, S. (1982) *Competitive comrades*. Berkeley and Los Angeles: University of California Press.

'ing-Toomey, S. (1988) Intercultural conflict styles: A face-negotiation theory. In Y.Y. Kim & W.B. Gudykunst (Eds), *Theories in intercultural communication*. Newbury Park, CA: Sage, pp. 213–35.

Williams, M. & Burden, R.L. (1997) *Psychology for language teachers: A social construc* *ivist approach*. Cambridge: Cambridge University Press.

Woike, B.A. (2008) A functional framework for the influence of implicit and explic motives on autobiographical memory. *Personality and Social Psychology Review, 12* 99–117.

Wong, J. K-K (2004) Are the learning styles of Asian international students culturall or contextually based? *International Education Journal*, 4 (4), 154–66.

Young, L.W.L. (1994) *Crosstalk and culture in Sino-American communication*. Cambridge Cambridge University Press.

11

Supporting Intercultural Learning: For Beginners' Chinese Language Learners at The Open University, UK

Inma Álvarez and Kan Qian

11.1 Introduction

It is no longer necessary to argue for the integration of a cultural dimension in foreign language learning. In the past few decades, theoretical pedagogical approaches in the field of language acquisition have consolidated the intimate link between these two educational dimensions, although effective practices are still in the process of being developed. Intercultural competence has become integral to the languages curriculum. It has been defined in a number of ways but it is commonly accepted as involving knowledge, skills and attitudes, all of which are tinted with values that 'are part of one's social identities' (Byram, Gribkova, and Starkey, 2002: 11). In particular the more precise concept of 'intercultural communicative competence', coined by Michael Byram (1997), with its emphasis on cultural mediation and intercultural speakers, has dominated much discussion about communication in foreign language teaching.

In the area of adult formal education, textbooks have often advanced knowledge-oriented cultural items that offer a limited view of the target culture (Singerman, 1988); this means that teachers need to add to, modify or mediate it in the classroom (Pulverness, 2003). This shortcoming of publications has received many criticisms in the past few years (e.g., Risager, 1991; McGrath, 2002) but in the meantime some useful suggestions have been made about how to improve the integration of culture in language learning textbooks and how teachers can promote dialogue of cultural perspectives (Cortazzi and Jin, 1999). Recent developments in communication technology have also facilitated communication across borders, and lessons have been learnt from online projects in higher education supporting students' intercultural encounters. The majority of research in this area has consisted of tandem or group learning projects linking students across institutions located in different countries with an emphasis on the use of the target language, mostly via e-mail (see, for instance, Belz, 2003; Hauck 2007; O'Dowd, 2003). More specifically, reports from projects explorin interactions in asynchronous online forums have pointed out increase 'cross-cultural sensitisation' among participants after the use of critica incidents (Truscott and Morley, 2001: 22), as well as students' commitmen to construct intercultural relationships through readings and discussion about their own native culture (Liaw, 2007: 237). On the one hand, studie on online forums have indicated a number of additional benefits to inte acting in this medium, so it has been suggested that online forums ca facilitate collaborative learning (Curtis and Lawson, 2001) and communica tion that is 'personal, dialogic, and open minded as to sources of knowledg (Hammond, 2000: 261). On the other hand, the same studies have also su gested some negative factors that should not be overlooked. Warnings hav been issued about the different expectations students could have about or line communication and how 'the ability to engage in communication at deep level of intercultural inquiry may be impeded by an online discours norm that often favours brevity over sustained attention' (Kern, Ware, an Warschauer, 2004: 253).

Both theory and empirical studies around language and intercultura competence have usually focused on intermediate or advanced studen who are already to some extent competent in the target language; therefor we know very little about pedagogical approaches and issues around ho intercultural aims can be successfully achieved at beginners' level. The are only a few research-based studies of beginners and intercultural learr ing. So far at this level, interest has focused on issues such as how languag teaching methodology can do more work with texts to explore cultura identity and subjectivity 'allowing a personal, dynamic and realistic dia logue with the target culture' (Ros i Solé, 2003: 149), with Internet base online tasks 'as a means of broadening the students' learning experienc and connection to target cultures' (Osuna and Meskill, 1998: 77), as well a with instant messaging interaction between beginners and native speake (Jin, 2008). It is important to bear in mind that adult beginners' linguisti skills might be inadequate for fluent written or oral communication, bu their background knowledge of the target cultures and their intercultura skills might be already quite developed. Another aspect of this group is tha unlike schoolchildren and university students whose motivation to lear a modern foreign language is closely linked with exams and public att tudes, distance adult learners choose to study a foreign language mainl for pleasure and intellectual challenge (Coleman, 2009). In fact, motivatio as well as previous knowledge have been identified as key to learners' att tudes towards other cultures (Baumann and Shelley, 2003). Therefore thes two factors are crucially important to bear in mind when researching adu learners. Indeed, for many decades, the experiences that adult learners brin with them to formal education have been highlighted as a valuable resourc whose potential impact should not be overlooked (Lindeman, 1961). On the other hand, some general characteristics of adult learners, such as their individual expectations, aspirations and intentions, having interests which compete with language learning, and having own patterns of learning, but also their experience, knowledge and value, have been identified as challenging aspects for teachers (Rogers and Horrocks, 1986).

This chapter reports on a study of beginners' Chinese language learners at the Open University in the United Kingdom. The research examines the role of reflective forums for culture learning and intercultural awareness within the context of adult distance language learning. It focuses on individual learners' cultural positioning through exchanges among a diverse group of peers and tries to establish to what extent they develop intercultural skills individually and as a group, as well as to what extent the learning of culture supports the learning of the language. Distance Chinese language learners comprise a 'relatively underreported group of learners' (Tasker, 2010: 154), and this is especially so in the area of intercultural learning. We hope our research will add to the understanding of the experience of Chinese language beginners studying at a distance, and will generate further interest in the field.

1.2 Context and background of research

The Open University (OU) is the largest university in the United Kingdom, providing supported distance learning to over 250,000 students. In response to the increasing demands for language learning through distance education, the Department of Languages introduced beginners' Chinese in its curriculum in November 2009. The pilot study reported here concerns participants who were the first cohort of students who studied the course in 2009–10.

1.2.1 Students' profile

Students on the beginners' Chinese course come from all parts of the United Kingdom and also from continental Western Europe. An enrolment survey (Figure 11.1) shows a profile which is atypical in relation to most full-time undergraduate programmes in other universities, though it is representative of distance learning courses at the OU and elsewhere. The female population was higher than the male one. These figures are in line with those of undergraduates in full-time education studying Chinese in campus-based British universities (HESA, 2011); however, among those studying other European languages the percentage of women was even higher. The age of this group was in line with the overall OU students' profile, ranging from under 25 to over 65 years old, with more than 60 per cent over 40. Similarly, the ethnic profile reflects a majority of white students. Finally, in terms of educational qualifications, compared with other OU courses the percentage

Gender	Male	45%
	Female	55%
Age	under 25:	10%
	25– 29:	10%
	30– 39:	20%
	40– 49:	19%
	50– 59:	19%
	60– 64:	11%
	over 65:	10%
Ethnic origin	White:	81%
	Asian:	7%
	Black:	2%
	Mixed:	2%
	Other:	7%
	Not known:	6%
Qualifications	No formal qualifications	3%
	Less than 2-A Levels	12%
	2+ A-Levels or equivalent	21%
	HE qualifications	37%
	Postgraduate qualifications	25%
	Not known	2%

Figure 11.1   Demographic information of the beginners' Chinese course n = 467
Source: Students Statistics Service, IET, enrolment data 2009, The Open University, UK.

of students with previously held undergraduate and postgraduate qualifica
tions was higher: more than half of these students already held a Highe
Education qualification.

In addition, students declared a wide range of reasons for learnin
Chinese. Results from a pre-course online survey completed by a sample c
170 students (a 69 per cent return rate of the 245 students who were ser
the questionnaire) showed that 50 per cent of students' motivation to lear
Chinese was mainly for pleasure and personal interest, or as an intelle
tual challenge; only 5.29 per cent studied Chinese as part of a wider degre
programme. The same survey data also suggested the presence of languag
diversity within this group. Although the majority were British with Englis
as their mother tongue (around 82 per cent), there were about 18 per cer
non-British students who lived in the United Kingdom or in other Europea
countries; 13.53 per cent had other European languages as mother tongue
1.76 per cent spoke Cantonese, and 4.12 per cent spoke other languages (th
total does not add up to 100 per cent because some respondents claime
two languages as their mother tongue: for example they were bilingual i
English and French).

1.2.2   Course model

The beginners' Chinese course at The Open University was designed according to a blended learning model 'that is facilitated by the effective combination of different modes of delivery, models of teaching and styles of learning, and founded on transparent communication amongst all parties involved' (Heinze and Procter, 2004). Using this model, the course includes attending a mixture of face-to-face and synchronous online tutorials, studying print and audio materials, interactive online language activities and completing assessments.

1.2.3   Learning outcomes and materials

The learning outcomes for the beginners' Chinese course included both linguistic and intercultural objectives. The course teaches Mandarin Chinese in its standardized spoken modern form and in simplified characters. The level of linguistic competence the course intends to achieve is comparable to A2 as defined by the Council of Europe's Common European Framework of Reference for Languages. Students are encouraged to engage in critical and cultural reflection and discussion through activities that present aspects of Chinese cultural traditions and beliefs; make explicit the relationship between standard Mandarin and other language varieties; and discuss the diversity of cultures within the Chinese-speaking communities. Aspects addressed are appropriate to the theme of a particular session of study in both the print materials and in a designated online discussion forum, named the 'Culture Forum'. These types of activities are aimed at encouraging students to attend first to the information presented and then to 'examine and evaluate their own habits, cultural context, ideas and conceptions' (Álvarez, 2011: 159). A few instances will help to illustrate how this is achieved in the print materials.

The course teaches Mandarin and, when appropriate, comparisons with other regional dialects are made in the language and grammar notes. For example, one language note draws students' attention to the use of the verbs for 'to drink' and 'to eat' and mentions that the phrase for '*to drink tea*' 喝茶 hē chá) is '*to eat tea*' (吃茶 chī chá) in the Shanghai dialect (OU, 2010: 31). Linguistic facts like this make students aware of other forms and expressions and accents that they might encounter while interacting with Chinese speakers. By combining the teaching of the language and the culture, this puts the learning of language in context and helps students understand why certain expressions are the way they are, besides raising their awareness of linguistic diversity. Another example is the introduction of the Chinese concept of beauty in a culture note (OU, 2008: 18) which explains the positive cultural connotation of the phrase 你胖了 ('you have put on weight'). This is appropriate for this session because it teaches adjectives such as 'thin' and 'fat'. Students are thus alerted to the traditional positive

文化   **Chinese perspectives on the past and future**

To a certain extent, Chinese time expressions reflect cultural perspectives on the past and future. The past is known and therefore seen as crystal clear, whereas the future is unknown and thus unpredictable. So the phrase for 'the day before yesterday' is 前天 *qiántiān*, which literally means 'front day', implying that you can see the past event in front of your eyes, while the phrase for 'the day after tomorrow' is 后天 *hòutiān*, which literally means 'behind day' because the day has not arrived and is something your eyes cannot yet see, hence it is behind you.

想一想

The Chinese language reflects the fact that the past is 'seen' and the future 'unseen'. How do the concepts of past and future work in your culture, and how might you explain it to a Chinese person learning your language? If, for instance, you say, 'This time next year, I'll be in Beijing', does that imply confidence in the future or just personal determination? Do you, or does anyone you know, use superstitious or religious formulae like 'touch wood' or 'God willing' when you speak of the future?

Figure 11.2   Culture note, book 2, session 27 with 想一想 *xiăng yi xiăng* section

meaning of this expression in Chinese which might well contrast with th use and meaning of this sentence in their own culture(s).

Many of the culture notes that appear in the main course books are fo lowed by a section named 想一想 *xiăng yi xiăng*, meaning 'Have a thin where explicit questions are asked to invite students to reflect and engage i critical thinking (Figure 11.2).

It was hoped that this type of reflective activity would foster intercultur awareness, with information and questioning that went beyond stereo types and might counter a uniform image of articulations and objects fro a single culture. Focusing on a critical cultural approach to thinking, n only about the target and students' own cultures but also about a variety of others as well, the activities also aimed at the promotion of self-questioning in order to achieve self-knowledge, regardless of individual students' origins and backgrounds.

1.2.4   Online intercultural interactions through online forums

The cultural information and questioning in the culture notes attempt to activate individual critical thinking and reflection which is also encouraged through peer interaction through an online forum. The forum initially replicated 17 cultural reflective activities from the books that students could expand on or, if they wished, they could also add new ones. Learners were encouraged to provide their own answers to the questions asked and react and respond to each others' answers. In fact, to these activities, students added another 22 threads on culturally related topics which went beyond the original learning expectations formulated in the forum. But at beginner level students are not yet able to read a complex text nor conduct discussions about the target culture in the target language; therefore as this is a UK course, English was used as the lingua franca for information, questions, answers and discussions.

In addition to the culture forum, students were encouraged to participate in a general course forum for general course-related issues, and in a café forum for arranging social activities and meeting up (either virtually or face to face). Participation in all three forums was voluntary. Close scrutiny of these forums reveals that students used them more freely than intended and

L197-09K > Culture forum   Update this Forum

This forum is for you to share and discuss your thoughts raised by the culture notes and in particular the 想一想 xiǎng yi xiǎng 'have a think' sections.   Guide to forum

Add a new discussion topic

Discussion	Started by	Replies	Unread ✓	Last post
Chinese authors	S1	1	0	S5 9 Oct 2010. 20:5
chicken feet? how about Jellyfish, tripe, fish head	S2	2	0	S6 30 Sep 2010. 15:
Festivals	S3	4	0	T2 20 Sep 2010. 18:
Chinese Literature-Dream of the Red Chamber	T1	11	0	S7 19 Sep 2010. 23:
Session 18: The influence of Cantonese on Mandarin	CTM	10	0	S8 29 Jul 2010. 09:4
Chinese painter	S1	1	0	S9 23 Jul 2010. 19:0
Session 27 Chinese perspectives on the past and future	CTM	1	0	S10 3 Jul 2010. 21:34
Session 32 Karaoke	CTM	1	0	S2 2 Jul 2010. 18:06
Session 36 The Great Wall and the Yellow River	CTM	0	0	CTM 2 Jul 2010. 10:56
Session 35 Etiquette for giving gifts	CTM	0	0	CTM 2 Jul 2010. 10:55
China's Most Honourable City (Ancient Xi'an)	T1	1	0	T1 21 Jun 2010. 09:
Journey to the East - York Art Gallery China Exhibition to 5/9/10	S4	0	0	S4 18 Jun 2010. 14:
Chinese films: Zhang Yimou	S1	6	0	S11 11 Jun 2010. 23:

Figure 11.3   Front page of the culture forum showing a list of topical threads

Note: Original contributors' names are deleted. S=student; T=tutor; CTM=course team member.

Session 10: Differences between spoken dialects
CTM   · 1 Oct 2009, 20:01

想一想 *Xiǎng yi xiǎng*

What do you think are the reasons for such huge language variations between two neighbouring cities? What is your view regarding the promotion of a standard form of a language?

Read by | Edit | Delete | Reply (quote) | ☐ S

S12   · 10 Oct 2009, 09:25

I think China is such a big place, that it isn't surprising.

In Europe, there are different dialects of French spoken in France, Switzerland and Belgium, although probably not as different as sor the dialects in China. But there are also languages like Italian, Spanish, Portuguese, French and Romanian that all came from Latin.

When I moved to Scotland, I had to learn a lot of words that my in-laws used in conversation -- plus the differences between British English and American English!

cheers

Kathy

Show parent | Read by | Edit | Split | Delete | Reply (quote) | ☐ S

S13   · 16 Oct 2009, 22:00

Ey up mi duks, art a'reit? Or to translate from Derbyshire dialect into some more usual form of English, hello my friends, how are doing? Check this weeks papers for the companies employing translators for Glasweegan, no surprise at all dialects exist in China they do here on this little island as well!

Show parent | Read by | Edit | Split | Delete | Reply (quote) | ☐ S

T3   · 30 Oct 2009, 15:39

Language variations--they could be languages or dialects. John DeFrancis *(The Chinese Language)* coined the word 'regionalect' to represent the regional speech (fangyan 方言) , and he thinks dialects should be referred to those 'mutually intelligible sub-varieties o regionalects.'

Figure 11.4   An extract within a particular discussion topic from the course material

there were cross postings, that is, discussions pertinent to one forum wer posted in another one. This study examines the culture forum and a sma sample of postings in the course forum that are related to cultural issues.

The culture forum evoked considerable participation, as recorded onlin in the forum itself: from the beginning of the course in November 2009 t the end of September 2010, there were altogether 43 discussion topics wit over 180 posts on the culture forum. Of the 39 cultural discussion topics, 1 were linked with the 'Have a think' sections in the books, and the rest wer new threads generated by students themselves. Any new discussion topi and the most recent post appeared at the top of the screen (Figure 11.3).

The forums were designed very much for peer-to-peer communicatior but they were also open to tutors who, from time to time, participated i discussions (Figure 11.4).

The occasional contribution from some tutors and course team member helped to keep the forum active, and students could feel that the forum wa supported by staff. There were 19 posts from three tutors, two of whom cor tributed regularly. The course team members contributed 18 posts altogethe 17 of which were the cultural activities linked with the book (Figure 11.4).

11.3   Methodology

Our research approach to the intercultural development of this group c beginners' Chinese learners focuses fundamentally on how analysis of ind viduals' discourses reveals their intercultural skills, although aspects of hov person develops them through exchanges with others are also considered. Julie Belz (2003) points out that studies of intercultural exchanges have not paid much attention to the actual language use, but that a critical interpretation of the development of interculturality can be gained through linguistic examination. The research reported here is a qualitative study at the micro level of the discourse of individual students. It is mainly exploratory as well as descriptive of students' interculturality individually, but also of how interculturality emerges interpersonally. For this, we identify aspects of intercultural discourse that implicate others and examine how these are accepted, rejected or ignored. Conclusions are also informed by some quantitative aspects of students' profiles and their active participation in the forums.

The research sought to answer the following questions:

. What intercultural skills do adults of beginners' Chinese have?
. To what extent do these students develop personal views of the target cultures while studying the language?
. How do the students mutually influence their own intercultural competence through forum participation?

1.3.1 Data collection

For this study, student quantitative and qualitative data were collected from a number of sources. Quantitative information was obtained through:

. statistics automatically captured by the forum software that records numerically individual students' postings;
. pre-course and post-course questionnaires sent out to students on a wide range of issues to do with distance language learning (see Appendix 11.1); and
. beginners' Chinese student profiles provided by the university's student statistics service. Qualitative data were obtained from: (a) voluntary entries in the forums which were logged according to the activity in a specific topical thread; and (b) from semi-structured but open-ended conversational telephone interviews, which were recorded and later transcribed (see Appendix 11.2 for sample questions).

Of the 245 students who were sent the pre-course online questionnaire, 170 completed it (a 69 per cent return rate). For the post-course survey, 247 students were approached, and 130 completed it (a 55.6 per cent return rate). Of 130 who completed the post-course survey, 118 students, that is, 90.8 per cent, had visited the forums regularly or occasionally during the course of their study (either reading the messages or participating). For follow-up telephone interviews, 15 students volunteered to participate, of whom only one had never visited any of the forums, and one other had not visited the culture forum. Of those 14 students who visited the forums, one never posted but visited regularly to read others' postings, and 13 spent more time reading others' messages than contributing. Only one student spent roughly equal amounts of time contributing and reading others' messages.

11.3.2   Data analysis

Data collected from the different sources were connected during the process of analysis in order to identify salient aspects of students' intercultural skills. Forum and interview data were examined from a discourse analysis perspective, that is, a perspective that 'focuses on talk and texts as social practices and on the resources that are drawn on to enable those practices' (Potter, 1996: 129).

For this discourse analysis, two researchers examined students' forum postings and transcriptions of interview statements, and manually coded and categorized specific words and expressions that revealed components of students' interculturality – that is, aspects of their knowledge, attitudes of curiosity and openness, skills of interpreting and relating, skills of discovery and interaction as well as their critical cultural awareness to evaluate themselves and others (Byram, 1997). The data were searched for demonstration as well as development of those intercultural components. Topical content was not studied in any depth but it was looked at because it could provide insights on aspects such as students' stereotypical images of Chinese cultures. Contextualization cues (e.g., intonation, non-verbal language, etc.) were not relevant to the written medium offered by forums and were not taken into consideration in the analysis of the interviews.

In addition, this investigation searched for evidence of whether students were having intercultural influences on each other through writing that is communicative, as well as for evidence of the extent to which the medium was suitable for supporting specifically those influences. Michael Hammond (2000) has identified a number of features characteristic of communicative discussion:

1. keeps an open mind on the value of different types of knowledge
2. takes a critical stance to theoretical knowledge
3. is reflective
4. adopts a cautious tone
5. seeks dialogue and debate with others in the group
6. strikes a personal note through the message
7. contributions have a loose structure

These characteristics, he observes, 'require support and a willingness on the part of the learner to take risks' (Hammond, 2000: 261). The first five of these characteristics (open-mindedness, critical stance, reflexivity, caution and seeking a dialogue) and the demands on the learner to take risk early overlap with desirable intercultural traits and values. In the analysis, students' discourses were scrutinized for signs of any of these. The last two characteristics were contemplated in the interpretation of the data in order to assess the suitability of the medium for supporting students' intercultural development and mutual influence. Interview questions also prompted learners to comment explicitly on whether they felt others had helped them to make up their minds on specific topics.

One of the limitations of this research is the voluntary nature of all the activities recorded and analysed, so findings reported refer to self-selected groups who might happen to be the most interculturally competent of the cohort. As over 80 per cent of our students are white British adults highly educated, our sample only reflects this group.

In the presentation of the findings, students' identities have been anonymized by referring to them with an S plus a number. Forum entries should be assumed as taken from the culture forum unless otherwise specified.

1.4 Findings

The analysis of the data focused mainly on linguistic cues from forum entries that signalled presence or development of personal or interpersonal intercultural skills. The examination of student discourses led to the identification of discursive categories that suggested that intercultural skills were used and developed but these categories were not validated through quantification of linguistic recurrences. The approach taken is more exploratory and searches for language use that provides evidence of interculturality in action. These words and phrases have been italicized in the quotes used.

It is also important to state that, in the process of identifying and classifying language expressions that signal different intercultural components, it became evident that many of these were not by any means clear-cut. Some of the language used could correspond to several intercultural categories, that is, there were cues that reflected multiple intercultural skills at play. We also found that there were very few commonalities in the ways in which individual students expressed their views, which means that in this sample group we could not identify common patterns of how interculturality is conveyed through language, although language clearly marked the use and development of intercultural skills.

1.4.1 Intercultural skills in action

The forum data reveal that asking specific questions can encourage students to go beyond the course content to further research into certain aspects of culture and support the development of their intercultural skills. As we will see, a single question can trigger the functioning of a chain of competences, although sometimes the potential is not fully developed. For instance, one of the cultural activities was concerned with the Chinese lunar calendar

and, although there is some evidence of openness to acquiring new know
ledge, responses mainly consisted of presenting those findings. This postin
exemplifies such a result since information is presented as facts with no pe:
sonal critical analysis and no further elaboration is requested by others:

> *It is interesting* that there are even variations on the calendar for instanc
> the rent days. The Quarter Days are the traditional days in English la
> when rent payments become due. These are important to landlords as
> is still the practice today that commercial rents become due on the qua:
> ter days, quarterly in advance. They were taken from the Christian hol
> days; four specified days when certain payments are due. ... (S11)

However, most forum postings and answers from the interviews reveal
complex picture of intercultural skills being activated and developed, which
might be expected of motivated adult learners. For instance, in the follow
ing posting a student reveals skills of discovery, that is, the capacity to fin
out new information, as revealed in her expression '*I asked my friend ...*
These skills are linked to his attitude of curiosity expressed in the questio:
'*how do I ...?*' to a native Chinese speaker which in turn activates the skill c
relating, introduced by the formula '*they aren't ... we are*':

> The Chinese *aren't* rude, *we're* over polite. *I asked my friend* yesterday '*ho*
> *do I* end a telephone conversation?' She looked at me as if I'd asked th
> silliest question in the world. 'Just put the phone down'. (S14, cours
> forum)

The presence and development of interculturality were found in student
participation in a culture activity entitled, 'Differences between spoken diz
lects'. This discussion thread displays rich interactive postings. For instance
in the entry below *I think* ... and *it should not be...* express personal beliefs, i:
this case on a topic of the student's interest. The student articulated unam
biguously her position on this issue by using '*is important for*' and referred t
previous posts '*as said before is important to*' taking a critical stance to share
knowledge:

> *I think* standardised language *is important for* literacy and communicatio
> across regions, especially in a country as large as China but *it should n*
> *be* at the cost of the mother tongue, which *as said before is important t*
> identity and culture. (S15)

Another intervention in this thread states some facts a student discovere
by reading a survey but also shows that he is able to relate them to previou
knowledge of Chinese television. The student continues the dialogue wit
his peers in a tentative, explanatory tone. With the expressions '*Perhaps th*

ccounts for ...' and the use of the first person pronoun '*I would argue that
.*', the student reveals skills of interpreting as he is able to produce an ex-
lanation about the linguistic situation in China. Although his question
 rhetoric, as he immediately answers it himself, it can also be seen as an
 idirect invitation to others to reflect and make up their minds, that is, to
ctivate their critical cultural awareness based on their knowledge and the
 iformation provided:

> It [referring to a survey he had read] noted that many parts of China
> are now seeing a situation of what linguists call diglossia, where there
> is one public spoken language and one local dialect that is used among
> friends and family. *Perhaps this accounts for* the use of Chinese subti-
> tles on Chinese television (Chinese programmes intended for a native
> Chinese audience) .... So is a dialect a language? Well, considering the
> speaker of one is almost entirely unintelligible to a speaker of another,
> *I would argue that* it is, albeit related to the same 'parent' language.
> (S6)

 1 a different thread, a student shows a general intercultural attitude of
 uriosity and openness in her attempt to find a Chinese name for herself.
 ler expression '*I tried to look up ...*' reveals willingness to understand an out-
 ider's perspective on naming habits and construct a Chinese social iden-
ty. The fact that she specifies that she went about it with the help of a
 :hinese friend also suggests the presence of discovery skills which allow her
) have recourse to other people to find out information:

> *I tried to look up* a Chinese name[;] ... *my Chinese friend* was happy to do
> so and came up with 吴雨婷 and I asked my daughter if she liked it, who
> said it had something to do with rain ... said it suited me. (S10)

 1 the following forum entry, by the same student who was looking for
  Chinese name (S10), on the topic of Chinese perspectives on the past
 ind future, we find further evidence of this student's intercultural skills at
lay. Development of critical cultural awareness becomes obvious as pre-
ious beliefs are examined and a new view is considered, compared and
 nderstood by the student. In this contribution, the phrase '*The more I
 earn ... the more subtle it appears*' reflects a willingness to engage in a pro-
 ess of acquiring new knowledge, but also relate it to her own and evalu-
te it. Her intercultural attitude of readiness to suspend her own beliefs
 ; summarized in the statement '*it makes sense*' about the Chinese time
erspective. With that she is conveying understanding. More precisely, in
er expressions '*is an interesting one*', '*I hadn't before thought of ...*' she reveals
ealization and willingness to embrace a different cultural concept. In add-
ion, these expressions can also be interpreted as suggestive of skills of

discovery, and the phrase *'compared to ours'* is clearly an indication of he skills of relating:

> This idea of perception *is an interesting one*, events that are over bein 'seen' *I hadn't before thought of* events in this way, although *it makes sens The more I learn* of the Chinese language, *the more subtle it appears con pared to ours*. (S10)

In the literature on the intercultural dimension in foreign language edu cation, the skills of discovery have been linked to our capacity to acquir knowledge of habits, history, artefacts and so on, that might be similar c very different to what we know and value. But this knowledge discover has also been connected to an empathetic capacity in our responses. Th Intercultural Competence Assessment (INCA) project worked on the creatio of a framework that could explain and evaluate an individual's intercultura competence when working and interacting with a multicultural group. I describes three main characteristics of interculturality: openness (respec for otherness and tolerance of ambiguity), knowledge (knowledge discover and empathy) and adaptability (behavioural flexibility and communicativ awareness); and three levels of competence (basic, intermediate, full). A a basic level empathy means that one tends to see the cultural foreigner differences as curious and remains confused about the seemingly strang behaviours and their antecedents. Nonetheless, at this basic level, one trie to 'make allowances', while at an intermediate level, one 'tends increasingl to see things intuitively from the other's point of view' (INCA, 2004: 10 Signs of empathic development became apparent in a student's response t the telephone interview in which he revealed how the process of writing i the forum helped him to understand not only his own experiences but als the experiences that others in similar situations might have. Writing in th forum, as well as reading other people's postings, opened up for him th possibility of reflection and this, in turn, helped him to overcome his initia confusion and move on to see it from the point of view of the other:

> I'm a big believer in writing as a reflective tool for learning so I found tha actually writing up my own experience *helped me make sense* of my visit t China. When I came back, *I couldn't decide if* I enjoyed my visit or not...suc an alienating cultural experience. And in doing the course, thinking abou things, and sometimes writing them down and reading other people experiences, *I've come to realize that* it was actually one of the most impor ant two weeks I spent anywhere. *It helped me make sense of* my own exper ences, *and also helped me understand* my Chinese students' experiences c coming here, and my Chinese friends' experiences of coming to work an live here. It was very valuable from that point of view. (S14, interview)

In this interview statement, the student describes a change of attitud brought about by reflection and critical cultural awareness. He moves fror

n alienating feeling where he *'couldn't decide'* about his experience to an
ppreciation of the other people's perspective. His realization is evident in
he expressions *'helped me make sense'*, *'I've come to realize that'* and *'helped
1e understand'*. This declaration as a whole seems to support Olson's view
f writing as an activity that 'enables us to say and think things that we
ould not, or at least have not, said and thought without writing' (Olson,
995: 228). More specifically, the asynchronous nature of the interaction
ives participants time to think and reflect before they write down what
hey want to say, thus creating a 'special relationship between interaction
nd reflection' (Warschauer, 1997: 5). Indeed, Marie-Noelle Lamy and Robin
;oodfellow's (1999) research corroborated that asynchronous text-based
omputer conferencing can promote the sort of learning that integrates
•oth reflection and interaction.

It could be argued, therefore, that the text-based asynchronous forums
re well suited for cultural discussions in the language learning context:
/hen prompted by critical reflection they have a transformative potential
or students. Transformative learning is a powerful process of reconsider-
1g one's beliefs, past experiences and assumptions, critically and ration-
lly (Mezirow, 1991) or affectively and emotionally (Boyd and Myers, 1988).
igns of transformative learning appeared in our findings, at not only an
1dividual level, but also at an interpersonal level. Some forum entries
•rompted critical cultural awareness in other participants. In the following
xchange, one student's experience creates an opportunity for reactions that
how how learning can transform viewpoints. The response demonstrates
n open attitude and an ability to relate which becomes an evaluation of
elf in the expression *'we should be very tolerant'*. Here the implication is that
/e (Westerners), perhaps, are not tolerant enough and could learn from the
:hinese attitude towards language learners:

> There seems to be universal appreciation for anyone [W]estern attempt-
> ing to learn Chinese. If you try to speak Chinese to someone, then unless
> they are too busy, they will give you all the time and patience in the
> world. (S14, course forum)
>
> So now *we should be very tolerant* of all those Chinese students, etc., who
> come up to us in China wanting to speak in English. (S16 in response to
> S14, course forum)

n both the pre-course and post-course surveys, we asked students to com-
•lete the same statement: 'When learning a language, learning about the
ulture and customs of where it is spoken is ...'. In the pre-course survey,
2.14 per cent chose *essential*, and 40.48 per cent chose *very important*. The
igures in the post-course survey are very similar: 46.2 per cent completed
he statement with *essential* and 32.2 per cent with *very important*. This
1dicates that there is a slight shift to recognizing how culture learning is
ssential. More interestingly, students actually came with a very positive

attitude, which is probably why they embraced the opportunities to reflect and examine in the forum.

We will now discuss instances in the forum of students' dialogues that impacted on each other's intercultural competence.

11.4.2   Mutual intercultural influences

Whilst many students had had some experiences with Chinese-speaking cultures, the post-course survey revealed a significant proportion (33. per cent) whose only contact point with them was through doing this course. This group, 'disconnected' from the target cultures, was particularly keen to hear other students' experiences and views expressed in the forums. One student linked the acquisition of this knowledge through vicarious experience to his emotional engagement and level of motivation:

> *Hearing about* people's trips to China and their work in China was useful. ... For a significant number of people like me, they have no direct connection with the Chinese people[;] ... it is very important for them to get a kind of emotional connection with what it is they are learning, and so maintain motivation. (S5, interview)

Fortunately, the 'connected' group (those students with previous experience and knowledge of the Chinese language and cultures) were keen to share experiences with others. As one student put it:

> If I knew anything about anything, *I just contributed*. (S14, interview)

The following exchange between two students shows this dynamic at play. After reading a book about Chinese culture one student explains her understanding of the Chinese characters for 'up' and 'down'(上 and 下 respectively) which are used in time expressions to refer to the past and the future (e.g., 上个星期 'last week' and 下个星期 'next week'):

> [A]nd *I understood it as*: the past is the ancestors, they are in heaven. Heaven is up, (historically, in China, mountains, as their tops reach high near heaven, were sacred). The future has not happened, it is, literally, in the lap of the Gods, for all of us. Water is the staff of life, there is no future without it. There will be no new events without springs of water to drink, and to form rivers to irrigate the land to grow food. So, in a very literal sense, the future does need springs of water (from underground) to exist at all: thus the future IS down, only springing up when it becomes the present. *This might be helpful?* (S7)
>
> Wow, thank you [addressing S7], *I get it now*. That is a lovely poetic interpretation *I can relate to*. (S1 in response to S7)

his type of exchange exemplifies how students contribute to one anoth-
r's knowledge and understanding in what Martin Cortazzi and Lixian Jin
2006: 34–5) identify as student-to-student informal co-constructions of
:arning or 'chains of learning transmission'. The student who posted the
xplanatory note on this topic is showing not only intercultural knowledge
ut also a willingness to communicate efficiently through a cautious tone,
sing the expression '*I understood it as*', and introducing a final tentative
uestion, '*This might be helpful?*', showing key features of a communicative
iscussion that opens up the possibility of a dialogue between them. The
esponse, '*I get it now*', acknowledges understanding. As in most other occa-
ions, an explanation not only impacts on other people's knowledge but
lso on other intercultural skills. In this case, it seems to have an influence
n the respondent's attitude or 'ability to "decentre"' (Byram et al., 2002:
2), as reflected in her final comment: '*I can relate to*'.

In order to activate communicative discussions, questions that encour-
ged learners to reflect and share their own backgrounds, personal views
nd experiences were set up in the culture forum. Some discussion topics
ttracted active participation, revealing that students were willing to strike
personal note. For instance, in one thread of cultural exchanges around
amily names, local knowledge and personal information were disclosed
nd shared with the group:

> First names given to babies are actually an issue *here in Germany*... If you
> meet *people from my generation* (I was born in 1972).... (S17)
> *I'm American*, and we always used 'first name',... I worked *in Eritrea*,
> where... (S12)

n the culture forum, there were a considerable number of entries where
xperiential as well as discovered knowledge was shared with the group
f peers and thus, it became in turn new knowledge for other students.
n these communicative contributions of chains of learning, not only did
:arners learn about one anothers' backgrounds, but most importantly, in
erms of their intercultural awareness, they were increasing their cultural
nowledge, not only about Chinese, but also about a variety of different
ultures:

> Names are very interesting aren't they? I believe that here *in England* a
> person's occupation led to surnames such as 'Cook' 'Wright' and the
> family name on *my father's side* 'Clubbe' which means... (S11)
> *My father is* Korean, and *we have* Korean names as well as [W]estern
> names. The first name *is* the family name, the second name *is* the given
> name and the last part *is* the generation name. *It appears that* the order
> of the given and generation names are reversed *in the Chinese system*.
> (S18)

There are also forum entries where students referred to other scholars' wor or websites and this had an impact on others. A good example of this wa around the discussion of the concept of time which inspired students t search for knowledge beyond the course materials. In the following entr a student (S12) quoted a scholar's view in order to explain and compar the concept in the British and the Chinese culture. This demonstrates he ability to build knowledge of the social constructions of both the targe communities and her own, and an incipient skill of relating both culture through an explicit comparison that groups language communities in tw different sentences: 'English speakers ...' and 'Speakers of Mandarin' that ar contrasted by the conjunction 'however'. In addition, it can be argued tha by providing a name and a link, S12 tries to engage in a communicativ act with others, she offers them the possibility to check and reflect on tha knowledge, as indeed happened. The response to her message from S7 show that engagement:

> English speakers, (Lera Boroditsky explains), tend to see time on a hori zontal plane: The best years are ahead; he put his past behind him Speakers of Mandarin, however, tend to see time both horizontally and ve tically, with new events emerging from the ground like a spring of wate the past above and the future below. http://www.stanfordalumni.org news/magazine/2010/mayjun/features/boroditsky.html (S12)
>
> I remember that when [using S12's given name] originally mentione Lera Boroditsky on the forum and *I looked it up on the net* ... (S7)

An interesting finding in our analysis of students' exchanges in the forum was that there was a certain level of debate around a number of topics. In study on forum exchanges, David Curtis and Mike Lawson (2001) reporte that there were no signs of challenging others or offering explanation possibly due to not knowing each other. However, our analysis of the forun data shows that there were various friendly and constructive challenge among students despite the fact that they had never met. Examples of thi can be appreciated in the expressions '*very interesting, but*' and '*just to giv the other side of things*', used by one student, or '*not sure*' and '*looks a bit sus picious*', by another:

> I have found your responses all *very interesting but* if we look at it histor ically what you will find is that all cultures are treating the aged mor disrespectfully – the west just faster! Asia is having a rising problem wit this as well .... *just to give the other side of things* .... (S15)
>
> *Not sure I trust* that source though ... ? Some of those entries definitel *look a bit suspect [suspicious]*! Otherwise mostly Cantonese words/expres sions which is hardly surprising given Britain's relationship with Hon Kong, but still doesn't account for that much .... (S6)

these interventions can also be bound up with individual students' skills of interpreting and relating and critical cultural awareness. Although it is not clear from their discourses whether they developed them during the exchanges in the forum or whether they had already come to the course with solid competence. Statistics captured by the forum software that retains individual students' postings clearly indicate that there is a critical mass of about ten students who regularly contributed to the discussions. These students should have more influence on those who did not contribute but regularly read the postings. Amongst those who regularly contributed, it seems that there was an equal influence on each other.

1.4.3   Asynchronous forums for intercultural learning

A final consideration should be to look at the suitability of the activities and the medium for supporting students' development of intercultural learning both individually and as a group.

The asynchronous written nature of online discussion forums, such as the ones used in this course, provides an informal context for cultural debates among students. Examining the forum entries and the interview data offers plenty of evidence to support the claim that those who actively participated in the forum discussions demonstrated and/or developed their intercultural skills. Unfortunately, there was only evidence that this was the case for a minority of students (Students 5, 7, 10, 14, 15 and 16). Forum activities based on critical questioning of cultural aspects (including linguistic ones) seemed to support individual student's reflection and to encourage them to take a critical stance; they also had the potential to activate mutual influences on their interculturality. However, many students did not participate at all or participated very little in the forums, although they were experienced OU learners and experienced language students with good IT skills and independent learning skills.

The literature on forums has already highlighted some of the many complex factors that affect who participates and who does not. These factors include: time constraints, a sense of alienation, poorly developed ICT skills, personal study preferences, and the fact that forum activity was not part of any summative assessment and that students may perceive the medium as a permanent written text that puts them at risk of criticism (Hammond, 2000: 56) as well as distinct pedagogical online cultures that not all students feel comfortable with (Goodfellow and Hewling, 2005) due to the differences between their cultures of learning (Kumpulainen and Renshaw, 2007).

Silences are particularly important to conversational analysis and require an interpretation of what is not there and why that might be the case (Wood and Kroger, 2000). Analysis of the discourses in forums did not reveal any indication of why students had decided to keep silent about specific topics or even after a particular intervention from a peer. Our interview data indicate some of the specific reasons why some students did not visit or did not contribute to debates in the culture forum. But due to the fact that only one person interviewed did not participate in any forums at all, and only two visited forums less than ten times, the sample is too small to ascertain an exhaustive list of reasons.

Despite explicit questioning in the forum threads, for some students knowledge sharing was the main purpose of the forums, rather than personal reflection and development of cultural perspectives through group interaction. It seems that some students felt alienated if they had no previous knowledge to contribute. They opted for a passive role and just browsed through contributions rather than take the opportunity to have a presence in the forum and enter into a dialogue with their peers. One particular student perceived sharing of information in a negative way, as *'boasting'* (S19, interview). Another reason given for limited active participation was that others had already posted enough relevant information on the topic, as a student put it: 'There are so much there already. ... I didn't feel that I had anything extra to contribute' (S20 interview). Finally, a practical reason mentioned by some of them was that they had extremely busy schedules and had no time to converse online.

11.5   Conclusions

This study aimed to understand the effectiveness of specific educational approaches and tools to raise students' intercultural awareness in order to help foreign language teachers and material developers successfully achieve cultural and intercultural objectives.

The study identified that students were successfully using intercultural skills to mediate between their cultures and Chinese-speaking cultures through the reading of culture notes in the teaching materials, but especially when they were prompted with reflective questions and shared their views in communicative written discussions. It seems clear that at beginners' level, activities that support students' written narrations of their views, feelings and experiences using the language they are confident with ('English' in this case) can support the exercise of their intercultural awareness. However, it is hard to distinguish in most instances between the impact of the set activities on the development of their interculturality and the extent to which students were already quite confident intercultural individuals. We examined the data for clues of intercultural development, but we found that grasping this development is a very slippery task. When learners change their views, modify their attitudes, are they putting into action new or consolidated intercultural skills? Our response to this is that intercultural skills are constantly being practised and developed and, perhaps, it is less significant to ask whether students are developing intercultural skills with the help of specific activities than to ask whether we are developing and using the kinds of activities that support that practice. To this latter question, we believe we can answer affirmatively.

Acknowledgement

We would like to thank Joanne Fallows for her comments and corrections to the original manuscript.

Appendix 11.1: Course surveys

Relevant questions from pre-course survey

3	Have you had personal experience of or contact with any Chinese-speaking countries? Please put a cross against all the options that apply to you.		All that apply
	• I have been on holidays in a Chinese-speaking country		
	• I have lived in a Chinese-speaking country		☐
	• I have friends in a Chinese-speaking country		☐
	• I have work contacts in a Chinese-speaking country		☐
	• I have watched Chinese films, plays or TV (either in the original language or in translation)		☐
	• I have looked at Chinese newspapers or magazines		☐
	• I have met Chinese speakers in the UK (or another non-Chinese-speaking country)		☐
	• Some members of my family speak Chinese		☐
	• other		☐
4			All that apply
	My mother tongue is		☐
	• English		☐
	• Other European language		☐
	• Japanese/Korean		☐
	• Cantonese		☐
	• Other		☐
5	What are your reasons for studying 第一步[1] now? Put a cross against all the reasons that apply in the first column and against the most important reason in the second column.	All that apply	Most important
	• for pleasure or interest	☐	☐
	• to assist me in my present or future work	☐	☐
	• to be able to communicate with Chinese-speaking friends or family	☐	☐

• to be able to communicate when visiting a Chinese-speaking country	☐	☐
• to be able to live in a Chinese-speaking country	☐	☐
• to understand TV, radio, films or songs in Chinese	☐	☐
• to read newspapers, magazines or books in Chinese	☐	☐
• to help my children or grandchildren learn Chinese	☐	☐
• as an intellectual challenge	☐	☐
• as part of a wider programme (for instance, to obtain a degree)	☐	☐
• other	☐	☐

q20 – Please indicate how you would complete the following statement: When learning a language, learning about the culture and customs of countries where it is spoken is …

(Please select one only)

- Essential
- Very important
- Quite important
- Useful but not essential
- Not important at all

II Relevant questions from post-course survey

q13 – This question aims to find out how important 第一步 has been in developing your speaking skills, or whether and to what extent other contact with the language has been important, e.g., through work, friends, holidays, watching television.

(Please select the one option that applies to you most)

- 第一步 is my only contact with the Chinese language
- 第一步 is my main contact with the Chinese language
- I have other contacts with the Chinese language that are just as important as the course for the development of my speaking skills
- The course plays a subordinate role in the development of my speaking skills. Other contacts I have with the Chinese language are more important

q21 – Do you think that learning about other cultures and their customs can help you reflect on your own culture and customs?

(Please select one only)

Yes
No
Don't know

22 – Please indicate how you would complete the following statement: When learning a language, learning about the culture and customs of countries where it is spoken is ...

(Please select one only)

Essential
Very important
Quite important
Useful but not essential
Not important at all

23 – During the course, did you visit the forums (either reading the messages or contributing to the discussions)?

Yes
No

Appendix 11.2: Interview questions related to forum participation and learning about culture

Profile of students interviewed

Gender :	7 male
	8 female
Age range :	
0+	2
0+	3
0+	8
0+	2

Ethnic background: 13 British and 2 Europeans (1 Swedish and 1 Belgian)
Which forum did you visit most frequently? Were you mostly reading or contributing?
If you felt unable to contribute, what was it that prevented you from so doing?
Did you get any satisfaction when the discussion topic you initiated generated interest?

(Describe one topic that you particularly remember in relation to this)

Why did you use the forums (your reasons for participating in forum discussions)?

What did you get out of them?

What type of messages from others did you find useful?

In what ways did the forums help you in your learning of Chinese language and culture?

How important is for you the discussion of Chinese cultures? How did your own reflections on cultural issues help you learn the language?

Have the forum discussions changed your views or simply reinforced your existing views about Chinese cultures and/or languages?

When you asked a specific question on the forum, did you expect it to be answered by your fellow students, tutors or the course team?

Did you tend to agree with what was said on the forum? Were you concerned if you disagreed with others' views?

Note

1 This is the Chinese name for the beginners' course, which means 'The First Step'.

References

Álvarez, I. (2011) Learning about Chinese-speaking cultures at a distance. In J. Fenoulhet & C. Ros i Solé (Eds), *Mobility and localisation in language learning. A view from languages of the wider world*. Oxford: Peter Lang, pp. 145–72.

Baumann, U& Shelley, M. (2003) Adult learners of German at the Open University. Their knowledge of, and attitudes towards Germany. *Open Learning*, 18 (1), 61.

Belz, J. (2003) Linguistic perspectives on the development of intercultural competence in telecollaboration. *Language Learning & Technology*, 7 (2), 68–117.

Boyd, R.D. & Myers, J.G. (1988) Transformative education. *International Journal of Lifelong Education*, 7 (4), 261–84.

Byram, M. (1997) *Teaching and assessing intercultural communicative competence*. Clevendon: Multilingual Matters.

Byram, M., Gribkova, B. & Starkey, H. (2002) *Developing the intercultural dimension in language teaching. A practical introduction for teachers*. Strasbourg: Council of Europe.

Coleman, J.A. (2009) Why the British do not learn languages: Myths and motivation in the United Kingdom. *Language Learning Journal*, 37 (1), 111–27.

Cortazzi, M. & Jin, L. (1999) Cultural mirrors: Materials and methods in the EFL classroom. In E. Hinkel (Ed.), *Culture in second language teaching and learning*. Cambridge: Cambridge University Press, pp. 152–66.

Cortazzi, M. & Jin, L. (2006) Asking questions, sharing stories and identity construction: Sociocultural issues in narrative research. In S. Trahar (Ed.), *Narrative research on learning, comparative and international perpectives*. Oxford: Symposium Books, pp. 27–46.

Curtis, D.D. & Lawson, M.J. (2001) Exploring collaborative online learning. *Journal of Asynchronous Learning Networks*, 5 (1), 21–34.

oodfellow, R. & Hewling, A. (2005) Reconceptualising culture in virtual learning environments: From an 'essentialist' to a 'negotiated' perspective. *E-learning*, 2 (4), 355–67.

ammond, M. (2000) Communication within on-line forums: The opportunities, the constraints and the value of a communicative approach. *Computers & Education*, 35 (4), 251–62.

auck, M. (2007) Critical success factors in a TRIDEM exchange. *ReCALL*, 19 (02), 202–23.

einze, A. & Procter, C. (2004) *Reflections on the use of blended learning*. Paper presented at the Education in a Changing Environment Conference Proceedings, University of Salford.

ESA (2011) All HE students by level of study, subject of study, domicile and gender 2009/10, from http://www.hesa.ac.uk/index.php/content/view/1973/239/

NCA (2004) Assessor manual, from http://www.incaproject.org/

n, L. (2008) Using instant messaging interaction (IMI) in intercultural learning. In S. Sieloff Magnan (Ed.), *Mediating discourse online*. Amsterdam: John Benjamins Publishing Company, pp. 275–301.

ern, R., Ware, P. & Warschauer, M. (2004) Crossing frontiers: New directions in online pedagogy and research. *Annual Review of Applied Linguistics*, 24, 243–60.

umpulainen, K. & Renshaw, P. (2007) Cultures of learning. *International Journal of Educational Research*, 46 (3–4), 109–15. doi: 10.1016/j.ijer.2007.09.009.

amy, M.-N. & Goodfellow, R. (1999) Supporting language students' interactions in web-based conferencing. *Computer Assisted Language Learning*, 12 (5), 457–77.

iaw, M.-L. (2007) Constructing a 'third space' for EFL learners: Where language and cultures meet. *ReCALL*, 19 (02), 224–41.

indeman, E.C. (1961) *The meaning of adult education in the United States*. New York: Harvest House.

cGrath, I. (2002) *Materials evaluation and design for language teaching*. Edinburgh: Edinburgh University Press.

ezirow, J. (1991) *Transformative dimensions of adult learning*. San Francisco: Jossey-Bass.

'Dowd, R. (2003) Understanding the 'other side': Intercultural learning in a Spanish-English e-mail exchange. *Language Learning & Technology*, 7 (2), 118–44.

lson, D.R. (1995) Conceptualising the written word: An intellectual autobiography. *Written communication*, 12, 277–97.

suna, M.M. & Meskill, C. (1998). Using the world wide web to integrate Spanish language and culture: A pilot study. *Language Learning & Technology*, 1 (2), 71–92.

U (2008) *Skills for OU study*. Milton Keynes: The Open University.

U (2010) *L197 beginners' Chinese* (Book 1 and Book 2). Milton Keynes: The Open University.

otter, J. (1996) Discourse analysis and constructionist approaches: Theoretical background. In J. Richardson (Ed.), *Handbook of qualitative research methods for psychology and the social sciences*. Leicester: British Psychological Society, pp. 125–40.

ulverness, A. (2003) Materials for cultural awareness. In B. Tomlinson (Ed.), *Developing Materials for Language Teaching*. London: Continuum, pp. 426–38.

isager, K. (1991) Cultural references in European textbooks: An evaluation of recent tendencies. In D. Buttjes & M. Byram (Eds), *Mediating languages and cultures: Towards an intercultural theory of foreign language education*. Clevedon: Multilingual Matters, pp. 180–92.

ogers, A. & Horrocks, N. (1986) *Teaching adults* (4th edn). Glasgow: Open University Press.

Ros i Solé, C. (2003) Culture for beginners: A subjective and realistic approach fc
adult language learners. *Language & Intercultural Communication*, 3 (2), 141–50.

Singerman, A.J. (Ed.) (1988) *Towards a new integration of language and culture*
Middlebury, VT: Northeast Conference.

Tasker, I. (2010) Intermediate distance learners of Chinese look back: A survey study
In M.E. Everson & H.H. Shen (Eds), *Research among learners of Chinese as a foreig*
language. Honolulu, HI: National Foreign Language Resource Center, pp. 153–77.

Truscott, S. & Morley, J. (2001) Cross-cultural learning through computer-mediate
communication. *Language Learning Journal*, 24, 14–23.

Warschauer, M. (1997) Computer-mediated collaborative learning: Theory and prac
tice. *Modern Language Journal*, 81 (4), 470–81.

Wood, L.A. & Kroger, R.O. (2000) *Doing discourse analysis: Methods for studying actio*
in talk and text. Thousand Oaks: Sage.

12
Adjusting to Differing Cultures of Learning: The Experience of Semester-Long Exchange Students from Hong Kong

Jane Jackson

2.1 Introduction

Institutions of higher education across the globe are increasingly signing agreements to facilitate cross-border education. This is providing more opportunities for students to experience new ways of being; in some cases, this includes exposure to a second language on a daily basis. While many administrators are preoccupied with increasing the participation rate in international exchange programs, it is imperative that we pay attention to what actually transpires when students move to another cultural and linguistic context to study. By understanding the challenges they face in and outside of classrooms, educators will be in a better position to design pre-sojourn programs and determine the most effective ways to support the learning, intercultural experience and second language development during stays abroad.

This chapter reports on one phase of a study that is investigating the learning of undergraduate students from a Hong Kong university who took part in a semester-long exchange program in the 2009–10 academic year (Jackson, 2011a).While the study is examining multiple dimensions of their sojourn experience (e.g., academic, personal, [inter]cultural, professional, disciplinary learning), discussion centres on their emerging intercultural competence and responses to differing cultures of learning. Before focusing on the experiences and perceptions of the interviewees, I provide a brief overview of the theoretical underpinning for the study. I begin by exploring notions of 'cultures of learning' and then describe the Developmental Model of Intercultural Sensitivity (DMIS) and its application in study abroad research, including the present study.

12.2 Cultures of learning

Martin Cortazzi and Lixian Jin (1996, 1997, 2011), Jin and Cortazzi (1993) Heather Parris-Kidd and Jenny Barnett (2011), Jane Jackson (2002, 2003) and other educators have found that differing 'cultures of learning' may pose a challenge for students who travel overseas and enter an unfamiliar educational system and sociocultural setting. As Cortazzi and Jin (1997) explain:

> [A] culture of learning depends on the norms, values and expectations of teachers and learners relative to classroom activity.... It is not simply that overseas students encounter different ways of teaching and different expectations about learning; rather such encounters are juxtaposed with the cultures of learning they bring with them. (Cortazzi and Jin, 1997: 83)

The primary socialization of most learners takes place within a particular linguistic and sociocultural setting in their home country. It is in this context that they receive messages about what constitutes 'good' teaching and learning. They learn how to ask questions and discover when it is appropriate to do so in specific classroom situations. When exposed to a new culture of learning, whether at home or abroad, they may be confronted with behaviours and attitudes towards learning and teaching that are out of sync with their expectations. How they respond may then have a significant impact on their development.

My work on case method teaching and learning in Hong Kong uncovered tension between local students and international exchange students due to differing understandings about what constitutes appropriate behaviour in case discussions. American business professors who were acting as case leaders in this setting were also frustrated by the reticence of local students (Jackson, 2004). Although there were individual variations in the attitude toward participation, students who spoke up risked being branded as 'show offs' by their peers. The reticence phenomenon may be attributed to a complex mix of affective, sociocultural, and educational factors (e.g., lack of confidence in one's English language skills or 'points', 'habits' developed in the exam-oriented Hong Kong school system, lack of experience with discussion-based pedagogy, fear of standing out and losing face) (Jackson, 2003, 2004).

If local students find it challenging to adjust to case discussions in their home context, one might expect that they would face even more difficulty in an environment in which active discussions are the norm. One might also expect that a certain degree of openness to cultural difference would be necessary for student sojourners to fully engage in academic practices that are new to them.

2.3 The Developmental Model of Intercultural Sensitivity (DMIS)

The DMIS (Bennett, 1993), including recent interpretations by Mitch Hammer 2007, 2009a, 2009b), helped me to understand the exchange students' responses to differing cultures of learning. Derived from the analysis of 'real world' intercultural interactions, this model centres on the constructs of more monocultural ('ethnocentric') and more intercultural/global ('ethnorelative') mindsets (Bennett, 1993, 1997; Bennett and Bennett, 2004; Hammer, 2009b, 2009c; Landis et al., 2004). In the former, 'the worldview of one's own culture is central to all reality' (Bennett, 1993: 30), while the latter is linked to 'being comfortable with many standards and customs' and an ability to adapt behaviour and judgments to a variety of interpersonal settings' (ibid.: 26). Within the DMIS framework, intercultural sensitivity/competence entails personal and cognitive growth and the emergence of a mindset capable of understanding from within and from without both one's own culture and other cultures' (Bennett et al., 2003: 252), including differing cultures of learning in academic settings.

At the heart of this model is the belief that the way people view and respond to cultural difference (such as unfamiliar cultures of learning) impacts on the development of intercultural competence. More specifically, the DMIS posits that individuals move from more ethnocentric stages (*denial*, *polarization*) through *minimization* (a transitional orientation; Hammer, 2009a, 2009b, 2009c) to more ethnorelative stages of development (*acceptance*, *adaptation*, and *integration*) as they acquire intercultural competence. This development does not always follow a linear progression. Disturbing intercultural encounters or severe culture shock, for example, may exacerbate ethnocentric tendencies and impel individuals to temporarily retreat to a lower level of sensitivity.

Janet Bennett and Milton Bennett (2004) define intercultural competence as 'the ability to communicate effectively in cross-cultural situations and to relate appropriately in a variety of cultural contexts' (p. 149). The DMIS is based on the notion that ethnorelative world views are more effective in fostering the attitudes, knowledge and behaviour that facilitate successful intercultural communication and adjustment in unfamiliar cultural settings (Jackson, 2010; Kim, 2001, 2005). Many researchers investigating study abroad learning have found this model useful in explaining the intercultural development of student sojourners (e.g., Anderson et al., 2006; Engle and Engle, 2004; Jackson, 2009, 2010, 2011a, b; Medina, 2008; Paige et al., 2004; Pedersen, 2010; Vande Berg et al., 2004). Pre- and post-sojourn, these researchers have employed the Intercultural Development Inventory (IDI), a cross-culturally validated, empirically based survey which measures the stages of the DMIS (Hammer, 2009a, 2009b, 2009c; Hammer and Bennett, 2002; Hammer et al., 2003; Paige et al., 2003).

12.4   Background to study

Before focusing on the experiences of the Hong Kong sojourners, it i
important to have an understanding of the home institution's internatior
alization aims and efforts. The Chinese University of Hong Kong (CUHK
is a bilingual (Chinese–English), comprehensive research university with '
global vision and a mission to combine tradition with modernity, and t
bring together China and the West' (CUHK, 2006: 3). At present, it has mor
than 20,000 undergraduate and postgraduate students, including 3,000 wh
come from regions outside Hong Kong. Although the institution does no
have an explicit internationalization policy, the 2006 strategic plan indi
cates the attributes and skills expected of graduates, and several are linke
to intercultural/linguistic competence and global dimensions of learn
ing. For example, the document states that graduates are expected to hav
acquired: 'bilingual proficiency and effective communication skills', 'inter
cultural sensitivity and appreciation of other cultures', 'personal attributes
ethical values (e.g., interpersonal skills, civic and global responsibility)' an
'a global perspective (a broader perspective and deeper understanding of th
realities of the interconnectedness of world systems)'.

The number of CUHK students gaining some form of international experi
ence has increased significantly in recent years (Office of Academic Links
CUHK, 2010). In the 2009–10 academic year, 1,304 students participate
in some form of credit-bearing, international education (546 more than i
2005–06): 709 joined an exchange program (534 went abroad for a semeste
and 175 for a year), while 595 took part in a short-term, credit-bearing pro
gram. In addition, 1,800 students participated in other experiential learn
ing opportunities outside Hong Kong (e.g., community service, fieldwork
The university now has more than 200 exchange partners in 28 countries
regions and the number and diversity of incoming exchange students ha
also risen in recent years.

Since 2009, I have been examining the developmental trajectories of out
going semester-long exchange students from CUHK using a mixed-method
experimental design approach. In Jackson (2011a), the intercultural sensi
tivity development of 94 students who went abroad for the first semeste
of 2009–10 (the experimental group) was compared with 34 who were or
campus prior to going on exchange (the control group). Twenty-three of th
students in the experimental group were interviewed both before and afte
the sojourn. The remainder of this chapter focuses on their perceptions an
experiences with special attention paid to the following research questions

1. What is the level of intercultural sensitivity of the interviewees befor
   and after the semester-long sojourn?
2. What differing cultures of learning did they encounter? How did the
   respond?

. What are the implications for the pre-sojourn preparation of future exchange students and their support in receiving (host) institutions?

2.5   Method

2.5.1   Participants

Among the 23 interviewees, there were 16 females (69.6 per cent) and 7 males (30.4 per cent) with a mean age of 21.9 years. All were of Chinese ethnicity: 17 (73.9 per cent) were born in Hong Kong, 1 (4.3 per cent) in Macau and the other 5 (21.8 per cent) in Mainland China (Beijing, Shanghai or Guangzhou). 18 (78.3 per cent) spoke Cantonese as a first language, 4 (17.4 per cent) Putonghua, and 1 (4.3 per cent) student spoke both Cantonese and Putonghua fluently.

At the beginning of the 2009–10 academic year, 2 (8.7 per cent) were in their second year of study, 14 (60.9 per cent) in their third, and 7 (30.4 per cent) in their fourth. Their mean GPA (Grade Point Average) was 3.4. Their majors varied, as they came from different faculties: 12 (52.2 per cent) business administration, 5 (21.7 per cent) arts, 2 (8.7 per cent) social science, 2 (8.7 per cent) science, 1 (4.3 per cent) medicine, and 1 (4.3 per cent) education. The exchange programs they joined took place in a range of destinations: 13 (56.5 per cent) the United States, 2 (8.7 per cent) Singapore, 2 (8.7 per cent) South Korea, 2 (8.7 per cent) Czech Republic, 1 (4.3 per cent) Spain, 1 (4.3 per cent) Norway, 1 (4.3 per cent) New Zealand, and 1 (4.3 per cent) the United Kingdom. Similar to the full cohort, the United States was the most popular destination; for all students, their coursework would be in a second language (e.g., English). Three (13.0 per cent) had never ventured outside Hong Kong; 20 (87.0 per cent) had some travel experience, which typically consisted of a few days or weeks in Asia; 18 (78.3 per cent) had no form of education abroad, while 5 (21.7 per cent) had studied abroad; this study typically consisted of a short-term sojourn in an English-speaking country. Fifteen (65.2 per cent) had never taken a course in intercultural or cross-cultural communication, while 8 (34.8 per cent) had taken one or more courses in this area.

2.5.2   Instrumentation and procedures

The following section describes the instrumentation and procedures that were used to gather data before and after the semester abroad.

2.5.2.1   *Pre-test instrumentation and procedures*

In the pre-test phase, the IDI was administered on entry to provide a measure of the participants' intercultural sensitivity. They also completed the Pre-International Exchange Survey, an in-house instrument that consisted of 93 closed questions and an open-ended question. Topics covered included: reasons for studying abroad; aims, expectations, and level of preparedness for sojourn; concerns about living and studying abroad; previous international or education abroad experience; intercultural contact; perceptions of intercultural competence; second language proficiency and use; identity and family background (e.g., parents' level of education and international experience).

Prior to the sojourn, individual semi-structured interviews were conducted in Cantonese, English, or Putonghua, depending of the preference of the interviewee. The average length of the interviews was 80 minutes. Topics covered included: aims and expectations for the sojourn; intercultural contact; intercultural communication skills; perceptions of intercultural competence; identity; previous international experience and education abroad; level of preparedness for life/study abroad; second language proficiency (self-assessment; English language scores on TOEFL, IELTS assessments); and language use. The interviewees were also encouraged to discuss other issues related to the international exchange experience that interested them.

12.5.2.2   *Post-test instrumentation and procedures*

At the end of the exchange semester, the participants were again administered the IDI. They also completed the Post-International Exchange Survey, which consisted of 78 closed questions and 3 that were open-ended. To facilitate the assessment of their learning, the instrument included many items that were similar to those in the Pre-International Exchange Survey. Topics were varied: reasons for studying abroad; aims, expectations and level of preparedness for sojourn; assessment of goals achieved; challenges faced while living and studying abroad; benefits of previous international experience; second language proficiency and use; perceptions of intercultural sensitivity/competence; identity; and recommendations for the preparation of future exchange students.

After they had returned to Hong Kong, the 23 participants were re-interviewed to facilitate a deeper understanding of what actually happened when they were abroad. Similar to the first administration, the semi-structured interviews took place in English, Cantonese or Putonghua, again depending on the preference of the interviewee. The average length of the second interview was 90 minutes. Topics included: their overall impression of their international experience; perceptions of their academic and intellectual development; extracurricular activities and travel; intercultural contact and adjustment; intercultural communication skills; perception of their development in personal, social, academic, cognitive, and professional spheres; identity (change); second language development and usage; evaluation of level of preparedness; perception of needs; reentry challenges and adjustment; current intercultural contact and future plans; and recommendations for the preparation and support of future exchange students/returnees.

2.6   Data analysis

At the beginning of the study, a project database was set up in NVivo Bazeley, 2007; Richards, 2009); this qualitative software program facilitated the organization and triangulation of quantitative and qualitative data from different sources (e.g., interview transcripts, open-ended survey questions, IDI/CCAI survey results).

The analysis of the IDI surveys provided an indication of the actual and perceived levels of intercultural sensitivity of each participant. This permitted the tracking of changes in individuals as well as a comparison of the intercultural development of the 23 interviewees with the experimental group (N = 94) and control group (N = 34). The Pre- and Post- International Exchange Surveys were processed using SPSS and the IDIs by IDI, LLC.

An 'open coding' approach (Grbich, 2007) was employed to analyse the qualitative data (interview transcripts, open-ended survey questions); codes were devised to reflect what I saw in the material instead of limiting myself to predetermined categories (Berg, 2007). As I became familiar with the data and recognized relationships between items, categories were adjusted and new ones emerged. Since all of the surveys included the students' ID number, it was possible to link this data with the interview transcripts. By triangulating data types and sources, I discovered how the interviewees perceived cultural differences and adjusted to a new academic/social environment while on exchange.

2.7   Results

2.7.1   Overview

While data about a range of issues was gathered by way of multiple surveys and interviews, the following sub-sections focus on the pre- and post-IDI results and the analysis of the interview transcripts that shed light on the interviewees' response to different cultures of learning, especially class participation.

2.7.2   Overall IDI development

2.7.2.1   *Pre-test profile*

In the IDI, the *perceived orientation* (PO) of a group indicates where the group as a whole 'places itself' along the intercultural development continuum of denial, polarization (defence/reversal), minimization, acceptance, or adaptation (Hammer, 2009a; 2009b, 2009c). On entry, the perceived orientation of the 23 interviewees was 116.39 in acceptance, which is an ethnorelative stage.

The *development orientation* (DO) also provides an indication of 'the group's primary orientation toward cultural differences and commonalities along the continuum *as assessed by the IDI*' (Hammer, 2009c: 5). This orientation is the perspective that the group is most apt to draw on in inter cultural encounters. Similar to the perceived orientation, the developmen orientation can be denial, polarization (defence/reversal), minimization acceptance, or adaptation (ibid.). On entry, the interviewees' developmenta orientation was 77.80 (polarization: defence/reversal), an ethnocentric stage of development which indicates 'a judgmental orientation that views cul tural differences in terms of "us" and "them"' (ibid.: 4).

For this cohort, the *orientation gap* (OG), the difference between the per ceived orientation and developmental orientation, was 38.59. According to Hammer (2009c), a gap score of 7 points or higher indicates a meaningfu difference between the perceived orientation and the developmental orien tation. What this means is that before going on exchange, the interviewee significantly overestimated their intercultural competence and would likel have been very surprised by the discrepancy between their perceived orien tation and developmental orientation scores.

The IDI profiles also provide an indication of what Hammer (2009a) refer to as *trailing orientations* (TO), 'orientations that are "in back of" the group' Developmental Orientation (DO) on the intercultural continuum *that ar not "resolved"*' (ibid.: 5). In times of intercultural stress or conflict thes trailing issues may pull individuals back from their developmental orien tation for coping with cultural difference. The analysis of trailing orienta tions revealed that none of the worldviews of the interviewees was full resolved.

Leading orientations (LO) indicate the 'next step to take in the enhance ment of intercultural competence, in terms of the intercultural continuum As the interviewees' developmental orientation on entry was polarization defence/reversal, their leading orientations were minimization, acceptance and adaptation. Thus, their IDI profile was similar to the rest of the experi mental group, as well as the control group (Jackson, 2011a).

12.7.2.2   Post-test profiles

At the end of the semester, the interviewees again completed the IDI along with the remainder of the experimental group, as well as the control group This time their perceived orientation was 119.33, indicating a slight increase of 2.94 points. Both pre- and post-sojourn, the interviewees estimated thei level of intercultural sensitivity to be in acceptance, an ethnorelative stage

After a semester abroad, the developmental orientation of the interview ees increased to 86.44, a gain of 8.64 points; they had moved from polariza tion: defence/reversal to the low end of minimization, a transitional stage of development that 'highlights cultural commonality and universal value and principles' but 'may also mask deeper recognition and appreciation o cultural differences' (Hammer, 2009c: 4). The orientation gap was 32.89 still a great overestimation of their level of intercultural competence. A for trailing orientations, all orientations remained in transition except fo

he defence/denial orientation which was resolved (barely), indicating that
hese students were less apt to simplify and/or polarize cultural difference.
s their developmental orientation was now in minimization, their lead-
ng orientations were acceptance and adaptation. Similar to the full experi-
nental group, the interviewees as a whole had shifted in the direction of a
reater 'intercultural worldview'; the semester abroad appeared to have had
 positive impact on the development of their intercultural competence. By
ontrast, the control group regressed slightly (a reduction of 1.59 points in
O) (Jackson, 2011a).

2.7.3   The qualitative data

n the post-sojourn interview, the interviewees were encouraged to share their
iews about academic learning in the host institution; several questions probed
heir experience with differing cultures of learning. Interestingly, all of the
nterviewees, except for a female student who went to South Korea, identified
ctive class discussions as the greatest difference between their courses at CUHK
nd those at the host institution. The following comments were typical:

> The learning attitude in the U.S. was the most challenging to adjust to.
> At CUHK I became used to sitting and listening to a lecture but students
> there always ask questions and I felt bad when I didn't have one to ask.
> I was forced to generate questions as class participation counted for the
> grade, much more than in Hong Kong.
>
> (Male, third-year professional accountancy major,
> in the United States)

> The professors really encouraged us to be more interactive and actively
> participate in class. They didn't need to finish their own questions as the
> students were already raising their hands to answer them! People always
> say Hong Kong students are way too passive, but Singaporean students
> took the chance to express their ideas. At first, I was really shocked that
> students there were so enthusiastic and always raising their hands in dis-
> cussions. Of course, that's why I joined the exchange programme, right?
> To experience a whole different culture .... At CUHK, we don't participate
> much in class because no one wants to stand out.
>
> (Male, third-year business administration major, in Singapore)

n particular, many of the interviewees found it difficult to adjust to the fast
ace of discussions, especially in a second language:

> My English is not good enough to express myself fully .... The language
> problem was most apparent in discussions. I wasn't sure how to respond ....
> Three months was not adequate to solve this problem.
>
> (Male, third-year molecular biotechnology major, United States)

For some, like this professional accountancy major, fear was the first reac tion in these rather threatening situations:

> The management course I took was case-based and students were will ing to voice out their opinions in discussions. You had to at least rais your hand once in every lesson and write a participation card. At first I was really frightened. The students could express themselves fluentl but I wasn't able to express my thoughts clearly even though I had som ideas in mind…. Although I didn't improve a lot, I realized that peopl wouldn't reject you because of your poor English.
>
> (Male, third-year professional accountancy majo in the United States

Afraid of making mistakes and losing face, many found it difficult to fi in. They did not fully grasp the purpose of the discussions (e.g., to increas understanding, to encourage critical reflection) and felt ill-prepared:

> In Hong Kong, we are used to spoon-feeding and students in the US ar really active in learning…. It was stressful to speak in front of nativ speakers. There was a tutorial where I had to speak up every time and didn't want to look dumb. I had to make sure my grammar was right. also needed to read all the materials before going there as the content wa new and difficult for me. You couldn't contribute anything meaningful i you hadn't prepared well. The teachers didn't provide you with notes o ppt slides [PowerPoint] like they do at CUHK and memorizing your own notes wouldn't work. You really had to understand the concept to answe the questions.
>
> (Female, fourth-year English major, in the United States

Used to a more receptive style of learning, this English major found it dif ficult to keep up, as did a third-year student from her department who also went to the United States:

> The professors printed out an outline for us but never provided or mad any PowerPoints. When it was time to start the lesson, they just kept ask ing questions and summarized a bit. Students raised their hands and th professors recognized their names! I didn't get the chance to really diges what happened. Students there might not have PowerPoint but they wer well-prepared for discussions.

A similar experience led many interviewees to question the roles and wor ethic of lecturers who did not provide the level of support they had grown accustomed to in Hong Kong (e.g. PowerPoint slides, detailed lecture notes)

Early in the sojourn, others were also troubled by the communication styles of local students:

> The students there are more aggressive in discussions. They would oppose an idea immediately. They might not wait until you've finished your whole point and even show gestures and expressions that imply they think your ideas are wrong. I think our culture stresses a more modest character so that even if someone is not satisfied with your points, we seldom interrupt. At first, I was puzzled by their actions since I am, after all, a Hong Konger who is greatly affected by Chinese culture. I thought their behavior was really strange.... Then I realized that they wouldn't think you were impolite to interrupt as that was their habit. I began to appreciate their courage to express their own opinions. Also, when the discussion was over, they wouldn't feel upset about what somebody had said about their ideas. This model of learning is very good because it can train students to speak their minds without fearing undesirable consequences.... I tried to adjust my attitude and accept that I was just experiencing a new social environment. Things went much easier when I began to accept this.
>
> (Female, fourth-year social work major, in the United Kingdom)

In her interview, this returnee added: 'Because I was adapted to passive learning, I often accepted whatever someone said. But, gradually, after listening to different opinions, I learnt that I could also have my own ideas. I now encourage myself to think more and even challenge others' point of view'. She attributed her previous attitude and behaviour to the 'duck-ducking' learning mode in Hong Kong (a Chinese metaphor for teaching which points to very high levels of support for learning, similar to 'spoon-feeding'), as did the following second-year psychology major (male) who sojourned in Norway:

> The local students were very eager to ask questions but I couldn't think of any to ask, which made me wonder if there was some problems with me.... Maybe the reason is that I was taught like this for many years. While taking the HKCEE [the exam for university entrance], it was enough to succeed by studying the textbooks and getting to know the forms of assessment in the exams. You didn't need to discuss with others and you could even skip all the lessons and still get an A grade....

While initially uncomfortable in this environment, he persevered and reaped the benefits: 'My greatest gain from going abroad was that I became more active in discussions with professors and students, which is a good thing for me'. Other interviewees disclosed a similar shift in attitude and behaviour:

> As class participation was highly encouraged and included in our grading, some of us would force ourselves to be active and speak up in every single lesson. A bit stressful as this doesn't happen much in Hong Kong, but I soon got used to this practice.... You could see how people look at the same problem or issue from different perspectives.... When we study at CUHK we never have such an open discussion and we cannot think outside the box. But after hearing many ideas from others you may change your mind. It does make a difference.
>
> (Female, third-year mathematics major, in the United States)

A female second-year business administration student who went to Singapore commented: 'Before going abroad, I was a bit shy and preferred to ask questions after class or via e-mail. Because of the academic environment you were forced to be more active in class.... I enhanced my critical thinking skills and problem-solving skills'.... By the end of the sojourn, some surmised that their lecturers were trying to encourage them to 'think independently' and they expressed appreciation for this.

While most of the students became more active in discussions, this did not always occur. For example, a third-year business administration major who went to the United States revealed the following: 'Almost all of the courses there require intensive communication and discussion, so I just dropped the ones that I found very hard to cope with, so I was left with ones I could easily accept. Probably for this reason, I didn't find it difficult to adjust'. Her avoidance strategy limited her exposure to this mode of active learning; consequently, as she noted in her interview and survey, she experienced fewer gains in self-confidence, second language proficiency and intercultural communication skills than did her peers.

Active discussions were not the only challenges the exchange students faced. Several commented that they received less guidance and direction for tasks and assignments and were often unsure how to proceed, as the following excerpt illustrates:

> There were more essays and project work compared with CUHK. I didn't always understand what the teachers expected from us in those assignments.... When I did ask some questions, the lecturers responded, 'up to you'.... It was hard to grasp what they wanted. I didn't know how to deal with this so I just rushed through the assignments and submitted them.
>
> (Male, second-year professional accountancy major, in New Zealand)

When collaborating with local students on group projects and presentations, they also encountered a range of practices and attitudes that were new o them (e.g., differing expectations about roles and responsibilities). A full discussion of these elements is not possible due to space limitations. What is important to note is that a central element in their international exchange experience was differing cultures of learning, and their responses varied, due in part to their level of intercultural sensitivity, as well as to that of their hosts (both lecturers and students).

2.8   Outcomes and results

While abroad, most of the interviewees experienced symptoms of culture shock and initially found it difficult to adjust to less familiar academic practices and beliefs that were prevalent in the host institution (e.g., discussion-based pedagogy, differing teacher-student roles and relationships, unexpected attitudes towards learning, differing approaches to group work and differing expectations of support and independence). To cope, they employed a variety of strategies, ranging from avoidance to deliberate steps that would provide them with more opportunity to gain the skills and confidence needed to take a fuller role in the host academic environment (e.g., actively participate in class and case discussions).

The analysis of the interview transcripts revealed that those who acquired higher levels of intercultural sensitivity displayed more awareness of cultural elements in the host culture, including the rationale behind differing academic cultures of learning (e.g., discussion-based pedagogy). This finding lends support to the DMIS, which posits that 'as one's experience of cultural difference becomes more complex and sophisticated, one's competence in intercultural relations increases' (Intercultural Communication Institute, 2004). Those with a higher level of intercultural competence were more willing to suspend judgment and experiment with practices that were new to them; accordingly, in their estimation they experienced more gains in personal and academic growth as well as second language proficiency.

The analysis of the IDI scores and interview transcripts revealed that the participants significantly overestimated their level of intercultural sensitivity. On entry, most perceived their intercultural competence to be several IDI band levels above their actual developmental level. The pre-sojourn interviews indicated that most were very confident about their ability to interact successfully across cultures, even though they had had very little intercultural experience. Psychologists attribute such inflated self-perceptions to a range of factors, including the desire to maintain a positive self-image, using biased reference points, and lack of awareness of one's incompetence (Ditto and Lopez, 1992; Fischer et al., 2007; Taylor and Brown, 1994). Significantly, research indicates that metacognitive-awareness training can help individuals recognize limitations in their knowledge and skills, and provide direction for the setting of realistic goals for improvement (Kruger and Dunning,

1999). This suggests the potential benefits of pre-sojourn programming of this nature.

Similar to my ethnographic investigations of short-term sojourners from Hong Kong (Jackson, 2008, 2010a, 2011b), this study of semester-long exchange students revealed that a high level of proficiency in the host language does not ensure a similar level of intercultural sensitivity or competence. Study abroad researchers in other contexts have similar findings (e.g. Parris-Kidd and Barnett, 2011). It is naïve to expect intercultural competence to develop at the same pace as foreign language proficiency. An array of linguistic, sociocultural, psychological and environmental factors can impact on sojourner adjustment and participation in both academic and social arenas in the host culture, and this can lead to differences in their developmental trajectories.

12.9   Pedagogical implications

The findings of this study have implications for the preparation of exchange students for unfamiliar cultures of learning. The participants in this study had had limited preparation for their sojourn and prior to departure did not receive guidance on setting goals. Most had had limited intercultural contact and few had taken any formal courses in intercultural communication or comparative education. Their pre-sojourn orientation primarily focused on logistics (e.g., procedures for transferring credits, security).While useful, brief sessions of this nature cannot deal with complex intercultural communication issues or adequately prepare students for study and residence in another culture. More intensive, credit-bearing intercultural communication courses are needed to help students develop a framework to make sense of cultural difference, including exposure to differing cultures of learning. Such courses could usefully include teaching students ways to investigate social patterns of interaction in classroom contexts in the host institutions. This would extend the work of Celia Roberts and her colleagues (Roberts et al., 2001) and Jackson (2006); prior to the sojourn, students could learn to become ethnographers of cultures of learning and, in the process, become equipped to investigate systematically social contexts in host countries. Besides numerous intercultural benefits, this would likely accelerate their learning and help to ameliorate or remove some of the problems the students in this study experienced.

The findings from this study also have implications for educators in countries receiving international exchange students. While it is always important to be mindful of individual variations, an awareness of academic practices in different parts of the world can be very helpful. When newcomers are unsure what is expected of them and anxious in unfamiliar classroom situations, it is incumbent on host lecturers to take steps to put them at ease (e.g., to create a welcoming atmosphere conducive to ngagement, facilitate local and international student interaction). Making lements more explicit early on (e.g., discussing their expectations as well s the aims and benefits of discussion-based pedagogy) should benefit ewcomers as well as local students. It is also important to recognize that eticence among exchange students does not necessarily indicate a lack of nderstanding or proficiency in the host language. Multiple factors may ccount for this, as illustrated in this chapter. Patience and encouragement re essential.

To optimize the international exchange experience, much more work eeds to be done to better understand the developmental trajectories of tudent sojourners and the impact of various forms of intervention both t home and abroad (e.g., the effects of a pre-sojourn intercultural communication course or the adoption of a buddy system in the host culture). Vhile most of the students in the present study experienced modest gains n intercultural sensitivity during their stay abroad, as their stories attest, imply being present in the host culture does not ensure smooth adjustment o differing cultures of learning, second language enhancement or personal transformations. Theory-inspired, research-driven interventions may e necessary for student sojourners to fully benefit from an international xchange program.

Acknowledgements

his research was generously supported by a direct grant from the Chinese Jniversity of Hong Kong (CUHK) (#2010312) and a general research fund #444709) from the Research Grants Council of Hong Kong. I appreciate the participation of the exchange students and the assistance of the Office of Academic Links (OAL) at CUHK.

References

Anderson, P., Lawton, L., Rexeisen, R. & Hubbard, A. (2006) Short-term study abroad and intercultural sensitivity: A pilot study. *International Journal of Intercultural Relations*, 30, 457–69.

Bazeley, P. (2007) *Qualitative data analysis with NVivo*. London: Sage.

Bennett, J.M. & Bennett, M.J. (2004) Developing intercultural sensitivity: An integrative approach to global and domestic diversity. In D. Landis, J.M. Bennett and M.J. Bennett (Eds), *Handbook of Intercultural Training* (3rd edn). Thousand Oaks, CA: Sage, pp. 145–67.

Bennett, J.M. Bennett, M.J. & Allen, W. (2003) Developing intercultural competence in the language classroom. In D. Lange and M. Paige (Eds), *Culture as the core: Perspectives on culture in second language learning*. Greenwich, CT: Information Age Publishing, pp. 237–70.

Bennett, M.J. (1993) Towards ethnorelativism: A developmental model of intercultural sensitivity. In R.M. Paige (Ed.), *Education for the Intercultural Experience*. Yarmouth, ME: Intercultural Press, pp. 21–71.

Bennett, M.J. (1997) How not to be a fluent fool: Understanding the cultural dimensions of language. In A.E. Fantini (Vol. Ed.) & J.C. Richards (Series Ed.), *New Ways in Teaching Culture. New Ways in TESOL Series II: Innovative Classroom Techniques* Alexandria, VA: TESOL, pp. 16–21.

Berg, B.L. (2007) *Qualitative Research Methods for the Social Sciences* (6th edn). Boston Allyn and Bacon.

Cortazzi, M. & Jin, L. (1996) Cultures of learning: Language classrooms in China In H. Coleman (Ed.), *Society and the Language Classroom*. Cambridge: Cambridge University Press, pp. 169–206.

Cortazzi, M. & Jin, L. (1997) Communication for learning across cultures. In D. McNamara and R. Harris (Eds), *Overseas Students in Higher Education*. London Routledge, pp. 76–90.

Cortazzi, M. & Jin, L. (2011) Conclusions: What are we learning from research about Chinese learners? In L. Jin and M. Cortazzi (Eds), *Researching Chinese learners Skills, perceptions and intercultural adaptations*. Basingstoke: Palgrave Macmillan, pp 314–18.

CUHK (Chinese University of Hong Kong) (2006) The Chinese University of Hong Kong Strategic Plan, 1 February 2006. Hong Kong: CUHK. http://www.cuhk.edu hk/strategicplan/english/documents/cuhk-strategic-plan.pdf

Ditto, P.H. & Lopez, D.F. (1992) Motivated skepticism: Use of differential decision criteria for preferred and nonpreferred conclusions. *Journal of Personality and Social Psychology*, 91, 1–15.

Engle, L. & Engle, J. (2004) Assessing language acquisition and intercultural sensitivity development in relation to study abroad program design. *Frontiers: The Interdisciplinary Journal of Study Abroad*, X, 219–36.

Fischer, P., Greitemeyer, T. & Frey, D. (2007) Ego depletion and positive illusions Does the construction of positivity require regulatory resources? *Personal and Social Psychology Bulletin*, 33 (9), 1306–21.

Grbich, C. (2007) *Qualitative data analysis*. London: Sage.

Hammer, M.R. (2007) *The intercultural development inventory manual* (v. 3). Ocean Pines, MD, USA: IDI, LLC.

Hammer, M.R. (2009a) Intercultural Development Inventory (v. 3) (IDI). www.idiinventory.com

Hammer, M.R. (2009b) The intercultural development inventory: An approach for assessing and building intercultural competence. In M.A. Moodian (Ed.) *Contemporary leadership and intercultural competence: Exploring the cross-cultural dynamics within organizations*. Thousand Oaks, CA: Sage, pp. 203–17.

Hammer, M.R. (2009c) Intercultural Development Inventory (v. 3) (IDI) Education Group Profile Report. http://idiinventory.com/pdf/idi_sample.pdf

Hammer, M. & Bennett, M. (2002) *The Intercultural Development Inventory: Manual* Portland, OR: Intercultural Communication Institute.

Hammer, M., Bennett, M. & Wiseman, R. (2003) Measuring intercultural sensitivity: The intercultural development inventory. *International Journal of Intercultural Relations*, 27 (3), 421–43.

Intercultural Communication Institute (2004) *The Developmental Model of Intercultural Sensitivity*. Retrieved from http://www.intercultural.org.

Jackson, J. (2002) Diversity and the case leader: Linguistic, cultural, psychological and contextual insights. *Journal on Excellence in College Teaching*. Special Issue Teaching with Case Studies, 13, 87–102.

ackson, J. (2003) Case-based learning and reticence in a bilingual context: Perceptions of business students in Hong Kong. *System*, 31 (4), 457–69.

ackson, J. (2004) Case-based teaching in a bilingual context: Perceptions of business faculty in Hong Kong. *English for Specific Purposes*, 23 (3), 213–32.

ackson, J. (2006) Ethnographic preparation for short-term study and residence in the target culture. *The International Journal of Intercultural Relations*, 30 (1), 77–98.

ackson, J. (2008) *Language, identity, and study abroad: Sociocultural perspectives.* London: Equinox.

ackson, J. (2009) Intercultural learning on short-term sojourns. *Intercultural Education*, 20 (1–2), S59–71.

ackson, J. (2010) *Intercultural journeys: From study to residence abroad.* Basingstoke: Palgrave Macmillan.

ackson, J. (2011a) *Assessing the impact of a semester abroad using the IDI and semi-structured interviews,* (distinguished paper award) Proceedings of the 2nd Intercultural Development Inventory conference, Minneapolis, MN, USA.

ackson, J. (2011b) Host language proficiency, intercultural sensitivity and study abroad. *Frontiers: The Interdisciplinary Journal of Study Abroad*, XXI, 167–89.

in, L. & Cortazzi, M. (1993) Cultural orientation and academic language use. In D. Graddol, L. Thompson & M. Byram (Eds), *Language and Culture.* Clevedon: Multilingual Matters, pp. 84–97.

im, Y.Y. (2001) *Becoming intercultural: An integrative theory of communication and cross-cultural adaptation.* Thousand Oaks, CA: Sage.

im, Y.Y. (2005) Adapting to a new culture: An integrative communication theory. In W. Gudykunst (Ed.), *Theorizing about Intercultural Communication.* Thousand Oaks, CA: Sage, pp. 375–400.

ruger, J. & Dunning, D. (1999) Unskilled and unaware of it: How difficulties in recognizing one's own incompetence lead to inflated self-assessments. *Journal of Personality and Social Psychology*, 77 (6), 1121–34.

andis, D., Bennett, J.M. & Bennett, M.J. (Eds) (2004) *Handbook of intercultural training* (3rd edn). Thousand Oaks, CA: Sage.

Medina, A. (2008) *Intercultural sensitivity development in study abroad: Is duration a decisive element in cultural learning outcomes?* Saarbrücken, Germany: Verlag.

Office of Academic Links, CUHK (2010) *Office of Academic Links Annual Report on International Academic Relations and Education Activities 2009–10.* Hong Kong: OAL, The Chinese University of Hong Kong.

aige, R.M., Cohen, A.D. & Shively, R.L. (2004, Fall) Assessing language acquisition and intercultural sensitivity development in relation to study abroad program design features. *Frontiers: The Interdisciplinary Journal of Study Abroad*, X, 253–76.

aige, R.M., Jacobs-Cassuto, M., Yershova, Y.A. & DeJaeghere, J. (2003) Assessing intercultural sensitivity: An empirical analysis of the Hammer and Bennett intercultural development inventory. *International Journal of Intercultural Relations*, 27 (4), 467–86.

arris-Kidd, H. & Barnett, J. (2011) Cultures of learning and student participation: Chinese learners in a multicultural English class in Australia. In L. Jin and M. Cortazzi (Ed.), *Researching Chinese learners: Skills, perceptions and intercultural adaptations.* Basingstoke: Palgrave Macmillan, pp. 169–87.

edersen, P. (2010) Assessing intercultural effectiveness outcomes in a yearlong study abroad program. *International Journal of Intercultural Relations*, 34, 70–80.

Richards, L. (2009) *Handling qualitative data* (2nd edn). Thousand Oaks, CA: Sage.

Roberts, C., Byram, M., Barro, A., Jordan, S. & Street, B. (2001) *Language learners a* *ethnographers*. Clevedon: Multilingual Matters.

Taylor, S. & Brown, J. (1994) Positive illusions and well-being revisited: Separatin fact from fiction. *Psychological Bulletin*, 116 (1), 21–7.

Vande Berg, M., Balkcum, A., Scheid, M. & Whalen, B. (2004, Fall) The Georgetow University Consortium Project: A report from the halfway mark. *Frontiers: Th Interdisciplinary Journal of Study Abroad*, X, 101–16.

13

Internet-Mediated Intercultural English Language Teaching and Learning: An Overview of Challenges and Opportunities in China

Liang Wang

13.1   Introduction

In the Information Age the advent of Internet technologies has made it possible to transform language learning and teaching through online intercultural exploration and exchange. However, empirical evidence from researchers and practitioners worldwide shows that the pedagogical possibilities for intercultural language teaching and learning are often shaped and framed by the national and local visions of education, and by the social context for teaching and learning practices. Among the designs of Internet-mediated intercultural foreign language activities, cross-site collaboration with external support seems to prevail worldwide, especially between 'native speakers' and 'non-native speakers'. In tertiary English language teaching (ELT) in China, although similar cases are randomly reported, it is, on the whole, not clear what changes are taking place in Internet-mediated language classes, despite the fact that the goals of technology-enhanced education and developing intercultural communicative competence are both recognized in the latest national curricula, alongside other goals such as learner autonomy, creativity and critical thinking.

This chapter reports on research, conducted in 2008–09, into the situation of Internet-mediated intercultural English language teaching and learning in 24 higher education institutions in China. The research employs multi-stage and multi-site fieldwork and combines a survey approach, and a collective case study approach with four particular universities. It investigates the delivery of an intercultural dimension mediated by Internet technologies beyond the classroom. Combined data derive from 612 questionnaires (N = 63 teachers, 549 students), 45 interviews (N = 24 teachers/groups,

21 students/groups), two one-off and four continued observations, as well as the analysis of a number of documents. This breadth and depth will help to understand the sample cases.

Four cases – demonstrating a variety of institutional, individual, pedagogical and technological factors – are analysed to explore how Internet mediated practices might facilitate an intercultural approach to teaching and learning. These cases are in different student contexts: non-English major undergraduates taking a mixed curriculum in a language-specialist university; non-English undergraduates taking EAP/ESP modules in an international partnership institution; postgraduates taking an optional intercultural communication module in a language-specialist university's intercultural institute; and English majors taking an English literature course in a university specializing in sport science and education. Comparison suggest that, although these cases have differing characteristics, there are some commonalities regarding Internet-mediated activities which entail elements of an intercultural approach. These common elements are synthesized, in an original pedagogical framework for Internet-mediated intercultural teaching and learning, with a set of guiding principles. The framework advocates establishing an Internet-mediated intra-class community as the basis for undertaking intercultural language activities, which complement the prevailing telecollaborative model for ICC development. This outcome contributes to a fuller understanding of the design of Internet-mediated intercultural language activities.

13.2   The intercultural approach and Internet-mediated English language education

13.2.1   The rationale

This chapter reports on an investigation (2008–09) into the situation of Internet-mediated intercultural English language teaching and learning in higher education institutions (HEIs) in China. The aim is to enrich the research field of Internet-mediated intercultural language teaching and learning with perspectives from China's HEIs, which are little researched.

Here, the notion of 'culture' and the 'intercultural' involves a dual perspective to the research content and methodology. Culture is seen both as 'an abstract feature of a large community' and as being realized 'in the conduct of individual people' (Palfreyman, 2003: 8), in line with 'large-small culture' paradigms (Holliday, 1999: 237–8). As such, intercultural communication taking place at a collective level relies on 'interdiscourse communication' (Scollon and Scollon, 2001a, b; Piller, 2007). Hence, a typical monocultural class in my research is still viewed as an 'intercultural' class, as each participant represents some of the diversity of cultures within China.

3.2.2 An Internet-mediated approach to intercultural language teaching and learning

In China globalization has made English a means of international communication. The traditional role of culture in ELT, in which there has been an ideology of 'native-speakerism' in which the ideal standard is held to that of native speakers (Holliday, 2005), is challenged by two 'conflicting' trends: the blurring of national and linguistic boundaries' and 'the emergence of regional thinking and the revival of ethnic and regional cultures' (Kramsch and Sullivan, 1996: 200). This means ELT should be recontextualized with appropriate pedagogies with which to serve both the global and the local needs of learners.

For decades, ELT has taken place predominantly in the classroom rather than in 'a natural immersion environment' (Lamy and Hampel, 2007: 9), in which culture has been mostly understood within a 'large-culture' paradigm, as the structured knowledge and a system of public meanings (Roberts et al., 2001; Palfreyman, 2003) of a national/ethnic group. Cultural approaches such as background studies, comparison–contrast studies, and even communicative teaching which merges language and culture, often result in a reductionist over-generalization and conveying of a sense of otherness on 'foreign' educators, students and societies (Byram, 1997; O'Dowd, 2006). In contrast, other approaches, such as ethnography and study abroad (Roberts et al., 2001), involve experiential learning and direct contact with the target culture community. These approaches see culture as a constantly shifting and changing construct, although the mere exposure of learners to the language environment may not automatically produce heightened intercultural awareness (Dlaska, 2000).

Some scholars view culture as communication and discourse (Holliday, 1999; Scollon and Scollon, 2001a, b and Piller, 2007), trying to deconstruct collective culture into individual forms of expression and to distance reified cultural entities from individual identities. Such a discourse approach requires some ability, in the discourse of communication, to understand cultures as being socially constructed, to mediate between them, and to enhance the individual's capacity for identity formation, self-expression and reformulation (Block, 2007). Ron Scollon and Suzanne Scollon (ibid.) and Ingrid Piller (ibid.) also distinguish among cross-cultural communication, intercultural communication and interdiscourse communication, with this last reflecting non-essentialist assumptions.

Within ELT, an essentialist perspective has often accompanied many approaches, embedding a native-speaker model and target (Holliday, 1999). This is widely regarded as largely inappropriate and unattainable, because it not only overlooks the learner's own cultural identity but also risks losing it as a result of imitating the native speaker's conventions and norms in communication (Byram, 1997; Kramsch, 1998; Holliday, 1999; Alptekin, 2002).

Rather than taking a native-speaker model, language teachers and learner
need to develop an 'intercultural speaker' target (Byram, 1997; Kramsch
1998; Corbett, 2003; O'Dowd, 2006; Thorne, 2006). Ideally, an intercultura
speaker should be an autonomous learner, being able to interact with an
mediate between people of different cultural groups for the purpose of inter
cultural exploration, comparison, mediation and collaboration through
language and social practices (Byram, 1997; Kramsch, 1998; Corbett, 2003
2010). Hence, an intercultural approach takes both target and home culture
into account, aiming at developing learners' intercultural communicative
competence (ICC), including communicative competence and intercul
tural competence (Byram, 1997). Following this approach, Anwei Feng and
Mike Byram (2002: 63–7) believe that teaching materials should be multi
dimensionally represented to raise awareness of not only diverse product
and practices but also of different perspectives. John Corbett (2010: 2) add:
that the learners' own cultures can also be used as an extensive resource fo
interpreting texts.

The advent of Internet technologies has made it possible to foster an inter
cultural approach through online intercultural exploration and exchang
(Belz and Thorne, 2006; Block, 2007; Lamy and Hampel, 2007), as well a
intercultural community building (Corbett, 2010).

An array of approaches can be applied to Internet-mediated scenarios
For example, resource-based approaches offer both teachers and learner
the opportunity to develop the skills of discovery and selection of learning
materials (Benson, 2001: 113) for learning about cultural knowledge and
practices, and for raising awareness of different perspectives. Task-based and
project-based approaches have great strengths, in particular for telecollabo
ration design (Debski, 2006; Müller-Hartmann, 2007; O'Dowd and Ware
2009). Developing an online community for intercultural learning provide
a platform whereby learners can enrich their intercultural experience with
formal and informal learning (Corbett, 2010). All these approaches demand
consideration not only from technological and pedagogical points of view
but also from the socio-institutional and individual viewpoints of Internet
mediated intercultural activity.

A growing body of research and popular practice has established online
intercultural exchange for language and intercultural learning (see Belz and
Thorne, 2006; Furstenberg et al., 2001; Hauck and Stickler, 2006; Müller
Hartmann, 2000, 2006; O'Dowd and Eberbach, 2004; O'Dowd, 2006, 2007a
b; Levy, 2007; Guth and Helm, 2010). Four main models are identified: tel
ecollaboration, e-tandem learning, local learner-informant partnerships and
engagement in an established e-community (see Thorne, 2006). In brief: *tel
ecollaboration* is the model that offers international class-to-class exchange:
within institutionalized settings, requiring intensive coordination from syl
labus negotiation to technological preparation; the *e-tandem model* sets up
the pairing of individuals with an interest in learning each other's language

or mutual benefit through various online communication tools; the *learner-informant partnership* is organized via Internet connections between learners and local expert speakers of the target language as informants for consultation and communication; and the *e-community model* requires students' engagement in established online communities for exploration and exchange. All have the feature of including participants outside the classroom via Internet technologies for the purposes of achieving linguistic and pragmatic development; the better understanding of, and reflection on, one's own and other cultures; and mediation of the processes of intercultural communication.

However, with the exception of the e-community, these models often function between 'native speakers' and 'non-native speakers'. There is little research into other scenarios such as cross-site collaboration between non-native speakers of the target language and within-site Internet-mediated intercultural language activities.

3.3 English language education in China

China's modernization and international involvement have created a huge demand for all-round talents. Recent national syllabuses for both English majors and non-English majors include goals to cultivate professionals who possess ICC, together with sound language proficiency, creativity and the ability to solve problems (Ministry of Education, 2000, 2004), although a pedagogical framework is lacking (Zhang, 2007). A recent document (Dai, 2008: x) proposes that language graduates are expected to:

1. think carefully in a foreign language,
2. adapt to economic globalization processes and social challenges by using Chinese and the foreign language,
3. be critical and systematic in reasoning,
4. communicate with intercultural awareness,
5. use foreign languages to work innovatively and independently,
6. deal with foreign affairs with ideological and moral qualities,
7. compete against and cooperate with international society,
8. be critically aware of foreign cultures,
9. be familiar with Chinese and foreign thinking, and
10. observe different disciplines, cultures and philosophies with an integrative perspective.

These descriptors indicate that an intercultural dimension has been emerging as a guide to China's foreign language education, which basically sees ICC as an ability to interact with and mediate between 'Chinese culture' and 'foreign cultures'.

At the same time, with the advent of computers and network technologies, the pace of 'educational informationalization' (Huang et al., 2007) in

China's education sector has been accelerating. Strategically, the Chinese government realizes that a well-educated workforce with good IT capability will play a significant role in developing and sustaining economic strength. Practically, the government regards this transformation as a way of offsetting the inadequacy of educational resources to support university expansion (Huang et al., 2007). It is generally believed that computer and Internet technologies can enhance learner autonomy (Dai, 2008; Wang, 2008) so all levels of educational institutions have been urged to make efforts to integrate information and communication technologies, especially the Internet and intranet, into their educational agendas.

Another focus of effort is the construction of online teaching and learning materials known as a 'Quality Curricula Programme' (Huang et al., 2007: 226), which aims to share quality learning materials through online platforms. Among the 3,020 officially recognized courses (by May 2010), those 444 which were foreign language-related (mostly English) accounted for nearly 15 per cent. In the distance-education strand, altogether 68 universities have been authorized to set up programmes including English since the early 1990s (Kang and Song, 2007), providing learning materials, instruction, lectures and tutorials through educational media, including the Internet, to adult learners.

In terms of technological infrastructure, in addition to conventional classrooms equipped with a teacher-controlled computer, networked computer rooms and self-access centres where students can go online (intranet and Internet), wireless connection is available at many institutions, if not all. Nowadays, many student residences are also provided with a broadband connection to the Internet. However, neither service provision is free; students are often charged on an hourly basis.

Research activities in ICC development and computer/Internet technologies for language classes develop in parallel but seldom meet. On the one hand, there is theoretical contribution to interculturalizing ELT in China's HEIs (Zhang, 2007; Song, 2008), but this theme has not been intensively explored and often lacks support from empirical data. On the other hand, research into classroom interactions and the application of computer/Internet tools to language classes has been increasing. However, studies seem to show more interest in autonomous learning than in other aspects of ICC. There has been little reported evidence of the integration of textbooks, Internet technologies and tasks for intercultural teaching and learning (Wang and Coleman, 2009). In general, an integral perspective on research into how ICC development aligns with Internet technology remains little explored.

13.4   The study

13.4.1   Research design

This research involved multi-stage, multi-site fieldwork, combining a survey approach and a collective case study approach, to investigate university

Table 13.1 Research questions and instrument items

Research Questions	Q	I	O	D/LD
How are the ICC dimensions manifested in the language class?	TQ1–5 SQ1–5	TI1 , 2 SI1	O16	Statement, topics, objectives
What Internet tools are used for language activities?	TQ7, 8 SQ7, 8, 9	TI4 SI3	O13, 14, 15	Web pages, forums, online tools
How is the use of Internet tools shaped by local educational context?	TQ6, 9, 10 SQ6, 10	TI3, 5, 6 SI2, 5, 7	O4, 5, 6, 7, 8, 9, 10, 11, 16	Location of learning, context of learning
Can Internet-mediated practices evidenced in the study facilitate an intercultural approach to teaching and learning?		TI7, 8 SI4, 6, 8	O16	Experience, evidence

Notes: T – Teacher, S – Student, Q – Questionnaire, I – Interview, O – Observation, D/LD Document or Learning diary.

English language education. The survey was used to collect information about teachers' and students' perceptions, attitudes and practices as well as demographic data. It helped to identify potential targets worth following up as in-depth case studies. The multiple case studies focused on the interactions between teachers and learners of their Internet-mediated language teaching and learning activities. Such coverage allowed diverse contexts to be examined in order to identify both commonalities and particularities among cases (Hammersley, 2004). The research instruments (Table 13.1) consisted of a questionnaire survey, interviews and observation, and analysis of documents and learning diaries, with the intention not only to give 'a sense of richness and complexity to an inquiry' (Bryman, 2004: 1143) but also to triangulate or corroborate data gathered from different sources (Yin, 2003).

Questionnaire survey: Two self-completed questionnaires (Appendix 13.1) similar in content and structure were used for 63 teachers and 549 students to elicit comparable data on attitudes to and experiences of Internet-mediated intercultural activities. Both questionnaires were written in English, but the student version provided a Chinese translation to avoid misunderstanding. Most questionnaires were administered face-to-face, occasionally through e-mail delivery due to practical constraints.

Interviews: 45 semi-structured interviews (Appendix 13.2) were carried out with students and teachers in a flexible manner, focusing on teachers' (N = 26) and students' (N = 21) understandings of the goal of ICC, their use of Internet tools, their activity designs and the challenges. Interviews

were recorded with permission, and note-taking was employed as a com
plementary technique (Blaxter et al., 2001: 173).
- **Observations:** Observations were mainly conducted in physical setting
focusing on the facilities, the classroom interactions including som
online demonstrations, with as little researcher intervention as possible
Field notes were made where possible, either on-site or afterwards.
- **Document collection:** Documents collected covered materials such a
course syllabuses and appendices, teachers' lesson plans, student presen
tation files and assignments, and learning diaries (Appendix 13.3) for in
formant students to record their individual learning activities mediate
by the use of the Internet outside the class and to provide evidence of, fo
example, the URLs and search words used.

Via non-probability sampling methods such as networking sampling
opportunity sampling and purposeful sampling, 24 universities were site
for surveying and 4 were cases for focused examination. All claimed to hav
English classes 'with Internet mediation' and 'for cultural/intercultura
activities'. Data from different resources were analysed to identify key pa
terns within each research site, and to make comparisons for commonalitie
or differences across research sites (Warschauer, 2008: 55).

13.5 Reflections and limitations

As the investigator and primary instrument for gathering and analysing data
I was aware of my potential influence on the data collection and analysi
my presence was likely to affect the behaviour and attitude of the teacher
and students and the methods were inevitably subject to 'the subjectiv
perception and biases of both participants and researcher' (Merriam, 1998
22). Technically, the survey only included a small number of non-proba
bility samples of the whole population. This inevitably missed some othe
samples; for example, I was unaware of how some universities have been
piloting online interactive intercultural materials produced by textboo
publishers (Lixian Jin, personal communication, 13–12–2010). Practically
the constraints of time and frequent travel made it challenging to collec
systematic data from each site consistently. The diverse nature of the nego
tiations for access meant that it was problematic to follow a common set o
steps for data collection. The process of cross-site comparison and genera
ization may have reduced the site-specific features (Herriott and Firestone
1983).

13.6 Results

Diverse and complex as the situations were, results emerged concerning per
ceptions of the learning and teaching of ICC in language education, th

tual use of Internet technologies for language and cultural activities, and
ne practicalities of using such tools.

3.6.1 The survey

3.6.1.1 *The recognition and implementation of the ICC goal*

1 all the data sets, ICC was declared as a goal of English language education
1 response to the national guidelines. Mostly it is taken as the teaching
f knowledge about people and society from 'the target culture' and the
wareness of different cultural behaviours and perspectives. These interretations shaped the course syllabuses and textbooks, in which culture
vas largely treated as a component which was independent of language
kills, as evidenced by the separation of language skills-focused courses and
ulture-focused courses, especially in the College English education sec-
on. Teachers specializing in cross-(inter)cultural communication courses
)cused more on the concepts and theories, with an interest in critical inci-
ent analysis so as to raise their students' awareness. Understanding culture
nd intercultural communication at a personal level was not prioritized.

3.6.1.2 *The use of 'authentic' resources*

1 interviews, most teachers and students insisted that the priority in
nglish language education should be to develop native–speaker-like
nglish language proficiency. They prioritized input from 'the target cul-
ire' over that from their own culture. The demand for 'authentic' input
om native-speaker sources included both materials (textual, audio-visual,
raphic, etc.) and language partners. They often searched the Internet and
isited professional websites from 'the target culture' for updated materials
rhile acknowledging that it was challenging for them to search and select
nline resources effectively, considering the overabundance of online infor-
iation. In addition, both teachers and students held that it was ideal to
ommunicate with interlocutors from 'the target culture', although most
lasses had no opportunities to have overseas teachers or partner classes
hrough cross-site collaboration.

3.6.1.3 *The development of autonomy*

rom document analysis it is clear that, although the concept of 'autono-
ious learning' was used, in reality (as discovered through interview and
bservation) this equated to students' self-study with courseware-based
nline materials. The completion of campus network learning records was
ften a prerequisite for credits, and students had no choice but to follow
rigid process. Students were asked to learn from predetermined materi-
ls, using predesigned procedures, and helped by prefabricated hints and
nswers. In interviews students often revealed that they were 'frustrated' by
eing forced to do nothing more meaningful than getting scores and records

of 'online learning' in order to pass the assessment. With regard to qua
ity programmes such as the cross-(inter)cultural communication course
online spaces were only used as a means to distribute courses, rather than a
a platform for communication.

13.6.1.4   *The use of Internet tools for pedagogical purposes*

On the whole, using communication tools for pedagogical activities wa
rare, although the use of information and social networks for announce
ments and communication was relatively frequent. However, the applica
tions varied. From the interviews, teachers were generally eager to hav
an online pedagogical resource bank that would contain everything the
wanted to use for their language classes, although they knew this was ur
likely to be achieved. There was an overwhelming use of information too
(e.g., search engines) while the use of communication tools remained ma
ginal, constrained by time, class size, teaching goals, lack of access to net
worked computers and lack of co-operation. A few enthusiastic teacher
experimented with virtual learning environments or social networking fc
pedagogical activities, in combination with print materials. Outside clas
students accessed the Internet to complete extra tasks, independently or co
lectively, and at their own expense. This gave rise to student complaints c
extra costs and time, although they did spend time online for fun.

13.7   The cases

This section presents an analysis of four cases, as summarized in Table 13.2
They were cross-compared with a focus on Internet-mediated intercultura
teaching and learning.

Cases U4 (Case 1) and U17 (Case 4) had a monocultural environmen
whereas U22 (Case 2) and U14 (Case 3) had their international staff mem
bers as the primary source of intercultural communication. External inpu
for pedagogically oriented intercultural communication among these case
seemed rare. Technically, U22 offered the most convenient access to com
puters and the Internet, which was made an integral part of campus life
Unlike U14 and U17, in which computers and Internet access were under
provided, U4 seemed more generous in that it offered students some prepai
hours for using the university computer network.

Pedagogically, the ICC goal was interpreted differently according to
each course curriculum, as background knowledge (Case 1), intercultura
communication process (Case 2), empathy and critical thinking (Case 3
and human affective development (Case 4). Despite such diverse focuses
the pedagogical practices, mediated with the use of Internet technologies
seemed to share some common ground. In Cases 2, 3 and 4 teachers a
attached importance to group work and student presentation method
as ways of organizing learning activities, and all involved regular use o

formation and communication tools. In particular, in Cases 3 and 4, online discussions were organized with assessment purposes in mind, and students had a higher level of participation, in contrast to the students in Case 2, where there was no such official requirement for online discussion, given that the unsuccessful intercultural Wiki platform was voluntary. However, in Case 3, assessment on forum posts reshaped the discussion format so that students only contributed monologues and reflective essays without producing meaningful discussions and social interaction. Likewise, in Case 4 the implementation of peer assessment led to student disagreement and consequent partial withdrawal from online discussion. In Case 1, little evidence was seen regarding the use of Internet tools during observation. However, from teachers' and students' accounts, both parties revealed that they made considerable use of information tools to source information, with occasional use of social networking platforms.

In Cases 1 and 2 teachers engaged less with students' use of Internet tools or organized pedagogical activities than in Cases 3 and 4, where teachers made great efforts to extend their classroom teaching for the purpose of enhancing peer learning. Students unanimously agreed that using online resources was essential, yet showed contradictory attitudes towards the use of communication tools such as forums. However, a common element was that they aspired to meaningful and well-organized activities, with good resources and facilitation, although they did not welcome assessment-based tasks. At the same time, they were less willing to take the initiative or respond to each other, which implies that Internet technologies do not automatically initiate interdiscourse communication (between students). Instead, students preferred communication directly with 'native speakers', either online or on-site. For convenience, they chose to search and read learning materials in both languages, which indicates that there was a level of cross-cultural learning.

The four cases shared some similar practices in using the Internet for intercultural language activities. Firstly, locating and exploring information from professional websites were frequent and regular activities. Secondly, teachers and students maintained off-campus contact through e-mail and online networking. Thirdly, engaging students in pair/group presentations on specified or recommended topics appeared common practice (excluding Case 1). Fourthly, setting up an online learning environment emerged as a way of extending in-class discussion and furthering the aspiration to establish intercultural exchange (especially Cases 2 and). Fifthly, asynchronous communication tools were evidently employed differently to synchronous ones (excluding Case 1). Lastly, with regard to forum discussions in Cases 3 and 4, students predominantly used the forum as a medium to express their own ideas; interaction with each other was rarely evidenced.

Table 13.2 An overview of the key characteristics of the four cases

Cases	Institutional	Individual	Pedagogical	Technological
1. U4 – *Intensive Reading* with occasional Internet use	• The Centre of English Education's target of teaching some non-English majors with English major standards • The Centre's investment in digital resource purchase • The Centre's offer to students of prepaid cards for free use of the computers and network	• The informant teachers attach importance to integrated language skills • Students' needs identical to the teaching goal • Students' belief that it is beneficial to follow teachers' instruction	• Culture is an added-on component to integrated language skills in language programmes • Teacher-led instruction with occasional student presentation • Language-focused learning • Rarely direct use of the Internet in class	• The Internet accessible in class but not often used • Intranet available as a resource bank • Prepaid cards for free access to computer network on campus given but not used sufficiently
2. U22 – *Business English* and intercultural wiki	• English Language Centre adopting a British educational system • Institutional focus on English for academic and specific purposes • More international staff than Chinese staff • Regular extracurricular activities	• Frequent communication between teachers and students • Teachers responsive to students' needs and concerns • Students' high expectations due to their plans to study abroad • Students preference for 'native-speaker' teachers • Students' adaptation to a new educational culture	• Teachers' collaborative efforts for learning materials preparation with wide use of authentic audio-visual clips • Students' regular use of the search engines for external resources for group presentations • A wiki space for cross-site communication piloted but with low participation due to lack of constant facilitation and interaction	• The cost of Internet use covered by tuition fees • Computer rooms and network easily accessible • Intranet available for information delivery • Official e-mail accounts frequently used by all teachers and students

3. U14 – Google Groups-mediated *Cultural Analysis of Film*	• Intercultural Institute directed by American staff • Master's level programmes focusing on intercultural studies theory and research, not language proficiency-oriented • Google services used as an institution-wide convention	• The informant teacher's understanding of ICC in terms of critical thinking • The teacher's awareness of pitfalls in the use of Internet information and communication tools • Regular communication between teachers and students via e-mail • Students' heavy workloads as postgraduates	• No use of the Internet in class • The informant teacher's practice of using Google Groups for discussion • The teacher's minimal online intervention in forum discussion but readiness to provide resources • Students posting papers in the discussion forum without interaction	• No Internet connection available in the teaching buildings • Both library and residential network use charged
4. U17 – Moodle-mediated *English Literature* class	• English Department programmes sports-oriented • Lack of departmental interest in and support in incorporating Internet technologies in teaching and learning • ICC not a clear goal in the institutional agenda	• The informant teacher's enthusiasm in engaging students to use an e-forum in the literature class • The teacher's awareness of students' affective development through literature analysis • The teacher's constant support for her students' group work • Students' low confidence in the institution and their career prospects • Students lack of motivation to use Moodle	• The teacher's lecturing involving direct use of Internet resources • Students' presentations involving indirect use of Internet resources • Discussion forum used as a platform for self-expression (monologues) between participants, lacking reflective thinking • Discussion for assessment purposes • Little online intervention by the teacher in forum discussion	• No institutional network provided for pedagogical use • Internet accessible in the multimedia classroom • Both library and residential network use charged • Slow and unstable network connection at residence

13.8   Discussion

The cases show that overall the Internet has been primarily used outsid
class for information searching, networking, consultation and commun
cation. An integrated use of course materials and Internet tools for diffe
ent pedagogical purposes and practices has been identified. Although thes
efforts may be individual rather than representative, they mirror the cha
lenges and opportunities to develop a framework for Internet-mediate
intercultural language teaching and learning.

13.8.1   Challenges

The first challenge is that the manifestations of ICC goals lack a consisten
conceptual framework that clearly defines the basic concepts and delineate
the overarching goal and its sub-goals (Dörnyei, 2001: 26) in long-term lan
guage learning.

The second challenge relates to the views on accessing 'authentic' materi
als and 'native' speakers. While language quality in the materials may b
the reason, this bias against home-based materials may not justify the exclu
sion of home or other cultures.

The third challenge lies in the development of autonomous learnin
through the implementation of online courseware platforms for out-of-clas
self-study, especially in the College English education strand, which, in fact
hardly prepares students to adopt a flexible learning approach to the use o
external resources. This individualistic learning scenario suggests that on
line learning methods only encourage individual learning, overlooking th
social aspects of online learning (Zemsky and Massey, 2004, in O'Dowc
2007b: 21).

The fourth challenge shows that assessment seems problematic to pro
moting Internet-mediated teaching and learning in the Chinese contex
because students are often reluctant to contribute to discussions, even i
this is explicitly required.

Fifthly, technological availability does not guarantee pedagogical acces
sibility in class, plus the fact that students' Internet access is not free o
charge, although students tend to see this network access issue as the leas
serious barrier.

Last, but not least, it is the lack of time to use the Internet, both in an
outside class.

13.8.2   Opportunities

Despite the many existing constraints, it is possible that Internet-mediate
practices can lead to an intercultural approach to teaching and learning ir
Chinese contexts, provided that the pedagogical implications of Interne
use are well understood. As shown in the data, quite a few teachers use
the Internet by following their intuition or experience. However, ad ho

ractices and experiences in Internet-mediated teaching and learning do
ot necessarily answer what the dimensions of an intercultural approach
re, and why and how the Internet should be integrated.

3.8.3 A proposed framework

'ere, a distinctive feature has been identified: teachers and students are
1ostly involved in intra-class (intercultural) language activities with (lim-
ed) Internet mediation. These activities are characteristically resource-based
nd self-expression oriented, in contrast to cross-site, collaboration-based
1odels. I therefore propose that, based on the research, an intra-class com-
1unity model be developed to complement the cross-site collaborative
1odels (Figure 13.1).

In brief, the proposed framework in Figure 13.1 contributes to fostering
n Internet-mediated intercultural approach to teaching and learning, not
nly for its immediate application in a single-class context, but also in cross-
1te collaboration. The left side of the framework represents the actual ele-
1ents (in continuous lines) that are embodied in this research, in contrast
) those on the right side which show potential for further development
n broken lines), although these elements do exist in the literature. Taken
)gether, this conceptual framework entails three interwoven dimensions
f Internet-mediated intercultural language activities, that is, human par-
1cipants, pedagogy and pedagogical tools, with an orientation to skills and

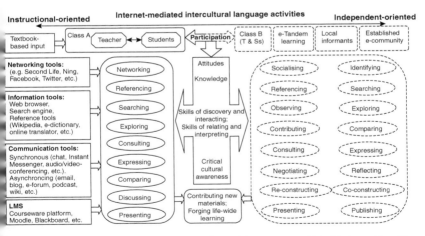

igure 13.1 The framework for process-oriented Internet-mediated intercultural lan-
'uage teaching and learning

practices in the process. The dynamics of these dimensions are explaine
below:

- First of all, with an Internet-mediated environment, the language clas
  (Class A) has opportunities to access enriched information and to realiz
  empowered communication (Warschauer et al., 2000; Debski, 200€
  Gu, 2006). Teachers and students are key participants to build up a
  Internet-mediated intra-class community in which they extend their face
  to-face communication to virtual contact, especially outside class, con
  plementing the limited classroom interactions. Such intra-class onlin
  community building is also conducive to fostering a 'greater classroon
  idea to streamline classroom instruction with 'co-curricular activitie
  (Liu, 2007c). This intra-class community can, and should, be seen as th
  starting point for organizing both online non-interactive activities an
  interactive activities. When it is well-established and conditions permit
  Class A may reach out to other communities or individuals by means c
  *inter-class telecollaboration, inter-group student–student tandem learning, loca
  informant-learner partnership,* and *mass participation in established e-con
  munities.*
- Secondly, Class A's pedagogical preparation integrates elements of Byram
  (1997) ICC model into language curricula. In particular, the two sets c
  skills, (skills of discovery and interacting; skills of relating and interpret
  ing) are important because through online interaction 'Intercultura
  Communication' (Piller, 2007) can be realized. With Internet mediatior
  the two sets of skills correspond with and contribute to a range of teach
  ing and learning practices (in ovals) that are summarized (yet remair
  open) from evidence shown here (the left column), as well as from exist
  ing literature (the right column). These skills-based practices are oriente
  towards intercultural exploration, exchange and reflection.
- Thirdly, for Class A, the instruction tools include textbook-based materi
  als and a menu of Internet technologies currently in use for intercultura
  learning. Unlike some Web-based projects which do not involve textboo
  use, in China textbook and print materials play a predominant role in
  educational contexts (Jin and Cortazzi, 2006; Wang and Coleman, 2009)
  Therefore, an integration of Internet resources into the textbook-base€
  materials enables extended information-seeking, communication, net
  working as communities and overall blended learning. Noticeably, it i
  not so much the Internet tools that can make a difference, but the kind
  of tasks and activities that teachers and students carry out with Interne
  mediation (Moore et al., 1998). The short-term objectives and the imme
  diate outcomes of Internet-mediated intercultural language teaching an€
  learning are, ideally, to contribute new learning materials and to suppor
  wider participation in learning through online community building
  interaction and collaboration.

lthough in reality each class, goal and context is unique, some general
rinciples should be adhered to in order to foster the regular use of Internet
ᵒols that are underpinned by an intercultural approach. EDITED

*The underpinning of 'Intercultural Communication' with a non-essentialist
perspective.* (Scollon and Scollon, 2001a, b; Piller, 2007). An intra-class
community can be either a monocultural society (Cases 1 and 4) or a
multicultural one (Cases 2 and 3). Whatever the situation, the relationship
and interaction (or interdiscourse communication) between the teacher
and students is the most vital element. When looking for a partner, participants should be open to those from the same national culture, the
target culture and other cultures.

The continuum of formal learning and flexible learning. This framework cor-
responds to the vision of learning from a formal classroom event to a
continuum of life-long learning contexts. While the former involves fixed
(even rigid) language curricula that do not seem yet to encompass an
intercultural approach to ELT (e.g., in China), it is through the Internet
that language programmes can be made more flexible in terms of conducting intercultural exploration, experiencing intercultural communication and socializing globally and locally through experiential learning.
Classrooms are no longer just the venue preparing for future careers but
rather a community in their own right, with a specific culture (Kohonen
et al., 2001).

Using textbook materials in conjunction with Internet resources. This framework highlights the importance of Internet mediation, but does not
downplay the use of textbook materials or other media resources. Rather,
it proposes integrating all the resources, including human resources.
While textbook materials are often considered out-of-date and may be
inadequate in terms of intercultural authenticity (Feng and Byram, 2002),
the content can be deliberately employed as a trigger for more creative
uses such as reconstruction into a more up-to-date and interculturally authentic version, with the assistance of Internet-mediated exploration and
communication.

3.8.3.1   *Internet-mediated intercultural activities*

Jnder such a framework, an Internet-mediated intercultural task (Corbett,
.010), based on Nunan's (1989, 2004) communicative task model, is
▌escribed below.

Intercultural-speaker goal: to develop intercultural speakers consistently
through linguistic development, intercultural exploration, intercultural
communication and social networking. In the Chinese context where collaboration with 'native-speaker' classes is rare, it is important to adopt a

non-essentialist view in order to understand the concept of culture i ELT as a construct that contains not only sociocultural knowledge of th concerned target groups, but also the individual person's perspectives an interpretations of a given event. Likewise, intercultural communicatio should be seen as a dynamic process of both personal engagements an social experience within concerned groups. If intercultural-speaker targe is the overall goal, activities should be designed within a clearly define model.

- *Intercultural representation as 'input'*: to include course materials, othe resources and Internet resources, and teachers' and students' (an online interlocutors') personal experiences and cultural perspective as input contributions. With a non-essentialist perspective or a sma culture paradigm (Holliday, 1999), teachers and students should shif from the notion of 'authenticity' to 'intercultural authenticity' (Fen, and Byram, 2002), that is, materials should be selected according t four criteria: 'intercultural representations', 'mediation of intention an interpretation', 'balance of diachrony and synchrony and image repre sentations', and 'principles of contrivance' (ibid.: 63). This may reduc the limitation of the wide search for 'authentic' information on cultura products and practices, which may be inadequate to provide student with the investigatory tools and skills to achieve an understanding c the perspectives (Moore et al., 1998; Warschauer et al., 2000) from th target culture as well as other cultures. In communication, they nee to be convinced that authenticity also means to include interpersona and intra-group communication by using the target language withi their own community. In this way, teachers and students potentiall can not only find useful materials for language activities in class, bu also interact, both collectively and individually, with different voice and opinions.

- *Internet-mediated activities*: according to a negotiated assessment scheme to design activities that are Internet-mediated (not Internet-based) t allow various types of in-class and out-of-class activities – non-inter active (for sourcing and referencing information), interactive (for syn chronous and asynchronous communication) and networking-oriente (for sharing and community building), together with activities withou Internet mediation. Teachers need to interweave their experience with students' cultures and, therefore, teaching becomes co-learning Similarly, student-initiated tasks often empower the students to be 'mas ters' of the process of managing information and knowledge and, in par ticular, of their own culture, which may go beyond the teacher's scop of knowledge.

- *Intra-class community roles*: to negotiate roles according to the activitie in contexts which facilitate community autonomy. Learner autonom should entail not only the development of strategies for independen learning, but also positive attitudes and cognitive abilities of interpersonal communication and collaboration in order to co-construct learning experiences with community autonomy, or group autonomy (Mangenot and Nissen, 2006).The teachers, besides their roles as instructor, organizer and facilitator of activities, manager of logistics and evaluator of assessment, should at the same time be good learners (Lewis, 2006), including updating his/her knowledge of new technologies. Meanwhile, teachers need to be willing to shift from being a knowledge authority to being a pedagogy authority and engage in a new dynamic relationship that aims at contributing to promoting community autonomy. Cases 2, 3 and 4 clearly indicate the importance of providing a sociocultural approach to language and intercultural learning in the Internet-mediated learning environment. An online community can be set up to extend contact to external professional communities for intercultural exchange (Corbett, 2010).

Settings: to allow flexible layout and equipment according to practical conditions so as to develop different activities both in and outside class, in face-to-face or virtual scenarios.

3.10 Implications and conclusions

Although this study has sampling limitations, the framework developed here may have the merit of transferability to similar institutional contexts, with implications for teachers and practitioners, both in China and elsewhere, for the conceptual and practical preparation of Internet-mediated intercultural language activities.

These findings suggest that teachers' individual interests must be sustained by institution-wide community building for intercultural language education. This relies on institutional commitment to internal collaboration through, for example, streamlining programme goals, sharing resources and conducting team-teaching/learning (Liu, 2007b; Tajino and Tajino, 2000). Externally, collaboration should also be sought to develop institutional educational ideologies and practices through intercultural communication for intercultural community building, especially with Internet facilitation, as the *eChina-UK Programme* (Spencer-Oatey, 2007) shows. Such reformulations of curricular structures often challenge existing language education policy and practice and require top-down effort.

Secondly, the findings indicate that teachers should receive adequate training in how to integrate Internet technologies with pedagogical designs for intercultural teaching and learning within such a framework. Therefore, establishing a set of curricular standards and teachers' performance standards is of vital importance, as a recent series of volumes for pre-tertiary English language teachers in China (Agor and Chen, 2007; Murphey and Chen, 2007) shows. To prepare for such standards, some practices are recommended with reference to this proposed framework. For intra-cla[ss] community development, one should consider:

- *Institutional preparation.* Teachers and administrators should discuss ho[w] to meet the curricular requirements, develop pedagogical design and se[e] institutional support for facility access.
- *Technical preparation.* Teachers can set up an online community withi[n] their classes. It is worth surveying students' habitual use of online too[ls] to identify possible activity designs and to apply to use institution-base[d] servers or free commercial ones to create a learning community platfor[m] with various functions.
- *Managerial preparation.* Teachers should enhance students' motivation b[y] creating individual profiles for online networking, netiquette establish[-] ment and content/task upload. Teachers should state clearly in advan[ce] specific goals, requirements and assessment criteria and allow negotiatio[n] with students and flexibility for improvement.
- *Pedagogical preparation.* Teachers should stimulate, monitor and maintai[n] online interaction with students by such means as grouping, supervisin[g] students and showcasing their learning activities with multi-perspective[s.] Students can provide interculturally represented learning resources to c[o-] build a resource bank.

Based on the intra-class community building, further collaboration ca[n] develop with external partners, from colleagues in the same institution to [a] cross-site partner class. Some other aspects are worth considering:

- *Networking preparation.* This can be done on-site between colleagues i[n] the same institution or online within professional communities throug[h] mailing lists and forums to seek partnership. Teachers need to identit[y] and network with potential partners to negotiate collaboration concern[-] ing pedagogical goals, methods, measures, resources, facilities, and s[o] forth.
- *Co-ordinating preparation.* Importantly, teachers on both sides need t[o] negotiate a workable schedule for communication and collaborative work[,] especially for telecollaborations. Task design and allocation to each sid[e] need to be balanced and mutually beneficial.

In this chapter, issues relating to Internet-mediated, ICC goal-oriented prac[-] tices in a variety of Chinese tertiary ELT classes have been investigated. [A] pedagogical framework has been proposed to enhance teachers' and learn[-] ers' understanding of the application of an Internet-mediated intercultura[l] approach to teaching and learning. However, considering China's size an[d] diversity, this framework, as an initial account of Internet-mediated intercul[-] tural teaching and learning, opens a door to understanding the complexit[y] f institutions and classrooms with more contextualized Internet-mediated ractices, for the purpose of developing language learners as intercultural peakers. Therefore, it remains important to find locally appropriate solutions to local problems (Liu, 2007a).

Appendix 13.1: Teacher questionnaire (sample)

Questionnaire for Teachers

am Liang Wang, doing a PhD work at the Open University, UK. This questionnaire ntends to investigate your perceptions and/or practices of using the Internet for your nglish language classes. There are no right or wrong answers. Please answer them onestly and to your best knowledge.

This questionnaire consists of three sections. If you DO NOT have any experience of using the Internet in your teaching practices, please complete **Section 1 (Perceptions)** and **Section 3 (Personal information)** only. Otherwise, please complete the whole questionnaire sections by following the instructions. When you omplete it, please save it and send it back to wanglpkcn@gmail.com.

Section 1: Please indicate your opinion by checking the box with a cross (X, move our mouse over the little square box and left click it) in the appropriate column.

-Strongly disagree;   2-Disagree;   3-Agree;   4-Strongly agree

No.	Statements	1	2	3	4
1	**In general, I think that using the Internet in language classes ...**				
	should be an essential element in the textbook-based language class.	☐	☐	☐	☒
	should be as important as textbook-based classroom teaching.	☐	☐	☐	☒
	should be complementary to textbook-based classroom teaching.	☐	☐	☐	☒
	will be more interesting than textbook-based classroom teaching.	☐	☐	☒	☐
	will be more time-consuming than textbook-based classroom teaching.	☐	☐	☒	☐
	will be more rewarding than textbook-based classroom teaching.	☐	☐	☒	☐
	will be less manageable than textbook-based classroom teaching.	☐	☒	☐	☐
	will be less practical than textbook-based classroom teaching.	☐	☒	☐	☐
	will allow great flexibility to textbook-based classroom teaching.	☐	☐	☐	☒
	will encourage more active learning than in textbook-based classroom.	☐	☐	☐	☒
	will improve learner autonomy.	☐	☐	☐	☒
	will be distracting from textbook-based classroom teaching.	☐	☒	☐	☐
2	**In my view, using the Internet for teaching English can ...**				
	enhance language proficiency in general.	☐	☐	☒	☐
	enable real language use.	☐	☐	☒	☐
	enrich cultural knowledge.	☐	☐	☐	☒
	foster skills in communication.	☐	☐	☒	☐
	develop awareness of one's home culture.	☐	☐	☒	☐
	enhance understandings of the target culture.	☐	☐	☒	☐
	bring about conflicts in cultural exchanges.	☐	☐	☒	☐
3	**I think that the involvement of the Internet in the language class can ...**				
	bring more up-to-date materials than the textbook does.	☐	☐	☒	☐
	introduce authentic materials about the target culture.	☐	☐	☐	☒
	enable students to have opportunities for authentic communication.	☐	☐	☐	☒
	enable students to develop reflective thinking.	☐	☐	☐	☒
	increase uncertainty in organising teaching and learning activities.	☐	☐	☒	☐
	increase anxiety in language classes	☐	☐	☒	☐

4	By using the Internet, I think it is important for me to...				
	explore more language materials for my students.	☐	☐	☒	☐
	explore more cultural knowledge for my students.	☐	☐	☒	☐
	organize my students to have intercultural exchange with partners from the target culture.	☐	☐	☒	☐
	support my students to communicate effectively with partners from the target culture.	☐	☐	☒	☐
	examine my students' learning outcomes	☐	☐	☒	☐
	help my students to socialize in the virtual learning community.	☐	☐	☒	☐
	provide technical support.	☐	☐	☒	☐
	collaborate effectively with the partner teacher.	☐	☐	☒	☐
5	By using the Internet, I think it is important for my students to...				
	search for language learning materials themselves.	☐	☐	☒	☐
	search for cultural materials themselves.	☐	☐	☒	☐
	have intercultural exchange with partner classes in line with my instruction.	☐	☐	☐	☒
	communicate with their own classmates.	☐	☐	☒	☐
	socialize with new people from the target culture.	☐	☐	☒	☐
	display online their learning outcomes.	☐	☐	☒	☐
	be skilled in Internet technologies.	☐	☐	☒	☐

Note: If you don't have any experience in using Internet tools, please skip over Section 2 and continue with Section 3.

Section 2: Please choose the answers which are the closest to the facts you know about your teaching experience by checking the box with a cross 'X' in the appropriate column.

1-Never Applicable;　2-Seldom Applicable;　3-Often Applicable;　4-Always Applicable

No.	Statements	1	2	3	4
6	**In preparing for activities, I like to use the Internet as a tool for...**				
	seeking information about linguistic knowledge (lexical and grammatical).	☐	☐	☒	☐
	seeking information about language skills training.	☐	☐	☒	☐
	seeking information about the target cultural knowledge.	☐	☐	☒	☐
	seeking information about home cultural knowledge.	☐	☐	☒	☐
	communicating with my class.	☐	☐	☒	☐
	my students to explore more of the target culture.	☐	☐	☒	☐
	my students to explore more of home culture.	☐	☐	☒	☐
	my students to communicate with the partner class from the target culture.	☐	☐	☒	☐
	my students to communicate with the partner class from home culture.	☐	☐	☒	☐
	displaying my class' learning outcomes.	☐	☐	☒	☐
	others (please specify here)	☐	☐	☐	☐
7	**I like to design online activities in class by using...**				
	individual Internet tools.	☐	☐	☒	☐
	Online learning system with a distance partner class.	☐	☐	☐	☒
	Online learning system (e.g. Blackboard) without a partner class.	☐	☐	☐	☒
	Others (please specify here)	☐	☐	☐	☐

8	I have the experience of using the following Internet tools for my language class:				
	browsers and search engines	☐	☐	☒	☐
	online reference tools (e.g. dictionary, Wikipedia)	☐	☐	☐	☒
	text-based web pages	☐	☐	☒	☐
	audio (podcasting)	☐	☐	☐	☒
	vlog (Youtube, Tudou)	☐	☐	☐	☒
	email	☐	☐	☒	☐
	e-forum (e.g. discussion board)	☐	☐	☒	☐
	blog	☐	☐	☐	☒
	chat-room	☐	☐	☒	☐
	instant messenger (e.g. MSN)	☐	☐	☒	☐
	videoconferencing	☐	☐	☐	☒
	wikis	☐	☐	☐	☒
	other (please specify here)	☐	☐	☐	☐
9	I engage my students in using...				
	online reference tools for vocabulary and grammar learning.	☐	☐	☒	☐
	browsers and search engines to access information on specific topics.	☐	☐	☐	☒
	online audio and video materials.	☐	☐	☐	☒
	emails to write to their partner class.	☐	☐	☐	☒
	e-forums to discuss topics with their classmates.	☐	☐	☐	☒
	e-forums to discuss topics with a partner class.	☐	☐	☐	☒
	chatting facilities (text, voice) to 'talk' to partners.	☐	☐	☒	☐
	videoconferencing to talk to partners.	☐	☐	☒	☐
	web page or blog for sharing learners' ideas.	☐	☐	☐	☒
	facebook/Hi5/Second Life for socialization	☐	☒	☐	☐
	other (Please specify here)	☐	☐	☐	☐
10	The main barriers to using Internet tools for intercultural activities are lack of...				
	funding.	☐	☐	☒	☐
	access to network.	☐	☐	☒	☐
	time in class.	☐	☐	☒	☐
	time outside class.	☐	☐	☒	☐
	technical support.	☐	☐	☒	☐
	pedagogical experience.	☐	☐	☒	☐
	participation by the learners or their partners.	☐	☐	☒	☐
	managerial experience in collaborating with partner teachers.	☐	☐	☒	☐
	other (Please specify here)	☐	☐	☐	☐

Section 3: Please complete this section about your personal situation. We need thes
details to classify responses to the survey, but your identity will never be revealed.

11	How long have you been a foreign language teacher?	17 years 4 months
12	How long have you been using Internet?	9 years 4 months
13	How long have you been using Internet tools for teaching?	8 years months
14	Have you been trained for using Internet tools for teaching?	Yes ☒ No ☐
15	If yes, is the training one-off or ongoing? (If 'No', please skip over)	One-off ☒ Ongoing ☐
16	Do you have your website (online space) for teaching and learning activities?	Yes ☒ No ☐
17	How much time do you spend on the Internet every day on average?	6 hours
18	Your name (Surname, First name):	
19	Your email	@yahoo.com.cn
20	Your institute	University of Sport

Thanks for your cooperation! Now don't forget to save and send it as an attachment t
wanglpken@gmail.com.

Appendix 13.2: Interview protocols

T – For teachers; S – For students

1. T – What is your institutional interpretation of this goal of developing
   learners' 'kuawenhua jiaojinengli' (ICC)?
   S – What is your understanding of 'kuawenhua jiaojinengli' (ICC) in language learning? How important do you think it is regarding your learning goals?
2. T – What course(s) are you teaching? Regarding your course(s), how would
   you specify the goal of developing ICC?
   S – What course are you learning regarding ICC goal? How would you
   understand it?
3. T/S – What network facilities are available for you in your institution and
   what are the conditions of using network for teaching?
4. T/S – What network technologies do you use regularly for teaching activities? How do you feel when using these technologies?
5. T/S – Please describe the ICC-oriented activity involving the use of network (What aims? What tools? Who to use? What sequence? In which
   situation? What assessment methods? etc.).
6. T/S – What are the problems in using network for teaching? What kind of
   support do you wish to obtain in order to prepare for activities involving
   the use of network?
7. T/S – In what ways does the use of network technologies meet the aims of
   ICC-oriented teaching and learning activities?
8. T/S – Would you please make suggestions to the activities you just
   described on how to improve it in terms of activity design?

Appendix 13.3: Learning diary – sample

Online Learning Experiences

The form below is for you to keep a learning diary of what and how you are doing with English learning, especially with the use of Internet tools. By keeping learning diaries, you will have the opportunities to:

- Record and reflect on what you have learned;
- Identify problems you have and what you do to solve them;
- Be able to get additional help.

Once you will have done an activity, please spend about 15 minutes filling in this form and save a copy to yourself (you need to copy the blank form for next use). Also please email a copy to wanglpkcn@gmail.com so that some feedback regarding your diary will be returned and your learning diary will be developed into learning dialog journal.

Your diaries will be helpful for giving a sense of your experience related to the use of Internet tools for English learning process. Please write in the following items to the best understanding you can You are expected to provide evidences.

Diary of English Learning Experiences	
Date written/sent:	20090421
Topic	**Visual literacy**
Objectives	**Presention for IC course**
Location of learning	**Home, dom and library**
Context of learning (individual/ collaborative)	**Mostly Individual**
Online tools (if any)	**Google, email**
Experience (actions, problems, achievements, your thought, feeling etc)	**Browse websites provided be our professor, Googled some info on relevant subjects, esp the ad photos** **Feeling: internet tools seem to be quite essential to our presentation preparation.**
Copies from online learning records (e.g. chat logos, key searched words and useful URLs)	**>>** **http://www.pomana.edu/Academics/courserelated/ classprojects/visual-lit/intro** **>>/intro.html;** **http://www.museumca.org/picturethis/visual.html** **>>http://astro.temple.edu/~ruby/wava/worth/svscom.html** **>>** **http://www.uiowa.edu/~commstud/resources/visualsites.html** **>>** **http://commfaculty.fullerton.edu/lester/courses/viscomlinks. html** **>http://www.wadsworth.com.com//communication_d/ templates/student_resources/053456** **>>7068_massey/media_literarcy/index.html** **>>http://power-points.blogspot.com/2005/09/really-bad-powerpoint-and-how-to-av** **>>oid.html**

References

Agor, B. & Chen, L. (Eds) (2007) *Integrating EFL standards into Chinese classroom set tings, senior level* (Vol. 3). Beijing: Foreign Language Teaching and Research Press.

Alptekin, C. (2002) Towards intercultural communicative competence in ELT. *EL: Journal*, 56 (1), 57–64.

Belz, J.A. & Thorne, S.L. (2006) Introduction: Internet-mediated intercultural foreign language education and the intercultural speaker. In J.A. Belz & S.L. Thorne (Eds) *AAUSC 2005: Internet-mediated Intercultural Foreign Language Education*. Boston Thomson Heinle, pp. ix–xxv.

Benson, P. (2001) *Teaching and researching autonomy in language learning.* Harlow Pearson Education Limited.

Blaxter, L., Hughes, C. & Tight, M. (2001) *How to research* (2nd edn). Maidenhead, UK Open University Press.

Block, D. (2007) *Second language identities.* London: Continuum.

Bryman, A. (2004) Triangulation. In M.S. Lewis-Beck, A. Bryman & T.F. Liao (Eds) *The Sage Encyclopedia of Social Science Research Methods*, Vol. 3. London, CA: Sage Publications, pp. 1142–3.

Byram, M. (1997) *Teaching and assessing intercultural communicative competence* Clevedon: Multilingual Matters Ltd.

Corbett, J. (2003) *An intercultural approach to English language teaching.* Clevedon Multilingual Matters Ltd.

Corbett, J. (2010) *Intercultural language activities.* Cambridge: CUP.

Dai, W. (Ed.) (2008) *Gaoxiao waiyu zhuanye jiaoyu fazhan baogao (1978–2008)* [A repor on foreign language major education development at higher educational institu tions (1978–2008)]. Shanghai: Shanghai Foreign Language Education Press.

Dlaska, A. (2000) Integrating culture and language learning in institution-wide lan guage programmes. *Language, Culture and Curriculum*, 13 (3), 247–63.

Debski, R. (2006) *Project-based language teaching with technology.* Sydney: Nationa Centre for English Language Teaching and Research.

Dörnyei, Z. (2001) *Motivational Strategies in the Language Classroom.* Cambridge: CUP

Feng, A. & Byram, M. (2002) Authenticity in college english textbooks – an intercul tural perspective. *RELC Journal*, 33 (2), 58–84.

Furstenberg, G., Levet, S., English, K. & Maillet, K. (2001) Giving a virtual voice to the silent language of culture: The *CULTURA* project. *Language Learning and Technology* 5 (1), 55–102.

Gu, P. (Ed.) (2006) *CALL theory and practice.* Shanghai: Fudan University Press.

Guth, S. and Helm, F. (Eds) (2010) *Telecollaboration 2.0: Language, literacies and inter cultural learning in the 21st century.* Bern: Peter Lang.

Hammersley, M. (2004) Case study. In M.S. Lewis-Beck, A. Bryman & T.F. Liao (Eds) *The Sage encyclopaedia of social science research methods*, Vol. 1. London, CA: Sage Publications, pp. 92–4.

Hauck, M. & Stickler, U. (2006) What does it take to teach online? *CALICO Journal* 23 (3), 463–75.

Herriott, R.E. & Firestone, W.A. (1983) Multisite qualitative policy research Optimizing description and generalizability. *Educational Researcher*, 12 (2), 14–19.

Holliday, A. (1999) Small cultures. *Applied Linguistics*, 20 (2), 237–64.

Holliday, A. (2005) *The struggle to teach English as an international language.* Oxford Oxford University Press.

Huang, R., Jiang, X. & Zhang, H. (2007) The informationization of higher education in China: Present situation and challenges. In H. Spencer-Oatey (Ed.), *e-Learning initiatives in China: Pedagogy, policy and culture.* Hong Kong: Hong Kong University Press, pp. 221–32.

in, L. & Cortazzi, M. (2006) Changing practices in Chinese cultures of learning. *Language, Culture and Curriculum,* 19 (1), 5–20.

ang, F. & Song, G. (2007) e-Learning in higher education in China: An overview. In Spencer-Oatey, H. (Ed.), *e-Learning initiatives in China: Pedagogy, policy and culture.* Hong Kong: Hong Kong University Press, pp. 11–32.

ohonen, V., Jaatinen, R., Kaikkonen, P. & Lehtovaara, J. (2001) *Experiential learning in foreign language education.* Harlow, UK: Pearson Education Limited.

ramsch, C. (1993) *Context and Culture in Language Teaching.* Oxford: Oxford University Press.

ramsch, C. (1998) The privilege of the intercultural speaker. In M. Byram & M. Fleming (Eds), *Language learning in intercultural perspective: Approaches through drama and ethnography.* Cambridge: Cambridge University Press, pp. 16–31.

ramsch, C. & Sullivan, P. (1996) Appropriate pedagogy. *ELT Journal,* 50 (3), 199–212.

amy, M.-N. & Hampel, R. (2007) *Online communication in language learning and teaching.* New York: Palgrave Macmillan.

evy, M. (2007) Culture, cultural learning, and new technologies: Towards a pedagogical framework. *Language Learning and Technology,* 11 (2), 104–27.

ewis, T. (2006) When teaching is learning: A personal account of learning to teach online. *CALICO Journal,* 23 (3), 581–600.

iu, J. (2007a) Introduction. In J. Liu (Ed.), *English language teaching in China: New approaches, perspectives and standards.* New York: Continuum, pp. 1–10.

iu, J. (2007b) Empowering non-native English-speaking teachers through collaboration with their native English-speaking colleagues in EFL settings. In J. Liu (Ed.), *English Language Teaching in China: New Approaches, Perspectives and Standards.* London and New York: Continuum, pp. 107–23.

iu, J. (2007c) Epilogue: Beyond communicative competence: A pedagogical perspective. In J. Liu (Ed.), *English language teaching in China: New approaches, perspectives and standards.* London and New York: Continuum, pp. 330–5.

angenot, F. & Nissen, E. (2006) Collective activity and tutor involvement in e-learning environments for language teachers and learners. *CALICO Journal,* 23 (3), 601–22.

erriam, S.B. (1998) *Qualitative research and case study applications in education. Revised and expanded from 'case study research in education'.* San Francisco: Jossey-Bass Publishers.

inistry of Education (2000) *Gaodeng Xuexiao Yingyu Zhuanye Yingyu Jiaoxue Dagang* [English course guidelines for HE English majors]. Shanghai: Shanghai Foreign Language Education Publishing House.

inistry of Education (2004) *Daxue Yingyu Kecheng Jiaoxue Yaoqiu* [College English course requirements], http://www.edu.cn/20040120/3097997.shtml (accessed 6 August 2007).

oore, Z., Morales, B. & Carel, S. (1998) Technology and teaching culture: Results of a state survey of foreign language teachers. *CALICO Journal,* 15 (1–3), 109–25.

üller-Hartmann, A. (2000) The role of tasks in promoting intercultural learning in electronic learning networks. *Language Learning and Technology,* 4 (2), 129–47.

üller-Hartmann, A. (2006) Learning how to teach intercultural communicative competence via telecollaboration: A model for language teacher education. In J.A. Belz & S.L. Thorne (Eds), *AAUSC 2005: Internet-mediated intercultural foreign language education.* Boston: Thomson Heinle, pp. 63–84.

Müller-Hartmann, A. (2007) Teacher role in telecollaboration: Setting up and managing exchanges. In R. O'Dowd (Ed.), *Online intercultural exchange: An introduction for foreign language teachers*. Clevedon: Multilingual Matters Ltd, pp. 167–92.

Murphey, T. & Chen, L. (Eds) (2007) *Portfolio-based teacher development and appraisal with teacher performance standards: Teachers' handbook*. Beijing: Beijing Foreign Language Teaching and Research Press.

Nunan, D. (1989) *Designing Tasks for the Communicative Classroom*. Cambridge: Cambridge University Press.

Nunan, D. (2004) *Task-based language teaching*. Cambridge: Cambridge University Press.

O'Dowd, R. (2006) *Telecollaboration and the development of intercultural communicative competence*. Munchen: Langenscheidt ELT GmbH.

O'Dowd, R. (2007a) Introduction in online intercultural exchange: In introduction for foreign language teachers. In R. O'Dowd (Ed.), *Online intercultural exchange: An introduction for foreign language teachers*. Clevedon: Multilingual Matters Ltd, pp. 3–16.

O'Dowd, R. (2007b) Foreign language education and the rise of online communication: A review of promises and realities. In R. O'Dowd (Ed.), *Online intercultural exchange: An introduction for foreign language teachers*. Clevedon: Multilingual Matters, pp. 17–37.

O'Dowd, R. & Eberbach, K. (2004) Guides on the side? Tasks and challenges for teachers in telecollaborative projects. *ReCALL*, 16 (1), 5–19.

O'Dowd, R. & Ware, P. (2009) Critical issues in telecollaborative task design. *Computer Assisted Language Learning*, 22 (2), 173–88.

Palfreyman, D. (2003) Introduction: culture and learner autonomy. In D. Palfreyman & R.C. Smith (Eds), *Learner autonomy across cultures: Language education perspectives*. Basingstoke and New York: Palgrave Macmillan Ltd, pp. 1–22.

Piller, I. (2007) Linguistics and intercultural communication. *Language and Linguistics Compass*, 1 (3), 208–26.

Roberts, C., Byram, M., Barro, A., Jordan, S. & Street, B. (2001) *Language learners as ethnographers*. Buffalo, N.Y.: Multilingual Matters.

Scollon, R. & Scollon, S.W. (2001a) *Intercultural communication: A discourse approach* (2nd edn). Oxford: Blackwell Publishers..

Scollon, R. & Scollon, S.W. (2001b) Discourse and intercultural communication. In D. Schiffrin, D. Tannen & H.E. Hamilton (Eds), *The handbook of discourse analysis*. Oxford: Blackwell Publishers, pp. 538–47.

Song, L. (2008) *Exploration of a conceptual framework for intercultural communicative English language teaching in China*. Unpublished PhD thesis, Shanghai International Studies University, Shanghai.

Spencer-Oatey, H. (2007) Introduction. In H. Spencer-Oatey (Ed.), *e-learning initiatives in China: Pedagogy, policy and culture*. Hong Kong: Hong Kong University Press.

Tajino, A. & Tajino, Y. (2000) Native and non-Native: What can they offer? Lessons from team-teaching in Japan. *ELT Journal*, 54 (1), 3–11.

Thorne, S.L. (2006) Pedagogical and praxiological lessons from internet-mediated intercultural foreign language education research. In J.A. Belz & S.L. Thorne (Eds), *AAUSC 2005: Internet-mediated intercultural foreign language education*. Boston: Thomson Heinle, pp. 2–32.

Wang, L. & Coleman, J.A. (2009) A Survey of internet-mediated intercultural foreign language education in China. *ReCALL*, 21 (1), 113–29.

Yang, S. (Ed.) (2008) *Gaoxiao daxue waiyu jiaoyu fazhan baogao (1978–2008)* [A report on college english education development (1978–2008)]. Shanghai: Shanghai Foreign Language Education Press.

Warschauer, M. (2008) Laptops and literacy: A multi-site case study. *Pedagogies: An International Journal*, 3, 52–67.

Warschauer, M., Shetzer, H. & Meloni, C. (2000) *Internet for English teaching*. USA: Teachers of English to Speakers of Other Languages, Inc.

Yin, R. (2003) *Case study research: Design and methods* (3rd edn). London: Sage Publications.

Zemsky, R. and Massey, W. (2004) *Thwarted Innovation: What happened to e-Learning and Why*. Pennsylvania: University of Pennsylvania.

Zhang, H.L. (2007) *Intercultural approach to foreign language teaching*. Shanghai: Shanghai Foreign Language Education Press.

Postscript

Lixian Jin and Martin Cortazzi

Here we give a few reflections on 'researching intercultural learning'. They are necessarily incomplete and provisional since that is how researching intercultural learning is. They are also brief, which intercultural learning should not be. We think about further research, culture, learning and language, about reflection and reflexivity, and teamwork.

Further research has already been suggested in most chapters. With a little thought and perhaps imagination most of the themes evident here and the precise focus adopted here and there can be researched elsewhere in other intercultural contexts. A proviso is: as long as the questions involved are relevant, worthwhile, feasible and useful – worth answering, in fact. Further research could look more closely within the various levels outlined in the introduction. Learning is not, obviously, confined to formal education, and there are many informal or non-formal learning situations, voluntary and perhaps temporary contexts in which we would benefit from research; some will provide insights for formal education. Similarly, there is plenty of work-related learning, staff development, induction and training in business, industrial and professional contexts in which researching intercultural learning is vital. And how about learning at home, with the family and friends, for shopping, sport, leisure or entertainment? Learning networks? We can begin to think further, as suggested in the introduction, that all learning might usefully be considered intercultural, either because it is so or because this provides a useful investigatory perspective.

The 'inter' of intercultural learning requires more analysis and research and it is likely that multiple answers will emerge about what 'inter' means: between whom? (Should it be 'trans', as some argue?) 'Inter' concerns which features of which cultures? Which kinds of cultures? For which people(s)? Since cultures are processes rather than objects, they are necessarily dynamic, shifting, combining and unifying, and distinguish themselves in evolving ways – or rather people have these attributes and qualities groups and communities to which we ascribe cultures. The nexus of culture(s) and learning(s) thus seems hugely complex and is often mediated by language. If language reflects, constructs and symbolizes features of culture and identity, as is easily argued in anthropological linguistics, then also culture reflects, constructs and symbolizes aspects of language and identity. Similarly, perhaps with learning, at least with some intercultural learning, there are these reciprocal relations of reflection, construction and symbolizing with culture and identity.

A characteristic of much of the research here is that it demands or elicits reflection and reflexivity: the first may be a focussed outward, thinking about interpretation of method and results and insights, while the second is perhaps more of an inward retrospective and ongoing consideration about the nature of the links between researcher(s) – research process(es) – and the researched participants, about the themes and interpretations of meanings forming this triangle. This is particularly needed in intercultural investigations. The relevant questions turn out to be not so much those initial research questions in every project but other, epistemological ones (What do I know? How do I know that?), and an ongoing conversation about research experience while engaged in it (What are we learning here? How are we learning that?). This inward turning towards ourselves is appropriate for us as readers, too, since readers bring academic, social and cultural expectations to their reading processes and, after all, reading can also be intercultural learning if we allow it to be. Reading reflexively might include notions of research as an account of X, an account for X, an account by Y within a context of Z, and as an account to, with, through … different audiences and voices. Here, we hope the voices of participants as well as researchers can be heard and interpreted, so that we reflect on them and take them to other contexts.

Many of these studies have underlined the crucial role of conversation, discussion and dialogue in intercultural learning. While these terms as used in the literature may sometimes be seen as more of a metaphor than action, it is clear that in this field both ways of viewing such terms may be productive: as metaphors they may give insights, illuminate, inspire through comparison; as activities they develop interactive talk with a purpose between participants, which these research studies show can be crucial for classroom learning. While this might seem obvious, if less practised, between teachers and students, some studies show this to be strongly the case between learners, where peer dialogue provides input which can also be intercultural in some contexts.

This interactive talk must be a feature of other characteristics of most studies here: collaboration and teamwork, which may be between researchers and participants or between researchers within a team. In some cases, certainly for ourselves as a team, this means the research activity is also

intercultural learning about cultures of learning, intercultural commun
cation in practice, and intercultural dialogue as metaphor or action, an
learning about ourselves. It is also learning research or improving ways o
doing and understanding research: in a reversal of our book title ... learnin
intercultural researching.

Index

Printed and bound in the United States of America.